Expository Thoughts on the Gospels

LUKE

VOLUME ONE

J. C. Ryle

THE BANNER OF TRUTH TRUST

THE BANNER OF TRUTH TRUST
3 Murrayfield Road, Edinburgh EH12 6EL
P.O. Box 621, Carlisle, Pennsylvania 17013, U.S.A.
*

First published 1858
First Banner of Truth Trust edition 1986
Reprinted 1997
ISBN 0 85151 497 9

*

Printed and bound in Finland
by WSOY – Book Printing Division

PREFACE.

THE volume now in the reader's hands, is a continuation of the "Expository Thoughts on the Gospels," of which two volumes have been already published.

The general design of the work has been so fully explained in the preface to the volume on St. Matthew, that it seems needless to say anything further on the subject. I will only remark that I have steadily adhered to the three-fold object, which I proposed to myself, when I first began. I have endeavoured to produce something which may meet the wants of heads of families in conducting family prayers,—of district visitors in reading to the sick and unlearned,—and of private students of the Bible who have neither large libraries nor much leisure. These three classes I have constantly kept in view. Their wants have been continually before my eyes. Whatever would be unsuitable to them I have diligently tried to avoid.

In one important respect the present volume will be found to differ from the two which have preceded it. I allude to the explanatory notes which I have appended to each portion of Scripture expounded. These notes are so numerous that some may think they occupy a disproportionate place in the volume. I trust however that the majority of readers will think that they are worth the space which they fill.

A few words on the nature of these notes may not be out of place. I am desirous to explain the object I have had in view in the preparation of them.

1. My first object has been to throw light on difficulties. I can say with a good conscience that I have endeavoured to examine every hard passage, and have never turned aside from any perplexing expression or text. I have striven to gather together all the information I could obtain on each difficulty, and to present it to the reader in a compact and lucid form. I do not for a moment pretend to say that I have explained everything. I am deeply conscious that I have left many a hard thing in St. Luke where I found it. But I can honestly say, that I have never shrunk from the discussion of difficulties. I have resolved that it should never be said, that I commented upon easy things, and left hard things untouched.

2. My second object has been to aid those readers who do not understand the Greek language. I have tried to point out the literal meaning of words in the original Greek, which, from various causes, our English translators have rendered less literally than they might have done. I have also noticed the varying translations, which in many cases, our translators have made of the same Greek word. In doing this, I would state distinctly that I wish to bring no accusation against our authorized version of the Bible, and that I have no sympathy with the movement for a revised version. I do not forget that any translation of the Bible, to be useful, must be written in a popular style, and that an excessively literal reading of many Greek expressions would sound very harsh to English ears. That the authorized English version has faults, weak points, and defects,

I fully allow. But after reading the existing attempts at revision, I confess that I feel very strong doubts whether we are likely to alter our version for the better. It appears to me the wiser course to "let well alone."

3. My third object has been to quote passages from approved writers, which throw light on subjects under discussion, and to name writers who may be referred to on special points, by those who have libraries and leisure. This is a department of the notes, I need hardly say, which might easily have been greatly enlarged, and I would have gladly enlarged it. Nothing, in fact, but the fear of making my work extend to an unreadable size, has made me refrain from giving many more quotations than I have already given. But I remember that we live in a hurrying age, and that it never was so true as it is now, that "a great book is a great evil."

4. My last object in these notes, has been to combat existing false doctrines and heresies, on every occasion; and to point out the answers to them which the text of Scripture supplies. I have never shrunk from exposing the utter contrariety to Scripture of the peculiar doctrines of Socinians, Neologians, Romanists, and Semi-Romanists. I have not been deterred from speaking out plainly by the dread of being thought "controversial." I have made no secret of my opinions. I have unhesitatingly avowed that I hold the plenary inspiration of every word of Holy Scripture, and that I thoroughly adhere to those views which are commonly called Protestant and Evangelical. I cannot, of course, expect that notes on Scripture, written on such principles, will satisfy all readers;—but that they are so written, I would not for a moment conceal.

On one point only I have carefully abstained from offering

any opinion. I refer to the vexed questions of the comparative claims of various readings, of the authority of manuscripts, and of the best Greek text of the New Testament. This is a field into which I decline to enter. Materials do not appear to me to exist at present for forming a decided opinion on the subject. The time may come when all existing manuscripts shall have been carefully collated, the Vatican text not excepted. The time may come, when a competent jury of reverent-minded Biblical scholars, shall weigh the merits of conflicting readings, and finally bring forth an indisputably true and correct text of the Greek Testament. The time has certainly not come yet, and I doubt much whether it ever will.* In the mean time, I frankly avow, that I am content to use Scholefield's version of the well-known edition of Stephens, A. D. 1550. I am not ignorant of its blemishes; but I am unable to see that any other text has thoroughly made out a claim to be regarded as the "textus receptus" in its place.†

It only remains for me to say, that in the preparation of these notes, as well as of the Expository Thoughts, I have made a diligent use of all the commentators within my reach, both ancient and modern. I add a list of them, which may prove interesting to some readers, and useful to those who want to know the names of writers who have commented on St. Luke.

* I look forward with much interest to Dr. Tregelles' promised edition of the Greek Testament, and expect much from it.

† It is due to readers who are not familiar with the subject on which I am here speaking, to remind them, that the "various readings," of which they sometimes hear so much, are after all of infinitesimally small importance. They often consist of omissions or additions of little words and particles, which in no case affect the sense of a passage. It is not too much to say, that the whole of the various readings in existence, do not affect a single doctrine or precept in the whole New Testament.

In giving this list, I trust my motives may not be mis-apprehended. My simple desire is to show that I have not written on St. Luke's Gospel in ignorance of other men's labours, and that when I disagree with them, it is not because I do not know what they have to say. The names of those writers whom I have consulted are as follows :—

1. *Fathers,*—Ambrose, Theophylact, Euthymius, Augustine's Sermons on the New Testament, and the Catena of Corderius.

2. *Foreign Protestant Commentators,*—Calvin, Brentius, Bucer, Bullinger, Beza, Pellican, Gualter, Chemnitius, Flavius, Illyricus, Piscator, Cocceius, De Dieu, Calovius, Aretius, Schottgen, Bengel, Heinsius, Olshausen, Stier.

3. *Foreign Roman Catholic Commentators,*—Jansenius, Barradius, Maldonatus, Cornelius à Lapide, Quesnel, Stella, Clarius, Novarinus.

4. *English Commentators,*—Trapp, Mayer, Cartwright, Lightfoot, Baxter, Ness, Leigh, Hammond, Poole's Synopsis and Annotations, Henry, Whitby, Burkitt, Gill, Pearce, Scott, A. Clarke, Barnes, Davidson, Alford, Wordsworth, Ford, Watson, Burgon, Major.

It would be easy to say something on the comparative value of many of these writers. At some future time I may attempt to do so. It is almost needless to say that many of them hold most erroneous opinions on many points, and that I do not recommend the use of all the commentaries that I have named. At present I will content myself with saying, that in reading Commentaries I have often been surprised to find light where I expected darkness, and darkness where I expected light.   I have also discovered that some of the best commentaries on Scripture are comparatively little known.

I now send forth this volume with an earnest prayer, that the Holy Ghost may bless it, and that God may be pleased to use it for His own glory and the benefit of many souls. My chief desire in this, and all my writings, is to exalt the Lord Jesus Christ and make Him beautiful and glorious in the eyes of men, and to promote the increase of repentance, faith, and holiness upon earth.   If this shall be the result of this volume, the labour that it has cost me will be more than repaid.

I have a strong conviction that we want more reverent, deep-searching study of the Scripture in the present day. Most of Christians see nothing beyond the surface of the Bible when they read it.—We want a more clear knowledge of Christ, as a living Person, a living Priest, a living Physician, a living Friend, a living Advocate at the right hand of God, and a living Saviour soon about to come again.   Most of Christians know little of Christianity but its skeleton of doctrines.—I desire never to forget these two things.   If I can do anything to make Christ and the Bible more honourable in these latter days, I shall be truly thankful and content.

J. C. RYLE.

August, 1858.

TABLE OF CONTENTS OF EXPOSITIONS.

TABLE OF CONTENTS OF NOTES.

CHAPTER I.

CHAPTER II.

CHAPTER III.

CHAPTER IV.

CHAPTER VII.

CHAPTER IX.

CHAPTER X.

EXPOSITORY THOUGHTS

ON THE GOSPELS.

LUKE I. 1—4.

1 Forasmuch as many have taken in hand to set forth in order a declaration of those things which are most surely believed among us,

2 Even as they delivered them unto us, which from the beginning were eyewitnesses, and ministers of the word;

3 It seemed good to me also, having had perfect understanding of all things from the very first, to write unto thee in order, most excellent Theophilus,

4 That thou mightest know the certainty of those things, wherein thou hast been instructed.

THE Gospel of St. Luke, which we now begin, contains many precious things which are not recorded in the other three Gospels. Such, for instance, are the histories of Zacharias and Elizabeth,—the angel's announcement to the Virgin Mary,—and, to speak generally, the whole contents of the first two chapters. Such, again, are the narratives of the conversion of Zacchæus and of the penitent thief,—the walk to Emmaus, and the famous parables of the Pharisee and Publican, the rich man and Lazarus, and the Prodigal Son. These are portions of Scripture for which every well-instructed Christian feels peculiarly thankful. And for these we are indebted to the Gospel of St. Luke.

The short preface which we have now read is a peculiar feature of St. Luke's Gospel. But we shall find, on examination, that it is full of most useful instruction.

In the first place, St. Luke gives us *a short, but valuable, sketch of the nature of a Gospel*. He calls it, " a declaration of those things which are most surely believed among us." It is a narrative of facts about Jesus Christ.

Christianity is a religion built upon facts. Let us never lose sight of this. It came before mankind at first in this shape. The first preachers did not go up and down the world, proclaiming an elaborate, artificial system of abstruse doctrines and deep principles. They made it their first business to tell men great plain facts. They went about telling a sin-laden world, that the Son of God had come down to earth, and lived for us, and died for us, and risen again. The Gospel, at its first publication, was far more simple than many make it now. It was neither more nor less than the history of Christ.

Let us aim at greater simplicity in our own personal religion. Let Christ and His Person be the sun of our system, and let the main desire of our souls be to live the life of faith in Him, and daily know Him better. This was St. Paul's Christianity. "To me to live is Christ." (Philipp. i. 21.)

In the second place, St. Luke draws a beautiful picture of *the true position of the apostles in the early church*. He calls them, "eye-witnesses and ministers of the word."

There is an instructive humility in this expression. There is an utter absence of that man-exalting tone which has so often crept into the Church. St. Luke gives the apostles no flattering titles. He affords not the slightest excuse to those who speak of them with idolatrous veneration, because of their office and nearness to our Lord.

He describes them as "eye-witnesses." They told men what they had seen with their own eyes, and heard with their own ears. (1 John i. 1.)—He describes them as "ministers of the word." They were servants of the word of the Gospel. They were men who counted it their highest privilege to carry about, as messengers, the tidings of God's love to a sinful world, and to tell the story of the cross.

Well would it have been for the Church and the world, if Christian ministers had never laid claim to higher dignity and honour than the apostles claimed for themselves. It is a mournful fact, that ordained men have constantly exalted themselves and their office to a most unscriptural position. It is a no less mournful fact, that people have constantly helped forward the evil, by a lazy acquiescence in the demands of priest-craft, and by contenting themselves with a mere vicarious religion. There have been faults on both sides. Let us remember this, and be on our guard.

In the third place, St. Luke describes *his own qualifications for the work of writing a Gospel.* He says that he "had perfect understanding of all things from the very first."

It would be mere waste of time to inquire from what source St. Luke obtained the information which he has given us in his Gospel. We have no good reason for supposing that he saw our Lord work miracles, or heard Him teach. To say that he obtained his information from the Virgin Mary, or any of the apostles, is mere conjecture and speculation. Enough for us to know that St. Luke wrote by inspiration of God. Unquestionably he did not neglect the ordinary means of getting knowledge. But the Holy Ghost guided him, no less than all other writers of the Bible, in his choice of matter. The Holy Ghost supplied him with thoughts, arrangement, sentences, and even words. And the result is, that what St. Luke wrote is not to be read as the "word of man," but the "word of God." (1 Thess. ii. 13.)

Let us carefully hold fast the great doctrine of the plenary inspiration of every word of the Bible. Let us never allow that any writer of the Old or New Testament could make even the slightest verbal mistake or error, when writing as he was "moved by the Holy Ghost." (2 Peter i. 21.) Let it be a settled principle with us in reading the Bible, that when we cannot understand a passage, or reconcile it with some other passage, the fault is not in the Book, but in ourselves. The adoption of this principle will place our feet upon a rock. To give it up is to stand upon a quicksand, and to fill our minds with endless uncertainties and doubts.

Finally, St. Luke informs us of *one main object he had in view in writing his Gospel.* It was that Theophilus "might know the certainty of those things wherein he had been instructed."

There is no encouragement here for those who place confidence in unwritten traditions, and the voice of the church. St. Luke knew well the weakness of man's memory, and the readiness with which a history alters its shape both by additions and alterations, when it depends only on word of mouth and report. What therefore does he do? He takes care to "write."

There is no encouragement here for those who are opposed to the spread of religious knowledge, and talk of ignorance as the "mother of devotion." St. Luke does not wish his friend to remain in doubt on any matter of his faith. He tells him that he wants him to "know the certainty of those things wherein he had been instructed."

Let us close the passage with thankfulness for the Bible. Let us bless God daily that we are not left dependent on man's traditions, and need not be led astray by ministers' mistakes. We have a written volume, which is "able to make us wise unto salvation, through faith which is in Christ Jesus." (2 Tim. iii. 15.)

Let us begin St. Luke's Gospel with an earnest desire to know more ourselves of the truth as it is in Jesus, and with a hearty determination to do what in us lies to spread the knowledge of that truth throughout the world.

NOTES. LUKE I. 1—4.

[*Gospel according to St. Luke.*] Our information concerning St. Luke is scanty. It is conjectured by some that he was one of the seventy disciples sent forth by our Lord, in addition to the twelve apostles. (Luke x. 1·) There seems no reason to doubt that he was the companion of St. Paul in his travels, and that he was a "physician." (Col. iv. 14.) Some have thought that his profession as a physician may be traced in his manner of describing our Lord's miraculous cures of diseases,—and his companionship of St. Paul in his manner of speaking on such subjects as God's glory, and Christ's love to sinners. It is generally agreed that his Gospel was written with a special reference to Gentile converts, rather than Jews. Origen, Jerome, Chrysostom, Ambrose, and others, suppose that St. Paul refers to Luke and his Gospel, in the words, "the brother whose praise is in the Gospel." (2 Cor. viii. 18.)—This however is very questionable.

1.—[*Many have taken in hand.*] Who these "many" were, we do not know. That they wrote with any but good intentions we have no right to say. St. Luke's meaning appears to be simply this, that they wrote without any divine call or inspiration. He certainly does not refer to Matthew and Mark. Ambrose remarks, " Matthew did not *take in hand*, nor Mark, nor John, nor Luke. They, the divine Spirit supplying them with abundance of all words and matter, accomplished what they began without any effort."

[*A declaration of those things*.] A glance at the Greek in this sentence, will show us that the word " of," must be taken as a preposition, and means "about," or "concerning."

[*most surely believed*.] The word so translated is rendered, when applied to Abraham, (Rom. iv. 21.) "fully persuaded," and when applied to the preaching of the Gospel, "fully known," (2 Tim. iv. 17.) Theophylact, in Suicer, defines it as meaning here, "things fully proved by many arguments."

2.—[*The Word*.] Some think that this means the Lord Jesus Christ, the "Word," who "was made flesh." John i. 14. It seems however more probable that we are to take it as the written word, or word of the Gospel. It is not clear that the Lord Jesus is ever called " the Word" by any New Testament writer, except John.

3.—[*From the very first*.] The Greek word so translated, means literally, "from above." It is so rendered in John iii. 31 : xix. 11 : James i. 17 : iii. 15 : iii. 17. Gomarus and Lightfoot think that it should be taken in this sense, and that it is an assertion of Luke's inspiration. The expression would then signify, "having accurately traced up all things under Divine inspiration, or teaching, from above." The majority of commentators agree with our translators. The Bible writers do not generally assert their own inspiration. The word in Acts xxvi. 5. is rendered, " from the beginning."

[*In order*.] We must carefully observe that this expression does not imply that Luke followed the chronological order of the chief events in our Lord's history, more than the other Evangelists. It rather signifies that he grouped together, and classified in an orderly way, the principal facts which he was inspired to record. Watson remarks, " Luke has less regard to chronological order than Matthew or Mark, and rather classifies the events, than narrates them in a series,—a method of composing history not uncommon with the writers of antiquity." A. Clarke gives an example of this in the life of Augustus, by Suetonius. Campbell says that the word translated ' in order,' "does not necessarily relate to time. The proper import of it is 'distinctly, particularly, as opposed to confusedly, generally.'"

[*Theophilus*.] We know nothing certain about this person. The prevailing opinion is, that he was some Christian Gentile, in a high position, to whom St. Luke, for wise reasons, unknown to us, was directed to address himself in writing his Gospel. The expression "most excellent," seems to indicate that he was no common person. It is the same expression which St. Paul used in addressing Felix and Festus. Acts xxiv. 3: xxvi. 5.

4.—["*Certainty.*"] This is the same word which is translated "safety" in Acts v. 23, and 1 Thess. v. 3.

LUKE I. 5—12.

5 There was in the days of Herod, the king of Judæa, a certain Priest named Zacharias, of the course of Abia: and his wife *was* of the daughters of Aaron, and her name *was* Elisabeth.

6 And they were both righteous before God, walking in all the commandments and ordinances of the Lord blameless.

7 And they had no child, because that Elisabeth was barren, and they both were *now* well stricken in years.

8 And it came to pass, that while he executed the Priest's office before God in the order of his course,

9 According to the custom of the Priest's office, his lot was to burn incense when he went into the temple of the Lord.

10 And the whole multitude of the people were praying without at the time of incense.

11 And there appeared unto him an angel of the Lord standing on the right side of the altar of incense.

12 And when Zacharias saw *him*, he was troubled, and fear fell upon him.

THE first event recorded in St. Luke's Gospel, is the sudden apppearance of an angel to a Jewish priest, named Zacharias. The angel announces to him that a son is about to be born to him, by a miraculous interposition, and that this son is to be the forerunner of the long-promised Messiah. The word of God had plainly foretold that when Messiah came, some one would go before Him to prepare His way. (Malachi iii. 1.) The wisdom of God provided that when this forerunner appeared, he should be born in the family of a priest.

We can form very little idea, at this period of the world, of the immense importance of this angel's announcement. To the mind of a pious Jew, it must have been glad tidings of great joy. It was the first communication from God to Israel since the days of Malachi.

It broke the long silence of four hundred years. It told
the believing Israelite that the prophetic weeks of Daniel
were at length fulfilled, (Dan. ix. 25.)—that God's
choicest promise was at length going to be accomplished,
—and that "the seed" was about to appear in whom all
the nations of the earth should be blessed. (Gen. xxii. 18.)
We must place ourselves in imagination in the position
of Zacharias, in order to give the verses before us their
due weight.

Let us mark, for one thing, in this passage, *the high
testimony which is borne to the character of Zacharias and
Elisabeth.* We are told that they were "both righteous
before God," and that "they walked in all the commandments and ordinances of the Lord blameless."

It matters little whether we interpret this "righteousness" as that which is imputed to all believers for their
justification, or that which is wrought inwardly in
believers by the operation of the Holy Ghost, for their
sanctification. The two sorts of righteousness are never
disjoined. There are none justified who are not sanctified, and there are none sanctified who are not justified.
Suffice it for us to know that Zacharias and Elisabeth
had grace when grace was very rare, and kept all the
burdensome observances of the ceremonial law with devout
conscientiousness, when few Israelites cared for them excepting in name and form.

The main thing that concerns us all, is the example
which this holy pair hold up to Christians. Let us all
strive to serve God faithfully, and live fully up to our
light, even as they did. Let us not forget the plain words
of Scripture, "He that doeth righteousness is righteous."

(1 John iii. 7.) Happy are those Christian families in which it can be reported that both husband and wife are "righteous," and exercise themselves to have a conscience void of offence toward God and toward men. (Acts xxiv. 16.)

Let us mark, for another thing, in this passage, *the heavy trial which God was pleased to lay on Zacharias and Elisabeth.* We are told that "they had no child." The full force of these words can hardly be understood by a modern Christian. To an ancient Jew they would convey the idea of a very weighty affliction. To be childless was one of the bitterest of sorrows. (1 Sam. i. 10.)

The grace of God exempts no one from trouble. "Righteous" as this holy priest and his wife were, they had a "crook in their lot." Let us remember this, if we serve Christ, and let us count trial no strange thing. Let us rather believe that a hand of perfect wisdom is measuring out all our portion, and that when God chastises us, it is to make us "partakers of his holiness." (Heb. xii. 10.) If afflictions drive us nearer to Christ, the Bible, and prayer, they are positive blessings. We may not think so now. But we shall think so when we wake up in another world.

Let us mark, for another thing, in this passage, the *means by which God announced the coming birth of John the Baptist.* We are told that "an angel of the Lord appeared to Zacharias."

The ministry of angels is undoubtedly a deep subject. Nowhere in the Bible do we find such frequent mention of them, as in the period of our Lord's earthly ministry. At no time do we read of so many appearances of angels, as about the time of our Lord's incarnation and entrance into the world. The meaning of this circumstance is sufficiently clear. It was meant to teach the church that Messiah was no angel, but the Lord of angels, as well as of men. Angels announced His coming. Angels proclaimed His birth. Angels rejoiced at His appearing. And by so doing they made it plain that He who came to die for sinners, was not one of themselves, but one far above them, the King of kings and Lord of lords.

One thing, at all events, about angels, we must never forget. They take a deep interest in the work of Christ, and the salvation which Christ has provided. They sung high praise when the Son of God came down to make peace by His own blood between God and man. They rejoice when sinners repent, and sons are born again to our Father in heaven. They delight to minister to those who shall be heirs of salvation. Let us strive to be like them, while we are upon earth,—to be of their mind, and to share their joys. This is the way to be in tune for heaven. It is written of those who enter in there, that they shall be " as the angels." (Mark xii. 25.)

Let us mark, lastly, in this passage, *the effect which the appearance of an angel produced on the mind of Zacharias.* We are told that he " was troubled, and fear fell upon him."

The experience of this righteous man here, tallies exactly with that of other saints under similar circumstances. Moses at the burning bush, and Daniel at the river of Hiddekel,—the women at the sepulchre, and John at the isle of Patmos,—all showed like fear to that of Zacharias. Like him, when they saw visions of things belonging to another world, they trembled and were afraid.

How are we to account for this fear? To that question there is only one answer. It arises from our inward sense of weakness, guilt, and corruption. The vision of an inhabitant of heaven reminds us forcibly of our own imperfection, and of our natural unfitness to stand before God. If angels are so great and terrible, what must the Lord of angels be?

Let us bless God, that we have a mighty Mediator between God and man, the man Christ Jesus. Believing on Him, we may draw near to God with boldness, and look forward to the day of judgment without fear. When the mighty angels shall go forth to gather together God's elect, the elect will have no cause to be afraid. To them the angels are fellow servants and friends. (Rev. xxii. 9.)

Let us tremble when we think of the terror of the wicked at the last day. If even the righteous are troubled by a sudden vision of friendly spirits, where will the ungodly appear, when the angels come forth to gather them like tares for the burning? The fears of the saints are groundless, and endure but for a little season. The fears of the lost, when once aroused, will prove well-grounded, and will endure for evermore.

NOTES. LUKE I. 5—12.

5.—[*Course of Abiah.*] There were twenty-four of these courses, or classes, of the sons of Aaron, among whom the temple service was divided. The course of Abijah, or Abia, at the original institution, was the eighth in order. 1 Chron. xxiv. 10. Bishop Hall remarks, "The successive terms of the legal ministration held on in a line never interrupted. Even in a forlorn and miserable church, there may be a personal succession. How little were the Jews better for this, when they had lost the Urim and Thummim, sincerity of doctrine and manners! This stayed with them even while they crucified Christ. It is the succession of truth and holiness that makes and justifies a church."

[*Daughters of Aaron.*] Watson remarks, "Yet she was cousin to Mary, who was of the tribe of Judah. This indicates the marriage of some predecessor into the other tribe. The priests might marry into any of the tribes of Israel; and the law restraining heiresses to marry into their own tribes, did not extend to other daughters, nor at all to the tribe of Levi, who had no share in the land."

6.—[*Ordinances.*] The Greek word so translated, is the word which the Septuagint version of the Old Testament uses for the word we translate "judgments." See Exod. xxi. 1 ; and xxiv. 3.

10.—[*The whole multitude of the people was praying without.*] Lightfoot remarks on this passage: "When the priest came in unto the holy place to offer incense, notice was given to all, by the sound of a little bell, that the time of prayers was now." Lightfoot. vol. xii. p. 16.

11.—[*Angel appeared.*] Bishop Hall remarks, "The presence of angels is no novelty, but their apparition. They are always with us, but rarely seen, that we may awfully respect their messages when they are seen."

LUKE I. 13—17.

13 But the angel said unto him, Fear not, Zacharias: for thy prayer is heard ; and thy wife Elisabeth shall bear thee a son, and thou shalt call his name John.

14 And thou shalt have joy and gladness; and many shall rejoice at his birth.

15 For he shall be great in the sight of the Lord, and shall drink neither wine nor strong drink ; and he shall be filled with the Holy Ghost, even from his mother's womb.

16 And many of the children of Israel shall he turn to the Lord their God.

17 And he shall go before him in the spirit and power of Elias, to turn the hearts of the fathers to the children, and the disobedient to the wisdom of the just ; to make ready a people prepared for the Lord.

WE have, in these verses, the words of the angel who appeared to Zacharias. They are words full of deep spiritual instruction.

We learn here, for one thing, that *prayers are not necessarily rejected, because the answer is long delayed.*

Zacharias, no doubt, had often prayed for the blessing of children, and, to all appearance, had prayed in vain. At his advanced time of life, he had probably long ceased to mention the subject before God, and had given up all hope of being a father. Yet the very first words of the angel show plainly that the bygone prayers of Zacharias had not been forgotten :—" Thy prayer is heard : thy wife Elisabeth shall bear thee a son."

We shall do well to remember this fact, whenever we kneel down to pray. We must beware of hastily concluding that our supplications are useless, and specially in the matter of intercessory prayer on behalf of others. It is not for us to prescribe either the time or the way in which our requests are to be answered. He who knows best the time for people to be born, knows also the time for them to be born again. Let us rather "continue in prayer," "watch unto prayer," "pray always, and not faint." "Delay of effect," says an old divine, "must not discourage our faith. It may be, God hath long granted, ere we shall know of His grant."

We learn, in the second place, that *no children cause such true joy, as those who have the grace of God.* It was a child about to be filled with the Holy Ghost, to whose father it was said, "Thou shalt have joy and gladness ; and many shall rejoice at his birth."

Grace is the principal portion that we should desire for our children. It is a thousand times better for them than beauty, riches, honours, rank, or high connexions. Till they have grace we never know what they may do. They may make us weary of our life, and bring down our grey hairs with sorrow to the grave. When they are converted, and not till then, they are provided for, both for time and eternity. "A wise son maketh a glad father." (Prov. x. 1.) Whatever we seek for our sons and daughters, let us first seek that they may have a place in the covenant, and a name in the book of life.

We learn, in the third place, *the nature of true greatness*. The angel describes it, when he tells Zacharias that his son "shall be great in the sight of the Lord."

The measure of greatness which is common among men is utterly false and deceptive. Princes and potentates, conquerors and leaders of armies, statesmen and philosophers, artists and authors,—these are the kind of men whom the world calls "great." Such greatness is not recognised among the angels of God. Those who do great things for God, they reckon great. Those who do little for God, they reckon little. They measure and value every man according to the position in which he is likely to stand at the last day.

Let us not be ashamed to make the angels of God our example in this matter. Let us seek for ourselves and our children that true greatness which will be owned and recognized in another world. It is a greatness which is within the reach of all,—of the poor as well as the rich, —of the servant as well as of the master. It does not depend on power or patronage, on money or on friends. It is the free gift of God to all who seek it at the Lord Jesus Christ's hands. It is the portion of all who hear Christ's voice and follow Him,—who fight Christ's battle and do Christ's work in the world. Such may receive little honour in this life. But great shall be their reward at the last day.

We learn, in the fourth place, that *children are never too young to receive the grace of God*. Zacharias is informed that his son "shall be filled with the Holy Ghost, even from his mother's womb."

There is no greater mistake than to suppose that infants, by reason of their tender age, are incapable of being operated upon by the Holy Spirit. The manner of His work upon a little child's heart, is undoubtedly mysterious and incomprehensible. But so also are all His works upon the sons of men. Let us beware of limiting God's power and compassion. He is a merciful God. With Him nothing is impossible.

Let us remember these things in connection with the subject of infant baptism. It is a feeble objection to say that infants ought not to be baptized, because they cannot repent and believe. If an infant can be filled with the Holy Ghost, he is surely not unworthy to be admitted into the visible church. Let us remember these things specially in the training of young children. We should always deal with them as responsible to God. We should never allow ourselves to suppose that they are too young to have any religion. Of course we must be reasonable in our expectations. We must not look for evidences of grace, unsuitable to their age and capacities. But we must never forget that the heart which is not too young to sin, is also not too young to be filled with the grace of God.

We learn, in the last place, from these verses, *the character of a really great and successful minister of God*. The picture is set before us in a striking manner by the angel's description of John the Baptist. He is one who

will "turn hearts,"—turn them from ignorance to knowledge, from carelessness to thoughtfulness, from sin to
God.—He is one who will "go before the Lord,"—he
will delight in nothing so much as being the messenger
and herald of Jesus Christ.—He is one who "will make
ready a people for the Lord." He will strive to gather
out of the world a company of believers, who will be
ready to meet the Lord in the day of His appearing.

For such ministers let us pray night and day. They
are the true pillars of a Church,—the true salt of the
earth,—the true light of the world. Happy is that
Church, and happy is that nation, which has many such
men. Without such men, learning, titles, endowments,
and splendid buildings, will keep no Church alive. Souls
will not be saved,—good will not be done,—Christ will
not be glorified, excepting by men full of the Holy Ghost.

NOTES. LUKE I. 13—17.

13.—[*His name John.*] The word John means "the grace, gift, or
mercy of the Lord." *Cruden.*

15 —[*Drink neither wine nor strong drink.*] From this it would
appear that John the Baptist was a Nazarite, or person separated by special vow to the Lord. See Num. vi. 3.

17.—[*Spirit and power of Elias.*] Theophylact properly remarks
on this expression, that "as Elias is the precursor of Christ's
second advent, so also John is the precursor of the first advent."
Let it be carefully noted that Gabriel does not say that John
shall be Elias himself, but that he shall go "in the spirit and
power of Elias." The real advent of Elias, to fulfil the prophecy
of Malachi, is, in all probability, a thing yet to come.

[*to turn the heart of the fathers to the children.*] This is a
dark and difficult expression, and one which seems to perplex
the commentators much. The most likely explanation is that of
De Dieu. He considers it to mean, "the fathers upon, or together
with, the children,"—that is, all ages, and all sorts of people,—
parents and children together. He supports this view by the
Septuagint version of Exodus xii. 8. Montanus, Vatablus,
Barradius, Hammond and Watson take the same view. So also
does Bengel, and quotes in support of it the Septuagint version
of Genesis xxxii. 11.

LUKE I. 18—25.

18 And Zacharias said unto the angel, Whereby shall I know this? for I am an old man, and my wife well stricken in years.

19 And the angel answering said unto him, I am Gabriel, that stand in the presence of God; and am sent to speak unto thee, and to shew thee these glad tidings.

20 And, behold, thou shalt be dumb, and not able to speak, until the day that these things shall be performed, because thou believest not my words, which shall be fulfilled in their season.

21 And the people waited for Zacharias, and marvelled that he tarried so long in the temple.

22 And when he came out, he could not speak unto them: and they perceived that he had seen a vision in the temple: for he beckoned unto them, and remained speechless.

23 And it came to pass, that, as soon as the days of his ministration were accomplished, he departed to his own house.

24 And after those days his wife Elisabeth conceived, and hid herself five months, saying,

25 Thus hath the Lord dealt with me in the days wherein he looked on *me*, to take away my reproach among men.

WE see in this passage, *the power of unbelief in a good man.* Righteous and holy as Zacharias was, the announcement of the angel appears to him incredible. He cannot think it possible that an old man like himself should have a son. "Whereby shall I know this?" he says, "for I am an old man, and my wife well stricken in years."

A well-instructed Jew, like Zacharias, ought not to have raised such a question. No doubt he was well acquainted with the Old Testament Scriptures. He ought to have remembered the wonderful births of Isaac, and Samson, and Samuel in old times. He ought to have remembered that what God has done once, he can do again, and that with Him nothing is impossible. But he forgot all this. He thought of nothing but the arguments of mere human reason and sense. And it often happens in religious matters, that where reason begins, faith ends.

Let us learn wisdom from the fault of Zacharias. It is a fault to which God's people in every age have been sadly liable. The histories of Abraham, and Isaac, and

Moses, and Hezekiah, and Jehoshaphat, will all show us that a true believer may sometimes be overtaken by unbelief. It is one of the first corruptions which came into man's heart in the day of the fall, when Eve believed the devil rather than God. It is one of the most deep-rooted sins by which a saint is plagued, and from which he is never entirely freed till he dies. Let us pray daily, "Lord increase my faith." Let us not doubt that when God says a thing, that thing shall be fulfilled.

We see furthermore, in these verses, *the privilege and portion of God's angels.* They carry messages to God's Church. They enjoy God's immediate presence. The heavenly messenger who appears to Zacharias, rebukes his unbelief by telling him who he is: "I am Gabriel, that stand in the presence of God; and am sent to speak unto thee."

The name "Gabriel" would doubtless fill the mind of Zacharias with humiliation and self-abasement. He would remember it was that same Gabriel, who 490 years before had brought to Daniel the prophecy of the seventy weeks, and had told him how Messiah should be cut off. (Dan. ix. 26.) He would doubtless contrast his own sad unbelief, when peaceably ministering as a priest in God's temple, with the faith of holy Daniel when dwelling a captive at Babylon, while the temple at Jerusalem was in ruins. Zacharias learned a lesson that day which he never forgot.

The account which Gabriel gives of his own office, should raise in our minds great searchings of heart. This mighty spirit, far greater in power and intelligence than we are, counts it his highest honour to "stand in God's

presence " and do His will. Let our aims and desires be in
the same direction. Let us strive so to live, that we may
one day stand with boldness before the throne of God,
and serve Him day and night in His temple. The way
to this high and holy position is open before us. Christ
has consecrated it for us by the offering of His own body
and blood. May we endeavour to walk in it during the
short time of this present life, that so we may stand in
our lot with God's elect angels in the endless ages of
eternity. (Dan. xii. 13.)

We see, finally, in this passage, *how exceeding sinful is
the sin of unbelief in the sight of God.* The doubts and
questionings of Zacharias brought down upon him a
heavy chastisement. "Thou shalt be dumb," says the
angel, "and not able to speak, because thou believest
not my words."—It was a chastisement peculiarly
suitable to the offence. The tongue that was not
ready to speak the language of believing praise was
struck dumb.—It was a chastisement of long continuance. For nine long months at least, Zacharias was
condemned to silence, and was daily reminded, that
by unbelief he had offended God.

Few sins appear to be so peculiarly provoking to God
as the sin of unbelief. None certainly have called down
such heavy judgments on men. It is a practical denial of
God's Almighty power to doubt whether he can do a thing,
when he undertakes to do it.—It is giving the lie to God
to doubt whether he means to do a thing, when He has
plainly promised that it shall be done.—The forty years
wanderings of Israel in the wilderness, should never be
forgotten by professing Christians. The words of St.

Paul are very solemn: "They could not enter in because of unbelief." (Heb. iii. 19.)

Let us watch and pray daily against this soul-ruining sin. Concessions to it rob believers of their inward peace,—weaken their hands in the day of battle,—bring clouds over their hopes,—make their chariot wheels drive heavily. According to the degree of our faith will be our enjoyment of Christ's salvation,—our patience in the day of trial,—our victory over the world. Unbelief, in short, is the true cause of a thousand spiritual diseases, and once allowed to nestle in our hearts, will eat as doth a canker. "If ye will not believe, ye shall not be established." (Isaiah vii. 9.) In all that respects the pardon of our sins, and the acceptance of our souls,—the duties of our peculiar station and the trials of our daily life,—let it be a settled maxim in our religion, to trust every word of God implicitly, and to beware of unbelief.

NOTES. LUKE I. 18—25.

18.—[*Whereby shall I know this.*] Let us note that there is a wide distinction between this question asked by Zacharias, and that asked by the Virgin Mary, at verse 34. The question of Zacharias implies a doubt of the whole thing announced by the angel. The question of Mary implies no doubt of the event, but is only directed to the manner of its accomplishment.

19.—[*Gabriel.*] The word Gabriel means "God is my strength," or "Man of God," or "strength of God." *(Cruden.)* It is the only clear example of an angel's name in the Bible. "Michael," in Dan. x. 21, and xii. 1, probably signifies the Lord Jesus, when compared with Rev. xii. 7.

20.—[*Dumb.*] By comparing this expression with verse 62, it would appear highly probable that Zacharias became deaf as well as dumb. Else, why should his friends communicate with him by signs?

LUKE I. 26—33.

26 And in the sixth month the angel Gabriel was sent from God unto a city of Galilee, named Nazareth,

27 To a virgin espoused to a man whose name was Joseph, of the house of David; and the virgin's name *was* Mary.

28 And the angel came in unto her, and said, Hail, *thou that art* highly favoured, the Lord *is* with thee: blessed *art* thou among women.

29 And when she saw *him*, she was troubled at his saying, and cast in her mind what manner of salutation this should be.

30 And the angel said unto her, Fear not, Mary: for thou hast found favour with God.

31 And, behold, thou shalt conceive in thy womb, and bring forth a son, and shalt call his name JESUS.

32 He shall be great, and shall be called the Son of the Highest: and the Lord God shall give unto him the throne of his father David:

33 And he shall reign over the house of Jacob for ever; and of his kingdom there shall be no end.

WE have in these verses, the announcement of the most marvellous event that ever happened in this world,—the incarnation and birth of our Lord Jesus Christ. It is a passage which we should always read with mingled wonder, love and praise.

We should notice, in the first place, *the lowly and unassuming manner in which the Saviour of mankind came amongst us.* The angel who announced His advent, was sent to an obscure town of Galilee, named Nazareth. The woman who was honoured to be our Lord's mother, was evidently in a humble position of life. Both in her station and her dwelling-place, there was an utter absence of what the world calls "greatness."

We need not hesitate to conclude, that there was a wise providence in all this arrangement. The Almighty counsel, which orders all things in heaven and earth, could just as easily have appointed Jerusalem to be the place of Mary's residence as Nazareth, or could as easily have chosen the daughter of some rich scribe to be our Lord's mother, as a poor woman. But it seemed good that it should not be so. The first advent of Messiah was to be an advent of humiliation. That humiliation was to begin even from the time of His conception and birth.

Let us beware of despising poverty in others, and of being ashamed of it if God lays it upon ourselves. The condition of life which Jesus voluntarily chose, ought always to be regarded with holy reverence. The common tendency of the day to bow down before rich men, and make an idol of money, ought to be carefully resisted and discouraged. The example of our Lord is a sufficient answer to a thousand grovelling maxims about wealth, which pass current among men. "Though He was rich, yet for our sakes He became poor." (2 Cor. viii. 9.)

Let us admire the amazing condescension of the Son of God. The Heir of all things not only took our nature upon Him, but took it in the most humbling form in which it could have been assumed. It would have been condescension to come on earth as a king and reign. It was a miracle of mercy passing our comprehension to come on earth as a poor man, to be despised, and suffer, and die. Let His love constrain us to live not to ourselves, but to Him. Let His example daily bring home to our conscience the precept of Scripture: "Mind not high things, but condescend to men of low estate." (Rom. xii. 16.)

We should notice, in the second place, *the high privilege of the Virgin Mary.* The language which the angel Gabriel addresses to her is very remarkable. He calls her " highly favoured." He tells her that "the Lord is with her." He says to her, "Blessed art thou among women."

It is a well-known fact, that the Roman Catholic Church pays an honour to the Virgin Mary, hardly inferior to that which it pays to her blessed Son. She is formally declared by the Roman Catholic Church to have been "conceived without sin." She is held up to Roman Catholics as an object of worship, and prayed to as a mediator between God and man, no less powerful than Christ Himself. For all this, be it remembered, there is not the slightest warrant in Scripture. There is no warrant in the verses before us now. There is no warrant in any other part of God's word.

But while we say this, we must in fairness admit, that no woman was ever so highly honoured as the mother of our Lord. It is evident that one woman only out of the countless millions of the human race, could be the means whereby God could be "manifest in the flesh," and the Virgin Mary had the mighty privilege of being that one. By one woman, sin and death were brought into the world at the beginning. By the child-bearing of one woman, life and immortality were brought to light when Christ was born. No wonder that this one woman was called " highly favoured " and " blessed."

One thing in connection with this subject should never be forgotten by Christians. There is a relationship to Christ within reach of us all,—a relationship far nearer than that of flesh and blood,—a relationship which belongs to all who repent and believe. " Whosoever shall do the will of God," says Jesus, " the same is my brother, and sister, and mother."—" Blessed is the womb that bare thee," was the saying of a woman one day. But what was the reply? " Yea! rather blessed are they

that hear the word of God and keep it." (Mark iii. 35 ;
Luke xi. 27.)

We should notice, finally, in these verses, *the glorious
account of our Lord Jesus Christ,* which the angel gives
to Mary. Every part of the account is full of deep
meaning, and deserves close attention.

Jesus "shall be great," says Gabriel. Of His greatness we know something already. He has brought in a
great salvation. He has shown Himself a Prophet greater
than Moses. He is a great High Priest. And He shall
be greater still when He shall be owned as a King.

Jesus "shall be called the Son of the Highest," says
Gabriel. He was so before He came into the world.
Equal to the Father in all things, He was from all
eternity the Son of God. But He was to be known and
acknowledged as such by the Church. The Messiah was
to be recognized and worshipped as nothing less than
very God.

"The Lord God shall give unto Him the throne of
his father David," says Gabriel, "and he shall reign over
the house of Jacob for ever." The literal fulfilment of
this part of the promise is yet to come. Israel is yet to
be gathered. The Jews are yet to be restored to their
own land, and to look to Him whom they once pierced, as
their King and their God. Though the accomplishment
of this prediction tarry, we may confidently wait for it.
It shall surely come one day and not tarry. (Hab. ii. 3.)

Finally, says Gabriel, "Of the kingdom of Jesus there
shall be no end." Before His glorious kingdom, the
empires of this world shall one day go down and pass away.
Like Nineveh, and Babylon, and Egypt, and Tyre, and

Carthage, they shall all come to nothing one day, and the saints of the most high shall take the kingdom. Before Jesus every knee shall one day bow, and every tongue confess that He is Lord. His kingdom alone shall prove an everlasting kingdom, and His dominion that which shall not pass away. (Dan. vii. 14, 27.)

The true Christian should often dwell on this glorious promise and take comfort in its contents. He has no cause to be ashamed of his Master. Poor and despised as he may often be for the Gospel's sake, he may feel assured that he is on the conquering side. The kingdoms of this world shall yet become the kingdoms of Christ. Yet a little time and He that shall come will come, and will not tarry. (Heb. x. 37.) For that blessed day let us patiently wait, and watch, and pray. Now is the time for carrying the cross, and for fellowship with Christ's sufferings. The day draws near when Christ shall take His great power and reign; and when all who have served Him faithfully shall exchange a cross for a crown.

NOTES. LUKE I. 26—33.

27.—[*A virgin espoused.*] Let us not fail to note the wise providence by which the mother of our Lord, though a virgin, was a virgin " espoused." It screened her reputation from unseemly remarks. It provided a helper and protector for her in her time of weakness and need.

28.—[*Highly favoured.*] The Romanist translation of this word, " full of grace," does not convey the meaning so well as our own translation, and is moreover liable to shameful perversion. In no way can the word bear the sense of one " full of grace to bestow on others." The truest sense is that of our marginal reading, " one much graced,"—one who has been made the object of much grace, but not one who has much grace to give. The Romish prayer, to the Virgin, beginning "Ave Maria," is a most unhappy perversion of Scripture. Bishop Hall remarks, "The angel salutes the virgin; he prays not to her. He salutes her, as a saint; he prays not to her as a goddess.

For us to salute her as he did were gross presumption, for neither are we as he was, neither is she as she was. If he that was a spirit, saluted her that was flesh and blood here on earth, it is not for us that are flesh and blood to salute her which is a glorious spirit in heaven. For us to pray to her in the angel's salutation, were to abuse the virgin, the angel, and the salutation."

29.—[*troubled.*] The Greek word here is very strong and intensive, and nowhere used in the New Testament, excepting in this place.

32, 33.—[*Throne of David—Reign over the house of Jacob.*] Let us beware of spiritualizing away the full meaning of these words. The "house of Jacob" does not mean all Christians. The "throne of David" does not mean the office of a Saviour to all Gentile believers. The words will yet receive a literal fulfilment, when the Lord Jesus comes the second time, and the Jews are converted. The promise of Gabriel is parallel with Jeremiah xxx. 9. The kingdom of which he speaks, is the glorious kingdom foretold in Daniel vii. 27, before which all other kingdoms are finally to be overthrown at Christ's second coming.

<hr>

LUKE I. 34—38.

34 Then said Mary unto the angel, How shall this be, seeing I know not a man?

35 And the angel answered and said unto her, The Holy Ghost shall come upon thee, and the power of the Highest shall overshadow thee: therefore also that holy thing which shall be born of thee shall be called the Son of God.

36 And, behold, thy cousin Elisabeth, she hath also conceived a son in her old age: and this is the sixth month with her, who was called barren.

37 For with God nothing shall be impossible.

38 And Mary said, Behold the handmaid of the Lord; be it unto me according to thy word. And the angel departed from her.

LET us mark, in these verses, *the reverent and discreet manner in which the angel Gabriel speaks of the great mystery of Christ's incarnation.* In reply to the question of the Virgin, "How shall this be?" He uses these remarkable words: "The Holy Ghost shall come upon thee, and the power of the Highest shall overshadow thee."

We shall do well to follow the example of the angel

in all our reflections on this deep subject. Let us ever
regard it with holy reverence, and abstain from those
unseemly and unprofitable speculations upon it, in which
some have unhappily indulged. Enough for us to know
that "the Word was made flesh," and that when the Son
of God came into the world, a real "body was prepared
for Him," so that He "took part of our flesh and blood,"
and was "made of a woman." (John i. 14; Heb. x. 5;
Heb. ii. 14; Gal. iv. 4.) Here we must stop. The
manner in which all this was effected is wisely hidden
from us. If we attempt to pry beyond this point, we
shall but darken counsel by words without knowledge;
and rush in where angels fear to tread. In a religion
which really comes down from heaven there must needs
be mysteries. Of such mysteries in Christianity, the
incarnation is one.

Let us mark, in the second place, *the prominent place
assigned to the Holy Ghost in the great mystery of the
incarnation*. We find it written, "The Holy Ghost shall
come upon thee."

An intelligent reader of the Bible will probably not fail
to remember, that the honour here given to the Spirit is
in precise harmony with the teaching of Scripture in other
places. In every step of the great work of man's redemption, we shall find special mention of the work of
the Holy Ghost. Did Jesus die to make atonement for
our sins? It is written that "through the eternal Spirit
He offered Himself without spot to God." (Heb. ix. 14.)
Did He rise again for our justification? It is written
that He "was quickened by the Spirit." (1 Peter iii. 18.)
Does He supply His disciples with comfort between the

time of His first and second advent? It is written that the Comforter, whom He promised to send is "the Spirit of truth." (John xiv. 17.)

Let us take heed that we give the Holy Ghost the same place in our personal religion, which we find Him occupying in God's word. Let us remember, that all that believers have, and are, and enjoy under the Gospel, they owe to the inward teaching of the Holy Spirit. The work of each of the three Persons of the Trinity is equally and entirely needful to the salvation of every saved soul. The election of God the Father, the blood of God the Son, and the sanctification of God the Spirit, ought never to be separated in our Christianity.

Let us mark, in the third place, *the mighty principle which the angel Gabriel lays down to silence all objections about the incarnation*. "With God nothing shall be impossible."

A hearty reception of this great principle is of immense importance to our own inward peace. Questions and doubts will often arise in men's minds about many subjects in religion. They are the natural result of our fallen estate of soul. Our faith at the best is very feeble. Our knowledge at its highest is clouded with much infirmity. And among many antidotes to a doubting, anxious, questioning state of mind, few will be found more useful than that before us now,—a thorough conviction of the almighty power of God. With Him who called the world into being and formed it out of nothing, everything is possible. Nothing is too hard for the Lord.

There is no sin too black and bad to be pardoned. The blood of Christ cleanseth from all sin.—There is no heart too hard and wicked to be changed. The heart of stone can be made a heart of flesh.—There is no work too hard for a believer to do. We may do all things through Christ strengthening us.—There is no trial too hard to be borne. The grace of God is sufficient for us.—There is no promise too great to be fulfilled. Christ's words never pass away, and what He has promised He is able to perform.—There is no difficulty too great for a believer to overcome. When God is for us, who shall be against us? The mountain shall become a plain.—Let principles like these be continually before our minds. The angel's receipt is an invaluable remedy. Faith never rests so calmly and peacefully as when it lays its head on the pillow of God's omnipotence.

Let us mark, in the last place, *the meek and ready acquiescence of the Virgin Mary in God's revealed will concerning her.* She says to the angel, "Behold the handmaid of the Lord; be it unto me according to thy word."

There is far more of admirable grace in this answer than at first sight appears. A moment's reflection will show us, that it was no light matter to become the mother of our Lord in this unheard of and mysterious way. It brought with it, no doubt, at a distant period great honour; but it brought with it for the present no small danger to Mary's reputation, and no small trial to Mary's faith. All this danger and trial the holy Virgin was willing and ready to risk. She asks no further questions. She raises no further objections. She accepts the honour laid upon her with all its attendant perils and inconveniences. "Behold," she says, "the handmaid of the Lord."

Let us seek in our daily practical Christianity to exercise the same blessed spirit of faith which we see here in the Virgin Mary. Let us be willing to go anywhere, and do anything, and be anything, whatever be the present and immediate inconvenience, so long as God's will is clear and the path of duty is plain. The words of good Bishop Hall on this passage are worth remembering. " All disputations with God after His will is known, arise from infidelity. There is not a more noble proof of faith than to captivate all the powers of our understanding and will to our Creator, and without all questionings to go blindfold whither He will lead us."

NOTES. LUKE I. 34—38.

36.—[*Behold thy cousin Elisabeth.*] We should mark how graciously the angel helps the faith of the Virgin Mary, by telling her of a fact which may serve to assist her in receiving his message. This is the manner of God's dealings. He knows our weakness. It is like our Lord calling for meat, and eating of a broiled fish and honey-comb, to satisfy his disciples of the material reality of his risen body.

LUKE I. 39—45.

39 And Mary arose in those days, and went into the hill country with haste, into a city of Juda;

40 And entered into the house of Zacharias, and saluted Elisabeth.

41 And it came to pass, that, when Elisabeth heard the salutation of Mary, the babe leaped in her womb; and Elisabeth was filled with the Holy Ghost.

42 And she spake out with a loud voice, and said, Blessed *art* thou among women, and blessed is the fruit of thy womb.

43 And whence *is* this to me, that the mother of my Lord should come to me?

44 For, lo, as soon as the voice of thy salutation sounded in mine ears, the babe leaped in my womb for joy.

45 And blessed *is* she that believed : for there shall be a performance of those things which were told her from the Lord.

WE should observe in this passage, *the benefit of fellowship and communion between believers.* We read of a visit paid by the Virgin Mary to her cousin Elisabeth. We are told in a striking manner how the hearts of both these holy women were cheered, and their minds lifted up by this interview. Without this visit, Elisabeth might never have been so filled with the Holy Ghost, as we are here told she was; and Mary might never have uttered that song of praise which is now known all over the Church of Christ. The words of an old divine are deep and true: "Happiness communicated doubles itself. Grief grows greater by concealing: joy by expression."

We should always regard communion with other believers as an eminent means of grace. It is a refreshing break in our journey along the narrow way to exchange experience with our fellow travellers. It helps us insensibly and it helps them, and so is a mutual gain. It is the nearest approach that we can make on earth to the joy of heaven. "As iron sharpeneth iron, so doth the countenance of a man his friend." We need reminding of this. The subject does not receive sufficient attention, and the souls of believers suffer in consequence. There are many who fear the Lord and think upon His name, and yet forget to speak often one to another. (Malachi iii. 16.) First let us seek the face of God. Then let us seek the face of God's friends. If we did this more, and were more careful about the company we keep, we should oftener know what it is to feel "filled with the Holy Ghost."

We should observe in this passage, *the clear spiritual knowledge which appears in the language of Elisabeth.* She uses an expression about the Virgin Mary which shews that she herself was deeply taught of God. She calls her "the mother of my Lord."

Those words "my Lord" are so familiar to our ears, that we miss the fulness of their meaning. At the time they were spoken they implied far more than we are apt to suppose. They were nothing less than a distinct declaration that the child who was to be born of the Virgin Mary was the long promised Messiah, the "Lord" of whom David in spirit had prophecied, the Christ of God. Viewed in this light, the expression is a wonderful example of faith. It is a confession worthy to be placed by the side of that of Peter, when he said to Jesus, "Thou art the Christ."

Let us remember the deep meaning of the words, "the Lord," and beware of using them lightly and carelessly. Let us consider that they rightly apply to none but Him who was crucified for our sins on Calvary. Let the recollection of this fact invest the words with a holy reverence, and make us careful how we let them fall from our lips. There are two texts connected with the expression which should often come to our minds. In one it is written, "No man can say that Jesus is the Lord but by the Holy Ghost." In the other it is written, "Every tongue shall confess that Jesus Christ is Lord, to the glory of God the Father." (1 Cor. xii. 3. Philipp. ii. 11.)

Finally, we should observe in these verses, *the high praise which Elisabeth bestows upon the grace of faith.* "Blessed," she says, "is she that believed."

We need not wonder that this holy woman should thus commend faith. No doubt she was well acquainted with the Old Testament Scriptures. She knew the great things that faith had done. What is the whole history of God's saints in every age but a record of men and women who obtained a good report by faith? What is the simple story of all from Abel downwards but a narrative of redeemed sinners who believed, and so were blessed? By faith they embraced promises. By faith they lived. By faith they walked. By faith they endured hardships. By faith they looked to an unseen Saviour, and good things yet to come. By faith they battled with the world, the flesh, and the devil. By faith they overcame, and got safe home. Of this goodly company the Virgin Mary was proving herself one. No wonder that Elisabeth said, "Blessed is she that believed."

Do we know anything of this precious faith? This, after all, is the question that concerns us. Do we know anything of the faith of God's elect, the faith which is of the operation of God? (Titus i. 2. Col. ii. 12.) Let us never rest till we know it by experience. Once knowing it, let us never cease to pray that our faith may grow exceedingly. Better a thousand times be rich in faith than rich in gold. Gold will be worthless in the unseen world to which we are all travelling. Faith will be owned in that world before God the Father and the holy angels. When the great white throne is set, and the books are opened, when the dead are called from their graves, and receiving their final sentence, the value of faith will at length be fully known. Men will learn then, if they never learned before, how true are the words, "Blessed are they that believed."

NOTES. LUKE I. 39—45.

39.—[*A city of Judah.*] It is thought by many that this city was Hebron, and by examining Joshua xxi. 9—11, we shall see there is considerable probability that it was. It is the place where Abraham, the father of the faithful, long dwelt, and the place where Sarah died. Gen. xiii. 18, and xxiii. 2. Few places in Palestine have been so highly honoured.

LUKE I. 46—56.

46 And Mary said, My soul doth magnify the Lord,

47 And my spirit hath rejoiced in God my Saviour.

48 For he hath regarded the low estate of his handmaiden : for, behold, from henceforth all generations shall call me blessed.

49 For he that is mighty hath done to me great things; and holy *is* his name.

50 And his mercy *is* on them that fear him from generation to generation.

51 He hath shewed strength with his arm; he hath scattered the proud in the imagination of their hearts.

52 He hath put down the mighty from *their* seats, and exalted them of low degree.

53 He hath filled the hungry with good things; and the rich he hath sent empty away.

54 He hath holpen his servant Israel, in remembrance of *his* mercy;

55 As he spake to our fathers, to Abraham, and to his seed for ever.

56 And Mary abode with her about three months, and returned to her own house.

THESE verses contain the Virgin Mary's famous hymn of praise, in the prospect of becoming the "mother of our Lord."—Next to the Lord's Prayer, perhaps, few passages of Scripture are better known than this. Wherever the Church of England Prayer-book is used, this hymn forms part of the evening service. And we need not wonder that the compilers of that Prayer-book gave it so prominent a place. No words can express more aptly the praise for redeeming mercy which ought to form part of the public worship of every branch of Christ's Church.

Let us mark, firstly, *the full acquaintance with Scripture which this hymn exhibits.* We are reminded as we read it, of many expressions in the book of Psalms. Above all, we are reminded of the song of Hannah, in the book of Samuel. (1 Sam. ii. 2, &c.) It is evident that the memory of the Blessed Virgin was stored with Scripture. She was familiar, whether by hearing or by reading, with the Old Testament. And so, when out of the abundance of her heart her mouth spoke, she gave vent to her feelings in Scriptural language. Moved by the Holy Ghost to break forth into praise, she chooses language which the Holy Ghost had already consecrated and used.

Let us strive, every year we live, to become more deeply acquainted with Scripture. Let us study it, search into it, dig into it, meditate on it, until it dwell in us richly. (Coloss. ii. 16.) In particular, let us labour to make ourselves familiar with those parts of the Bible which, like the book of Psalms, describe the experience of the saints of old. We shall find it most helpful to us in all our approaches to God. It will supply us with the best and most suitable language both for the expression of our wants and thanksgivings. Such knowledge of the Bible can doubtless never be attained without regular, daily study. But the time spent on such study is never mis-spent. It will bear fruit after many days.

Let us mark, secondly, in this hymn of praise, *the Virgin Mary's deep humility*. She who was chosen of God to the high honour of being Messiah's mother, speaks of her own "low estate," and acknowledges her need of a "Saviour." She does not let fall a word to show that she regarded herself as a sinless, "immaculate" person. On the contrary, she uses the language of one who has been taught by the grace of God to feel her own sins, and so far from being able to save others, requires a Saviour for her own soul. We may safely affirm that none would be more forward to reprove the honour paid by the Romish Church to the Virgin Mary, than the Virgin Mary herself.

Let us copy this holy humility of our Lord's mother, while we stedfastly refuse to regard her as a mediator, or to pray to her. Like her, let us be lowly in our own eyes, and think little of ourselves. Humility is the highest grace that can adorn the Christian character. It is a true saying of an old divine, that "a man has just so much Christianity as he has humility." It is the grace, which of all is most becoming to human nature. Above all, it is the grace which is within the reach of every converted person. All are not rich. All are not learned. All are not highly gifted. All are not preachers. But all children of God may be clothed with humility.

Let us mark, thirdly, *the lively thankfulness of the Virgin Mary.* It stands out prominently in all the early part of her hymn. Her "soul magnifies the Lord." Her "spirit rejoices in God." "All generations shall call her blessed." "Great things have been done for her." We can scarcely enter into the full extent of feelings which a holy Jewess would experience on finding herself in Mary's position. But we should try to recollect them as we read her repeated expressions of praise.

We too shall do well to walk in Mary's steps in this matter, and cultivate a thankful spirit. It has ever been a mark of God's most distinguished saints in every age. David, in the Old Testament, and St. Paul, in the New, are remarkable for their thankfulness. We seldom read much of their writings without finding them blessing and praising God. Let us rise from our beds every morning with a deep conviction that we are debtors, and that every day we have more mercies than we deserve. Let us look around us every week, as we travel through the world, and see whether we have not much to thank God for. If our hearts are in the right place, we shall never find any difficulty in building an Ebenezer. Well would it be if our prayers and supplications were more mingled with thanksgiving. (1 Sam. vii. 12. Phil. iv. 6.)

Let us mark, fourthly, *the experimental acquaintance with God's former dealings with His people, which the Virgin Mary possessed.* She speaks of God as One whose " mercy is on them that fear Him,"—as One who " scatters the proud, and puts down the mighty, and sends the rich empty away,"—as One who " exalteth them of low degree, and filleth the hungry with good things." She spoke, no doubt, in recollection of Old Testament history. She remembered how Israel's God had put down Pharaoh, and the Canaanites, and the Philistines, and Sennacherib, and Haman, and Belshazzar. She remembered how He had exalted Joseph, and Moses, and Samuel, and David, and Esther, and Daniel, and never allowed His chosen people to be completely destroyed. And in all God's dealings with herself,—in placing honour upon a poor woman of Nazareth,—in raising up Messiah in such a dry ground as the Jewish nation seemed to have become,—she traced the handiwork of Israel's covenant God.

The true Christian should always give close attention to Bible history, and the lives of individual saints. Let us often examine the "footsteps of the flock." (Cant. i. 8.) Such study throws light on God's mode of dealing with His people. He is of one mind. What He does for them, and to them, in time past, He is likely to do in time to come. Such study will teach us what to expect, check unwarrantable expectations, and encourage us when cast down. Happy is that man whose mind is well stored with such knowledge. It will make him patient and hopeful.

Let us mark, lastly, *the firm grasp which the Virgin Mary had of Bible promises.* She ends her hymn of praise by declaring that God has "blessed Israel in remembrance of His mercy," and that He has done "as He spake to our fathers, to Abraham and his seed for ever." These words show clearly that she remembered the old promise made to Abraham, "In thee shall all nations of the earth be blessed." And it is evident that in the approaching birth of her Son she regarded this promise as about to be fulfilled.

Let us learn from this holy woman's example, to lay firm hold on Bible promises. It is of the deepest importance to our peace to do so. Promises are, in fact, the manna that we should daily eat, and the water that we should daily drink, as we travel through the wilderness of this world. We see not yet all things put under us. We see not Christ, and heaven, and the book of life, and the mansions prepared for us. We walk by faith, and this faith leans on promises. But on those promises we may lean confidently. They will bear all the weight we can lay on them. We shall find one day, like the Virgin Mary, that God keeps His word, and that what He has spoken, so He will always in due time perform.

NOTES. LUKE I. 46—56.

47.—[*My Saviour.*] Let us not fail to notice the Virgin Mary's expressions of need of salvation. It would be difficult to find a more complete answer to the Romish doctrine respecting her, and especially the doctrine of the immaculate conception, than her language in this hymn.

51.—[*His arm.*] A remark of Whitby on this expression is worth notice. "God's great power is represented by His finger,—His greater by His hand,—His greatest by His arm. The production of lice was by the finger of God. Exod. viii. 19 ;—His other miracles in Egypt were wrought by His hand : Exod. iii. 20 ;—the destruction of Pharaoh and his host in the Red Sea, by His arm. Exod. xv. 6."

LUKE I. 57—66.

57 Now Elisabeth's full time came that she should be delivered ; and she brought forth a son.

58 And her neighbours and her cousins heard how the Lord had shewed great mercy upon her; and they rejoiced with her.

59 And it came to pass, that on the eighth day they came to circumcise the child ; and they called him Zacharias, after the name of his father.

60 And his mother answered and said, Not *so ;* but he shall be called John.

61 And they said unto her, There is none of thy kindred that is called by this name.

62 And they made signs to his father, how he would have him called.

63 And he asked for a writing table, and wrote, saying, His name is John. And they marvelled all.

64 And his mouth was opened immediately, and his tongue *loosed,* and he spake, and praised God.

65 And fear came on all that dwelt round about them : and all these sayings were noised abroad throughout all the hill country of Judæa.

66 And all they that heard *them* laid *them* up in their hearts, saying, What manner of child shall this be ? And the hand of the Lord was with him.

WE have in this passage the history of a birth, the birth of a burning and shining light in the Church, the forerunner of Christ Himself,—John the Baptist. The language in which the Holy Ghost describes the event is well worthy of remark. It is written that "The Lord shewed great mercy on Elisabeth." There was mercy in bringing her safely through her time of trial. There was mercy in making her the mother of a living child. Happy are those family circles, whose births are viewed in this light—as especial instances of "the mercy" of the Lord.

We see in the conduct of Elisabeth's neighbours and cousins, *a striking example of the kindness we owe to one another*. It is written that "They rejoiced with her."

How much more happiness there would be in this evil world, if conduct like that of Elisabeth's relations was more common! Sympathy in one another's joys and sorrows costs little, and yet is a grace of most mighty power. Like the oil on the wheels of some large engine, it may seem a trifling and unimportant thing, yet in reality it has an immense influence on the comfort and well-working of the whole machine of society. A kind word of congratulation or consolation is seldom forgotten. The heart that is warmed by good tidings, or chilled by affliction, is peculiarly susceptible, and sympathy to such a heart is often more precious than gold.

The servant of Christ will do well to remember this grace. It seems "a little one," and amidst the din of controversy, and the battle about mighty doctrines, we are sadly apt to overlook it. Yet it is one of those pins of the tabernacle which we must not leave in the wilderness. It is one of those ornaments of the Christian character which make it beautiful in the eyes of men. Let us not forget that it is enforced upon us by a special precept: "Rejoice with them that do rejoice, and weep with them that weep." (Rom. xii. 15.) The practice of it seems to bring down a special blessing. The Jews who came to comfort Mary and Martha at Bethany, saw the greatest miracle that Jesus ever worked.—Above all, it is commended to us by the most perfect example. Our Lord was ready both to go to a marriage feast, and to weep at a grave. (John ii. 1, &c. John xi. 1, &c.) Let us be ever ready to go and do likewise.

We see in the conduct of Zacharias in this passage, *a striking example of the benefit of affliction*. He resists the wishes of his relations to call his new-born son after his own name. He clings firmly to the name "John," by which the angel Gabriel had commanded him to be called. He shews that his nine months' dumbness had not been inflicted on him in vain. He is no longer faithless, but believing. He now believes every word that Gabriel had spoken to him, and every word of his message shall be obeyed.

We need not doubt that the past nine months had been a most profitable time to the soul of Zacharias. He had learned, probably, more about his own heart, and about God, than he ever knew before. His conduct shews it. Correction had proved instruction. He was ashamed of his unbelief. Like Job, he could say, "I have heard of thee by the hearing of the ear, but now mine eye seeth thee." Like Hezekiah, when the Lord left him, he had found out what was in his heart. (Job xlii. 5. 2 Chron. xxxii. 31.)

Let us take heed that affliction does us good, as it did to Zacharias. We cannot escape trouble in a sin-laden world. Man is born to trouble, as the sparks fly upwards. (Job v. 27.) But in the time of our trouble, let us make earnest prayer that we may " hear the rod and who hath appointed it," that we may learn wisdom by the rod, and not harden our hearts against God. "Sanctified afflictions," says an old divine, are "spiritual promotions." The sorrow that humbles us, and drives us nearer to God, is a blessing, and a downright gain. No case is more hopeless than that of the man who, in time of affliction, turns his back upon

God. There is an awful mark set against one of the
kings of Judah: "In the time of his distress he did
trespass yet more against the Lord : this is that king
Ahaz." (2 Chron. xxviii. 22.)

We see in the early history of John Baptist the *nature
of the blessing that we should desire for all young children.*
We read that "the hand of the Lord was with him."

We are not told distinctly what these words mean.
We are left to gather their meaning from the promise
that went before John before his birth, and the life that
John lived all his days. But we need not doubt that the
hand of the Lord was with John to sanctify and renew
his heart—to teach and fit him for his office—to strengthen
him for all his work as the forerunner of the Lamb of
God—to encourage him in all his bold denunciation of
men's sins—and to comfort him in his last hours, when
he was beheaded in prison. We know that he was filled
with the Holy Ghost from his mother's womb. We need
not doubt that from his earliest years the grace of the
Holy Ghost appeared in his ways. In his boyhood as
well as in his manhood the constraining power of a mighty
principle from above appeared in him. That power was
the "hand of the Lord."

This is the portion that we ought to seek for our
children. It is the best portion, the happiest portion, the
only portion that can never be lost, and will endure beyond the grave. It is good to have over them "the hand"
of teachers and instructors; but it is better still to have
"the hand of the Lord." We may be thankful if they
obtain the patronage of the great and the rich. But we
ought to care far more for their obtaining the favour of

God. The hand of the Lord is a thousand times better than the hand of Herod. The one is weak, foolish, and uncertain; caressing to day, and beheading to-morrow. The other is almighty, all-wise, and unchangeable. Where it holds it holds for evermore. Let us bless God that the Lord never changes. What He was in John the Baptist's days, He is now. What He did for the son of Zacharias, He can do for our boys and girls. But He waits to be entreated. If we would have the hand of the Lord with our children, we must diligently seek it.

NOTES. LUKE I. 57—66.

59.—[*Eighth day.*] This was in accordance with Leviticus xii. 3. If a child died uncircumcised before the eighth day, we find nothing in Scripture to warrant our saying that it was not saved. By parity of reason we may justly conclude that baptism is not absolutely necessary to the salvation of infants under the Christian dispensation. It is not the want of ordinances, but the contempt of them that destroys souls. Of this contempt a little infant cannot be guilty.

62.—[*Made signs.*] This expression seems to make it probable that Zacharias was deaf as well as dumb.

LUKE I. 67—80.

67 And his father Zacharias was filled with the Holy Ghost, and prophesied, saying,

68 Blessed *be* the Lord God of Israel; for he hath visited and redeemed his people,

69 And hath raised up an horn of salvation for us in the house of his servant David;

70 As he spake by the mouth of his holy prophets, which have been since the world began:

71 That we should be saved from our enemies, and from the hand of all that hate us;

72 To perform the mercy *promised* to our fathers, and to remember his holy covenant;

73 The oath which he sware to our father Abraham,

74 That he would grant unto us, that we being delivered out of the hand of our enemies, might serve him without fear,

75 In holiness and righteousness before him, all the days of our life.

76 And thou, child, shalt be called the prophet of the Highest: for thou shalt go before the face of the Lord to prepare his ways;

77 To give knowledge of salvation unto his people by the remission of their sins,

78 Through the tender mercy of our God; whereby the dayspring from on high hath visited us,

79 To give light to them that sit in darkness and *in* the shadow of death, to guide our feet into the way of peace.

80 And the child grew, and waxed strong in spirit, and was in the deserts till the day of his shewing unto Israel.

ANOTHER hymn of praise demands our attention in these verses. We have read the thanksgiving of Mary, the mother of our Lord. Let us now read the thanksgiving of Zacharias, the father of John the Baptist. We have heard what praises the first advent of Christ drew from the Virgin of the house of David. Let us now hear what praise it draws from an aged priest.

We should notice, firstly, *the deep thankfulness of a Jewish believer's heart, in the prospect of Messiah's appearing.* Praise is the first word that falls from the mouth of Zacharias as soon as his dumbness is removed, and his speech restored. He begins with the same expression with which St. Paul begins several of his epistles : "Blessed be the Lord."

At this period of the world we can hardly understand the depth of this good man's feelings. We must imagine ourselves in his position. We must fancy ourselves seeing the fulfilment of the oldest promise in the Old Testament, —the promise of a Saviour, and beholding the accomplishment of this promise brought near to our own door. We must try to realize what a dim and imperfect view men had of the Gospel before Christ actually appeared, and the shadows and types passed away. Then perhaps we may have some idea of the feelings of Zacharias when he cried out, "Blessed be the Lord."

It may be feared that Christians have very low and inadequate conceptions of their amazing privileges in living under the full light of the Gospel. We have probably a very faint idea of the comparative dimness and twilight of the Jewish dispensation. We have a very feeble notion of what a church must have been before the incarnation of Christ. Let us open our eyes to the extent of our obligations. Let us learn from the example of Zacharias, to be more thankful.

We should notice, secondly, in this hymn of praise, *how much stress Zacharias lays on God's fulfilment of His promises.* He declares that God has "visited and redeemed his people," speaking of it in the manner of the prophets as a thing already accomplished, because sure to take place. He goes on to proclaim the instrument of this redemption,—"a horn of salvation,"—a strong Saviour of the house of David. And then he adds that all this is done, "as He spake by the mouth of His holy prophet,—to perform the mercy promised,—to remember His holy covenant,—and the oath which He sware to our father Abraham."

It is clear that the souls of Old Testament believers fed much on God's promises. They were obliged to walk by faith far more than we are. They knew nothing of the great facts which we know about Christ's life, and death, and resurrection. They looked forward to redemption as a thing hoped for, but not yet seen,—and their only warrant for their hope was God's covenanted word. Their faith may well put us to shame.—So far from disparaging Old Testament believers, as some are disposed to do, we ought to marvel that they were what they were.

Let us learn to rest on promises and embrace them as Zacharias did. Let us not doubt that every word of God about His people concerning things future, shall as surely be fulfilled as every word about them has been fulfilled concerning things past. Their safety is secured by promise. The world, the flesh, and the devil, shall never prevail against any believer.—Their acquittal at the last day is secured by promise. They shall not come into condemnation, but shall be presented spotless before the Father's throne.—Their final glory is secured by promise. Their Saviour shall come again the second time, as surely as He came the first,—to gather His saints together and to give them a crown of righteousness.—Let us be persuaded of these promises. Let us embrace them and not let them go. They will never fail us. God's word is never broken. He is not a man that He should lie. We have a seal on every promise which Zacharias never saw. We have the seal of Christ's blood to assure us, that what God has promised God will perform.

We should notice, thirdly, in this hymn, *what clear views of Christ's kingdom Zacharias possessed.* He speaks of being "saved and delivered from the hands of enemies," as if he had in view a temporal kingdom and a temporal deliverer from Gentile power. But he does not stop here. He declares that the kingdom of Messiah, is a kingdom in which His people are to " serve Him without fear, in holiness and righteousness before Him." This kingdom, He proclaimed, was drawing nigh. Prophets had long foretold that it would one day be set up. In the birth of his son John the Baptist, and the near approach of Christ, Zacharias saw this kingdom close at hand.

The foundation of this kingdom of Messiah was laid by the preaching of the Gospel. From that time the Lord Jesus has been continually gathering out subjects from an evil world. The full completion of the kingdom is an event yet to come. The saints of the Most High shall one day have entire dominion. The little stone of the

Gospel-kingdom shall yet fill the whole earth.   But whether in its incomplete or complete state, the subjects of the kingdom are always of one character.   They "serve God without fear."   They serve God " in holiness and righteousness."

Let us give all diligence to belong to this kingdom. Small as it seem now, it will be great and glorious one day.   The men and women who have served God in " holiness and righteousness " shall one day see all things put under them.   Every enemy shall be subdued, and they shall reign for ever in that new heaven and earth, wherein dwelleth righteousness.

We should notice, finally, *what clear views of doctrine Zacharias enjoyed.*   He ends his hymn of praise by addressing his infant son John the Baptist.   He foretells that he shall " go before the face " of Messiah, and " give knowledge of the salvation" that He is about to bring in,— a salvation which is all of grace and mercy,—a salvation of which the leading privileges are "remission of sins," "light," and "peace."

Let us end the chapter by examining what we know of these three glorious privileges.   Do we know anything of pardon?   Have we turned from darkness to light? Have we tasted peace with God?   These, after all, are the realities of Christianity.   These are the things, without which church-membership and sacraments save no one's soul.   Let us never rest till we are experimentally acquainted with them.—Mercy and grace have provided them.   Mercy and grace will give them to all who call on Christ's name.—Let us never rest till the Spirit witnesses with our spirit that our sins are forgiven us,—that we

have passed from darkness to light, and that we are
actually walking in the narrow way, the way of peace.

NOTES. LUKE I. 67—80.

69.—[*An horn of salvation.*] Henry Venn remarks, "The horn
of an animal is its weapon for defence and vengeance, its orna-
ment and beauty too. It is used therefore in the prophetic style,
to denote the power of the strongest empires. In the same
sense we are to understand it here. By this image the exceeding greatness of the Redeemer's strength, and the never-ceasing
exertion of it in behalf of His church are signified."—*Venn on
the prophecy of Zacharias.*

70.—[*He spake by the mouth of his holy prophets.*] Let us note
that it is expressly said that "God spake" by the prophets.
When we read their words, we read the words of God. Burgon
gives the following apt quotation from Hooker :—"They neither
spake nor wrote any word of their own, but uttered syllable by
syllable as the Spirit put it into their mouths; no otherwise
than as the harp or the lute doth give a sound according to the
discretion of his hands that holdeth and striketh it with skill."

71, 74.—[*Our enemies.*] We are left to gather from other sources,
who are meant by these "enemies." It is highly improbable that
the expression is to be taken only in a spiritual sense, and that
Zacharias only means that Christ delivers His believing people
from the world, the flesh, and the devil. It is far more probable
that the prophecy of Zacharias, speaking, as he did, when filled
with the Holy Ghost, looks far forward into all time, and includes
both the second and the first advents of Jesus Christ. In this view
the expression "enemies" includes not only the spiritual enemies
from whom Jesus delivers His people now, but the literal
enemies from whom He will deliver His redeemed Church, and
the scattered tribes of Israel, at His future second appearing.

78.—[*Dayspring.*] This must mean Christ Himself. He is called
in Malachi, "the Sun of righteousness," and in Peter, "the
day-star," and in Revelation, "the bright and morning star."
(Mal. iv. 2. 2 Peter i. 19. Rev. xxii. 16.) All are figurative
expressions, teaching the same grand truth, that "Christ is the
light of the world." (John viii. 12.)

LUKE II. 1—7.

1 And it came to pass in those days, that there went out a decree from Cæsar Augustus, that all the world should be taxed.

2 *(And* this taxing was first made when Cyrenius was governor of Syria.)

3 And all went to be taxed, every one into his own city.

4 And Joseph also went up from Galilee, out of the city of Nazareth, into Judæa, unto the city of David, which is called Bethlehem; (because he was of the house and lineage o David:)

5 To be taxed with Mary his espoused wife, being great with child.

6 And so it was, that, while they were there, the days were accomplished that she should be delivered.

7 And she brought forth her firstborn son, and wrapped him in swaddling clothes, and laid him in a manger; because there was no room for them in the inn.

WE have, in these verses, the story of a birth,—the birth of the incarnate Son of God, the Lord Jesus Christ. Every birth of a living child is a marvellous event. It brings into being a soul that will never die. But never since the world began was a birth so marvellous as the birth of Christ. In itself it was a miracle:—"God was manifest in the flesh." (1 Tim. iii. 16.) The blessings it brought into the world were unspeakable:—it opened to man the door of everlasting life.

In reading these verses, let us first notice *the times when Christ was born.* It was in the days when Augustus, the first Roman emperor, made "a decree that all the world should be taxed."

The wisdom of God appears in this simple fact. The sceptre was practically departing from Judah. (Gen. xlix. 10.) The Jews were coming under the dominion and taxation of a foreign power. Strangers were beginning to rule over them. They had no longer a really independent government of their own. The "due time" had come for the promised Messiah to appear. Augustus taxes "the world," and at once Christ is born.

It was a time peculiarly suitable for the introduction of

Christ's Gospel. The whole civilized earth was at length governed by one master. (Dan. ii. 40.) There was nothing to prevent the preacher of a new faith going from city to city, and country to country. The princes and priests of the heathen world had been weighed in the balances and found wanting. Egypt, and Assyria, and Babylon, and Persia, and Greece, and 'Rome, had all successively proved that "the world by wisdom knew not God." (1 Cor. i. 21.) Notwithstanding their mighty conquerors, and poets, and historians, and architects, and philosophers, the kingdoms of the world were full of dark idolatry. It was indeed "due time" for God to interpose from heaven, and send down an almighty Saviour. It was "due time" for Christ to be born. (Rom. v. 6.)

Let us ever rest our souls on the thought, that times are in God's hand. (Psalm xxxi. 15.) He knows the best season for sending help to His church, and new light to the world. Let us beware of giving way to over anxiety about the course of events around us, as if we knew better than the King of kings what time relief should come. "Cease, Philip, to try to govern the world," was a frequent saying of Luther to an anxious friend. It was a saying full of wisdom.

Let us notice, secondly, *the place where Christ was born.* It was not at Nazareth of Galilee, where His mother, the Virgin Mary, lived. The prophet Micah had foretold that the event was to take place at Bethlehem. (Micah v. 2.) And so it came to pass. At Bethlehem Christ was born.

The overruling providence of God appears in this simple fact. He orders all things in heaven and earth.

He turns the hearts of kings whithersoever He will. He overruled the time when Augustus decreed the taxing. He directed the enforcement of the decree in such a way, that Mary must needs be at Bethlehem when "the days were accomplished that she should be delivered." Little did the haughty Roman emperor, and his officer Cyrenius, think that they were only instruments in the hand of the God of Israel, and were only carrying out the eternal purposes of the King of kings. Little did they think that they were helping to lay the foundation of a kingdom, before which the empires of this world would all go down one day, and Roman idolatry pass away. The words of Isaiah, upon a like occasion, should be remembered, "He meaneth not so, neither doth his heart think so." (Isaiah x. 7.)

The heart of a believer should take comfort in the recollection of God's providential government of the world. A true Christian should never be greatly moved or disquieted by the conduct of the rulers of the earth. He should see with the eye of faith a hand overruling all that they do to the praise and glory of God. He should regard every king and potentate,—an Augustus, a Cyrenius, a Darius, a Cyrus, a Sennacherib,—as a creature who, with all his power, can do nothing but what God allows, and nothing which is not carrying out God's will. And when the rulers of this world "set themselves against the Lord," he should take comfort in the words of Solomon, "There be higher than they." (Eccles. v. 8.)

Let us notice, lastly, *the manner in which Christ was born.* He was not born under the roof of His mother's house, but in a strange place, and at an "inn." When born, He was not laid in a carefully prepared cradle. He was "laid in a manger, because there was no room in the inn."

We see here the grace and condescension of Christ. Had He come to save mankind with royal majesty, surrounded by His Father's angels, it would have been an act of undeserved mercy. Had He chosen to dwell in a palace, with power and great authority, we should have had reason enough to wonder. But to become poor as the very poorest of mankind, and lowly as the very lowliest,—this is a love that passeth knowledge. It is unspeakable and unsearchable. Never let us forget that through this humiliation Jesus has purchased for us a title to glory. Through His life of suffering, as well as His death, He has obtained eternal redemption for us. All through His life He was poor for our sakes, from the hour of His birth to the hour of His death. And through His poverty we are made rich. (2 Cor. viii. 9.)

Let us beware of despising the poor, because of their poverty. Their condition is one which the Son of God has sanctified and honoured, by taking it voluntarily on Himself. God is no respecter of persons. He looks at the hearts of men, and not at their incomes. Let us never be ashamed of the cross of poverty, if God thinks fit to lay it upon us. To be godless and covetous is disgraceful, but it is no disgrace to be poor. A mean dwelling place, and coarse food, and a hard bed, are not pleasing to flesh and blood. But they are the portion which the Lord Jesus Himself willingly accepted from the day of His entrance into the world. Wealth ruins far more souls than poverty. When the love of money begins to creep over us, let us think of the manger at Bethlehem, and of Him who was laid in it.   Such thoughts may deliver us from much harm.

NOTES. LUKE II. 1—7.

1.—[*Cæsar Augustus.*]   This is that Octavius who, after the defeat of Antony and Cleopatra at Actium, took the government of the Roman Empire into his own hands, and was, properly speaking, the first Cæsar, or Roman Emperor.

[*The world.*]   Some think that the Greek word so translated, is specially applied in the New Testament, to Judæa and the countries surrounding it.   There is no sufficient proof of this. It cannot be taken in this limited sense in Acts xvii. 31, and Rev. xii. 9, and need not be so taken here.

[*Taxed.*]   The word so translated, might be equally well rendered "enrolled."   It is so in the margin.   In the only other place in the New Testament, where it is used, it is translated "written."   Heb. xii. 23.

2.—[*This taxing was first made, &c.*]   There is a well-known difficulty connected with this verse, which calls for a few remarks. According to uninspired writers, Cyrenius or Quirinius, as he is called by Latin authors, was not governor of Syria, until eight or ten years after Christ was born.   How can this be reconciled with St. Luke's statement?   The following explanations have been given.

Some say that the name of Cyrenius has got into the text by mistake, and that we ought to read instead of it, either Quintilius or Saturninus, who were the two governors preceding Cyrenius. But it is a most unsatisfactory proceeding to alter texts, in order to meet difficulties.   In the present case there is no warrant for the alteration.

Some say that the explanation is to be found in the word translated, "was made," and that it ought to be rendered, "took effect."   The sense would then be, that "this enrolling, or taxing, though ordered now, only first *took effect* when Cyrenius was governor."

Some say that the word translated, "first," should have been translated, "prior to," or "before."   The sense would then be, "this taxing was *before* that made under Cyrenius."   For such a translation there is authority in John i. 15 and 30.

Some say that there were two taxings, in both of which Cyrenius was officially concerned, though not exactly in the same capacity on both occasions,—and that St. Luke was aware of this, and expressly inserts the word "first," to show which of the two taxings he meant. In favour of this view, it must be remembered that St. Luke was infinitely more likely to be correct about a matter of fact, than any uninspired historians, and that we have no right to assume, where he differs from them, that they are correct, and he incorrect. Moreover, it is a striking fact, that Justin Martyr, who lived in the second century, distinctly asserts three times that Christ was born under Cyrenius. Wordsworth says that, "the researches of Zumpt have enhanced the probability that Quirinius, who was governor of Cilicia, was also governor of Syria at the time of the nativity."

3.—[*All went to be taxed.*] Quesnel remarks, "Augustus imagines that he is busied in advancing the glory of his name, and the lustre of his reign. And yet his orders, by means of others more powerful and absolute than his, become subservient to the accomplishment of prophecies, of which he is altogether ignorant, —to the birth of a king whom he will never know,—and to the establishment of a monarchy, which will subject his and all others to itself. This is what happens in all ages, and men take no notice of it."

On this taxing being a fulfilment of Genesis xlix. 10, Watson observes, "Nothing can be more strikingly in proof, that the sceptre was departing from Judah, and the government of Herod was rather nominal than real. Julian the apostate objected to Christ's claim, that He was by virtue of this very enrolment born one of Cæsar's subjects, not knowing how truly this illustrated the ancient prophecy of Jacob, that his birth and the departing of the sceptre from Judah should be coincident."

4.—[*Lineage.*] The word so translated is rendered in the only other places where it is used, "kindred," or "family." Acts iii. 25. Ephes. iii. 15.

7.—[*Her first-born Son.*] The words so translated are more emphatic in the Greek language, They would be rendered more literally, "her Son, the first-born one."

[*Wrapped Him in swaddling clothes.*] On this expression, the Fathers, and most Romish writers, have built the idea that our Lord's birth was a childbirth without labour or pain. Such an idea is, to say the least, an unprofitable conjecture. There is nothing mentioned here which a mother, in Mary's position, in an Eastern climate, might not have done for herself without aid. There is no need of imagining and inventing miraculous circumstances in our Lord's incarnation, beside those which are fully revealed.

[*A manger.*] The word so translated is rendered, "a stall," in the only other place where it is used in the New Testament. Luke xii. 15. It admits of considerable doubt whether the common idea that our Lord was laid in the trough out of which cattle feed, is really correct. There is no certain proof that the expression means anything more than that he was "laid in the stable, because there was no room in the house." Some think that this manger was one of those hair cloths, out of which horses, in those countries, are fed. There is strong reason for supposing that the whole transaction took place in a cave, such as many which are to be found in Judæa.

[*No room in the Inn.*] One fact should be carefully noted here, which is often entirely overlooked. In the providence of God the birth of Christ was attended with as much publicity as a birth could possibly be attended with. It took place at an inn, and an inn crowded with strangers from all parts. Imposture was thus rendered impossible. The event was patent to many witnesses, and could never be denied. The Son of God was really incarnate, and literally and really born of a woman, like any of ourselves. Had the birth taken place quietly at Nazareth, or in some private house at Bethlehem, in thirty years time the whole event would probably have been denied.

LUKE II. 8—20.

8 And there were in the same country shepherds abiding in the field, keeping watch over their flock by night.

9 And, lo, the angel of the Lord came upon them, and the glory of the Lord shone round about them : and they were sore afraid.

10 And the angel said unto them, Fear not : for, behold, I bring you good tidings of great joy, which shall be to all people.

11 For unto you is born this day in the city of David a Saviour, which is Christ the Lord.

12 And this *shall be* a sign unto you ; Ye shall find the babe wrapped in swaddling clothes, lying in a manger.

13 And suddenly there was with the angel a multitude of the heavenly host praising God, and saying,

14 Glory to God in the highest, and on earth peace, good will toward men.

15 And it came to pass, as the angels were gone away from them into heaven, the shepherds said one to another, Let us now go even unto Bethlehem, and see this thing which is come to pass, which the Lord hath made known unto us.

16 And they came with haste, and found Mary, and Joseph, and the babe lying in a manger.

17 And when they had seen *it*, they made known abroad the saying which was told them concerning this child.

18 And all they that heard *it* wondered at those things which were told them by the shepherds.

19 But Mary kept all these things, and pondered *them* in her heart.

20 And the shepherds returned, glorifying and praising God for all the things that they had heard and seen, as it was told unto them.

WE read, in these verses, how the birth of the Lord Jesus was first announced to the children of men. The birth of a king's son is generally made an occasion of

public revelling and rejoicing. The announcement of
the birth of the Prince of Peace was made privately, at
midnight, and without anything of worldly pomp and
ostentation.

Let us mark *who they were to whom the tidings
first came that Christ was born.* They were "shepherds abiding in the field near Bethlehem, keeping
watch over their flocks by night." To shepherds—not
to priests and rulers,—to shepherds—not to Scribes and
Pharisees, an angel appeared, proclaiming, "unto you is
born this day a Saviour, which is Christ the Lord."

The saying of St. James should come into our mind,
as we read these words: "Hath not God chosen the poor
of this world, rich in faith and heirs of the kingdom,
which he hath promised to them that love him." (James
ii. 5.) The want of money debars no one from spiritual
privileges. The things of God's kingdom are often hid
from the great and noble, and revealed to the poor. The
busy labour of the hands need not prevent a man being
favoured with special communion with God. Moses was
keeping sheep,—Gideon was threshing wheat,—Elisha
was ploughing, when they were severally honoured by
direct calls and revelations from God. Let us resist the
suggestion of Satan, that religion is not for the working
man. The weak of the world are often called before the
mighty. The last are often first, and the first last.

Let us mark, secondly, *the language used by the angel in
announcing Christ's birth to the shepherds.* He said, "I
bring you good tidings of great joy, which shall be to all
people."

We need not wonder at these words. The spiritual

darkness which had covered the earth for four thousand years, was about to be rolled away. The way to pardon and peace with God was about to be thrown open to all mankind. The head of Satan was about to be bruised. Liberty was about to be proclaimed to the captives, and recovering of sight to the blind. The mighty truth was about to be proclaimed that God could be just, and yet, for Christ's sake, justify the ungodly. Salvation was no longer to be seen through types and figures, but openly, and face to face. The knowledge of God was no longer to be confined to the Jews, but to be offered to the whole Gentile world. The days of heathenism were numbered. The first stone of God's kingdom was about to be set up. If this was not "good tidings," there never were tidings that deserved the name.

Let us mark, thirdly, *who they were that first praised God, when Christ was born.* They were angels, and not men,—angels who had never sinned, and needed no Saviour,—angels who had not fallen, and required no redeemer, and no atoning blood. The first hymn to the honour of "God manifest in the flesh," was sung by "a multitude of the heavenly host."

Let us note this fact. It is full of deep spiritual lessons. It shows us what good servants the angels are. All that their heavenly Master does pleases and interests them.—It shows us what clear knowledge they have. They know what misery sin has brought into creation. They know the blessedness of heaven, and the privilege of an open door into it.—Above all, it shows us the deep love and compassion which the angels feel towards poor lost man. They rejoice in the glorious prospect of many souls being saved, and many brands plucked from the burning.

Let us strive to be more like-minded with the angels. Our spiritual ignorance and deadness appear most painfully in our inability to enter into the joy which we see them here expressing. Surely if we hope to dwell with them for ever in heaven, we ought to share something of their feelings while we are here upon earth. Let us seek a more deep sense of the sinfulness and misery of sin, and then we shall have a more deep sense of thankfulness for redemption.

Let us mark, fourthly, *the hymn of praise which the heavenly host sung in the hearing of the shepherds.* They said, "Glory to God in the highest, and on earth peace, good will towards men."

These famous words are variously interpreted. Man is by nature so dull in spiritual things, that it seems as if he cannot understand a sentence of heavenly language, when he hears it. Yet a meaning may be drawn from the words which is free from any objection, and is not only good sense, but excellent theology.

"Glory to God in the highest!" the song begins. Now is come the highest degree of glory to God, by the appearing of His Son Jesus Christ in the world. He by His life and death on the cross will glorify God's attributes,—justice, holiness, mercy, and wisdom,—as they never were glorified before. Creation glorified God, but not so much as redemption.

"Peace on earth!" the song goes on. Now is come to earth the peace of God which passeth all understanding, —the perfect peace between a holy God and sinful man, which Christ was to purchase with His own blood,—the peace which is offered freely to all mankind,—the peace which, once admitted into the heart, makes men live at peace one with another, and will one day overspread the whole world.

"Good will towards men!" the song concludes. Now is come the time when God's kindness and good will towards guilty man is to be fully made known. His power was seen in creation. His justice was seen in the flood. But His mercy remained to be fully revealed by the appearing and atonement of Jesus Christ.

Such was the purport of the angels' song. Happy are they that can enter into its meaning, and with their hearts subscribe to its contents. The man who hopes to dwell in heaven, should have some experimental acquaintance with the language of its inhabitants.

Let us mark, ere we leave the passage, *the prompt obedience to the heavenly vision* displayed by the shepherds. We see in them no doubts, or questionings, or hesitation. Strange and improbable as the tidings might seem, they at once act upon them. They went to Bethlehem in haste. They found every thing exactly as it had been told them. Their simple faith received a rich reward. They had the mighty privilege of being the first of all mankind, after Mary and Joseph, who saw with believing eyes the new-born Messiah. They soon returned, "glorifying and praising God" for what they had seen.

May our spirit be like their's! May we ever believe implicitly, act promptly, and wait for nothing, when the path of duty is clear! So doing, we shall have a reward

like that of the shepherds. The journey that is begun
in faith, will generally end in praise.

8.—[*Shepherds abiding in the field, &c.*] It has been argued from
these words, that our Lord could not have been born on Christmas
day, because it was not the custom of the Jews to keep flocks in
the field in winter. It may be doubted whether the argument is
quite conclusive. At any rate, Jacob complains of "frost by
night," when he kept the flock of Laban, in the neighbouring
country of Padan Aram. (Gen. xxxi. 40.) However, it is an
undeniable fact that the precise month or day of our Lord's
nativity is not known. Every month in the year has found its
advocates, in the conjectures made on the subject. Certainty
about it there is none. Had it been good for us to know the
day, God would have told us. For keeping Christmas we have no
authority, but that of the church.

10.—[*All people.*] It may be questioned whether this expression
was not meant to apply specially and primarily to the Jews. It
would be translated more literally, "to all the people."

12.—[*The babe.*] There can be no doubt that this expression
would have been better translated, "a babe." The whole context, no less than the absence of the Greek article, shows the
propriety of this.

14.—[*Good will.*] The word and thing here are the same that we
find in Ephes. i. 5, 9. The meaning is that "good will and
good pleasure of God" towards man, which is revealed in His
Son Jesus Christ.—It is the same as the "kindness and love of
God" in Titus iii. 4, and the "love of God" in John iii. 16.

15.—[*See this thing which is come to pass.*] The word translated
"this thing," might also be rendered "this saying." The commentary of Ambrose on this passage is a curious proof that the
Fathers were anything but infallible. He actually regards "this
thing" as the personal Word, the Son of God! A very slight
acquaintance with Greek will show that this sense of the word
is impossible. Even the Romish commentator Barradius is
obliged to confess, that in this comment Ambrose erred.

16.—[*They came with haste.*] There is a touching comment on this
conduct of the shepherds, in a letter of Bishop Hooper's to
certain "godly and faithful prisoners, which were taken together
at prayer in a house in Bow Churchyard." He says, "Read the
second chapter of St. Luke, and there ye shall see how the
shepherds that watched their sheep all night, as soon as they
heard that Christ was born at Bethlehem, by and bye must go

to see him. They did not reason nor debate with themselves who should keep the wolf from the sheep in the mean time, but did as they were commanded, and committed their sheep to him whose pleasure they obeyed. So let us do, now we be called; let us commit all other things unto him that called us. He will take heed that all things shall be well. He will help the husband; he will comfort the wife. He will guide the servants; he will keep the house; he will preserve the goods; yea, rather than it should be undone, he will wash the dishes, and rock the cradle. Cast, therefore, all your care upon God."—*Hooper's Works. Parker Edit.* vol. ii. 617.

LUKE II. 21—24.

21 And when eight days were accomplished for the circumcising of the child, his name was called JESUS, which was so named of the angel before he was conceived in the womb.

22 And when the days of her purification according to the law of Moses were accomplished, they brought him to Jerusalem, to present *him* to the Lord;

23 (As it is written in the law of the Lord, Every male that openeth the womb shall be called holy to the Lord;)

24 And to offer a sacrifice according to that which is said in the law of the Lord, A pair of turtledoves or two young pigeons.

THE first point which demands our attention in this passage, is *the obedience which our Lord rendered, as an infant, to the Jewish law.* We read of His being circumcised on the eighth day. It is the earliest fact which is recorded in His history.

It is mere waste of time to speculate, as some have done, about the reason why our Lord submitted to circumcision. We know that "in Him was no sin," either original or actual. (1 John iii. 5.) His being circumcised was not meant in the least as an acknowledgment that there was any tendency to corruption in His heart. It was not a confession of inclination to evil, and of need of grace to mortify the deeds of His body. All this should be carefully borne in mind.

Let it suffice us to remember that our Lord's circumcision was a public testimony to Israel, that according to the flesh He was a Jew, made of a Jewish woman, and "made under the law." (Galat. iv. 4.) Without it He would not have fulfilled the law's requirements. Without it He could not have been recognized as the son of David, and the seed of Abraham. Let us remember, furthermore, that circumcision was absolutely necessary before our Lord could be heard as a teacher in Israel. Without it He would have had no place in any lawful Jewish assembly, and no right to any Jewish ordinance. Without it He would have been regarded by all Jews as nothing better than an uncircumcised Gentile, and an apostate from the faith of the fathers.

Let our Lord's submission to an ordinance which He did not need for Himself, be a lesson to us in our daily life. Let us endure much, rather than increase the offence of the Gospel, or hinder in any way the cause of God. The words of St. Paul deserve frequent pondering;—"Though I be free from all men, yet have I made myself servant unto all, that I might gain the more, and unto the Jews I became as a Jew, that I might gain the Jews: to them that are under the law, as under the law, that I might gain them that are under the law." —"I am made all things to all men, that I might by all means save some." (1 Cor. ix. 19—22.) The man who wrote these words walked very closely in the footsteps of His crucified Master.

The second point which demands our attention in this passage, is *the name by which our Lord was called, by God's special command.* "His name was called Jesus, which was so named by the angel, before He was conceived in the womb."

The word Jesus means simply "Saviour." It is the same word as "Joshua" in the Old Testament. Very striking and instructive is the selection of this name. The Son of God came down from heaven to be not only the Saviour, but the King, the Lawgiver, the Prophet, the Priest, the Judge of fallen man. Had He chosen any one of these titles, He would only have chosen that which was His own. But He passed by them all. He selects a name which speaks of mercy, grace, help, and deliverance for a lost world. It is as a deliverer and Redeemer that He desires principally to be known.

Let us often ask ourselves what our own hearts know of the Son of God. Is He our Jesus, our Saviour? This is the question on which our salvation turns. Let it not content us to know Christ as one who wrought mighty miracles, and spake as never man spake,—or to know Him as One who is very God, and will one day judge the world. Let us see that we know Him experimentally, as our Deliverer from the guilt and power of sin, and our Redeemer from Satan's bondage. Let us strive to be able to say, "This is my Friend : I was dead, and He gave me life : I was a prisoner, and He set me free."—Precious indeed is this name of Jesus to all true believers ! It is "as ointment poured forth." (Cant. i. 3.) It restores them when conscience-troubled. It comforts them when cast down. It smooths their pillows in sickness. It supports them in the hour of death. "The name of the Lord is a strong tower : the righteous runneth into it, and is safe." (Prov. xviii. 10.)

The last point which demands our attention in this passage, is *the poor and humble condition of our Lord's*

mother, the Virgin Mary. This is a fact which, at first
sight, may not stand out clearly in the form of these
verses. But a reference to the twelfth chapter of Leviticus will at once make it plain. There we shall see, that
the offering which Mary made was specially appointed
to be made by poor people:—"If she be not able to bring
a lamb, then she shall bring two turtles, or two young
pigeons." In short, her offering was a public declaration
that she was poor. (Lev. xii. 6.)

Poverty, it is manifest, was our Lord's portion upon
earth, from the days of His earliest infancy. He was
nursed and tended as a babe, by a poor woman. He
passed the first thirty years of His life on earth, under
the roof of a poor man. We need not doubt that He ate
a poor man's food, and wore a poor man's apparel, and
worked a poor man's work, and shared in all a poor man's
troubles. Such condescension is truly marvellous. Such
an example of humility passes man's understanding.

Facts like these ought often to be laid to heart by poor
people. They would help to silence murmuring and
complaining, and go far to reconcile them to their hard
lot. The simple fact that Jesus was born of a poor woman,
and lived all his life on earth among poor people, ought
to silence the common argument that "religion is not for
the poor." Above all it ought to encourage every poor
believer in all his approaches to the throne of grace in
prayer. Let him remember in all his prayers that his
mighty Mediator in heaven is accustomed to poverty, and
knows by experience the heart of a poor man. Well
would it be for the world if working men could only see
that Christ is the true poor man's friend!

21.—[*Circumcising of the child.*] Bishop Hall remarks, " He that came to be sin for us, would in our persons be legally unclean, that by satisfying the law he might take away our uncleanness. Though he were exempted from the ordinary conditions of our birth, yet he would not deliver himself from those ordinary rites that implied the weakness and blemishes of humanity. He would fulfil one law, to abrogate it; another, to satisfy it. He that was above the law, would come under the law, to free us from the law."

[*Named of the angel before he was conceived.*] Poole remarks, in his annotations, " We read of four under the Old Testament, to whom God gave names before they were born : Isaac,—Gen. xvii. 19; Josiah,—1 Kings xiii. 2; Ishmael,—Gen. xvi. 11; Cyrus,—Isai. xliv. 28; and in the New Testament we read of two :—John the Baptist and Jesus Christ. Which lets us know the certainty to God of future contingencies; for though the parents of Ishmael, Isaac, and John the Baptist, imposed those names in obedience to the command of God, and there was but a small time betwixt the giving of the names and the births, yet the case was otherwise as to Josiah and Cyrus."

24.—[*Two young pigeons.*] Lightfoot says that this was called, in the Hebrew language, " The offering of the poor, which if a rich man offered he did not do his duty."

LUKE II. 25—35.

25 And, behold, there was a man in Jerusalem, whose name *was* Simeon ; and the same man *was* just and devout, waiting for the consolation of Israel : and the Holy Ghost was upon him.

26 And it was revealed unto him by the Holy Ghost, that he should not see death, before he had seen the Lord's Christ.

27 And he came by the spirit into the temple : and when the parents brought in the child Jesus, to do for him after the custom of the law,

28 Then took he him up in his arms, and blessed God, and said,

29 Lord, now lettest thou thy servant depart in peace, according to thy word :

30 For mine eyes have seen thy salvation,

31 Which thou hast prepared before the face of all people ;

32 A light to lighten the Gentiles, and the glory of thy people Israel.

33 And Joseph and his mother marvelled at those things which were spoken of him.

34 And Simeon blessed them, and said unto Mary his mother, Behold, this *child* is set for the fall and rising again of many in Israel; and for a sign which shall be spoken against;

35 (Yea, a sword shall pierce through thy own soul also,) that the thoughts of many hearts may be revealed.

We have in these verses the history of one whose name

is nowhere else mentioned in the New Testament, a "just
and devout man" named Simeon.   We know nothing of
his life before or after the time when Christ was born.
We are only told that he came by the Spirit into the
temple, when the child Jesus was brought there by His
mother, and that he "took him up in his arms and blessed
God" in words which are now well-known all over the
world.

We see, in the case of Simeon, *how God has a believing
people even in the worst of places, and in the darkest times.*
Religion was at a very low ebb in Israel when Christ
was born.   The faith of Abraham was spoiled by the
doctrines of Pharisees and Sadducees.   The fine gold had
become deplorably dim.   Yet even then we find in the
midst of Jerusalem a man "just and devout,"—a man
"upon whom is the Holy Ghost."

It is a cheering thought that God never leaves Himself
entirely without a witness. Small as His believing church
may sometimes be, the gates of hell shall never completely prevail against it. The true church may be driven
into the wilderness, and be a scattered little flock, but it
never dies.   There was a Lot in Sodom and an Obadiah
in Ahab's household, a Daniel in Babylon and a Jeremiah in Zedekiah's court;—and in the last days of the
Jewish Church, when its iniquity was almost full, there
were godly people, like Simeon, even in Jerusalem.

True Christians, in every age, should remember this
and take comfort. It is a truth which they are apt to forget,
and in consequence to give way to despondency. "I only
am left," said Elijah, "and they seek my life to take it
away." But what said the answer of God to him, "Yet

have I left me seven thousand in Israel." (1 Kings xix. 14, 18.) Let us learn to be more hopeful. Let us believe that grace can live and flourish, even in the most unfavourable circumstances. There are more Simeons in the world than we suppose.

We see in the song of Simeon *how completely a believer can be delivered from the fear of death;* "Lord," says old Simeon, "now lettest thou thy servant depart in peace." He speaks like one for whom the grave has lost its terrors, and the world its charms. He desires to be released from the miseries of this pilgrim-state of existence, and to be allowed to go home. He is willing to be "absent from the body and present with the Lord." He speaks as one who knows where he is going when he departs this life, and cares not how soon he goes. The change with him will be a change for the better, and he desires that his change may come.

What is it that can enable a mortal man to use such language as this? What can deliver us from that "fear of death" to which so many are in bondage? What can take the sting of death away?—There is but one answer to such questions. Nothing but strong faith can do it. Faith laying firm hold on an unseen Saviour,—faith resting on the promises of an unseen God,—faith, and faith only, can enable a man to look death in the face, and say, "I depart in peace." It is not enough to be weary of pain, and sickness, and ready to submit to anything for the sake of a change. It is not enough to feel indifferent to the world, when we have no more strength to mingle in its business, or enjoy its pleasures. We must have something more than this, if we desire to depart in

real peace. We must have faith like old Simeon's, even
that faith which is the gift of God. Without such faith
we may die quietly, and there may seem "no bands in
our death." (Psalm lxxiii. 4.) But, dying without such
faith, we shall never find ourselves at home, when we
wake up in another world.

We see, furthermore, in the song of Simeon, *what clear
views of Christ's work and office some Jewish believers
attained, even before the Gospel was preached.* We find
this good old man speaking of Jesus as "the salvation
which God had prepared,"—as "a light to lighten the
Gentiles, and the glory of his people Israel." Well
would it have been for the letter-learned Scribes and
Pharisees of Simeon's time, if they had sat at his feet,
and listened to his word.

Christ was indeed "a light to lighten the Gentiles."
Without Him they were sunk in gross darkness and
superstition. They knew not the way of life. They
worshipped the works of their own hands. Their wisest
philosophers were utterly ignorant in spiritual things.
"Professing themselves to be wise they became fools."
(Rom. i. 22.) The Gospel of Christ was like sun-rise to
Greece and Rome, and the whole heathen world. The
light which it let in on men's minds on the subject
of religion, was as great as the change from night to day.

Christ was indeed "the glory of Israel." The descent
from Abraham,—the covenants,—the promises,—the law
of Moses,—the divinely ordered Temple service,—all these
were mighty privileges. But all were as nothing compared to the mighty fact, that out of Israel was born
the Saviour of the world. This was to be the highest

honour of the Jewish nation, that the mother of Christ
was a Jewish woman, and that the blood of One "made
of the seed of David, according to the flesh," was to make
atonement for the sin of mankind.   (Rom. i. 3.)

The words of old Simeon, let us remember, will yet
receive a fuller accomplishment.   The "light" which he
saw by faith, as he held the child Jesus in his arms,
shall yet shine so brightly that all the nations of the
Gentile world shall see it.—The "glory" of that Jesus
whom Israel crucified, shall one day be revealed so
clearly to the scattered Jews, that they shall look on
Him whom they pierced, and repent, and be converted.
The day shall come when the veil shall be taken from
the heart of Israel, and all shall "glory in the Lord."
(Isai. xlv. 25.) For that day let us wait, and watch, and
pray. If Christ be the light and glory of our souls, that
day cannot come too soon.

We see, lastly, in this passage, *a striking account of
the results which would follow when Jesus Christ and His
Gospel came into the world.* Every word of old Simeon
on this subject deserves private meditation. The whole
forms a prophecy which is being daily fulfilled.

Christ was to be "a sign spoken against." He was
to be a mark for all the fiery darts of the wicked one.
He was to be "despised and rejected of men." He and
His people were to be a "city set upon a hill," assailed
on every side, and hated by all sorts of enemies. And
so it proved. Men who agreed in nothing else have
agreed in hating Christ. From the very first, thousands
have been persecutors and unbelievers.

Christ was to be the occasion of "the fall of many in

Israel." He was to be a stone of stumbling and rock of offence to many proud and self-righteous Jews, who would reject Him and perish in their sins. And so it proved. To multitudes among them Christ crucified was a stumbling-block, and His Gospel " a savour of death." (1 Cor. i. 23 ; 2 Cor. ii. 16.)

Christ was to be the occasion of " rising again to many in Israel." He was to prove the Saviour of many who, at one time, rejected, blasphemed, and reviled Him, but afterwards repented and believed. And so it proved. When the thousands who crucified him repented, and Saul who persecuted Him was converted, there was nothing less than a rising again from the dead.

Christ was to be the occasion of " the thoughts of many hearts being revealed." His Gospel was to bring to light the real characters of many people. The enmity to God of some,—the inward weariness and hunger of others, would be discovered by the preaching of the cross. It would show what men really were. And so it proved. The Acts of the Apostles, in almost every chapter, bear testimony that in this, as in every other item of his prophecy, old Simeon spoke truth.

And now what do we think of Christ ? This is the question that ought to occupy our minds. What thoughts does He call forth in our hearts ? This is the inquiry which ought to receive our attention. Are we for Him, or are we against Him ? Do we love Him, or do we neglect Him ? Do we stumble at His doctrine, or do we find it life from the dead ? Let us never rest till these questions are satisfactorily answered.

25.—[*A man whose name was Simeon.*] Some learned men hold that this Simeon was a man of great note in Jerusalem, the son of Hillel, and father of Gamaliel. Henry says, "the Jews say that he was endued with a prophetic spirit, and that he was turned out of his place because he witnessed against the common opinion of the Jews concerning the temporal kingdom of the Messiah." All this, to say the least, is doubtful.

[*The consolation of Israel.*] This was a name applied by the Jews to the Messiah. Lightfoot says, "the whole nation waited for the consolation of Israel; insomuch that there was nothing more common with them, than to swear by the desire which they had of seeing it."

[*The Holy Ghost...upon him.*] Let us not fail to note that this was before the death and ascension of Christ, and the outpouring of the Spirit on the day of Pentecost. We must never forget that Old Testament saints were taught by the Holy Ghost as really as believers after the Gospel was set up, though not in such full measure.

29.—[*Lettest depart.*] The idea is that of loosing a person from a chain, or giving a prisoner release from captivity.

30.—[*Salvation.*] The word so translated is only used here and in three other places:—Luke iii. 6; Acts xxviii. 28; and Ephes. vi. 17. It is a more abstract, energetic word than the one commonly so translated.

31.—[*All people.*] The expression here is different from that in verse 10. It would be more literally and correctly rendered in this place, "all peoples."

32.—[*Light to...the Gentiles...glory of...Israel.*] Ford quotes Dr. Richard Clerke's remarks on this verse, "It is noted by the learned that the sweet singer of this song doth put the Gentile before the Jew, because the second calling, the conversion of the Jews to Christ, shall not be till the fulness of the Gentiles be come in."

33.—[*Of him.*] Let it be noted carefully that "of" in this place means "about," or "concerning."

34.—[*Simeon blessed them.*] From this expression some have supposed that Simeon was at least a chief priest, if not the high priest. There is nothing to justify the supposition. As one specially inspired by the Holy Ghost to prophecy, Simeon was doing nothing more, in blessing them, than any prophet would have done, whether a priest or not.

35.—[*A sword shall pierce, &c.*] The simplest explanation of these words is, that Simeon foretells sorrow coming on the Virgin Mary, as cutting and heart-piercing as a sword. This was spe-

cially fulfilled when she stood by the cross, and saw her Son
dying there.   Might not our Lord be reminding her of this
prophecy, when in that solemn hour He commended her to His
disciple John, saying, "Behold thy mother,"—in order that she
might have a friend in her time of need?

LUKE II. 36—40.

36 And there was one Anna, a pro-
phetess, the daughter of Phanuel, of
the tribe of Aser: she was of a great
age, and had lived with an husband
seven years from her virginity;
37 And she *was* a widow of about
four-score and four years, which departed not from the temple, but served
God with fastings and prayers night
and day.
38 And she coming in that instant
gave thanks likewise unto the Lord,
and spake of him to all them that
looked for redemption in Jerusalem.
39 And when they had performed
all things according to the law of the
Lord, they returned into Galilee, to
their own city Nazareth.
40 And the child grew, and waxed
strong in spirit, filled with wisdom:
and the grace of God was upon him.

THE verses we have now read introduce us to a servant
of God whose name is nowhere else mentioned in the
New Testament.   The history of Anna, like that of
Simeon, is related only by St. Luke.   The wisdom of God
ordained that a woman as well as a man should testify
to the fact that Messiah was born.   In the mouth of two
witnesses it was established that Malachi's prophecy was
fulfilled, and the messenger of the covenant had suddenly
come to the Temple. (Malachi iii. 1.)

Let us observe, in these verses, *the character of a holy
woman before the establishment of Christ's Gospel.*   The
facts recorded about Anna are few and simple.   But
we shall find them full of instruction.

Anna was a woman of irreproachable character.   After
a married life of only seven years duration, she had spent
eighty-four years as a lone widow.   The trials, desola-
tion, and temptation of such a condition were probably

very great. But Anna by grace overcame them all. She answered to the description given by St. Paul. She was "a widow indeed." (1 Tim. iv. 5.)

Anna was a woman who loved God's house. "She departed not from the temple." She regarded it as the place where God especially dwelt, and toward which every pious Jew in foreign lands, like Daniel, loved to direct his prayers. "Nearer to God, nearer to God," was the desire of her heart, and she felt that she was never so near as within the walls which contained the ark, the altar, and the holy of holies. She could enter into David's words, "my soul longeth, yea, even fainteth for the courts of the Lord." (Psalm lxxxiv. 2.)

Anna was a woman of great self-denial. She "served God with fastings night and day." She was continually crucifying the flesh and keeping it in subjection by voluntary abstemiousness. Being fully persuaded in her own mind that the practice was helpful to her soul, she spared no pains to keep it up.

Anna was a woman of much prayer. She "served God with prayer night and day." She was continually communing with Him, as her best Friend, about the things that concerned her own peace. She was never weary of pleading with Him on behalf of others, and, above all, for the fulfilment of His promises of Messiah.

Anna was a woman who held communion with other saints. So soon as she had seen Jesus, she "spake of Him" to others whom she knew in Jerusalem, and with whom she was evidently on friendly terms. There was a bond of union between her and all who enjoyed the same hope. They were servants of the same master, and travellers to the same home.

And Anna received a rich reward for all her diligence in God's service, before she left the world. She was allowed to see Him who had been so long promised, and for whose coming she had so often prayed. Her faith was at last changed to sight, and her hope to certainty. The joy of this holy woman must indeed have been "unspeakable and full of glory." (1 Peter i. 8.)

It would be well for all Christian women to ponder the character of Anna, and learn wisdom from it. The times, no doubt, are greatly changed. The social duties of the Christian are very different from those of the Jewish believer at Jerusalem. All are not placed by God in the condition of widows. But still, after every deduction, there remains much in Anna's history which is worthy of imitation. When we read of her consistency, and holiness, and prayerfulness, and self-denial, we cannot but wish that many daughters of the Christian Church would strive to be like her.

Let us observe, secondly, in these verses, *the description given of saints in Jerusalem in the time when Jesus was born*. They were people "who looked for redemption."

Faith, we shall always find, is the universal character of God's elect. These men and women here described, dwelling in the midst of a wicked city, walked by faith, and not by sight. They were not carried away by the flood of worldliness, formality, and self-righteousness around them. They were not infected by the carnal expectations of a mere worldly Messiah, in which most Jews indulged. They lived in the faith of patriarchs and prophets, that the coming Redeemer would bring in holiness and righteousness, and that His principal victory would be over sin and the devil. For such a Redeemer they waited patiently. For such a victory they earnestly longed.

Let us learn a lesson from these good people. If they, with so few helps and so many discouragements, lived such a life of faith, how much more ought we with a finished Bible and a full Gospel. Let us strive, like them, to walk by faith and look forward. The second advent of Christ is yet to come. The complete "redemption of this earth from sin, and Satan, and the curse, is yet to take place. Let us declare plainly by our lives and conduct, that for this second advent we look and long. We may be sure that the highest style of Christianity even now, is to " wait for redemption," and to love the Lord's appearing. (Rom. viii. 23 ; 2 Tim. iv. 8.)

Let us observe, lastly, in these verses, *what clear proof we have that the Lord Jesus was really and truly man, as well as God.* We read, that when Mary and Joseph returned to their own city Nazareth, "the child grew and waxed strong in spirit."

There is, doubtless, much that is deeply mysterious in the Person of the Lord Jesus. How the same Person could be at once perfect God and perfect man, is a point that necessarily passes our understanding. In what manner and measure, and in what proportion at the early part of His life, that divine knowledge which He doubtless possessed, was exerc ied, we cannot possibly explain. It is a high thing. We cannot attain unto it.

One thing, however, is perfectly clear, and we shall

do well to lay firm hold upon it. Our Lord partook
of everything that belongs to man's nature, sin only
excepted. As man He was born an infant. As man
He grew from infancy to boyhood. As man He yearly
increased in bodily strength and mental power, during
His passage from boyhood to full age. Of all the sinless
conditions of man's body, its first feebleness, its after
growth, its regular progress to maturity, He was in the
fullest sense a partaker. We must rest satisfied with
knowing this. To pry beyond is useless. To know this
clearly is of much importance. A want of settled knowledge of it has led to many wild heresies.

One comfortable practical lesson stands out on the
face of this truth, which ought never to be overlooked.
Our Lord is able to sympathize with man in every stage
of man's existence, from the cradle to the grave. He
knows by experience the nature and temperament of the
child, the boy, and the young man. He has stood in
their place. He has occupied their position. He knows
their hearts. Let us never forget this in dealing with
young people about their souls. Let us tell them confidently, that there is One in heaven at the right hand
of God, who is exactly suited to be their Friend. He
who died on the cross was once a boy Himself, and feels
a special interest in boys and girls, as well as in grown
up people.

NOTES. LUKE II. 36—40.

36.—[*A prophetess.*] This is a remarkable expression, and only
used on one other occasion in the New Testament. Rev. ii. 20.
If the word is to be taken in its fullest sense, it seems to show
that the spirit of prophecy, which had been withheld for nigh
four hundred years since Malachi's time, was being restored to

Israel when Christ was born. But as the word "prophet" does not necessarily imply, in the New Testament, the power of fore-telling things to come, so also it may be with the word "pro-phetess."

[*Tribe of Aser.*] This is remarkable, when we remember that Asher was one of the ten tribes, who were carried into captivity, and never returned. We must conclude that a scattered rem-nant of them were, in some way, mixed up with Judah and Benjamin, and with them returned from Babylon after the captivity.

38.—[*Spake of Him...to all, &c.*] It is worthy of remark, that this presentation of our Lord in the temple, appears to have been the primary fulfilment of the prophecy of Malachi iii. 1, "The Lord shall suddenly come to his temple." It was indeed a sudden unostentatious coming. The only witnesses, appa-rently, were an old man and an old woman,—and the only attendants a poor woman and her equally poor husband,—and the form in which the Lord appeared was as a little infant in arms! How little we should have expected this! How many prophecies may be fulfilling around us at this very time! God's ways are truly not as our ways.

39.—[*Returned into Galilee...to...Nazareth.*] Two important in-cidents in our Lord's history come in here, which St. Luke passes over, not necessarily because he was ignorant of them, but simply because he was not inspired to write of them. Those incidents are the visit of the wise men from the East, and the flight into Egypt. Joseph and Mary appear to have returned to Bethlehem after the presentation in the temple, though it is quite possible that they may have gone to Nazareth for a short time. They, probably, returned to Bethlehem under a sense of duty, as if the Messiah ought to dwell in the place where it was prophecied He should be born. There at Bethle-hem, they were visited by the wise men from the East. From thence, being supplied by their gifts with the means of journey-ing, they fled into Egypt, to escape the anger of Herod. From Egypt, after the death of Herod, they returned to Nazareth.

There are doubtless other views propounded on this somewhat difficult subject. The one above stated appears to be by far the most reasonable, and to involve the fewest difficulties.

If Mary and Joseph had remained at Bethlehem till the visit of the wise men, and after their visit had gone up to Jerusalem, they would have been deliberately plunging into danger, by going to the place where Herod was.

If the presentation in the temple did not take place till after the visit of the wise men, and the reception of their gifts, it does not seem likely that Mary's offering would only have been a pair of pigeons.

LUKE II. 41—52.

41 Now his parents went to Jerusalem every year at the feast of the Passover.

42 And when he was twelve years old, they went up to Jerusalem after the custom of the feast.

43 And when they had fulfilled the days, as they returned, the child Jesus tarried behind in Jerusalem; and Joseph and his mother knew not of it.

44 But they, supposing him to have been in the company, went a day's journey; and they sought him among *their* kinsfolk and acquaintance.

45 And when they found him not, they turned back again to Jerusalem, seeking him.

46 And it came to pass, that after three days they found him in the temple, sitting in the midst of the doctors, both hearing them, and asking them questions.

47 And all that heard him were astonished at his understanding and answers.

48 And when they saw him, they were amazed: and his mother said unto him, Son, why hast thou thus dealt with us? behold, thy father and I have sought thee sorrowing.

49 And he said unto them, How is it that ye sought me? wist ye not that I must be about my Father's business?

50 And they understood not the saying which he spake unto them.

51 And he went down with them, and came to Nazareth, and was subject unto them: but his mother kept all these sayings in her heart.

52 And Jesus increased in wisdom and stature, and in favour with God and man.

THESE verses should always be deeply interesting to a reader of the Bible. They record the only fact which we know about our Lord Jesus Christ during the first thirty years of His life on earth, after His infancy. How many things a Christian would like to know about the events of those thirty years, and the daily history of the house at Nazareth! But we need not doubt that there is wisdom in the silence of Scripture on the subject. If it had been good for us to know more, more would have been revealed.

Let us, first, draw from the passage *a lesson for all married people*. We have it in the conduct of Joseph and Mary, here described. We are told that "they went to Jerusalem every year, at the feast of the passover." They regularly honoured God's appointed ordinances, and they honoured them together. The distance from Nazareth to Jerusalem was great. The journey, to poor people without any means of conveyance, was, doubtless, troublesome and fatiguing. To leave house and home for ten days or a fortnight was no slight expense. But God had given Israel a command, and Joseph and Mary strictly obeyed it. God had appointed an ordinance for their spiritual good, and they regularly kept it. And all that they did concerning the passover they did together. When they went up to the feast, they always went up side by side.

So ought it to be with all Christian husbands and wives. They ought to help one another in spiritual things, and to encourage one another in the service of God. Marriage, unquestionably, is not a sacrament, as the Romish Church vainly asserts. But marriage is a state of life which has the greatest effect on the souls of those who enter into it. It helps them upwards or downwards. It leads them nearer to heaven or nearer to hell. We all depend much on the company we keep. Our characters are insensibly moulded by those with whom we pass our time. To none does this apply so much as to married people. Husbands and wives are continually doing either good or harm to one another's souls.

Let all who are married, or think of being married, ponder these things well. Let them take example from the conduct of Joseph and Mary, and resolve to do likewise. Let them pray together, and read the Bible together, and go to the house of God together, and talk to one another about spiritual matters. Above all, let them beware of throwing obstacles and discouragements in one another's way about means of grace. Blessed are those husbands who say to their wives as Elkanah did to Hannah, "Do all that is in thy heart." Happy are those wives who say to their husbands as Leah and Rachel did to Jacob, "Whatsoever God hath said unto thee, do." (1 Sam. i. 23; Gen. xxxi. 16.)

Let us, secondly, draw from the passage, *an example for all young persons.* We have it in the conduct of our Lord Jesus Christ, when He was left by Himself in Jerusalem at the age of twelve years. For four days He was out of sight of Mary and Joseph. For three days they "sought him sorrowing," not knowing what had befallen Him. Who can imagine the anxiety of such a mother at losing such a child?—And where did they find Him at last? Not idling His time away, or getting into mischief, as many boys of twelve years old do. Not in vain and unprofitable company. "They found him in the temple of God,—sitting in the midst" of the Jewish teachers, "hearing" what they had to say, and "asking questions" about things He wished to be explained.

So ought it to be with the younger members of Christian families. They ought to be steady and trustworthy behind the backs of their parents, as well as before their faces. They ought to seek the company of the wise and prudent, and to use every opportunity of getting spiritual knowledge, before the cares of life come on them, and while their memories are fresh and strong.

Let Christian boys and girls ponder these things well, and take example from the conduct of Jesus at the age of only twelve years. Let them remember, that if they are old enough to do wrong, they are also old enough

to do right; and that if able to read story-books and
to talk, they are also able to read their Bibles and
pray. Let them remember, that they are accountable
to God, even while they are yet young, and that it is
written that God "heard the voice of a lad." (Gen. xxi.
17.) Happy indeed are those families in which the
children "seek the Lord early," and cost their parents
no tears. Happy are those parents who can say of their
boys and girls, when absent from them, "I can trust
my children that they will not wilfully run into sin."

Let us, in the last place, draw from this passage, *an
example for all true Christians*. We have it in the solemn
words which our Lord addressed to His mother Mary,
when she said to Him, "Son, why hast thou dealt with
us thus?"—"Wist ye not," was the reply, "that I
must be about my father's business." A mild reproof
was evidently implied in that reply. It was meant to
remind His mother, that He was no common person,
and had come into the world to do no common work. It
was a hint, that she was insensibly forgetting that He
had come into the world in no ordinary way, and that
she could not expect Him to be ever dwelling quietly
at Nazareth. It was a solemn remembrancer that, as
God, He had a Father in heaven, and that this heavenly
Father's work demanded His first attention.

The expression is one that ought to sink down deeply
into the hearts of all Christ's people. It should supply
them with a mark at which they should aim in daily life,
and a test by which they should try their habits and
conversation. It should quicken them when they begin
to be slothful. It should check them when they feel

inclined to go back to the world.—" Are we about our
Father's business? Are we walking in the steps of Jesus
Christ?"—Such questions will often prove very hum-
bling, and make us ashamed of ourselves. But such
questions are eminently useful to our souls. Never is a
Church in so healthy a condition as when its believing
members aim high, and strive in all things to be like
Christ.

NOTES. LUKE II.˙41—52.

42.—[*Twelve years old.*] This age appears to have been regarded
by the Jews as a kind of turning point out of the state of child-
hood. Lightfoot quotes a saying from one of the Rabbinical
writers: "Let a man deal gently with his son, till he comes to
be twelve years old; but from that time let him descend with
him into his way of living,—that is, let him diligently keep
him close to that way, rule, and act, by which he may get his
living."

44.—[*Company.*] The word so translated is only used in this
place. It specially means a company of persons on a journey.

    [*Supposing...went a day's journey.*] An explanation of this is
given by Bede, in a passage quoted by Corderius. He says it
was the custom in going to and returning from Jewish feasts, for
the men to walk by themselves, and the women by themselves.
In this way Joseph might easily "suppose" that Jesus was with
Mary, and Mary "suppose" that He was with Joseph.

46.—[*After three days.*] Bishop Hall remarks, "Where wert thou,
O blessed Jesus, for the space of these three days? Where
didst thou bestow thyself, or who tended thee, while thou wert
thus alone in Jerusalem?—Whether it pleased thee to exercise
thyself thus early with the difficulties of a stranger, or to provide
miraculously for thyself, I inquire not, since thou revealest not.
Only this I know, that hereby thou intendest to teach thy parents
that thou couldest live without them, and that not out of any
indigency, but out of a gracious dispensation, thou wouldest
ordinarily depend upon their care."

    [*Sitting in...midst of...doctors, &c.*] The common expression,
"Christ disputing with the doctors," is utterly destitute of foundation in this passage. It conveys an improper and incorrect
idea, and ought to be discouraged among Christians. There is
not the slightest trace in the account before us of any "dispute"
at all.

48.—[*Why hast thou dealt with us thus.*] There is evidence of in-firmity in this language of the Virgin Mary to our Lord. She seems here, as on other occasions, to have shown herself to be like other holy women,—a being who needed a Saviour herself, and therefore unable to save others.

49.—[*About my Father's business.*] These words so translated would admit of being rendered, "in my Father's house," and many commentators are strongly in favour of that sense being given to them. But, on the whole, our own English translation seems the best and most comprehensive. The proposed trans-lation cramps and limits our Lord's words, by confining their application to one thing, "my father's house." The translation "my father's business" embraces a far wider range of thought, and is more in keeping with the general depth and fulness of our Lord's sayings.

51.—[*was subject.*] The words imply a continual habit during His residence at Nazareth, and not a single isolated act.

52.—[*Increased in wisdom and stature.*] A sentence from Poole's Annotations on this subject, is worth reading: "If any ask how He who was the eternal wisdom of the Father, who is the only one God, increased in wisdom, they must know that all things in Scripture which are spoken of Christ, are not spoken with respect to His entire Person, but with respect to the one or other nature united in that Person. He increased in wisdom, as He did in age or stature, with respect to His human, not His divine nature. And as God daily magnified His grace and favour towards Him, so He gained Him favour with the un-righteous and people of Galilee."

LUKE III. 1—6.

1 Now in the fifteenth year of the reign of Tiberius Cæsar, Pontius Pi-late being governor of Judæa, and Herod being tetrarch of Galilee, and his brother Philip tetrarch of Ituræa and of the region of Trachonitis, and Lysanias the tetrarch of Abilene,

2 Annas and Caiaphas being the High Priests, the word of God came unto John the son of Zacharias in the wilderness.

3 And he came into all the country about Jordan, preaching the baptism of repentance for the remission of sins.

4 As it is written in the book of the words of Esaias the prophet, saying, The voice of one crying in the wil-derness, Prepare ye the way of the Lord, make his paths straight.

5 Every valley shall be filled, and every mountain and hill shall be brought low; and the crooked shall be made straight, and the rough ways *shall be* made smooth;

6 And all flesh shall see the salva-tion of God.

THESE verses describe the beginning of the Gospel of Christ. It began with the preaching of John the Baptist.

The Jews could never say, that when Messiah came, He came without notice or preparation. He graciously sent a mighty forerunner before His face, by whose ministry the attention of the whole nation was awakened.

Let us notice first, in this passage, *the wickedness of the times when Christ's Gospel was brought into the world.* The opening verses of the chapter tell us the names of some who were rulers and governors in the earth, when the ministry of John the Baptist began. It is a melancholy list, and full of instruction. There is hardly a name in it which is not infamous for wickedness. Tiberius, and Pontius Pilate, and Herod, and his brother, and Annas, and Caiaphas, were men of whom we know little or nothing but evil. The earth seemed given into the hands of the wicked. (Job ix. 24.) When such were the rulers, what must the people have been?—Such was the state of things when Christ's forerunner was commissioned to begin preaching. Such were the times when the first foundation of Christ's church was brought out and laid. We may truly say, that God's ways are not our ways.

Let us learn never to despair about the cause of God's truth, however black and unfavourable its prospects may appear. At the very time when things seem hopeless, God may be preparing a mighty deliverance. At the very season when Satan's kingdom seems to be triumphing, the "little stone, cut without hands," may be on the point of crushing it to pieces. The darkest hour of the night is often that which just precedes the day.

Let us beware of slacking our hands from any work of God, because of the wickedness of the times, or the number and power of our adversaries. "He that observeth the wind shall not sow, and he that regardeth the clouds shall not reap." (Eccles. xi. 4.) Let us work on, and believe that help will come from heaven, when it is most wanted. In the very hour when a Roman emperor, and ignorant priests, seemed to have everything at their feet, the Lamb of God was about to come forth from Nazareth, and set up the beginnings of His kingdom. What He has done once, He can do again. In a moment He can turn His church's midnight into the blaze of noon day.

Let us notice, secondly, in this passage, *the account which St. Luke gives of the calling of John the Baptist into the ministry*. We are told that, "the word of God came to John, the son of Zacharias." He received a special call from God to begin preaching and baptizing. A message from heaven was sent to his heart, and under the impulse of that message, he undertook his marvellous work.

There is something in this account which throws great light on the office of all ministers of the Gospel. It is an office which no man has a right to take up, unless he has an inward call from God, as well as an outward call from man. Visions and revelations from heaven, of course we have no right to expect. Fanatical claims to special gifts of the Spirit must always be checked and discouraged. But an inward call a man must have, before he puts his hand to the work of the ministry. The word of God must "come to him," as really and truly as it came to John the Baptist, before he undertakes to "come to the word." In short, he must be able to profess with a good conscience, that he is "inwardly moved by

the Holy Ghost" to take upon him the office of a minister.
The man who cannot say this, when he comes forward
to be ordained, is committing a great sin, and running
without being sent.

Let it be a part of our daily prayers, that our churches
may have no ministers excepting those who are really
called of God. An unconverted minister is an injury
and burden to a church. How can a man speak of truths
which he has never tasted ? How can he testify of a
Saviour whom he has never seen by faith, and never laid
hold on for his own soul ? The pastor after God's own
heart, is a man to whom the word of God has come. He
runs confidently, because he has tidings. He speaks
boldly, because he has been sent.

Let us notice, lastly, in this passage, *the close connection between true repentance and forgiveness.* We are told
that John the Baptist came "preaching the baptism of repentance for the remission of sins." The plain meaning
of this expression is, that John preached the necessity of
being baptized, in token of repentance, and that he told
his hearers that except they repented of sin, their sins
would not be forgiven.

We must carefully bear in mind, that no repentance
can make atonement for sin. The blood of Christ, and
nothing else, can wash away sin from man's soul. No
quantity of repentance can ever justify us in the sight of
God. "We are accounted righteous before God, only for
the sake of our Lord Jesus Christ, by faith, and not for
our own works or deservings." It is of the utmost importance to understand this clearly. The trouble that
men bring upon their souls, by misunderstanding this
subject, is more than can be expressed.

But while we say all this, we must carefully remember that without repentance no soul was ever yet saved. We must know our sins, mourn over them, forsake them, abhor them, or else we shall never enter the kingdom of heaven. There is nothing meritorious in this. It forms no part whatever of the price of our redemption. Our salvation is all of grace, from first to last. But the great fact still remains, that saved souls are always penitent souls, and that saving faith in Christ, and true repentance toward God, are never found asunder. This is a mighty truth, and one that ought never to be forgotten.

Do we ourselves repent? This, after all, is the question which most nearly concerns us. Have we been convinced of sin by the Holy Ghost? Have we fled to Jesus for deliverance from the wrath to come? Do we know anything of a broken and contrite heart, and a thorough hatred of sin? Can we say, "I repent," as well as "I believe?" If not, let us not delude our minds with the idea that our sins are yet forgiven. It is written, "Except ye repent, ye shall all likewise perish." (Luke xiii. 3.)

NOTES. LUKE III. 1—6.

1.—[*Ituræa, Trachonitis, Abilene.*] These were districts lying to the north and north-east of Palestine.

2.—[*Annas and Caiaphas being high priests.*] We know, from the Bible, that there could not, properly speaking, be two high priests at the same time. The office, in the best days of Israel, was held by one man, and held for life. But in the time of our Lord's earthly ministry there seems to have been much irregularity connected with the high priest's office, and the Romans probably deposed some from it for political reasons. The result was that there were frequently others beside the actual high priest still living, who had filled the office before. Annas was father-in-law to Caiaphas. (John xviii. 13.)

5.—[*Every valley shall be filled, &c.*] These and similar expressions in this verse must certainly receive a figurative interpretation. It is no literal pulling down of mountains, or filling up of valleys, that is here meant. The sense of the prophecy evidently is, that difficulties and obstacles as great as mountains and valleys in the way of a king's march, shall go down before the progress of the Gospel of Christ.

6.—[*All flesh shall see, &c.*] This is a prophecy which is not yet fully accomplished. It is to receive its completion when the kingdom of Christ is fully set up at His second advent, and all know Him from the least to the greatest. It is one among many examples, that the prophets of the Old Testament often spoke of both advents at once. and foretold the complete victories of the second appearing of Jesus, in the same breath with the partial victories of His first appearing. Some began to " see the great salvation " as soon as the Gospel was first preached. A little flock was taken out at once. All shall finally see the salvation of God from the least to the greatest.

LUKE III. 7.—14.

7 Then said he to the multitude that came forth to be baptized of him, O generation of vipers, who hath warned you to flee from the wrath to come?

8 Bring forth therefore fruits worthy of repentance, and begin not to say within yourselves, We have Abraham to *our* father : for I say unto you, That God is able of these stones to raise up children unto Abraham.

9 And now also the axe is laid unto the root of the trees : every tree therefore which bringeth not forth good fruit is hewn down, and cast into the fire.

10 And the people asked him, saying, What shall we do then?

11 He answereth and saith unto them, He that hath two coats, let him impart to him that hath none ; and he that hath meat, let him do likewise.

12 Then came also Publicans to be baptized, and said unto him, Master, what shall we do?

13 And he said unto them, Exact no more than that which is appointed you.

14 And the soldiers likewise demanded of him, saying, And what shall we do? And he said unto them, Do violence to no man, neither accuse *any* falsely ; and be content with your wages.

WE have, in these verses, a specimen of John the Baptist's ministry. It is a portion of Scripture which should always be specially interesting to a Christian mind. The immense effect which John produced on the Jews, however temporary, is evident, from many expressions in the Gospels. The remarkable testimony which our Lord bore to John, as "a prophet greater than any born of woman," is well-known to all Bible readers. What then was the character of John's ministry? This is the question to which the chapter before us supplies a practical answer.

We should first mark *the holy boldness with which John addresses the multitudes who came to his baptism.* He speaks to them as "a generation of vipers." He saw the rottenness and hypocrisy of the profession that the crowd around him were making, and uses language descriptive of their case. His head was not turned by popularity. He cared not who was offended by his words. The spiritual disease of those before him was desperate, and of long standing, and he knew that desperate diseases need strong remedies.

Well would it be for the Church of Christ, if it possessed more plain-speaking ministers, like John the Baptist, in these latter days. A morbid dislike to strong language,—an excessive fear of giving offence,—a constant flinching from directness and plain speaking, are, unhappily, too much the characteristics of the modern Christian pulpit. Personality and uncharitable language are no doubt always to be deprecated. But there is no charity in flattering unconverted people, by abstaining from any mention of their vices, or in applying smooth epithets to damnable sins. There are two texts which are too much forgotten by Christian preachers. In one it is written, "Woe unto you when all men shall speak well of you." In the other it is written, "If I yet pleased men, I should not be the servant of Christ." (Luke vi. 26 ; Gal. i. 10.)

We should mark, secondly, *how plainly John speaks to*

his hearers about hell and danger. He tells them that
there is a "wrath to come." He speaks of "the axe"
of God's judgments, and of unfruitful trees being cast
into "the fire."

The subject of hell is always offensive to human nature.
The minister who dwells much upon it, must expect to
find himself regarded as coarse, violent, unfeeling, and
narrow-minded. Men love to hear "smooth things," and
to be told of peace, and not of danger. (Isai. xxx. 10.)
But the subject is one that ought not to be kept back, if we
desire to do good to souls. It is one that our Lord Jesus
Christ brought forward frequently in His public teaching.
That loving Saviour, who spoke so graciously of the way
to heaven, has also used the plainest language about the
way to hell.

Let us beware of being wise above that which is written, and more charitable than Scripture itself. Let the
language of John the Baptist be deeply graven in our
hearts. Let us never be ashamed to avow our firm
belief, that there is a "wrath to come" for the impenitent,
and that it is possible for a man to be lost as well as to
be saved. To be silent on the subject is positive
treachery to men's souls. It only encourages them to
persevere in wickedness, and fosters in their minds the
devil's old delusion, "Ye shall not surely die." That
minister is surely our best friend who tells us honestly
of danger, and warns us, like John the Baptist, to "flee
from the wrath to come." Never will a man flee till he
sees there is real cause to be afraid. Never will he seek
heaven till he is convinced that there is risk of his falling
into hell. The religion in which there is no mention of

hell, is not the religion of John the Baptist, and of our Lord Jesus, and His apostles.

We should mark, thirdly, *how John exposes the uselessness of a repentance which is not accompanied by fruits in the life.* He said to the multitude, who came to be baptized, "Bring forth fruits worthy of repentance." He tells them that "Every tree which bringeth not forth good fruit is hewn down."

This is a truth which should always occupy a prominent place in our Christianity. It can never be impressed on our minds too strongly, that religious talking and profession are utterly worthless, without religious doing and practice. It is vain to say with our lips that we repent, if we do not at the same time repent in our lives. It is more than vain. It will gradually sear our consciences, and harden our hearts. To say that we are sorry for our sins is mere hypocrisy, unless we show that we are really sorry for them, by giving them up. Doing is the very life of repentance. Tell us not merely what a man says in religion. Tell us rather what he does. "The talk of the lips," says Solomon, "tendeth only to penury." (Prov. xiv. 23.)

We should mark, fourthly, *what a blow John strikes at the common notion, that connection with godly people can save our souls.* "Begin not to say," he tells the Jews, "we have Abraham to our Father; for I say unto you that God is able of these stones to raise up children unto Abraham."

The strong hold that this notion has obtained on the heart of man, in every part of the world, is an affecting proof of our fallen and corrupt condition. Thousands have always been found, in every age of the church, who have believed that connection with godly men made them acceptable in the sight of God. Thousands have lived and died in the blind delusion, that because they were allied to holy people by ties of blood or church-membership, they might themselves hope to be saved.

Let it be a settled principle with us, that saving religion is a personal thing. It is a business between each man's own soul and Christ. It will profit us nothing at the last day, to have belonged to the Church of Luther, or Calvin, or Cranmer, or Knox, or Owen, or Wesley, or Whitfield.—Had we the faith of these holy men? Did we believe as they believed, and strive to live as they lived, and to follow Christ as they followed Him? These will be the only points on which our salvation will turn. It will save no man to have had Abraham's blood in his veins, if he did not possess Abraham's faith and do Abraham's works.

We should remark, lastly, in this passage, *the searching test of sincerity which John applied to the consciences of the various classes who came to his baptism.* He bade each man who made a profession of repentance, to begin by breaking off from those sins which specially beset him. The selfish multitude must show common charity to each other. The publicans must " exact no more than their due. " The soldiers must " do violence to no man, and be content with their wages." He did not mean that, by so doing, they would atone for their sins, and make their peace with God. But he did mean that, by so doing, they would prove their repentance to be sincere.

Let us leave the passage with a deep conviction of the wisdom of this mode of dealing with souls, and specially with the souls of those who are beginning to make a profession of religion. Above all, let us see here the right way to prove our own hearts. It must not content us to cry out against sins to which, by natural temperament, we are not inclined, while we deal gently with other sins of a different character. Let us find out our own peculiar corruptions. Let us know our own besetting sins. Against them let us direct our principal efforts. With these let us wage unceasing war. Let the rich break off from the rich man's sins, and the poor from the sins of the poor. Let the young man give up the sins of youth, and the old man the sins of age. This is the first step towards proving that we are in earnest, when we first begin to feel about our souls. Are we real? Are we sincere? Then let us begin by looking at home, and looking within.

NOTES. LUKE III. 7—14.

8.—[*Bring forth fruit.*] It is worthy of remark, that the word translated " bring forth," is the same that is used by St. John, when he speaks of "committing sin," and "doing righteousness." (1 John iii. 4, 7.) Both there and here is implied a continued habit, and not a single act.

[*We have Abraham to our father.*] A passage in Stella, the Spanish commentator on the Gospel of St. Luke, on this expression, is worth quoting:—" There are many monks who imitate these Jews, saying, we have Benedict, Augustine, Jerome, Francis, or Dominic for our father, just as they said, We have Abraham to our father. They relate to others the marvellous doings of the founders of their order, and cry up their praises with wonderful commendation. They say, our order has so many holy men enrolled in the catalogue of saints, so many Popes, so many Cardinals, so many bishops, so many teachers. In them they rejoice and vain-gloriously boast, while they themselves have degenerated from the true excellencies of their founders, by iniquity and laxity of morals.   To all these we may deservedly say what Christ said to the Jews, 'If ye are Abraham's children, do the works of Abraham.'"

[*God is able of these stones, &c.*] The meaning of this expression is simply this: "Think not that God will not have a people to show forth His praise, if He cuts you off and does not save you.   Even if you were all cast off, He could raise up *a family for Himself* of true believers from these stones."   The calling of the Gentiles was evidently implied.

14.—[*what shall we do.*] Our English version hardly gives the full sense of the original Greek here.   It should rather be, "and we, what shall we do?"

[*do violence.*] The word so translated is found nowhere else in the New Testament.   It signifies "to put in fear, or to shake, by violent conduct."

[*accuse falsely.*] This word is only found in one other place, and there it is rendered, "take by false accusation."   It occurs in the remarkable profession of Zacchæus after his conversion. (Luke xix. 8.)

Let it be carefully noted that John the Baptist says not a word to shew that the work of the tax-gatherer or the soldier is unlawful in the sight of God.

LUKE III. 15—20.

15 And as the people were in expectation, and all men mused in their hearts of John, whether he were the Christ, or not;

16 John answered, saying unto *them* all, I indeed baptize you with water; but one mightier than I cometh, the latchet of whose shoes I am not worthy to unloose; he shall baptize you with the Holy Ghost and with fire:

17 Whose fan *is* in his hand, and he will throughly purge his floor, and will gather the wheat into his garner; but the chaff he will burn with fire unquenchable.

18 And many other things in his exhortation preached he unto the people.

19 But Herod the tetrarch, being reproved by him for Herodias his brother Philip's wife, and for all the evils which Herod had done,

20 Added yet this above all, that he shut up John in prison.

WE learn, firstly, from these verses, *that one effect of a faithful ministry is to set men thinking*. We read concerning John the Baptist's hearers, that "the people were in expectation, and all men mused in their hearts of John, whether he were the Christ, or not."

The cause of true religion has gained a great step in a parish, or congregation, or family, when people begin to think. Thoughtlessness about spiritual things is one great feature of unconverted men. It cannot be said, in many cases, that they either like the Gospel, or dislike it. But they do not give it a place in their thoughts. They never "consider." (Isaiah i. 3.)

Let us always thank God when we see a spirit of reflection on religious subjects coming over the mind of an unconverted man. Consideration is the high road to conversion. The truth of Christ has nothing to fear from sober examination. We court inquiry. We desire to have its claims fully investigated. We know that its fitness to supply every want of man's heart and conscience is not appreciated in many cases, simply because it is not known. Thinking, no doubt, is not faith and repentance. But it is always a hopeful symptom. When hearers of the Gospel begin "to muse in their hearts," we ought to bless God and take courage.

We learn, secondly, from these verses, *that a faithful minister will always exalt Christ*. We read that when John saw the state of mind in which his hearers were, he told them of a coming One far mightier than himself. He refused the honour which he saw the people ready to give him, and referred them to Him who had the "fan in his hand," the Lamb of God, the Messiah.

Conduct like this will always be the characteristic of a true "man of God." He will never allow anything to be credited to him, or his office, which belongs to his divine Master. He will say like St. Paul, "we preach not ourselves, but Christ Jesus, the Lord, and ourselves your servants for Jesus' sake." (2 Cor. iv. 5.) To commend Christ dying, and rising again for the ungodly,—to make known Christ's love and power to save sinners,—this will be the main object of his ministry. " He must increase but I must decrease," will be a ruling principle in all his preaching. He will be content that his own name be forgotten, so long as Christ crucified is exalted.

Would we know whether a minister is sound in the faith, and deserving of our confidence, as a teacher ? We have only to ask a simple question, Where is Christ in his teaching ?—Would we know whether we ourselves are receiving benefit from the preaching we attend ? Let us ask whether its effect is to magnify Christ in our esteem ? A minister who is really doing us good will make us think more of Jesus every year we live.

We learn, thirdly, from these verses, *the essential difference between the Lord Jesus and even the best and holiest of His ministers.* We have it in the solemn words of John the Baptist :—" I indeed baptize you with water : —He shall baptize you with the Holy Ghost."

Man, when ordained, can administer the outward ordinances of Christianity, with a prayerful hope, that God will graciously bless the means which he has Himself appointed. But man cannot read the hearts of those to whom he ministers. He can preach the Gospel faithfully to their ears, but he cannot make them receive it into their consciences. He can apply baptismal water to their foreheads, but he cannot cleanse their inward nature. He can give the bread and wine of the Lord's Supper into their hands, but he cannot enable them to eat Christ's body and blood by faith. Up to a certain point he can go, but he can go no further. No ordination, however solemnly conferred, can give man power to change the heart. Christ, the great Head of the Church, can alone do this by the power of the Holy Ghost. It is His peculiar office to do it, and it is an office which He has deputed to no child of man.

May we never rest till we have tasted by experience the power of Christ's grace upon our souls! We have been baptized with water. But have we also been baptized with the Holy Ghost.—Our names are in the baptismal register. But are they also in the Lamb's book of life?—We are members of the visible Church. But are we also members of that mystical body of which Christ alone is the Head?—All these are privileges which Christ alone bestows, and for which all who would be saved must make personal application to Him. Man cannot give them. They are treasures laid up in Christ's hand. From Him we must seek them by faith and prayer, and believing we shall not seek in vain.

We learn, fourthly, in these verses, *the change that Christ will work in His visible Church at His second appearing.* We read in the figurative words of His forerunner, "that he will throughly purge his floor, and gather the wheat into his garner; but the chaff he will burn with fire unquenchable."

The visible Church is now a mixed body. Believers and unbelievers, holy and unholy, converted and unconverted, are now mingled in every congregation, and often sit side by side. It passes the power of man to separate them. False profession is often so like true, and grace is often so weak and feeble, that, in many cases, the right

discernment of character is an impossibility. The wheat and
the chaff will continue together until the Lord returns.

But there will be an awful separation at the last day.
The unerring judgment of the King of kings shall at
length divide the wheat from the chaff, and divide them
for evermore. The righteous shall be gathered into a
place of happiness and safety. The wicked shall be cast
down to shame and everlasting contempt. In the great
sifting day, every one shall go to his own place.

May we often look forward to that day, and judge
ourselves, that we be not judged of the Lord. May we
give all diligence to make our calling and election sure,
and to know that we are God's "wheat." A mistake in
the day that the floor is "purged," will be a mistake that
is irretrievable.

We learn, lastly, from these verses, that *the reward of
God's servants is often not in this world*. St. Luke closes
his account of John the Baptist's ministry, by telling us
of his imprisonment by Herod. The end of that imprisonment we know from other parts of the New Testament. It led at last to John being beheaded.

All true servants of Christ must be content to wait for
their wages. Their best things are yet to come. They
must count it no strange thing, if they meet with hard
treatment from man. The world that persecuted Christ
will never hesitate, to persecute Christians. "Marvel not
if the world hate you." (1 John iii. 13.)

But let us take comfort in the thought that the great
Master has laid up in heaven for His people such things
as pass man's understanding. The blood that His saints
have shed in His name will all be reckond for one day.

The tears that often flow so freely in consequence of the unkindness of the wicked, will one day be wiped from all faces. And when John the Baptist, and all who have suffered for the truth are at last gathered together, they will find it true that heaven makes amends for all.

NOTES. LUKE III. 15—20.

15.—[*mused.*] The word so translated is generally rendered "reasoned."

16.—[*I indeed baptize with water.*] We must not fail to observe that the contrast John the Baptist draws here, is not, as the Roman Catholic writers say, between his baptism and Christian baptism, but between his power as a mere man to administer an outward ordinance, and the power of Christ the Son of God to affect the heart.

We must be careful that we do not underrate the value of John's baptism. We have no proof that any of the apostles ever received any other baptism than that of John. To say that the baptism of Christian ministers always confers grace, "ex opere operato," and that the baptism of John never conferred grace, is to say what cannot be proved either by Scripture or experience. The value of John's baptism is well defended by Brentius, in his Homilies on this chapter. Spanheim ably discusses the whole question, and concludes that the distinction between the baptism of John and the baptism of Christ was "not essential but accidental," that is, not in its essence but in its accidents or circumstances.

[*Baptize with fire.*] The meaning of this expression is doubtful, and has never been fully cleared up. Some confine it entirely to the descent of the Holy Ghost on the day of Pentecost, when "cloven tongues like as of fire" sat upon each person present on the occasion. (Acts ii. 3.) Others confine it entirely to the converting operation of the Holy Ghost, purifying and refining the heart as fire purifieth gold. Both views are probably included.

19.—[*But Herod &c.*] The mention of John's imprisonment in this part of St. Luke's Gospel, before the event actually took place, is a striking example of St. Luke's mode of "writing in order." (Luke i. 3.) He is on the subject of John the Baptist and his ministry, and he therefore takes occasion to explain how that ministry was brought to an end, before turning to another subject.

LUKE III. 21—38.

21 Now when all the people were baptized, it came to pass, that Jesus also being baptized, and praying, the heaven was opened,

22 And the Holy Ghost descended in a bodily shape like a dove upon him, and a voice came from heaven, which said, Thou art my beloved Son ; in thee I am well pleased.

23 And Jesus himself began to be about thirty years of age, being (as was supposed) the son of Joseph, which was *the son* of Heli,

24 Which was *the son* of Matthat, which was *the son* of Levi, which was *the son* of Melchi, which was *the son* of Janna, which was *the son* of Joseph,

25 Which was *the son* of Mattathias, which was *the son* of Amos, which was *the son* of Naum, which was *the son* of Esli, which was *the son* of Nagge.

26 Which was *the son* of Maath, which was *the son* of Mattathias, which was *the son* of Semei, which was *the son* of Joseph, which was *the son* of Juda,

27 Which was *the son* of Joanna, which was *the son* of Rhesa, which was *the son* of Zorobabel, which was *the son* of Salathiel, which was *the son* of Neri,

28 Which was *the son* of Melchi, which was *the son* of Addi, which was *the son* of Cosam, which was *the son* of Elmodam, which was *the son* of Er,

29 Which was *the son* of Jose, which was *the son* of Eliezer, which was *the son* of Jorim, which was *the son* of Matthat, which was *the son* of Levi,

30 Which was *the son* of Simeon, which was *the son* of Juda, which was *the son* of Joseph, which was *the son* of Jonan, which was *the son* of Eliakim,

31 Which was *the son* of Melea, which was *the son* of Menan, which was *the son* of Mattatha, which was *the son* of Nathan, which was *the son* of David,

32 Which was *the son* of Jesse, which was *the son* of Obed, which was *the son* of Booz, which was *the son* of Salmon, which was *the son* of Naason,

33 Which was *the son* of Aminadab, which was *the son* of Aram, which was *the son* of Esrom, which was *the son* of Phares, which was *the son* of Juda,

34 Which was *the son* of Jacob, which was *the son* of Isaac, which was *the son* of Abraham, which was *the son* of Thara, which was *the son* of Nachor,

35 Which was *the son* of Saruch, which was *the son* of Ragau, which was *the son* of Phalec, which was *the son* of Heber, which was *the son* of Sala,

36 Which was *the son* of Cainan, which was *the son* of Arphaxad, which was *the son* of Sem, which was *the son* of Noe, which was *the son* of Lamech,

37 Which was *the son* of Mathusala, which was *the son* of Enoch, which was *the son* of Jared, which was *the son* of Maleleel, which was *the son* of Cainan,

38 Which was *the son* of Enos, which was *the son* of Seth, which was *the son* of Adam, which was *the son* of God.

WE see in the passage before us, *the high honour the Lord Jesus has put on baptism.* We find that among others who came to John the Baptist, the Saviour of the world came, and was " baptized."

An ordinance which the Son of God was pleased to use, and afterwards to appoint for the use of His whole

Church, ought always to be held in peculiar reverence by His people. Baptism cannot be a thing of slight importance, if Christ Himself was baptized. The use of baptism would never have been enjoined on the Church of Christ, if it had been a mere outward form, incapable of conveying any blessing.

It is hardly necessary to say that errors of every sort and description abound on the subject of baptism. Some make an idol of it, and exalt it far above the place assigned to it in the Bible. Some degrade it and dishonour it, and seem almost to forget that it was ordained by Christ Himself. Some limit the use of it so narrowly that they will baptize none unless they are grown up, and can give full proof of their conversion. Some invest the baptismal water with such magic power, that they would like missionaries to go into heathen lands and baptize all persons, old and young indiscriminately, and believe that however ignorant the heathen may be, baptism must do them good. On no subject, perhaps, in religion, have Christians more need to pray for a right judgment and a sound mind.

Let it suffice us to hold firmly the general principle, that baptism was graciously intended by our Lord to be a help to His Church, and "a means of grace," and that when rightly and worthily used, we may confidently look upon it for a blessing. But let us never forget that the grace of God is not tied to any sacrament, and that we may be baptized with water, without being baptized with the Holy Ghost.

We see, secondly, in this passage, *the close connection that ought to exist between the administration of baptism and prayer.* We are specially told by St. Luke, that when our Lord was baptized He was also "praying."

We need not doubt that there is a great lesson in this fact, and one that the Church of Christ has too much overlooked. We are meant to learn that the baptism which God blesses must be a baptism accompanied by prayer. The sprinkling of water is not sufficient. The use of the name of the blessed Trinity is not enough. The form of the sacrament alone conveys no grace. There must be something else beside all this. There must be "the prayer of faith." A baptism without prayer, it may be confidently asserted, is a baptism on which we have no right to expect God's blessing.

Why is it that the sacrament of baptism appears to bear so little fruit? How is it that thousands are every year baptized, and never give the slightest proof of having received benefit from it? The answer to these questions is short and simple. In the vast majority of baptisms there is no prayer except the prayer of the officiating minister. Parents bring their children to the font, without the slightest sense of what they are doing. Sponsors stand up and answer for the child, in evident ignorance of the nature of the ordinance they are attending, and as a mere matter of form. What possible reason have we for expecting such baptisms to be blessed by God? None! none at all! Such baptisms may well be barren of results. They are not baptisms according to the mind of Christ. Let us pray that the eyes of Christians on this important subject may be opened. It is one on which there is great need of change.

We see, thirdly, in these verses, *a remarkable proof of*

the doctrine of the Trinity. We have all the Three Persons of the Godhead spoken of, as co-operating and acting at one time. God the Son begins the mighty work of His earthly ministry, by being baptized. God the Father solemnly accredits Him as the appointed Mediator, by a voice from heaven. God the Holy Ghost descends "in a bodily shape like a dove" upon our Lord, and by so doing declares that this is He to whom "the Father gives the Spirit without measure." (John iii. 34.)

There is something deeply instructive, and deeply comforting in this revelation of the blessed Trinity, at this particular season of our Lord's earthly ministry. It shows us how mighty and powerful is the agency that is employed in the great business of our redemption. It is the common work of God the Father, God the Son, and God the Holy Ghost. All Three Persons in the Godhead are equally concerned in the deliverance of our souls from hell. The thought should cheer us, when disquieted and cast down. The thought should hearten and encourage us, when weary of the conflict with the world, the flesh, and the devil. The enemies of our souls are mighty, but the Friends of our souls are mightier still. The whole power of the triune Jehovah is engaged upon our side. "A three-fold cord is not easily broken." (Eccles. iv. 12.)

We see, fourthly, in these verses, a *marvellous proclamation of our Lord's office as Mediator between God and man*. A voice was heard from heaven at His baptism, "which said, Thou art my beloved Son; in thee I am well pleased." There is but One who could say this. It was the voice of God the Father.

These solemn words no doubt contain much that is deeply mysterious. One thing however about them is abundantly clear. They are a divine declaration, that our Lord Jesus Christ is the promised Redeemer, whom God from the beginning undertook to send into the world, and that with His incarnation, sacrifice, and substitution for man, God the Father is satisfied and well pleased. In Him, He regards the claim of His holy law as fully discharged. Through Him, He is willing to receive poor sinful man to mercy, and to remember his sins no more.

Let all true Christians rest their souls on these words, and draw from them daily consolation. Our sins and shortcomings are many and great. In ourselves we can see no good thing. But if we believe in Jesus, the Father sees nothing in us that He cannot abundantly pardon. He regards us as the members of His own dear Son, and, for His Son's sake, He is well pleased.

We see, lastly, in these verses, *what a frail and dying creature is man.* We read at the end of the chapter a long list of names, containing the genealogy of the family in which our Lord was born, traced up through David and Abraham to Adam. How little we know of many of the seventy-five persons, whose names are here recorded! They all had their joys and sorrows, their hopes and fears, their cares and troubles, their schemes and plans, like any of ourselves. But they have all passed away from the earth, and gone to their own place. And so will it be with us. We too are passing away, and shall soon be gone.

For ever let us bless God, that in a dying world we

are able to turn to a living Saviour. "I am he," says
Jesus, "that liveth and was dead, and behold I am alive
for evermore." "I am the resurrection and the life."
(Rev. i. 18 ; John xi. 25.) Let our main care be, to be
one with Christ and Christ with us. Joined to the Lord
Jesus by faith we shall rise again to live for evermore.
The second death shall have no power over us. "Because
I live," says Christ, "ye shall live also." (John xiv. 19.)

NOTES. LUKE III. 21—38.

23.—[*Thirty years of age.*] This was the age, be it remembered·
at which Levites were first permitted to do work in the tabernacle. (Num. iv. 3.)

[*Joseph, which was the son of Heli, &c.*] Every careful reader
of the Bible knows well that there is a great difficulty connected
with the genealogy of our Lord. The difficulty lies in the
entire variance between that part of the genealogy which lies
between David and Joseph, as recorded by St. Luke, and
the same part of it as recorded by St. Matthew. Between
Abraham and David the two genealogies agree. Between
David and Joseph they almost entirely differ. How can this
difference be reconciled? This is a question on which learned
men have written volumes, and failed to convince one another.
A few simple remarks must suffice. Those who wish to study
the subject will find it thoroughly discussed by Gomarus, Spanheim, South, Calovius, and A. Clarke.

The first, but least probable explanation, is this. The persons
mentioned in the genealogy from David to Joseph had all two
names. Matthew gives one of their names, Luke gives the
other. But both enumerate the same persons, and both give
the genealogy of Joseph. This explanation will satisfy very
few people. The difference between the number of names given
by Luke, compared to the number given by Matthew, is of itself
an insuperable objection. It seems waste of time to dwell on
this solution of the question.

The second, and more probable explanation of the difficulty,
is this. The mother of Joseph the husband of Mary, married
two husbands. Of one husband Joseph was the son by birth.
Of the other he was the son by adoption. The two genealogies
in the two Gospels, are the genealogies of these two husbands.
Each evangelist ends his genealogy in Joseph, but Luke traces
it through Heli, and Matthew through Jacob. Joseph was the

natural son of one, and the adopted son of the other. This
explanation is that which satisfied the early fathers, and is commonly known as that of Julius Africanus. It is, however, in
spite of its antiquity, open to several serious objections. It is
difficult to see why Joseph's genealogy should be repeated by
Luke, in a Gospel written specially for Gentile converts, and
why the genealogy of our Lord's own mother should be entirely
passed over by both evangelists.

The third, and most probable explanation of the difficulty, is
to regard Luke's genealogy as the genealogy of Mary, and not
of Joseph. Heli was the father of Mary, and the father-in-law,
by his marriage, of Joseph. It is not said that Heli "begat"
Joseph; and that the Greek does not necessarily mean Joseph
was "his son," is clear from the expressions used about Mary
and Jude. in two other places of the New Testament. (Mark
xvi. 1. and Acts i. 15.) It is Mary's family, therefore, and
not Joseph's, that St. Luke describes, and Joseph's family,
and not Mary's, that is described by St. Matthew.

There are doubtless some difficulties in the way of this explanation. But there seem to be far greater difficulties in
the way of any other. In leaving the question, I may be allowed
to remark, that the view I venture to maintain is that of Brentius,
Gomarus, Chemnitius, Spanheim, Surenhusius, Poole, Bengel,
Paræus, Lightfoot, Calovius, Gill, Burkitt, Henry, Scott, and
Clarke, among Protestants, — and of Jansenius, Barrradius,
Stella, and others, among Roman Catholics. It is also a
remarkable fact, that Rabbinical writers, quoted by Lightfoot,
speaking of Mary in very reproachful terms, distinctly call her,
"the daughter of Heli."

36.—[*The son of Cainan.*] There is a serious difficulty connected
with this name. It is not to be found in the genealogy from Noah
to Abraham, as recorded in the Hebrew version of Gen. xi. 12.,
although it is found in the Septuagint Greek version. The
question at once arises,—Why did St. Luke put the name here?
How are we to reconcile Moses and St. Luke?

The solutions of this difficulty are various, and a complete
settlement of the question will probably never be attained.
One thing only is certain, and that is, that neither Moses nor St.
Luke could have made a real mistake, because both were inspired.
Some think that St. Luke does not pretend to do more than
copy out the genealogy which was commonly received, and
guards himself against the charge of endorsing its errors and
mistakes, by the use of the expression at the outset, "as was
supposed." They consider this expression to apply to the whole
genealogy.—Some think that the name has been omitted in
the Hebrew text of Genesis, by mistake of a transcriber.—Some
think that St. Luke purposely put the name in the genealogy, in
order to consult the feelings of those who only knew the Sept-

uagint version of the Old Testament.—Some think that the name has crept into St Luke's Gospel by the error of some transcriber, who knew nothing of Hebrew, and only knew the old Testament from the Septuagint version, and that St. Luke originally did not insert Cainan's name.—This last solution is maintained by Spanheim, Capellus, Grotius, Calovius, Rivetus, Leigh, and Surenhusius, and is perhaps the most probable one. One argument in support of it is the fact that the name is omitted in Beza's manuscript, though it must be admitted that on this point his manuscript stands almost alone.

In leaving the difficult subject of these questions connected with our Lord's genealogy, we shall do well to ponder the sensible remarks of Mr. Burgon : " It is humbly suggested that a few difficulties of this class may have been suffered to find place in Holy Writ, in order to exercise the faith of persons who, while they feel such intellectual trials keenly, are but little affected by those which imperil the salvation of the ordinary class of mankind."

LUKE IV. 1—13.

1 And Jesus being full of the Holy Ghost returned from Jordan, and was led by the Spirit into the wilderness,

2 Being forty days tempted of the devil.   And in those days he did eat nothing : and when they were ended, he afterward hungered.

3 And the devil said unto him, If thou be the Son of God, command this stone that it be made bread.

4 And Jesus answered him, saying, It is written, That man shall not live by bread alone, but by every word of God.

5 And the devil, taking him up into an high mountain, shewed unto him all the kingdoms of the world in a moment of time.

6 And the devil said unto him, All this power will I give thee, and the glory of them : for that is delivered unto me; and to whomsoever I will I give it.

7 If thou therefore wilt worship me, all shall be thine.

8 And Jesus answered and said unto him, Get thee behind me, Satan : for it is written, Thou shalt worship the Lord thy God, and him only shalt thou serve.

9 And he brought him to Jerusalem, and set him on a pinnacle of the temple, and said unto him, If thou be the Son of God, cast thyself down from hence :

10 For it is written, He shall give his angels charge over thee, to keep thee :

11 And in *their* hands they shall bear thee up, lest at any time thou dash thy foot against a stone.

12 And Jesus answering said unto him, It is said, Thou shalt not tempt the Lord thy God.

13 And when the devil had ended all the temptation, he departed from him for a season.

THE first event recorded in our Lord's history, after His baptism, is His temptation by the devil.   From a season

of honour and glory He passed immediately to a season
of conflict and suffering. First came the testimony of
God the Father, " Thou art my beloved Son." Then
came the sneering suggestion of Satan, " If thou be the
Son of God." The portion of Christ will often prove
the portion of Christians. From great privilege to great
trial there will often be but a step.

Let us first mark in this passage, *the power and unwearied malice of the devil.*

That old serpent who tempted Adam to sin in Paradise,
was not afraid to assault the second Adam, the Son of
God. Whether he understood that Jesus was "God
manifest in the flesh" may perhaps be doubted. But that
he saw in Jesus One who had come into the world to
overthrow his kingdom, is clear and plain. He had seen
what happened at our Lord's baptism. He had heard
the marvellous words from heaven. He felt that the
great Friend of man was come, and that his own dominion
was in peril. The Redeemer had come. The prison door
was about to be thrown open. The lawful captives were
about to be set free. All this, we need not doubt, Satan
saw, and resolved to fight for his own. The prince
of this world would not give way to the Prince of peace
without a mighty struggle. He had overcome the
first Adam in the garden of Eden ;—why should he not
overcome the second Adam in the wilderness ? He had
spoiled man once of Paradise ;—why should he not spoil
him of the kingdom of God.

Let it never surprise us, if we are tempted by the devil.
Let us rather expect it, as a matter of course, if we are
living members of Christ. The Master's lot will be the

lot of His disciples. That mighty spirit who did not
fear to attack Jesus himself, is still going about as a
roaring lion, seeking whom he may devour. That murderer and liar who vexed Job, and overthrew David and
Peter, still lives, and is not yet bound. If he cannot
rob us of heaven, he will at any rate make our journey
thither painful. If he cannot destroy our souls, he will
at least bruise our heels. (Gen. iii. 15.) Let us beware
of despising him, or thinking lightly of his power. Let us
rather put on the whole armour of God, and cry to the
strong for strength. "Resist the devil and he will flee
from you." (James iv. 7.)

Let us mark secondly, *our Lord Jesus Christ's ability
to sympathize with those that are tempted.* This is a truth
that stands out prominently in this passage. Jesus has
been really and literally tempted Himself.

It was meet that He who came "to destroy the works of
the devil," should begin His own work by a special conflict
with Satan. It was meet that the great Shepherd and
bishop of souls should be fitted for His earthly ministry
by strong temptation, as well as by the word of God and
prayer. But above all, it was meet that the great High
Priest and advocate of sinners should be one who has
had personal experience of conflict, and has known what
it is to be in the fire. And this was the case with Jesus.
It is written that He "suffered being tempted." (Heb.
ii. 18.) How much He suffered, we cannot tell. But
that His pure and spotless nature did suffer intensely,
we may be sure.

Let all true Christians take comfort in the thought
that they have a Friend in heaven, who can be touched

with the feeling of their infirmities. (Heb. iv. 15.) When they pour out their hearts before the throne of grace, and groan under the burden that daily harasses them, there is One making intercession who knows their sorrows. Let us take courage. The Lord Jesus is not an "austere man." He knows what we mean when we complain of temptation, and is both able and willing to give us help.

Let us mark thirdly, *the exceeding subtlety of our great spiritual enemy, the devil.* Three times we see him assaulting our Lord, and trying to draw Him into sin. Each assault shewed the hand of a master in the art of temptation. Each assault was the work of one acquainted by long experience with every weak point in human nature. Each deserves an attentive study.

Satan's first device was to persuade our Lord to distrust His Father's providential care. He comes to Him, when weak and exhausted with forty days hunger, and suggests to Him to work a miracle, in order to gratify a carnal appetite. Why should He wait any longer? Why should the Son of God sit still and starve? Why not "command this stone to become bread?"

Satan's second device was to persuade our Lord to grasp at worldly power by unlawful means. He takes Him to the top of a mountain and shows Him "all the kingdoms of the world in a moment of time." All these he promises to give Him, if He will but "fall down and worship him." The concession was small. The promise was large. Why not by a little momentary act, obtain an enormous gain?

Satan's last device was to persuade our Lord to an act of presumption. He takes Him to a pinnacle of the

temple and suggests to Him to "cast Himself down." By
so doing he would give public proof that He was one sent
by God.   In so doing He might even depend on being
kept from harm.   Was there not a text of Scripture,
which specially applied to the Son of God, in such a
position ?   Was it not written that "angels should bear
Him up?"

On each of these three temptations it would be easy
to write much.   Let it be sufficient to remind ourselves,
that we see in them the three favourite weapons of the
devil.   Unbelief, worldliness, and presumption are three
grand engines which he is ever working against the soul of
man, and by which he is ever enticing him to do what
God forbids, and to run into sin.   Let us remember this,
and be on our guard. The acts that Satan suggests to us to
do, are often in appearance trifling and unimportant.
But the principle involved in each of these little acts, we
may be sure, is nothing short of rebellion against God.
Let us not be ignorant of Satan's devices.

Let us mark lastly, *the manner in which our Lord
resisted Satan's temptations.*   Three times we see Him
foiling and baffling the great enemy who assaulted Him.
He does not yield a hair's breadth to him.   He does not
give him a moment's advantage.   Three times we see
Him using the same weapon, in reply to his temptations ;
—"the sword of the Spirit, which is the word of God."
(Ephes. vi. 17.)   He who was "full of the Holy Ghost,"
was yet not ashamed to make the Holy Scripture His
weapon of defence, and His rule of action.

Let us learn from this single fact, if we learn nothing
else from this wondrous history, the high authority of

the Bible, and the immense value of a knowledge of its contents. Let us read it, search into it, pray over it, diligently, perseveringly, unweariedly. Let us strive to be so thoroughly acquainted with its pages, that its texts may abide in our memories, and stand ready at our right hand in the day of need. Let us be able to appeal from every perversion and false interpretation of its meaning, to those thousand plain passages, which are written as it were with a sunbeam. The Bible is indeed a sword, but we must take heed that we know it well, if we would use it with effect.

NOTES. LUKE IV. 1—13.

1.—[*Led by the Spirit.*] The word translated "led," is the same that we find in Rom. viii. 14, Gal. v. 18, applied to the influence of the Holy Ghost on the hearts of believers. Our Lord, be it noted, did not seek conflict with the devil, but was "led" to it.

[*the wilderness.*] We are not told where this wilderness was. Some have conjectured that it was the wilderness near Sinai, through which Israel journeyed. There seems no foundation for this idea. It is more probable that it was that uninhabited part of Judæa where John the Baptist's ministry began.

2.—[*forty days tempted of the devil.*] This part of our Lord's temptation, we may suppose, was mental and spiritual. The length of time mentioned is the same as that recorded in the history of the fast of Moses and Elijah.

3.—[*The devil said.*] It is plain that Satan now appeared to our Lord in a visible form. In what form we are not told. Some have supposed that he appeared as an angel of light; some that he came as an aged hermit, or as a Scribe or Pharisee. All this is mere conjecture. We need not doubt that he, who appeared to Eve in the form of a serpent, chose that form, which was most likely to serve his purpose, in appearing to our Lord.

The question has often been asked, whether the whole temptation of our Lord was a real thing or only a vision. That it was a real temptation appears clear from every expression in the history of it. Curious speculations have been raised as to the manner in which our Lord was taken to "the top of a mountain," and brought to "the pinnacle of the temple." These are matters which we cannot explain. Let it suffice us to believe that the circumstances related, really, literally, and actually took place.

[*That it may be made bread.*] Let it be noted that the first temptation contained an appeal to a fleshly appetite, like the temptation in Eden. Adam and Eve were tempted to eat unlawfully, and so also was our Lord.

4.—[*It is written.*] This text, we should mark, as well as the two others quoted by our Lord in reply to the devil, were taken from the Pentateuch. All three texts were from one book, Deuteronomy,—and two from one chapter, the sixth.

[*By every word.*] The meaning here is not strictly " by every spoken or written word," but by every thing which God is pleased to create, or command, or appoint, for man's sustenance, just as quails were commanded to come, and manna appointed to fall from heaven, to feed Israel. The Greek word translated " word," is in three places translated " thing." (Luke i. 37 ; ii. 15, 19.)

5.—[*All the kingdoms of the world.*] This expression must probably be taken with large qualification, unless we take " the world " in the limited sense of Palestine and the adjacent countries. From no single mountain could all the kingdoms of the world be literally seen at once. If our Lord did really see them, it must have been by means of a vision made to pass before His eyes. This however seems very improbable.

[*A moment of time.*] Lightfoot quotes a Rabbinical definition of a moment. The Rabbins consider it to be " the 58,888th part of an hour."

6.—[*This power will I give Thee.*] Let it be noted, that as the devil promised liberally to Eve, " Ye shall be as Gods," so he promised liberally to our Lord. But as his promise to Eve was a lie, so his promise to our Lord was a deception. He promised that which he had no power to give. He is undoubtedly called " prince of this world," but he has no power to give dominion over it without God's permission.

7.—[*Worship me.*] The marginal reading seems to give the sense of the word more fully,—" fall down before me," that is, " fall down and worship."

8.—[*Get thee behind me, Satan.*] These are precisely the words, let it be noted, which our Lord addressed to Simon Peter, when Peter would fain have dissuaded Him from the cross. (Matt. xvi. 23.) It may be observed, while remarking on this expression, that the temptation which St. Luke relates second, is related by St. Matthew as occuring last. It seems probable that the order of St. Matthew is that in which the several temptations occurred, and the expression of our Lord to Satan appears strong internal evidence of this.

For what reason St. Luke departs from the order observed by St. Matthew we do not know. Spanheim, in his Dubia Evangelica, discusses the question, but throws little light on it.

9.—[*Pinnacle of the temple.*] This is supposed to have been a turret, or high part of the temple-building, overhanging a deep valley. Josephus describes the place, and says, that "if any looked down, his eyes would grow dizzy, not being able to reach to so vast a depth."

10.—[*It is written.*] Let it be carefully noted, that the devil can quote Scripture, when it suits his purpose. There is no good thing which may not be abused.

[*To keep thee.*] From the earliest ages the comment has been made on these words, that Satan omitted the important expression which follows them, "In all thy ways;" and that the omission was intentional in order to favour his misapplication of the text. Perhaps more has been made of the omission than is quite warrantable. The quotations from the Old Testament in the New, even when made by holy and good men, are not always so full as we should have expected. At any rate, it is a striking fact that our Lord does not notice the misquotation, but simply quotes in reply another text.

Leighton's remarks on this point are worth reading. "Our Saviour teaches us that our better way, either with perverse men, in asserting their errors, or with Satan in his assaulting us with misalleged scripture, is not so much to subtilize about the place or words abused. It may be so cunningly done sometimes, that we cannot well find it out; but this downright sure way beats off the sophistry with another place, clearly and plainly carrying that truth which he opposes and we adhere to. Though thou canst not clear the sense of an obscure text, thou shalt always find a sufficient guard in another that is clearer."

13.—[*He departed from him.*] Two things should always be remembered in reading the history of our Lord's temptation.

For one thing, we have a clear proof of the personality of Satan. If the devil be not a person, judging from the whole history of the passage, there is no meaning in words. He "speaks," he "takes," he "shews," he offers to "give," he "brings," he "sets," he "departs." These expressions can only be used about a person.

For another thing, we see the folly of labouring to make out, as some commentators do, the person who was present at each act in our Lord's history, and supplied the four Gospel writers with the materials which they used in composing their narratives. Who, we may well ask, was present when all this temptation took place? From what source did Matthew and Luke obtain their information?—There is but one answer to these questions. They got it, like everything else which they wrote, from the inspiration of God. The theory that they were dependent on the reports of human witnesses in any part of their writings, is utterly unsatisfactory, and in the history of our Lord's temptation, entirely breaks down.

LUKE IV. 14—22.

14 And Jesus returned in the power of the Spirit into Galilee: and there went out a fame of him through all the region round about.

15 And he taught in their synagogues, being glorified of all.

16 And he came to Nazareth, where he had been brought up: and, as his custom was, he went into the synagogue on the sabbath day, and stood up for to read.

17 And there was delivered unto him the book of the prophet Esaias. And when he had opened the book, he found the place where it was written,

18 The Spirit of the Lord is upon me, because he hath anointed me to preach the Gospel to the poor; he hath sent me to heal the brokenhearted, to preach deliverance to the captives, and recovering of sight to the blind, to set at liberty them that are bruised,

19 To preach the acceptable year of the Lord.

20 And he closed the book, and he gave it again to the minister, and sat down. And the eyes of all them that were in the synagogue were fastened on him.

21 And he began to say unto them, This day is this Scripture fulfilled in your ears.

22 And all bare him witness, and wondered at the gracious words which proceeded out of his mouth. And they said, Is not this Joseph's son?

THESE verses relate events which are only recorded in the Gospel of St. Luke. They describe the first visit which our Lord paid, after entering on His public ministry, to the city of Nazareth, where He had been brought up. Taken together with the two verses which immediately follow, they furnish an awfully striking proof, that "the carnal mind is enmity against God." (Rom. viii. 7.)

We should observe, in these verses, *what marked honour our Lord Jesus Christ gave to public means of grace.* We are told that "He went into the synagogue of Nazareth on the Sabbath day, and stood up to read" the Scriptures. In the days when our Lord was on earth, the Scribes and Pharisees were the chief teachers of the Jews. We can hardly suppose that a Jewish synagogue enjoyed much of the Spirit's presence and blessing under such teaching. Yet even then we find our Lord visiting a synagogue, and reading and preaching in it. It was the place where His Father's day and word were publicly recognized, and, as such, He thought it good to do it honour.

We need not doubt that there is a practical lesson for
us in this part of our Lord's conduct. He would have
us know that we are not lightly to forsake any assembly
of worshippers, which professes to respect the name, the
day, and the book of God. There may be many things
in such an assembly which might be done better. There
may be a want of fulness, clearness, and distinctness in
the doctrine preached. There may be a lack of unction
and devoutness in the manner in which the worship is
conducted. But so long as no positive error is taught,
and there is no choice between worshipping with such an
assembly, and having no public worship at all, it becomes
a Christian to think much before he stays away. If
there be but two or three in the congregation who meet
in the name of Jesus, there is a special blessing promised.
But there is no like blessing promised to him who tarries
at home.

We should observe, for another thing, in these verses,
*what a striking account our Lord gave to the congregation
at Nazareth, of His own office and ministry.* We are
told that He chose a passage from the book of Isaiah, in
which the prophet foretold the nature of the work
Messiah was to do when He came into the world. He
read how it was foretold that He would "preach the
Gospel to the poor,"—how He would be sent to "heal
the broken hearted,"—how He would "preach deliverance to the captives, sight to the blind, and liberty to the
bruised,"—and how He would "proclaim that a year of
jubilee to all the world had come." And when our Lord
had read this prophecy, He told the listening crowd
around Him, that He Himself was the Messiah of whom

these words were written, and that in Him and in His Gospel the marvellous figures of the passage were about to be fulfilled.

We may well believe that there was a deep meaning in our Lord's selection of this special passage of Isaiah. He desired to impress on his Jewish hearers, the true character of the Messiah, whom He knew all Israel were then expecting. He well knew that they were looking for a mere temporal king, who would deliver them from Roman dominion, and make them once more first among the nations. Such expectations, He would have them understand, were premature and wrong. Messiah's kingdom at His first coming was to be a spiritual kingdom over hearts. His victories were not to be over worldly enemies, but over sin. His redemption was not to be from the power of Rome, but from the power of the devil and the world. It was in this way, and in no other way at present, that they must expect to see the words of Isaiah fulfilled.

Let us take care that we know for ourselves in what light we ought chiefly to regard Christ. It is right and good to reverence Him as very God. It is well to know Him as Head over all things—the mighty Prophet,—the Judge of all,—the King of kings. But we must not rest here, if we hope to be saved. We must know Jesus as the Friend of the poor in spirit, the Physician of the diseased heart, the Deliverer of the soul in bondage. These are the principal offices He came on earth to fulfil. It is in this light we must learn to know Him, and to know Him by inward experience, as well as by the hearing of the ear. Without such knowledge we shall die in our sins.

We should observe, finally, *what an instructive example we have in these verses of the manner in which religious teaching is often heard.* We are told that when our Lord had finished His sermon at Nazareth, His hearers "bare Him witness, and wondered at the gracious words which proceeded out of His mouth." They could not find any flaw in the exposition of Scripture they had heard. They could not deny the beauty of the well-chosen language to which they had listened. "Never man spake like this man." But their hearts were utterly unmoved and unaffected. They were even full of envy and enmity against the Preacher. In short, there seems to have been no effect produced on them, except a little temporary feeling of admiration.

It is vain to conceal from ourselves that there are thousands of persons, in Christian churches, in little better state of mind than our Lord's hearers at Nazareth. There are thousands who listen regularly to the preaching of the Gospel, and admire it while they listen. They do not dispute the truth of what they hear. They even feel a kind of intellectual pleasure in hearing a good and powerful sermon. But their religion never goes beyond this point. Their sermon-hearing does not prevent them living a life of thoughtlessness, worldliness, and sin.

Let us often examine ourselves on this important point. Let us see what practical effect is produced on our hearts and lives by the preaching which we profess to like. Does it lead us to true repentance towards God, and lively faith towards our Lord Jesus Christ? Does it excite us to weekly efforts to cease from sin, and to resist the devil? These are the fruits which sermons ought to produce, if they are really doing us good.   Without such fruit, a mere barren admiration is utterly worthless. It is no proof of grace.   It will save no soul.

NOTES. LUKE IV. 14—22.

14.—[*Fame of him.*]   Here, as in other places, the word "of" is used by our translators in the sense of "about," or "concerning."

16.—[*He came to Nazareth.*]   The date of this visit to Nazareth is not precisely known.   There seems strong internal evidence that it did not take place immediately after the temptation.   If this had been the case, we should not find the expression, "as his custom was," or reference to His works at Capernaum.   The simple explanation appears to be, that St. Luke, having made a general statement of our Lord's practice of teaching "in the synagogues," takes occasion to describe what took place when he taught in the synagogue of Nazareth,—not only as an interesting event in itself, but as an illustration of our Lord's method of proceeding when He visited a synagogue.

17.—[*Opened the book.*]   The word "opened" would be more literally translated "unfolded," or "unrolled."—A book in the times when our Lord was upon earth, was a scroll of parchment rolled up, and in no respect resembled a modern book.

20.—[*Closed the book.*]   The word "closed" here, would be more literally rendered, "folded up," or "rolled up."

[*The Minister.*]   We must not suppose that this word means the preacher, or teacher, of the synagogue.   It means the officer or attendant appointed to take charge of the sacred writings.

21.—[*He began to say.*]   It is evident that the full exposition of the passage in Isaiah, which our Lord gave, has been withheld from us.   The words which are recorded in this verse are probably the beginning of what our Lord said, and form the key-note of His sermon.   The sermon itself is not recorded.

LUKE IV. 22—32.

22 And all bare him witness, and wondered at the gracious words which proceeded out of his mouth.   And they said, Is not this Joseph's son?

23 And he said unto them, Ye will surely say unto me this proverb, Physician, heal thyself : whatsoever we have heard done in Capernaum, do also here in thy country.

24 And he said, Verily I say unto you, No prophet is accepted in his own country.

25 But I tell you of a truth, many widows were in Israel in the days of Elias, when the heaven was shut up three years and six months, when great famine was throughout all the land ;

26 But unto none of them was Elias sent, save unto Sarepta, *a city* of Sidon, unto a woman *that was* a widow.

27 And many lepers were in Israel in the time of Eliseus the prophet; and none of them was cleansed, saving Naaman the Syrian.

28 And all they in the synagogue, when they heard these things, were filled with wrath,

29 And rose up, and thrust him out of the city, and led him unto the brow of the hill whereon their city was built, that they might cast him down headlong.

30 But he passing through the midst of them went his way,

31 And came down to Capernaum, a city of Galilee, and taught them on the sabbath days.

32 And they were astonished at his doctrine: for his word was with power.

THREE great lessons stand out on the face of this passage. Each deserves the close attention of all who desire spiritual wisdom.

We learn for one thing, *how apt men are to despise the highest privileges, when they are familiar with them.* We see it in the conduct of the men of Nazareth when they had heard the Lord Jesus preach. They could find no fault in His sermon. They could point to no inconsistency in His past life and conversation. But because the Preacher had dwelt among them thirty years, and His face, and voice, and appearance were familiar to them, they would not receive His doctrine. They said to one another, " Is not this Joseph's son ? " Is it possible that one so well-known as this man can be the Christ ?—And they drew from our Lord's lips the solemn saying, " No prophet is accepted in his own country."

We shall do well to remember this lesson in the matter of ordinances and means of grace. We are always in danger of undervaluing them, when we have them in abundance. We are apt to think lightly of the privilege of an open Bible, a preached Gospel, and the liberty of meeting together for public worship. We grow up in the midst of these things, and are accustomed to have them without trouble. And the consequence is that we often hold them very cheap, and underrate the extent of our mercies. Let us take heed to our own spirit in the use of sacred things. Often as we may read the Bible, let us never read it without deep reverence. Often as we hear the name of Christ, let us never forget that He is the One Mediator, in whom is life. Even the manna that came down from heaven was at length scorned by Israel, as "light bread." (Num. xxi. 5.) It is an evil day with our souls, when Christ is in the midst of us, and yet, because of our familiarity with His name, is lightly esteemed.

We learn for another thing, *how bitterly human nature dislikes the doctrine of the sovereignty of God.* We see this in the conduct of the men of Nazareth, when our Lord reminded them that God was under no obligation to work miracles among them. Were there not many widows in Israel in the days of Elijah? No doubt there were. Yet to none of them was the prophet sent. All were passed over in favour of a Gentile widow at Sarepta. —Were there not many lepers in Israel in the days of Elisha? No doubt there were. Yet to none of them was the privilege of healing granted. Naaman the Syrian was the only one who was cleansed.—Such doctrine as this was intolerable to the men of Nazareth. It wounded their pride and self-conceit. It taught them that God was no man's debtor, and that if they themselves were passed over in the distribution of His mercies, they had no right to find fault. They could not bear it. They were "filled with wrath." They thrust our Lord out of their city, and had it not been for an exercise of miraculous power on His part, they would doubtless have put Him to a violent death.

Of all the doctrines of the Bible none is so offensive to human nature as the doctrine of God's sovereignty. To be told that God is great, and just, and holy, and pure, man can bear. But to be told that " he hath mercy on whom He will have mercy,"—that He " giveth no account of His matters,"—that it is "not of him that willeth, nor of him that runneth, but of God that showeth mercy,"—these are truths that natural man cannot stand. They often call forth all his enmity against God, and fill him with wrath. Nothing, in short, will make him submit to them but the humbling teaching of the Holy Ghost.

Let us settle it in our minds that, whether we like it or not, the sovereignty of God is a doctrine clearly revealed in the Bible, and a fact clearly to be seen in the world. Upon no other principle can we ever explain why some members of a family are converted, and others live and die in sin,—why some quarters of the earth are enlightened by Christianity, and others remain buried in heathenism. One account only can be given of all this. All is ordered by the sovereign hand of God. Let us pray for humility in respect of this deep thing. Let us remember that our life is but a vapour, and that our best knowledge compared to that of God is perfect folly. Let us be thankful for such light as we enjoy ourselves, and use it diligently while we have it. And let us not doubt that at the last day the whole world shall be convinced, that He who now " gives no account of His matters " has done all things well.

We learn, lastly, from this passage, *how diligently we ought to persevere in well doing, notwithstanding discouragements.* We are doubtless meant to draw this lesson from the conduct of our Lord, after His rejection at Nazareth. Nothing moved by the treatment He received, He patiently works on. Thrust out of one place, He passes on to another. Cast forth from Nazareth He comes to Capernaum, and there " teaches on the sabbath days."

Such ought to be the conduct of all the people of Christ. Whatever the work they are called to do, they should patiently continue in it, and not give up for want of success. Whether preachers, or teachers, or visitors, or missionaries, they must labour on and not faint. There is often more stirring in the hearts and consciences of people than those who teach and preach to them are at all aware of. There is preparatory work to be done in many a part of God's vineyard, which is just as needful as any other work, though not so agreeable to flesh and blood. There must be sowers as well as reapers. There must be some to break up the ground and pick out the stones, as well as some to gather in the harvest. Let each labour on in his own place. The day comes when each shall be rewarded according to his work. The very discouragements we meet with enable us to show the world that there are such things as faith and patience. When men see us working on, in spite of treatment like that which Jesus met at Nazareth, it makes them think. It convinces them that, at all events, we are persuaded that we have truth on our side.

NOTES. LUKE IV. 22—32.

22.—[*Bare him witness.*] The meaning of this appears to be that they could not deny the truth, correctness, and reasonableness of what He said.

[*Joseph's son.*] This expression shows us in what light our

Lord was regarded at Nazareth, and how little the miraculous circumstances of His conception and birth were generally known.

23.—[*This proverb.*] Let it be noted here that our Lord answers one proverb by another. It is a singular peculiarity about proverbs, that they can generally be found in defence of either side of a question. The men of Nazareth were ready to quote a proverb to prove that our Lord should work miracles first at home. Our Lord reminds them that there was another proverb, which taught that teachers were more valued anywhere rather than at home.

25.—[*Days of Elias.*] Let us not fail to note that our Lord speaks of the times of Elijah, and the events which happened in them, as realities. His language is one among many strong arguments to prove that the historical books of the Old Testament are authentic, and not mere collections of instructive fables, as some have dared to assert.

28.—[*Filled with wrath.*] Two reasons may be assigned for the violent anger of the men of Nazareth. One was the doctrine of God's sovereignty in saving sinners. The other was the favour shown to Gentiles instead of Jews, of which our Lord reminded them, with an evident intention of warning them that the same thing would happen again.

30.—[*Passing through the midst of them.*] That this was a miracle is clear. In what way it was effected we are not told. Enough for us to know that His enemies could not lay hands upon Him against His will, and that when finally He was delivered up to be crucified, it was only because He was willing to allow Himself to be slain.

LUKE IV. 33—44.

33 And in the synagogue there was a man, which had a spirit of an unclean devil, and cried out with a loud voice,

34 Saying, Let us alone; what have we to do with thee, *thou* Jesus of Nazareth? art thou come to destroy us? I know thee who thou art; the Holy One of God.

35 And Jesus rebuked him, saying, Hold thy peace, and come out of him. And when the devil had thrown him in the midst, he came out of him, and hurt him not.

36 And they were all amazed, and spake among themselves, saying, What a word *is* this! for with authority and power he commandeth the unclean spirits, and they come out.

37 And the fame of him went out into every place of the country round about.

38 And he arose out of the synagogue, and entered into Simon's house. And Simon's wife's mother was taken with a great fever; and they besought him for her.

39 And he stood over her, and re-

buked the fever; and it left her: and immediately she arose and ministered unto them.

40 Now when the sun was setting, all they that had any sick with divers diseases brought them unto him; and he laid his hands on every one of them, and healed them.

41 And devils also came out of many, crying out, and saying, Thou art Christ the Son of God. And he rebuking *them* suffered them not to speak : for they knew that he was Christ.

42 And when it was day, he departed and went into a desert place : and the people sought him, and came unto him, and stayed him, that he should not depart from them.

43 And he said unto them, I must preach the kingdom of God to other cities also : for therefore am I sent.

44 And he preached in the synagogues of Galilee.

WE should notice, in this passage, *the clear religious knowledge possessed by the devil and his agents.* Twice in these verses we have proof of this. "I know thee who thou art, the holy one of God," was the language of an unclean devil in one case.—"Thou art Christ the son of God," was the language of many devils in another.—Yet this knowledge was a knowledge unaccompanied by faith, or hope, or charity. Those who possessed it were miserable fallen beings, full of bitter hatred both against God and man.

Let us beware of an unsanctified knowledge of Christianity. It is a dangerous possession, but a fearfully common one in these latter days. We may know the Bible intellectually, and have no doubt about the truth of its contents. We may have our memories well stored with its leading texts, and be able to talk glibly about its leading doctrines. And all this time the Bible may have no influence over our hearts, and wills, and consciences. We may, in reality, be nothing better than the devils.

Let it never content us to know religion with our heads only. We may go on all our lives saying, "I know that, and I know that," and sink at last into hell,

with the words upon our lips.   Let us see that our
knowledge bears fruit in our lives.   Does our knowledge
of sin make us hate it?   Does our knowledge of Christ
make us trust and love Him?   Does our knowledge of
God's will make us strive to do it?   Does our knowledge
of the fruits of the Spirit make us labour to show
them in our daily behaviour?   Knowledge of this kind
is really profitable.   Any other religious knowledge will
only add to our condemnation at the last day.

We should notice, secondly, in this passage, *the almighty power of our Lord Jesus Christ*.   We see sicknesses and devils alike yielding to His command.   He
rebukes unclean spirits, and they come forth from the
unhappy people whom they had possessed.   He rebukes
a fever, and lays his hands on sick people, and at once
their diseases depart, and the sick are healed.

We cannot fail to observe many like cases in the four
Gospels.   They occur so frequently that we are apt to
read them with a thoughtless eye, and forget the mighty
lesson which each one is meant to convey.   They are all
intended to fasten in our minds the great truth that
Christ is the appointed Healer of every evil which sin
has brought into the world.   Christ is the true antidote
and remedy for all the soul-ruining mischief which Satan
has wrought on mankind.   Christ is the universal physician to whom all the children of Adam must repair, if
they would be made whole.   In Him is life, and health,
and liberty.   This is the grand doctrine which every
miracle of mercy in the Gospel is ordained and appointed
to teach.   Each is a plain witness to that mighty fact,
which lies at the very foundation of the Gospel.   The

ability of Christ to supply to the uttermost every want
of human nature, is the very corner-stone of Christianity.
Christ, in one word, is "all." (Coloss. iii. 11.) Let the
study of every miracle help to engrave this truth deeply
on our hearts.

We should notice, thirdly, in these verses, *our Lord's
practice of occasional retirement from public notice into
some solitary place.* We read, that after healing many
that were sick and casting out many devils, "he departed
and went into a desert place." His object in so doing is
shown by comparison with other places in the Gospels.
He went aside from His work for a season, to hold
communion with His Father in heaven, and to pray.
Holy and sinless as His human nature was, it was a
nature kept sinless in the regular use of means of grace,
and not in the neglect of them.

There is an example here which all who desire to
grow in grace and walk closely with God would do well
to follow. We must make time for private meditation,
and for being alone with God. It must not content us
to pray daily and read the Scriptures,—to hear the
Gospel regularly and to receive the Lord's Supper. All
this is well. But something more is needed. We should
set apart special seasons for solitary self-examination and
meditation on the things of God. How often in a year
this practice should be attempted each Christian must
judge for himself. But that the practice is most desirable
seems clear both from Scripture and experience. We
live in hurrying bustling times. The excitement of daily
business and constant engagements keeps many men in a
perpetual whirl, and entails great peril on souls. The

neglect of this habit of withdrawing occasionally from worldly business is the probable cause of many an inconsistency or backsliding which brings scandal on the cause of Christ. The more work we have to do the more we ought to imitate our Master. If He, in the midst of His abundant labours, found time to retire from the world occasionally, how much more may we? If the Master found the practice necessary, it must surely be a thousand times more necessary for His disciples.

We ought to notice, lastly, in these verses, *the declaration of our Lord as to one of the objects of His coming into the world.* We read that He said, "I must preach the kingdom of God to other cities also : for therefore was I sent."

An expression like this ought to silence for ever the foolish remarks that are sometimes made against preaching. The mere fact that the eternal Son of God undertook the office of a preacher, should satisfy us that preaching is one of the most valuable means of grace. To speak of preaching, as some do, as a thing of less importance than reading public prayers or administering the sacraments, is, to say the least, to exhibit ignorance of Scripture. It is a striking circumstance in our Lord's history, that although He was almost incessantly preaching, we never read of His baptizing any person. The witness of John is distinct on this point: "Jesus baptized not." (John iv. 2.)

Let us beware of despising preaching. In every age of the Church, it has been Gods's principal instrument for the awakening of sinners and the edifying of saints. The days when there has been little or no preaching have been days when there has been little or no good

done in the Church. Let us hear sermons in a prayerful
and reverent frame of mind, and remember that they are
the principal engines which Christ Himself employed,
when He was upon earth. Not least, let us pray daily for
a continual supply of faithful preachers of God's word.
According to the state of the pulpit will always be the
state of a congregation and of a Church.

NOTES. LUKE IV. 33—44.

33.—[*An unclean devil.*] This expression is one which occurs
frequently in the Gospels. It is probably intended to teach the
awful truth that works of uncleanness, in breach of the seventh
commandment, are works which Satan especially labours to
promote. It may also teach us that those who were given over
to satanic possession, were often people who had been specially
addicted to sins of uncleanness and impurity.

34.—[*What have we to do with thee ?*] The words so translated are
the same expression that we find used by our Lord to His
mother at the marriage of Cana in Galilee. (John ii. 4.) It
seems impossible to avoid the conclusion that they imply something of rebuke.

35.—[*Hold thy peace.*] The literal meaning of the word so translated is, " Be muzzled." (1 Cor. ix. 9 ; 1 Tim v. 18.) It is the
same expression that our Lord addresses to the stormy sea,
(Mark iv. 39,) where it is rendered "Be still."

[*Thrown him into the midst.*] This is one of those expressions
in the Gospels, which show clearly that satanic possession was
a distinct thing from lunacy, epilepsy, or any other common form
of mental or physical disease

36.—[*All amazed.*] The word would be translated more literally,
"amazement was upon all." The expression is one peculiar to
St. Luke, (Luke v. 9 ; Acts iii .10,) and specially describes that
state of mind which is produced in people by the sight of something supernatural or divine.

[*What a word is this.*] Scholefield says that this would be
better translated, "What is this word ?"

37.—[*The fame.*] The word so rendered is translated in the only
other place where it is used, " the sound." " A sound from
heaven," Acts ii. 2, and the "sound of a tempest," Heb. xii. 19.

38.—[*Simon's wife's mother.*] Let it be carefully noted here that
the Apostle Simon Peter was a married man. The Romish
doctrine of the celibacy of the clergy finds no countenance in
the Bible.

39.—[*Stood over.*] The word so rendered is more commonly translated, "coming in," "coming upon," and "standing by." Luke
ii. 9, 38, and Acts xxii. 20, and xxiii. 11. The present is the
only place where it is translated, "standing over."

39.—[*Immediately she arose and ministered.*] The completeness of
our Lord's cures is shown in this expression. It is notorious
that fevers leave people too weak for any exertion, even when
they begin to recover and are out of danger.

LUKE V. 1—11.

1 And it came to pass, that, as the people pressed upon him to hear the word of God, he stood by the lake of Gennesaret,

2 And saw two ships standing by the lake: but the fishermen were gone out of them, and were washing *their* nets.

3 And he entered into one of the ships, which was Simon's, and prayed him that he would thrust out a little from the land. And he sat down, and taught the people out of the ship.

4 Now when he had left speaking, he said unto Simon, Launch out into the deep, and let down your nets for a draught.

5 And Simon answering said unto him, Master, we have toiled all the night, and have taken nothing: nevertheless at thy word I will let down the net.

6 And when they had this done, they inclosed a great multitude of fishes: and their net brake.

7 And they beckoned unto *their* partners, which were in the other ship, that they should come and help them. And they came, and filled both the ships, so that they began to sink.

8 When Simon Peter saw *it*, he fell down at Jesus' knees, saying, Depart from me; for I am a sinful man, O Lord.

9 For he was astonished, and all that were with him, at the draught of the fishes which they had taken:

10 And so *was* also James, and John, the sons of Zebedee, which were partners with Simon. And Jesus said unto Simon, Fear not; from henceforth thou shalt catch men.

11 And when they had brought their ships to land, they forsook all, and followed him.

WE have, in these verses, the history of what is commonly called the miraculous draught of fishes. It is a remarkable miracle on two accounts.—For one thing, it shows us our Lord's complete dominion over the animal creation. The fish of the sea are as much obedient to His will, as the frogs, and flies, and lice, and locusts, in the plagues of Egypt. All are His servants, and all obey His commands.—For another thing, there is a singular similarity between this miracle,

worked at the beginning of our Lord's ministry, and
another which we find Him working after His resurrection, at the end of His ministry, recorded by St. John.
(John xxi. 1., &c.) In both we read of a miraculous
draught of fishes. In both the Apostle Peter has a prominent place in the story. And in both there is, probably,
a deep spiritual lesson, lying below the outward surface
of the facts described.

We should observe, in this passage, *our Lord Jesus
Christ's unwearied readiness for every good work*. Once
more we find Him preaching to a people who "pressed
upon him to hear the word of God." And where does
He preach? Not in any consecrated building, or place
set apart for public worship, but in the open air;—not
in a pulpit constructed for a preacher's use, but in a
fisherman's boat. Souls were waiting to be fed. Personal inconvenience was allowed no place in His consideration. God's work must not stand still.

The servants of Christ should learn a lesson from their
Master's conduct on this occasion. We are not to wait
till every little difficulty or obstacle is removed, before we
put our hand to the plough, or go forth to sow the seed
of the word. Convenient buildings may often be wanting for assembling a company of hearers. Convenient
rooms may often not be found for gathering children to
school. What, then, are we to do? Shall we sit still
and do nothing? God forbid! If we cannot do all we
want, let us do what we can. Let us work with such
tools as we have. While we are lingering and delaying
souls are perishing. It is the slothful heart that is
always looking at the hedge of thorns and the lion in

the way. (Prov. xv. 19 ; xxii. 13.) Where we are and as we are, in season or out of season, by one means or by another, by tongue or by pen, by speaking or by writing, let us strive to be ever working for God. But let us never stand still.

We should observe, secondly, in this passage, *what encouragement our Lord gives to unquestioning obedience.* We are told, that after preaching He bade Simon "launch out into the deep and let down his net for a draught." He receives an answer which exhibits in a striking manner the mind of a good servant. "Master," says Simon, "we have toiled all the night and have taken nothing : nevertheless, at thy word I will let down the net." And what was the reward of this ready compliance with the Lord's commands? At once, we are told, "they enclosed a great multitude of fishes : and their net brake."

We need not doubt that a practical lesson for all Christians is contained under these simple circumstances. We are meant to learn the blessing of ready unhesitating obedience to every plain command of Christ. The path of duty may sometimes be hard and disagreeable. The wisdom of the course we propose to follow may not be apparent to the world. But none of these things must move us. We are not to confer with flesh and blood. We are to go straight forward when Jesus says, " go ; " and do a thing boldly, unflinchingly, and decidedly, when Jesus says, " do it." We are to walk by faith and not by sight, and believe that what we see not now to be right and reasonable, we shall see hereafter. So acting, we shall never find in the long run that we are losers.

So acting, we shall find, sooner or later, that we reap a great reward.

We should observe, thirdly, in this passage, *how much a sense of God's presence abases man and makes him feel his sinfulness.* We see this strikingly illustrated by Peter's words, when the miraculous draught convinced him that One greater than man was in his boat. We read that "he fell down at Jesus' knees, saying, depart from me; for I am a sinful man, O Lord."

In measuring these words of Peter, we must of course remember the time at which they were spoken. He was, at best, but a babe in grace, weak in faith, weak in experience, and weak in knowledge. At a later period in his life he would, doubtless, have said, "Abide with me," and not, "depart." But still, after every deduction of this kind, the words of Peter exactly express the first feelings of man when he is brought into anything like close contact with God. The sight of divine greatness and holiness makes him feel strongly his own littleness and sinfulness. Like Adam after the fall, his first thought is to hide himself. Like Israel under Sinai, the language of his heart is, "let not God speak with us, lest we die." (Exod. xx. 19.)

Let us strive to know more and more, every year we live, our need of a mediator between ourselves and God. Let us seek more and more to realize that without a mediator our thoughts of God can never be comfortable, and the more clearly we see God the more uncomfortable we must feel. Above all, let us be thankful that we have in Jesus the very Mediator whose help our souls require, and that through Him we may draw near to God with boldness, and cast fear away. Out of Christ God is a consuming fire. In Christ He is a reconciled Father. Without Christ the strictest moralist may well tremble, as he looks forward to his end. Through Christ the chief of sinners may approach God with confidence, and feel perfect peace.

We should observe, lastly, in this passage, *the mighty promise which Jesus holds out to Peter :* "Fear not," He says, "from henceforth thou shalt catch men."

That promise, we may well believe, was not intended for Peter only but for all the Apostles,—and not for all the Apostles only, but for all faithful ministers of the Gospel who walk in the Apostles' steps. It was spoken for their encouragement and consolation. It was intended to support them under that sense of weakness and unprofitableness by which they are sometimes almost overwhelmed. They certainly have a treasure in earthen vessels. (2 Cor. iv. 7.) They are men of like passions with others. They find their own hearts weak and frail, like the hearts of any of their hearers. They are often tempted to give up in despair, and to leave off preaching. But here stands a promise, on which the great Head of the Church would have them daily lean : "Fear not, thou shalt catch men."

Let us pray daily for all ministers that they may be true successors of Peter and his brethren, that they may preach the same full and free Gospel which they preached, and live the same holy lives which they lived. These are the only ministers who will ever prove successful fishermen. To some of them God may give more honour, and to others less. But all true and faithful preachers of the Gospel have a right to believe that their labour shall not prove in vain. They may often preach the Word with many tears, and see no result of their labour. But God's word shall not return void. (Isai. lv. 11.) The last day shall show that no work for God was ever thrown away. Every faithful fisherman shall find his Master's words made good : "Thou shalt catch men."

NOTES. LUKE V. 1—11.

4.—[*Launch out into the deep.*] Let us note that this command must have been peculiarly trying to a fisherman's faith. The deep waters are not generally the waters in which fish are taken in lakes.

6.—[*Their net brake.*] The word rendered "brake" would have been better translated, "began to break," just as a similar word in the next verse is translated, "began to sink." That the net did not actually break, is clear from the context. It "was breaking," or "on the point of breaking."

10.—[*Thou shalt catch men.*] It has been often remarked, and with much justice, that the Greek word translated "catch," means literally "take alive." It is only used here and in one other place, 2 Tim. ii. 26, a passage which is often much misinterpreted, but rightly understood is a remarkable parallel to our Lord's words in this place.

Let us not forget, in reading this miracle, that holy and good men in every age have seen in it a remarkable type and emblem of the history of Christ's Church in the world. They have regarded the ships as emblems of the Churches,—the fishers of Ministers,—the net of the Gospel,—the sea of the world,—the shore of eternity,—and the miraculous draught of the success attending work done in strict compliance with Christ's word. There may be truth in all this. But it needs to be cautiously and delicately used. The habit of allegorizing and seeing hidden meanings in plain language of Scripture has often done great harm.

LUKE V. 12—16.

12 And it came to pass, when he was in a certain city, behold a man full of leprosy : who seeing Jesus fell on *his* face, and besought him, saying, Lord, if thou wilt, thou canst make me clean.

13 And he put forth *his* hand, and touched him, saying, I will : be thou

clean. And immediately the leprosy departed from him.

14 And he charged him to tell no man: but go, and shew thyself to the Priest, and offer for thy cleansing, according as Moses commanded, for a testimony unto them.

15 But so much the more went there a fame abroad of him : and great multitudes came together to hear, and to be healed by him of their infirmities.

16 And he withdrew himself into the wilderness, and prayed.

WE see in this passage, *our Lord Jesus Christ's power over incurable diseases.* "A man full of leprosy," applies to Him for relief, and is at once healed. This was a mighty miracle. Of all ills which can afflict the body of man, leprosy appears to be the most severe. It affects every part of the constitution at once. It brings sores and decay upon the skin, corruption into the blood, and rottenness into the bones. It is a living death, which no medicine can check or stay. Yet here we read of a leper being made well in a moment. It is but one touch from the hand of the Son of God, and the cure is effected. One single touch of that almighty hand ! "And immediately the leprosy departed from him."

We have in this wonderful history a lively emblem of Christ's power to heal our souls. What are we all but lepers spiritually in the sight of God ? Sin is the deadly sickness by which we are all affected. It has eaten into our constitution. It has infected all our faculties. Heart, conscience, mind, and will, all are diseased by sin. From the sole of our foot to the crown of our head, there is no soundness about us, but wounds, and bruises, and putrifying sores. (Isaiah i. 6.) Such is the state in which we are born. Such is the state in which we naturally live. We are in one sense dead long before we are laid in the grave. Our bodies may be healthy and active, but our souls are by nature dead in trespasses and sins.

Who shall deliver us from this body of death? Let us thank God that Jesus Christ can. He is that divine Physician, who can make old things pass away and all things become new. In Him is life. He can wash us thoroughly from all the defilement of sin in His own blood. He can quicken us, and revive us by His own Spirit. He can cleanse our hearts, open the eyes of our understandings, renew our wills, and make us whole. Let this sink down deeply into our hearts. There is medicine to heal our sickness. If we are lost it is not because we cannot be saved. However corrupt our hearts, and however wicked our past lives, there is hope for us in the Gospel. There is no case of spiritual leprosy too hard for Christ.

We see secondly, in this passage, *our Lord Jesus Christ's willingness to help those that are in need.* The petition of the afflicted leper was a very touching one. "Lord," he said, "if thou wilt, thou canst make me clean." The answer he received was singularly merciful and gracious. At once our Lord replies, "I will: be thou clean."

Those two little words, "I will," deserve special notice. They are a deep mine, rich in comfort and encouragement to all labouring and heavy laden souls. They show us the mind of Christ towards sinners. They exhibit His infinite willingness to do good to the sons of men, and His readiness to show compassion. Let us always remember, that if men are not saved, it is not because Jesus is not willing to save them. He is not willing that any should perish, but that all should come to repentance.—He would have all men to be saved and come to the knowledge of the truth.—He has no pleasure

in the death of him that dieth.—He would have gathered
Jerusalem's children, as a hen gathereth her chickens, if
they would only have been gathered. He would, but
they would not.—The blame of the sinner's ruin must be
borne by himself. It is his own will, and not Christ's
will, if he is lost for ever. It is a solemn saying of our
Lord's, "Ye will not come unto me that ye might have
life." (2 Pet. iii. 9. 1 Tim. ii. 5. Ezek. xviii. 32.
Matt. xxiii. 37. John v. 40.)

We see, thirdly, in this passage, *what respect our Lord
Jesus Christ paid to the ceremonial law of Moses.* He
bids the leper "go and show himself to the priest,"
according to the requirement in Leviticus, that he may
be regularly pronounced clean. He bids him offer an
offering on the occasion of his doing so, "according as
Moses commanded." Our Lord knew well that the
ceremonies of the Mosaic law were only shadows and
figures of good things to come, and had in themselves no
inherent power. He knew well that the last days of the
Levitical institutions were close at hand, and that they
were soon to be laid aside for ever. But so long as they
were not abrogated He would have them respected.
They were ordained by God Himself. They were pictures and lively emblems of the Gospel. They were not
therefore to be lightly esteemed.

There is a lesson here for Christians, which we shall
do well to remember. Let us take heed that we do not
despise the ceremonial law, because its work is done.
Let us beware of neglecting those parts of the Bible,
which contain it, under the idea that the believer in the
Gospel has nothing to do with them. It is true that the

darkness is past, and the true light now shineth. (1 John ii.
8.) We have nothing to do now with altars, sacrifices, or
priests. Those who wish to revive them are like men who
light a candle at noon day. But true as this is, we must
never forget that the ceremonial law is still full of instruction. It contains that same Gospel in the bud, which we
now see in full flower. Rightly understood we shall always
find it throwing strong light on the Gospel of Christ.
The Bible reader who neglects to study it, will always
find at last that by the neglect his soul has suffered
damage.

We see, lastly, in this passage, *our Lord Jesus Christ's
diligence about private prayer*. Although " great multitudes came together to hear, and to be healed by him of
their infirmities," He still made time for secret devotion.
Holy and undefiled as He was, He would not allow the
demands of public business to prevent regular private
intercourse with God. We are told that "He withdrew
himself into the wilderness and prayed."

There is an example set before us here, which is much
overlooked in these latter days. There are few professing
Christians, it may be feared, who strive to imitate Christ
in this matter of private devotion. There is abundance
of hearing, and reading, and talking, and profession, and
visiting, and almsgiving, and subscribing to societies, and
teaching at schools. But is there, together with all this,
a due proportion of private prayer? Are believing men
and women sufficiently careful to be frequently alone
with God? These are humbling and heart-searching
questions. But we shall find it useful to give them an
answer.

Why is it that there is so much apparent religious working, and yet so little result in positive conversions to God,—so many sermons, and so few souls saved,—so much machinery, and so little effect produced,—so much running hither and thither, and yet so few brought to Christ? Why is all this? The reply is short and simple. There is not enough private prayer. The cause of Christ does not need less working, but it does need among the workers more praying. Let us each examine ourselves, and amend our ways. The most successful workmen in the Lord's vineyard, are those who are like their Master, often and much upon their knees.

NOTES. LUKE V. 12—16.

12.—[*A man full of leprosy.*] Gill, in his commentary on this passage, gives a long list of the symptoms and indications of leprosy, as laid down by Galen, Aretæus, Pontanus, Ægineta, Cardan, and others. Those who wish to study the subject are recommended to read what he has compiled. It will be found more interesting to medical men than to general readers.

The disease of leprosy is still to be found in some parts of the world, though comparatively unknown in England. There is said to be a small island on the coast of South Africa, near the Cape of Good Hope, which is appropriated by the Colonial Government to lepers. It is mentioned in "M'Cheyne's Memoirs," p. 200.

13.—[*I will.*] It is remarked by Mr. Burgon that this "is the saying of God, and of God only,—the saying of Him, whose almighty will is the cause of all things. When His servants wrought miracles, far different were the phrases they used. Joseph says, 'It is not in me: God shall give Pharaoh an answer of peace.'" Gen. xli. 16.

16.—[*Withdrew himself.*] Gualter remarks on this expression that it should teach ministers of the Gospel to beware of too much familiarity, and too frequent public intercourse with their hearers. He considers that excessive familiarity between ministers and hearers leads to contempt, and that habits of privacy and retirement are on every account essential to a minister's position.

[*and prayed.*] This frequent mention of our Lord's praying is peculiar to St. Luke. Wordsworth remarks, "a similar instance is seen in his narrative of our Lord's baptism, and of the trans-figuration. (Luke iii. 21. and ix. 28, 29.) The Gentiles, for whom St. Luke's Gospel was especially designed, needed instruction in the duty and benefits of prayer. Accordingly this subject occupies a prominent place in his Gospel. It is eminently the Gospel of prayer." See Luke vi. 12. ix. 18, 28. xi. 1. xviii. 1. xxii. 41, 46.

LUKE V. 17.—26.

17 And it came to pass on a certain day, as he was teaching, that there were Pharisees and doctors of the law sitting by, which were come out of every town of Galilee, and Judæa, and Jerusalem : and the power of the Lord was *present* to heal them.

18 And, behold, men brought in a bed a man which was taken with a palsy : and they sought *means* to bring him in, and to lay *him* before him.

19 And when they could not find by what *way* they might bring him in because of the multitude, they went upon the housetop, and let him down through the tiling with *his* couch into the midst before Jesus.

20 And when he saw their faith, he said unto him, Man, thy sins are forgiven thee.

21 And the Scribes and the Pharisees began to reason, saying, Who is this which speaketh blasphemies ? Who can forgive sins, but God alone ?

22 But when Jesus perceived their thoughts, he answering said unto them, What reason ye in your hearts ?

23 Whether is easier, to say, Thy sins be forgiven thee ; or to say, Rise up and walk ?

24 But that ye may know that the Son of man hath power upon earth to forgive sins, (he said unto the sick of the palsy,) I say unto thee, Arise, and take up thy couch, and go unto thine house.

25 And immediately he rose up before them, and took up that whereon he lay, and departed to his own house, glorifying God.

26 And they were all amazed, and they glorified God, and were filled with fear, saying, We have seen strange things to day.

A THREEFOLD miracle demands our attention in these verses. At one and the same time, we see our Lord forgiving sins, reading men's thoughts, and healing a palsy. He that could do such things, and do them with such perfect ease and authority, must indeed be very God. Power like this was never possessed by man.

Let us mark, firstly, in this passage, *what pains men will take about an object when they are in earnest.* The friends of a man, sick with the palsy, desired to bring him to Jesus that he might be cured. At first they were unable to do it, because of the crowd by which our Lord was surrounded. What, then, did they do? "They went upon the house-top, and let him down through the tiling, with his couch, into the midst before Jesus." At once their object was gained. Our Lord's attention was drawn to their sick friend, and he was healed. By pains, and labour, and perseverance, his friends succeeded in obtaining for him the mighty blessing of a complete cure.

The importance of pains and diligence, is a truth that meets our eyes on every side. In every calling, and vocation, and trade, we see that labour is one great secret of success. It is not by luck or accident that men prosper, but by hard working. Fortunes are not made without trouble and attention, by bankers and merchants. Practice is not secured without diligence and study, by lawyers and physicians. The principle is one with which the children of this world are perfectly familiar. It is one of their favourite maxims, that there are "no gains without pains."

Let us thoroughly understand that pains and diligence are just as essential to the well-being and prosperity of our souls as of our bodies. In all our endeavours to draw near to God, in all our approaches to Christ, there ought to be the same determined earnestness which was shewn by this sick man's friends. We must allow no difficulties to check us, and no obstacle to keep us back from anything which is really for our spiritual good. Specially must we bear this in mind in the matter of regularly reading the Bible, hearing the Gospel, keeping the Sabbath holy, and private prayer. On all these points we must beware of laziness and an excuse-making spirit. Necessity must

be the mother of invention. If we cannot find means of
keeping up these habits in one way, we must in another.
But we must settle it in our minds, that *the thing shall be
done.* The health of our souls is at stake. Let the crowd
of difficulties be what it may, we must get through it.
If the children of this world take such pains about a
corruptible crown, we ought to take far more pains about
one that is incorruptible.

Why is it that so many people take no pains in religion?
How is it that they can never find time for praying,
Bible reading, and hearing the Gospel? What is the
secret of their continual string of excuses for neglecting
means of grace? How is it that the very same men who
are full of zeal about money, business, pleasure, or
politics, will take no trouble about their souls?—The
answer to these questions is short and simple. These
men are not in earnest about salvation. They have no
sense of spiritual disease. They have no consciousness of
requiring a Spiritual Physician. They do not feel that
their souls are in danger of dying eternally. They see
no use in taking trouble about religion. In darkness
like this thousands live and die. Happy indeed are
they who have found out their peril, and count all things
loss if they may only win Christ, and be found in Him!

Let us mark, secondly, *the kindness and compassion of
our Lord Jesus Christ.* Twice in this passage we see
Him speaking most graciously to the poor sufferer who
was brought before Him. At first He addresses to him
those marvellous and heart-cheering words, " Man, thy
sins are forgiven thee." Afterwards he adds words,
which in point of comfort, must have been second only to

the blessing of forgiveness. "Arise," He says, "and take up thy couch, and go unto thine house." First He assures him that his soul is healed. Then He tells him that his body is cured, and sends him away rejoicing.

Let us never forget this part of our Lord's character. Christ's loving kindness to His people never changes, and never fails. It is a deep well, of which no one ever found the bottom. It began from all eternity, before they were born. It chose, called, and quickened them when they were dead in trespasses and sins. It drew them to God and changed their character, and put a new will in their minds, and a new song in their mouths. It has borne with them in all their waywardness and shortcomings. It will never allow them to be separated from God. It will flow ever forward, like a mighty river, through the endless ages of eternity. Christ's love and mercy must be a sinner's plea when he first begins his journey. Christ's love and mercy will be his only plea when he crosses the dark river and enters home. Let us seek to know this love by inward experience, and prize it more. Let it constrain us more continually to live, not to ourselves, but to Him who died for us and rose again.

Let us mark, lastly, *our Lord Jesus Christ's perfect knowledge of the thoughts of men.* We read that when the Scribes and Pharisees began to reason secretly among themselves, and privately charge our Lord with blasphemy, He knew what they were about and put them to an open shame. It is written, that "He perceived their thoughts."

It should be a daily and habitual reflection with us that we can keep nothing secret from Christ. To Him apply the words of St. Paul, "all things are naked and

opened to the eyes of him with whom we have to do."
(Heb. iv. 13.) To Him belong the solemn expressions of
the 139th Psalm,—the Psalm which every Christian
should often study. There is not a word in our mouths,
nor an imagination in our hearts, but Jesus knows it
altogether. (Psalm cxxxix. 4.)

How many searchings of heart this mighty truth
ought to awaken within us! Christ ever sees us! Christ
always knows us! Christ daily reads and observes our acts,
words, and thoughts!—The recollection of this should
alarm the wicked and drive them from their sins. Their
wickedness is not hid, and will one day be fearfully exposed,
except they repent!—It should frighten hypocrites out
of their hypocrisy. They may deceive man, but they
are not deceiving Christ!—It should quicken and comfort
all sincere believers. They should remember that a loving
Master is looking at them, and should do all as in His
sight. Above all, they should feel that, however mocked
and slandered by the world, they are fairly and justly
measured by their Saviour's eye. They can say, "Thou
Lord who knowest all things, knowest that I love Thee."
(John xxi. 17.)

NOTES. LUKE V. 17—26.

17.—[*To heal them.*] We must not suppose that this means "to
heal the Pharisees." Mr. Burgon remarks: "To heal whom? The
Pharisees and doctors of the law? Clearly not. The truth is,
the whole scene rose up before the Evangelist, while he wrote, so
that he used the word 'them,' with reference to the many sick
persons who had been brought to our Saviour on this occasion,
and were waiting for an opportunity of being healed."

19.—[*Let him down through the tiling.*] In order to understand
this we must remember the construction of houses in the countries
where our Lord preached. It was, and is now, a common practice
to construct them with a flat roof, and a small square or court-

yard in the midst of the building. Access was obtained to the roof by a stair-case outside, so that a person might ascend to the roof without entering the house. Around the sides of the court-yard a shelter was provided, extending from the walls of the house towards the middle. Sometimes this shelter was made of canvass or cloth, sometimes of light tiling. The use of this shelter was to enable people to sit in the open air of the court-yard, and at the same time to be protected against the rain or sun.

In the case before us, our Lord appears to have been preaching and teaching in the court-yard of the house, under cover of the tiling projecting from one of the sides. The friends of the paralytic man being unable to make their way into the court-yard, because of the crowd, carried him up the stair-case outside the building, and so reached the flat roof of the house. They then removed that portion of the tiling which was above the place where our Lord was preaching, and let down their friend in his bed by ropes into the court-yard below.

Unless we entirely dismiss from our minds all conceptions of a house drawn from the construction of houses in England, the whole history of the circumstances of the miracle must be unintelligible. Bearing in mind what Eastern houses both were and are, it becomes clear and plain.

26.—[*They were all amazed.*] The word so rendered might be more literally translated, "Amazement took them all." The word used for amazement is the same that is translated in three places as "a trance." (Acts x. 10. xi. 5. and xxii. 17.) Suicer quotes Epiphanius to show that it is the word used concerning "the highest sort of admiration or wonder."

[*Strange things.*] The word so translated is only used in this place in the New Testament. It is literally "paradoxes," things contrary to all common opinion and ordinary experience.

LUKE V. 27—32.

27 And after these things he went forth, and saw a Publican, named Levi, sitting at the receipt of custom: and he said unto him, Follow me.

28 And he left all, rose up, and followed him.

29 And Levi made him a great feast in his own house: and there was a great company of Publicans and of others that sat down with them.

30 But their Scribes and Pharisees murmured against his disciples, saying, Why do ye eat and drink with Publicans and sinners?

31 And Jesus answering said unto them, They that are whole need not a physician; but they that are sick.

32 I came not to call the righteous, but sinners to repentance.

THE verses we have now read, ought to be deeply interesting to every one who knows the value of an

immortal soul, and desires salvation. They describe the
conversion and experience of one of Christ's earliest
disciples. We too are all by nature born in sin, and need
conversion. Let us see what we know of the mighty
change. Let us compare our own experience with that
of the man whose case is here described, and by comparison
learn wisdom.

We are taught, in this passage, *the power of Christ's
calling grace.* We read that our Lord called a publican
named Levi to become one of His disciples. This man
belonged to a class who were a very proverb for wickedness among the Jews. Yet even to him our Lord says,
"Follow me."—We read furthermore, that such mighty
influence on Levi's heart accompanied our Lord's words,
that although "sitting at the receipt of custom," when
called, he at once "left all, rose up, followed" Christ,
and became a disciple.

We must never despair of any one's salvation, so long
as he lives, after reading a case like this. We must
never say of any one that he is too wicked, or too hardened, or too worldly to become a Christian. No sins are
too many, or too bad, to be forgiven. No heart is too hard
or too worldly, to be changed. He who called Levi still
lives, and is the same that He was 1800 years ago.
With Christ nothing is impossible.

How is it with ourselves? This, after all, is the grand
question. Are we waiting, and delaying, and hanging
back, under the idea that the cross is too heavy, and that
we can never serve Christ? Let us cast such thoughts
away at once and for ever. Let us believe that Christ
can enable us by His Spirit to give up all, and come out

from the world. Let us remember that He who called
Levi never changes. Let us take up the cross boldly,
and go forward.

We are taught, secondly, in this passage, *that conversion
is a cause of joy to a true believer.* We read, that when
Levi was converted he "made a great feast in his own
house." A feast is made for laughter and merriment.
(Eccles. x. 19.) Levi regarded the change in himself as an
occasion of rejoicing, and wished others to rejoice with him.

We can easily imagine that Levi's conversion was a
cause of grief to his worldly friends. They saw him
giving up a profitable calling, to follow a new teacher
from Nazareth! They doubtless regarded his conduct
as a grievous piece of folly, and an occasion for sorrow
rather than joy. They only looked at his temporal losses
by becoming a Christian. Of his spiritual gains they
knew nothing. And there are many like them. There
are always thousands of people who, if they hear of a
relation being converted, consider it rather a misfortune.
Instead of rejoicing, they only shake their heads and
mourn.

Let us, however, settle it in our minds that Levi did
right to rejoice, and if we are converted, let us rejoice
likewise. Nothing can happen to a man which ought to
be such an occasion of joy, as his conversion. It is a
far more important event than being married, or coming
of age, or being made a nobleman, or receiving a great
fortune. It is the birth of an immortal soul! It is the
rescue of a sinner from hell! It is a passage from life
to death! It is being made a king and priest for evermore! It is being provided for, both in time and eternity!

It is adoption into the noblest and richest of all families, the family of God! Let us not heed the opinion of the world in this matter. They speak evil of things which they know not. Let us, with Levi, consider every fresh conversion as a cause for great rejoicing. Never ought there to be such joy, gladness, and congratulation, as when our sons, or daughters, or brethren, or sisters, or friends, are born again and brought to Christ. The words of the prodigal's father should be remembered :— "It was meet that we should make merry and be glad : for this thy brother was dead, and is alive again ; and was lost, and is found." (Luke xv. 32.)

We are taught, thirdly, in this passage, *that converted souls desire to promote the conversion of others.* We are told that when Levi was converted, and had made a feast on the occasion, he invited "a great company of publicans" to share it. Most probably these men were his old friends and companions. He knew well what their souls needed, for he had been one of them. He desired to make them acquainted with that Saviour who had been merciful to himself. Having found mercy, he wanted them also to find it. Having been graciously delivered from the bondage of sin, he wished others also to be set free.

This feeling of Levi will always be the feeling of a true Christian. It may be safely asserted that there is no grace in the man who cares nothing about the salvation of his fellow men. The heart which is really taught by the Holy Ghost, will always be full of love, charity, and compassion. The soul which has been truly called of God, will earnestly desire that others may experience the same calling. A converted man will not wish to go to heaven alone.

How is it with ourselves in this matter? Do we know anything of Levi's spirit after his conversion? Do we strive in every way to make our friends and relatives acquainted with Christ? Do we say to others, as Moses to Hobab, "Come with us, and we will do you good?" (Num. x. 29.) Do we say as the Samaritan woman, "Come, see a man that told me all that ever I did?" Do we cry to our brethren as Andrew did to Simeon, "We have found the Christ?"—These are very serious questions. They supply a most searching test of the real condition of our souls. Let us not shrink from applying it. There is not enough of a missionary spirit amongst Christians. It should not satisfy us to be safe ourselves. We ought also to try to do good to others. All cannot go to the heathen, but every believer should strive to be a missionary to his fellow men. Having received mercy, we should not hold our peace.

We are taught, lastly, in this passage, *one of the chief objects of Christ's coming into the world.* We have it in the well-known words, "I came not to call the righteous, but sinners, to repentance."

This is that great lesson of the Gospel which, in one form or another, we find continually taught in the New Testament. It is one which we can never have too strongly impressed upon our minds. Such is our natural ignorance and self-righteousness in religion, that we are constantly losing sight of it. We need to be frequently reminded, that Jesus did not come merely as a teacher, but as the Saviour of that which was utterly lost, and that those only can receive benefit from Him who will confess that they are ruined, bankrupt, hopeless, miserable sinners.

Let us use this mighty truth, if we never used it before. Are we sensible of our own wickedness and sinfulness? Do we feel that we are unworthy of anything but wrath and condemnation? Then let us understand that we are the very persons for whose sake Jesus came into the world. If we feel ourselves righteous, Christ has nothing to say to us. But if we feel ourselves sinners, Christ calls us to repentance. Let not the call be made in vain.

Let us go on using this mighty truth, if we have used it in time past. Do we find our own hearts weak and deceitful? Do we often feel that "when we would do good, evil is present with us?" (Rom. vii. 21.) It may be all true, but it must not prevent our resting on Chrst. He "came into the world to save sinners," and if we feel ourselves such, we have warrant for applying to, and trusting in Him to our life's end. One thing only let us never forget:—Christ came to call us *to repentance*, and not to sanction our continuing in sin.

NOTES. LUKE V. 27—32.

27.—[*A Publican named Levi.*] The person called Levi here, is called Matthew in St. Matthew's Gospel, and Levi in St. Mark's. It is almost universally agreed that it is one and the same person, Matthew the apostle. Like some others in the Bible, he had two names.

It is hardly necessary to observe that a publican means a collector of public taxes.

[*At the receipt of custom.*] The Greek word so translated does not necessarily mean that Levi was in the very act of receiving money. It might be rendered with equal correctness,

"At the place where taxes were received." This seems the more probable meaning.

28.—[*He left all, rose up, &c.*] We must be careful not to suppose that Levi neglected his duty to the government, and inflicted loss on his employers, by this sudden action here recorded, in leaving his post. It is highly probable that, like many tax gatherers and toll collectors, he hired the tolls, at the place where our Lord found him, by the year, and paid in advance. This being the case, if he chose to leave his post, he did so entirely at his own loss, but the government was not defrauded. Watson remarks, "Had Levi been a government servant hired at a salary like our custom-house officers, to collect the duties, he must in justice have remained until a successor was appointed. But having himself purchased the tolls and dues for a given period, he was at liberty to throw up the office of exacting them at pleasure."

29.—[*A great feast.*] The word translated "feast," is only used here and Luke xiv. 13. It means a kind of large reception banquet, such as only wealthy people could give, and at which the guests were numerous. The worldly sacrifice which Levi made in becoming Christ's disciple, was probably greater than that made by any of the apostles.

32.—[*Call...to repentance.*] Let it be carefully noted here, as well as elsewhere, that our Lord's call to sinners is not a bare call to become his disciples, but a call " to repentance."

Stella, the Spanish annotator, remarks on this verse. "You must not understand from this, that Christ found some who were righteous. For the sentence of Paul is true; "all have sinned." Christ calls these Scribes and Pharisees righteous, not because they were really so, but only according to the common estimation and appearance of them."

LUKE V. 33—39.

33 And they said unto him, Why do the disciples of John fast often, and make prayers, and likewise *the disciples* of the Pharisees; but thine eat and drink?

34 And he said unto them, Can ye make the children of the bridechamber fast, while the bridegroom is with them?

35 But the days will come, when the bridegroom shall be taken away from them, and then shall they fast in those days.

36 And he spake also a parable unto them; No man putteth a piece of a new garment upon an old; if otherwise, then both the new maketh a rent, and the piece that was *taken* out of the new agreeth not with the old.

37 And no man putteth new wine into old bottles; else the new wine will burst the bottles, and be spilled, and the bottles shall perish.

38 But new wine must be put into new bottles; and both are preserved.

39 No man also having drunk old *wine* straightway desireth new: for he saith, The old is better.

WE should observe in these verses, that *men may disagree on the lesser points of religion, while they agree on its weightier matters.* We have this brought out in the alleged difference between the disciples of John the Baptist, and the disciples of Christ. The question was put to our Lord, "Why do the disciples of John fast often, and make prayers, and likewise the disciples of the Pharisees, but thine eat and drink?"

We cannot suppose that there was any essential difference between the doctrines held by these two parties of disciples. The teaching of John the Baptist was doubtless clear and explicit upon all the main points necessary to salvation. The man who could say of Jesus, "Behold the Lamb of God, which taketh away the sin of the world," was not likely to teach his followers anything contrary to the Gospel. His teaching of course lacked the fulness and perfection of his divine Master's teaching, but it is absurd to suppose that it contradicted it. Nevertheless there were points of practice on which his disciples differed from those of Christ. Agreeing, as they doubtless did, about the necessity of repentance, and faith, and holiness, they disagreed about such matters as fasting, eating, drinking, and manner of public devotion. One in heart, and hope, and aim, as they were about the weightier matters of inward religion, they were not entirely of one mind about outward matters.

We must make up our minds to see differences of this kind among Christians so long as the world stands. We may regret them much, because of the handle they give to an ignorant and prejudiced world. But they will exist, and are one of the many evidences of our fallen condition. About church government, about the manner of conducting public worship, about fasts and feasts, and saint's days, and ceremonials, Christians have never been entirely of one mind, even from the days of the apostles. On all these points the holiest and ablest servants of God have arrived at different conclusions. Argument, reasoning, persuasion, persecution, have all alike proved unable to produce unity.

Let us, however, bless God that there are many points on which all true servants of God are thoroughly agreed. About sin and salvation, about repentance, and faith, and holiness, there is a mighty unity among all believers, of every name, and nation, and people, and tongue. Let us make much of these points in our own personal religion. These, after all, are the principal things which we shall think of in the hour of death, and the day of judgment. On other matters we must agree to differ. It will signify little at the last day what we thought about fasting, and eating, and drinking, and ceremonies. Did we repent, and bring forth fruits meet for repentance ? Did we behold the Lamb of God by faith, and receive Him as our Saviour ? All, of every church, who are found right on these points, will be saved. All, of every church, who are found wrong on these points, will be lost for evermore.

We should observe, secondly, in these verses, *the name by which our Lord Jesus Christ speaks of Himself.* Twice He calls Himself " the Bridegroom."

The name " bridegroom," like every name applied to our Lord in the Bible, is full of instruction. It is a name peculiarly comforting and encouraging to all true

Christians. It teaches the deep and tender *love* with
which Jesus regards all sinners of mankind, who believe in
Him. Weak, and unworthy, and short-coming as they
are in themselves, He feels towards them a tender affection, even as a husband does towards his wife.—It
teaches the close and intimate *union*, which exists between
Jesus and believers. It is something far nearer than the
union of king and subject, master and servant, teacher
and scholar, shepherd and sheep. It is the closest of all
unions, the union of husband and wife,—the union of
which it is written, "what God hath joined together, let
no man put asunder."—Above all, the name teaches
that entire *participation* of all that Jesus is and has,
which is the privilege of every believer. Just as the
husband gives to his wife his name, makes her partaker
of his property, home, and dignity, and undertakes all
her debts and liabilities, so does Christ deal with all true
Christians. He takes on Himself all their sins. He
declares that they are a part of Himself, and that he who
hurts them hurts Him. He gives them, even in this
world, such good things as pass man's understanding.
And He promises that in the next world they shall sit
with Him on His throne, and go out from His presence
no more.

If we know anything of true and saving religion, let
us often rest our souls on this name and office of Christ.
Let us remember daily, that the weakest of Christ's
people are cared for with a tender care that passeth
knowledge, and that whosoever hurts them is hurting the
apple of Christ's eye. In this world we may be poor
and contemptible, and laughed at because of our reli-

gion. But if we have faith, we are precious in the sight of Christ. The Bridegroom of our soul will one day plead our cause before the whole world.

We should observe, lastly, in these verses, how *gently and tenderly Christ would have His people deal with young and inexperienced Christians.* He teaches us this lesson by two parables, drawn from the affairs of daily life. He shows the folly of sewing "new cloth on an old garment," or of putting "new wine into old bottles." In like manner, He would have us know, there is a want of harmony between a new dispensation and an old one. It is vain to expect those who have been trained and taught under one system, to become immediately used to another system. On the contrary, they must be led on by degrees, and taught as they are able to bear.

The lesson is one which all true Christians would do well to lay to heart, and none perhaps so much as Christian ministers and Christian parents. Forgetfulness of it often does much harm to the cause of truth. The hard judgments and unreasonable expectations of old disciples have often driven back and discouraged young beginners in the school of Christ.

Let us settle it in our minds, that grace must have a beginning in every believer's heart, and that we have no right to say a man has no grace, because it does not come to full ripeness at once. We do not expect a child to do the work of a full-grown man, though he may one day, if he lives long enough. We must not expect a learner of Christianity to show the faith, and love, and knowledge of an old soldier of the cross. He may become by and bye a mighty champion of the truth.

But at first we must give him time.   There is great need
of wisdom in dealing with young people about religion,
and, generally speaking, with all young disciples.   Kindness, and patience, and gentleness, are of the first
importance.   We must not try to pour in the new wine
too quickly, or it will run over.   We must take them by
the hand, and lead them on gently.   We must beware
of frightening, or hurrying them, or pressing them on
too fast.   If they have only got hold of the main principles of the Gospel, let us not set them down as godless,
because of a few lesser matters.   We must bear with
much weakness and infirmity, and not expect to find old
heads on young shoulders, or ripe experience in those
who are only babes.   There was deep wisdom in Jacob's
saying, "If men should over-drive them one day, all the
flock will die." (Gen. xxxiii. 13.)

NOTES. LUKE V. 33—39.

33.—[*Thine eat and drink.*]   We must not suppose from this expression, that the disciples of our Lord were charged with
neglecting to pray.   A careless reader might fancy it was so.
It is evident from the whole tone of our Lord's answer, that this
was not the charge brought against them.   The real charge was,
that our Lord's disciples " did not fast."

34.—[*Bridechamber...bridegroom.*]   There is a peculiar beauty in
our Lord's use of these figures about Himself and His people,
when we remember that John the Baptist himself had used
them when speaking of Him to his own disciples. (John iii. 29.)
If any of John's disciples were among those who questioned
Him on this question, His expression would doubtless remind
them of their master's teaching.

35—[*Then shall they fast.*]   This expression has led many to suppose that from the time when our Lord Jesus Christ left the
world, literal fasting from meats and drinks at certain seasons,
was to be the duty of all Christians.
There seems no ground for this sweeping conclusion.   That
fasting and abstinence were occasionally practised by believers
after our Lord's ascension is clear and plain.   That all who

may find the practice useful and helpful to their souls at the present day are right in fasting, if they do it without ostentation, is also plain. But the utter absence of any direct injunction, or command to keep fasts in the Church of Christ, either in the Acts or Epistles, and specially in the Epistles to Timothy and Titus, makes it clear that the matter is one which should be handled with caution, and on which every one must be "persuaded in his own mind."

The words before us appear to have a deeper meaning than any mere abstinence from food. They seem to foretell that the period of time between our Lord's first and second advent must be a time of mourning and humiliation to all true believers. They describe the state of mind in which all true Christians should live until their Lord returns. It is a time for daily and hourly self-denial, and mortification. The time of fulness and satisfaction cannot be till we see the Bridegroom amongst us again.

36.—[*He spake also a parable.*] The parables of the new piece on the old garment, and the new wine into old bottles, are not without difficulty. It is curious to observe how variously they are interpreted and applied to the subject matter in dispute between our Lord and the Pharisees, by commentators on this passage.

It appears to me that, as in many of our Lord's parables, so in the two before us, we must be careful not to press particular expressions too far, or to seek a spiritual meaning for each individual portion of the whole.

The general truth our Lord desires to enforce on His hearers is the acknowledged incongruity between things old and new, and the unreasonableness of expecting persons accustomed to one system immediately to adopt another as soon as it appears. If we insist on going beyond this point, and must assign a meaning to "the patch," "the rent" and the like, I think we shall only darken counsel, and take nothing by our toil. At any rate all who have attempted it, appear to me to have failed.

39.—[*The old is better.*] It seems very likely that in this concluding verse our Lord specially refers to the disciples of John the Baptist. They had drunk of the "old wine" of John's teaching, and could hardly be expected to become straightway attached to the "new wine" of our Lord's kingdom.

Wordsworth remarks, that the beginning of this sentence is a pure Iambic verse, and may perhaps be a poetical proverb adopted by our Lord, of which St. Luke here gives the Greek form. He reminds us that even when our Lord appeared to Saul, on the way to Damascus, He condescended to use a Gentile proverb. (Acts ix. 5.)

LUKE VI. 1—5.

1 And it came to pass on the second sabbath after the first, that he went through the corn fields ; and his disciples plucked the ears of corn, and did eat, rubbing *them* in *their* hands.

2 And certain of the Pharisees said unto them, Why do ye that which is not lawful to do on the sabbath days ?

3 And Jesus answering them said, Have ye not read so much as this, what David did, when himself was an hungred, and they which were with him ;

4 How he went into the house of God, and did take and eat the shewbread, and gave also to them that were with him ; which it is not lawful to eat but for the Priests alone ?

5 And he said unto them, That the Son of man is Lord also of the sabbath.

WE should notice in this passage, *what excessive importance hypocrites attach to trifles.* We are told that on a certain Sabbath day our Lord was passing "through the cornfields." His disciples, as they followed Him, "plucked the ears of corn, and did eat, rubbing them in their hands." At once the hypocritical Pharisees found fault, and charged them with committing a sin. They said, "Why do ye that which is not lawful to do on the Sabbath days ?" The mere act of plucking the ears of corn of course they did not find fault with. It was an action sanctioned by the Mosaic law. (Deut. xxiii. 25.) The supposed fault with which they charged the disciples, was the breach of the fourth commandment. They had done work on the Sabbath, by taking and eating a handful of food.

This exaggerated zeal of the Pharisees about the Sabbath, we must remember, did not extend to other plain commandments of God. It is evident from many expressions in the Gospels, that these very men, who pretended such strictness on one little point, were more than lax and indifferent about other points of infinitely greater importance. While they stretched the commandment about the Sabbath beyond its true meaning, they openly trampled on

the tenth commandment, and were notorious for covetousness. (Luke xvi. 14.)   But this is precisely the character
of the hypocrite.   To use our Lord's illustration, in
somethings he makes ado about straining out of his cup
a gnat, while in other things he can swallow a camel.
(Matt. xxiii. 24.)

It is a bad symptom of any man's state of soul, when
he begins to put the second things in religion in the first
place, and the first things in the second, or the things
ordained by man above the things ordained by God.
Let us beware of falling into this state of mind.
There is something sadly wrong in our spiritual condition,
when the only thing we look at in others is their outward Christianity, and the principal question we ask is,
whether they worship in our communion, and use our
ceremonial, and serve God in our way.—Do they repent
of sin? Do they believe on Christ? Are they living
holy lives ? These are the chief points to which our
attention ought to be directed. The moment we begin
to place anything in religion before these things, we are
in danger of becoming as thorough Pharisees as the
accusers of the disciples.

We should notice, secondly, in this passage, *how
graciously our Lord Jesus Christ pleaded the cause of His
disciples, and defended them against their accusers.* We
are told that He answered the cavils of the Pharisees
with arguments by which they were silenced, if not convinced. He did not leave His disciples to fight their
battle alone. He came to their rescue, and spoke for them.

We have in this fact a cheering illustration of the
work that Jesus is ever doing on behalf of His people.

There is one, we read in the Bible, who is called " the accuser of the brethren, who accuses them day and night," even Satan, the prince of this world. (Rev. xii. 10.) How many grounds of accusation we give him, by reason of our infirmity! How many charges he may justly lay against us before God! But let us thank God that believers "have an Advocate with the Father, Jesus Christ the righteous," who is ever maintaining the cause of His people in heaven, and continually making intercession for them. Let us take comfort in this cheering thought. Let us daily rest our souls on the recollection of our great Friend in heaven. Let our morning and evening prayer continually be, "Answer for me, answer for me, O Lord my God."

We should notice lastly, in these verses, *the clear light which our Lord Jesus Christ throws on the real requirements of the fourth commandment.* He tells the hypocritical Pharisees, who pretended to such strictness in their observance of the Sabbath, that the Sabbath was never intended to prevent works of necessity. He reminds them how David himself, when suffering from hunger, took and ate that shew bread, which ought only to be eaten by the priests, and how the act was evidently allowed of God, because it was an act of necessity. And He argues from David's case, that He who permitted His own temple rules to be infringed, in cases of necessity, would doubtless allow work to be done on His own Sabbath days, when it was work for which there was really a need.

We should weigh carefully the nature of our Lord Jesus Christ's teaching about the observance of the

Sabbath, both here and in other places. We must not allow ourselves to be carried away by the common notion that the Sabbath is a mere Jewish ordinance, and that it was abolished and done away by Christ. There is not a single passage of the Gospels which proves this. In every case where we find our Lord speaking upon it, He speaks against the false views of it, which were taught by the Pharisees, but not against the day itself. He cleanses and purifies the fourth commandment from the man-made additions by which the Jews had defiled it, but never declares that it was not to bind Christians. He shews that the seventh day's rest was not meant to prevent works of necessity and mercy, but He says nothing to imply that it was to pass away, as a part of the ceremonial law.

We live in days when anything like strict Sabbath observance is loudly denounced, in some quarters, as a remnant of Jewish superstition. We are boldly told by some persons, that to keep the Sabbath holy is legal, and that to enforce the fourth commandment on Christians, is going back to bondage. Let it suffice us to remember, when we hear such things, that assertions are not proofs, and that vague talk like this has no confirmation in the word of God. Let us settle it in our minds, that the fourth commandment has never been repealed by Christ, and that we have no more right to break the Sabbath day, under the Gospel, than we have to murder and to steal. The architect who repairs a building, and restores it to its proper use, is not the destroyer of it, but the preserver. The Saviour who redeemed the Sabbath from Jewish traditions, and so frequently explained its true meaning, ought never to be regarded as the enemy of the fourth commandment. On the contrary, He has "magnified it, and made it honourable."

Let us cling to our Sabbath, as the best safeguard of our Country's religion. Let us defend it against the assaults of ignorant and mistaken men, who would fain turn the day of God into a day of business and pleasure. Above all, let us each strive to keep the day holy ourselves. Much of our spiritual prosperity depends, under God, on the manner in which we employ our Sundays.

NOTES. LUKE VI. 1—5.

1.—[*Second Sabbath after the first.*] The meaning of this expression has entirely puzzled all commentators. It is nowhere used in Scripture, excepting in this place. All explanations of it are nothing better than conjectures. Cornelius à Lapide gives a summary of these conjectures, which, if it proves nothing else, is a clear proof that there is no such thing as "unanimous consent of the Fathers" in the interpretation of Scripture. He mentions, among other things, that Jerome once asked Gregory Nazianzen what this Sabbath was, and received for answer, that he would teach him in church when it would be impossible to contradict him.

Some think that this second-first Sabbath (for so the Greek expression would be translated more correctly) was the Pentecost Sabbath. They suppose that the Jews had three principal Sabbath days in the year,—the first at the Feast of the Passover, the second at the Feast of Pentecost, and the third at the Feast of Tabernacles. And they consider that the Sabbath here mentioned is the "second great Sabbath," or Pentecost Sabbath.

Some think that this second-first Sabbath, was the first Sabbath after the second day of unleavened bread in the Jewish Passover week. This second day in the passover week was the day when the first ripe sheaf of barley was waved by the priest before the Lord, to consecrate the harvest. (Levit. xxiii. 10—12.) The Sabbath here spoken of would then be the first Sabbath after the first sheaf of harvest had been cut.

I offer no opinion on the difficulty. It is probably one that will never be settled till the Lord comes. If the ears of corn which the disciples plucked were wheat, the first explanation seems most probable. If, on the other hand, they were barley, the second seems most likely to be correct. The question, happily, is one which affects no point of doctrine, and may safely be left alone.

3.—[*What David did.*] Here, as in other places, let us not fail to observe how our Lord refers to things recorded in Old Testament Scriptures, as well-attested and acknowledged historical facts. The infidel notion, that the Old Testament narratives are nothing better than amusing fables, and fictions invented to convey useful lessons, is a notion that finds no foot-hold, or countenance in the New Testament. He that strikes at the authority of the Old Testament, will find at last, whether he means it or not, that he is striking also at the authority of the New.

[*When himself was an hungered.*] This is an expression which should be carefully noted in considering passages like that now before us, in which our Lord teaches the true spirit of Sabbath observance. The case of positive necessity, it should be observed, is carefully shown. It was a case of "hunger." This, and this only, justified the departure from a divine law. In this spirit we ought to consider the often mooted question, what may and what may not be done on the Christian Sunday. When Sunday is deliberately made a day for doing secular things which need not necessarily be done on Sunday, and might easily have been done before Sunday, there is an open breach of the fourth commandment. Neither here, nor elsewhere, does our Lord Jesus Christ sanction such use of the Sunday. The works that He sanctions, are works of necessity and mercy, not of money-making, business, pleasure-seeking, and amusement.

5.—[*The Son of man...Lord of the sabbath.*] The meaning of this expression has been already fully considered in my note on St. Mark. At present it may suffice to say, that I consider "the Son of man" to mean what the expression always means in the New Testament, the Lord Jesus Christ Himself.—The words, "Lord of the Sabbath," were not meant to imply that our Lord, by virtue of His divine authority, would alter, abrogate, or let down the law of the fourth commandment. They mean that Jesus is "Lord of the Sabbath," to deliver it from Jewish traditions, to protect it from superstitious views of its observance, and to show the true spirit and manner in which it was always intended to be kept.

LUKE VI. 6—11.

6 And it came to pass also on another sabbath, that he entered into the synagogue and taught: and there was a man whose right hand was withered.

7 And the Scribes and Pharisees watched him, whether he would heal on the sabbath day; that they might find an accusation against him.

8 But he knew their thoughts, and

said to the man which had the withered hand, Rise up, and stand forth in the midst. And he arose and stood forth.

9 Then said Jesus unto them, I will ask you one thing; Is it lawful on the sabbath days to do good, or to do evil? to save life, or to destroy it?

10 And looking round about upon them all, he said unto the man, Stretch forth thy hand. And he did so: and his hand was restored whole as the other.

11 And they were filled with madness; and communed one with another what they might do to Jesus.

THESE verses contain another example of our Lord Jesus Christ's mode of dealing with the Sabbath question. Once more we find Him coming into collision with the vain traditions of the Pharisees, about the observance of the fourth commandment. Once more we find Him clearing the day of God from the rubbish of human traditions, and placing its requirements on the right foundation.

We are taught in these verses, *the lawfulness of doing works of mercy on the Sabbath day*. We read that before all the Scribes and Pharisees our Lord healed a man with a withered hand on the Sabbath. He knew that these enemies of all righteousness were watching to see whether He would do it, in order that they might "find an accusation against him." He boldly asserts the right of doing such works of mercy, even on the day when it is said, "thou shalt do no manner of work." He openly challenges them to show that such a work was contrary to the law. "I will ask you one thing," He says, "Is it lawful on the Sabbath days to do good, or to do evil?— to save life or to destroy?" To this question His enemies were unable to find an answer.

The principle here laid down, is one of wide application. The fourth commandment was never meant to be so interpreted, as to inflict injury on man's body. It was intended to admit of adaptation to that state of things which sin has brought into the world. It was not meant to forbid showing kindness on the Sabbath to the afflicted, or attending to the wants of the sick. We may drive in a carriage to minister comfort to the dying. We may stay away from public worship, in order to fetch a doctor, or be useful in a sick room. We may visit the fatherless and widow in trouble. We may preach, and teach, and instruct the ignorant. These are works of mercy. We may do them, and yet keep the Sabbath holy. They are not breaches of God's law.

One thing, however, we must carefully remember. We must take heed that we do not abuse the liberty which Christ has given us. It is in this direction that our danger chiefly lies in modern times. There is little risk of our committing the error of the Pharisees, and keeping the Sabbath more strictly than God intended. The thing to be feared is the general disposition to neglect the Sabbath, and to rob it of that honour which it ought to receive. Let us take heed to ourselves in this matter. Let us beware of making God's day a day for visiting, feasting, journeying, and pleasure parties. These are not works of necessity or mercy, whatever a self-willed and unbelieving world may say. The person who spends his Sundays in such ways as these, is sinning a great sin, and proving himself entirely unprepared for the great rest in heaven.

We are taught, secondly, in these verses, *the perfect knowledge that our Lord Jesus Christ possesses of men's thoughts.* We see this in the language used about Him, when the Scribes and Pharisees were watching Him. We read that "He knew their thoughts."

Expressions like this are among the many evidences

of our Lord's divinity. It belongs to God only to read hearts. He who could discern the secret intents and imaginations of others, must have been more than man. No doubt He was man like ourselves in all things, sin only excepted. This we may freely grant to the Socinian, who denies the divinity of Christ. The texts the Socinian quotes, in proof of our Lord's manhood, are texts which we believe and hold as fully as himself. But there are other plain texts in Scripture which prove that our Lord was God as well as man. Of such texts the passage before us is one. It shows that Jesus was "God over all blessed for ever." (Rom. ix. 5.)

Let the remembrance of our Lord's perfect knowledge always exercise a humbling influence upon our souls. How many vain thoughts, and worldly imaginations, pass through our minds every hour, which man's eye never sees! What are our own thoughts at this moment? What have they been this very day, while we have been reading, or listening to this passage of Scripture? Would they bear public examination? Should we like others to know all that passes in our inner man? These are serious questions, and deserve serious answers. Whatever we may think of them, it is a certain fact that Jesus Christ is hourly reading our hearts. Truly we ought to humble ourselves before Him, and cry daily, "Who can tell how oft he offendeth?"—"Cleanse thou me from secret faults."—"God be merciful to me a sinner!"

We are taught, lastly, in these verses, *the nature of the first act of faith, when a soul is converted to God.* The lesson is conveyed to us in a striking manner, by the history of the cure which is here described. We read that our Lord said to the man whose hand was witherd, "Stretch forth thy hand." The command, at first sight, seems unreasonable, because the man's obedience was apparently impossible. But the poor sufferer was not stopped by any doubts or reasonings of this kind. At once we read that he made the attempt to stretch forth his hand, and, in making it, was cured. He had faith enough to believe that He who bade him stretch forth his hand, was not mocking him, and ought to be obeyed. And it was precisely in this act of implicit obedience, that he received a blessing. " His hand·was restored whole as the other."

Let us see in this simple history, the best answer to those doubts, and hesitations, and questionings, by which anxious inquirers often perplex themselves, in the matter of coming to Christ.—"How can they believe ?" they ask us,—" How can they come to Christ ? How can they lay hold on the hope set before them ?"—The best answer to all such inquiries, is to bid men do as he did who had the withered hand. Let them not stand still reasoning, but act. Let them not torment themselves with metaphysical speculations, but cast themselves, just as they are, on Jesus Christ. So doing, they will find their course made clear. How, or in what manner, we may not be able to explain. But we may boldly make the assertion, that in the act of striving to draw near to God, they shall find God drawing near to them, but that if they deliberately sit still, they must never expect to be saved.

NOTES. LUKE VI. 6—11.

8.—[*Stand forth in the midst.*]   Here we have a striking example of the publicity of our Lord's miracles.   He performs the cure of a disease with a few words, in the presence of a large assembly of persons unfriendly to Him, and in the face of open day.   He does not do it suddenly or hurriedly. He does it in such a manner that the attention of the whole assembly is necessarily concentrated on the thing done.

These things should be carefully noted.   Herein lies the great difference between the miracles wrought by Christ and His apostles, and the pretended miracles of Mahomet, or the lying miracles of the Church of Rome.   Those who wish to see this point fully worked out should read Leslie's "Short and easy method with Deists."

10.—[*Stretch forth thy hand.*]   Ford gives a quotation from Fuller on this passage, which is worth reading.   "God's commands are grants.   When He enjoins us, Repent, or Believe, it is only to draw from us a free acknowledgement of our impotence to perform His commands.   This confession being made, what He enjoins, He will enable us to do.   Man's owning his weakness is the only stock for God to graft thereon the grace of His assistance."

11.—[*Madness.*]   The word so translated, is only used in one other place, 2 Tim. iii. 9., and is there translated "folly."   The sense we now put on the word "madness," is probably stronger than the Greek word here bears.

LUKE VI. 12—19.

12 And it came to pass in those days, that he went out into a mountain to pray, and continued all night in prayer to God.

13 And when it was day, he called *unto him* his disciples : and of them he chose twelve, whom also he named apostles ;

14 Simon, (whom he also named Peter,) and Andrew his brother, James and John, Philip and Bartholomew,

15 Matthew and Thomas, James the *son* of Alphæus, and Simon called Zelotes,

16 And Judas *the brother* of James, and Judas Iscariot, which also was the traitor.

17 And he came down with them, and stood in the plain, and the company of his disciples, and a great multitude of people out of all Judæa and Jerusalem, and from the sea coast of Tyre and Sidon, which came to hear him, and to be healed of their diseases ;

18 And they that were vexed with unclean spirits : and they were healed.

19 And the whole multitude sought to touch him : for there went virtue out of him, and healed *them* all.

THESE verses describe the appointment of our Lord Jesus Christ's twelve apostles.   That appointment was the beginning of the Christian ministry. It was the first ordination, and an ordination conducted by the Great Head of the Church Himself. Since the day when the events here recorded took place, there have been many thousand ordinations. Myriads of bishops, elders, and deacons have been called to the office of the ministry, and often with far more pomp and splendour than we read of here. But never was there so solemn an ordination as this. Never were men ordained who have done so much for the church and the world as these twelve apostles.

Let us observe, firstly, in these verses, that *when our Lord ordained His first ministers, He did it after much prayer*. We read that He "went out into a mountain to pray, and continued all night in prayer to God. And when it was day, He called unto Him His disciples, and of them He chose twelve, whom also He named apostles."

We need not doubt that there is a deep significance in this special mention of our Lord's praying upon this occasion. It was intended to be a perpetual lesson to the Church of Christ. It was meant to shew the great importance of prayer and intercession on behalf of ministers, and particularly at the time of their ordination. Those to whom the responsible office of ordaining is committed, should pray that they may "lay hands suddenly on no man." Those who offer themselves for ordination, should pray that they may not take up work for which they are unfit, and not run without being sent. The lay members of the Church, not least, should pray that none may be ordained, but men who are inwardly moved by the Holy

Ghost.—Happy are those ordinations, in which all concerned have the mind that was in Christ, and come together in a prayerful spirit!

Do we desire to help forward the cause of pure and undefiled religion in the world? Then let us never forget to pray for ministers, and especially for young men about to enter the ministry. The progress of the Gospel, under God, will always depend much on the character and conduct of those who profess to preach it. An unconverted minister can never be expected to do good to souls. He cannot teach properly what he does not feel experimentally. From such men let us pray daily that the Church may be delivered. Converted ministers are God's special gift. Man cannot create them. If we would have good ministers, we must remember our Lord's example, and pray for them. Their work is heavy. Their responsibility is enormous. Their strength is small. Let us see that we support them, and hold up their hands by our prayers. In this, and in too many other cases, the words of St. James are often sadly applicable, "Ye have not, because ye ask not." (James iv. 2.) We do not ask God to raise up a constant supply of converted young men to fill our pulpits, and God chastises our neglect by withholding them.

Let us observe, secondly, *how little we are told of the worldly position of the first ministers of the Christian Church.* Four of them, we know, were fishermen. One of them, at least, was a publican. Most of them, probably, were Galileans. Not one of them, so far as we can see from the New Testament, was great, or rich, or noble, or highly connected. Not one was a Pharisee, or

Scribe, or Priest, or Ruler, or Elder among the people. All were, apparently, "unlearned and ignorant men." (Acts iv. 13.) All were poor.

There is something deeply instructive in the fact which is now before us. It shows us that our Lord Jesus Christ's kingdom was entirely independent of help from this world. His Church was not built by might, or by power, but by the Spirit of the living God. (Zech. iv. 6.)—It supplies us with an unanswerable proof of the divine origin of Christianity. A religion which turned the world upside down, while its first preachers were all poor men, must needs have been from heaven. If the apostles had possessed money to give their hearers, or been followed by armies to frighten them, an infidel might well deny that there was anything wonderful in their success. But the poverty of our Lord's disciples cuts away such arguments from beneath the infidel's feet. With a doctrine most unpalatable to the natural heart,—with nothing whatever to bribe or compel obedience,—a few lowly Galileans shook the world, and changed the face of the Roman empire. One thing only can account for this. The Gospel of Christ, which these men proclaimed, was the truth of God.

Let us remember these things, if we ever strive to do any work for Christ, and beware of leaning on an arm of flesh. Let us watch against the secret inclination, which is natural to all, to look to money, or learning, or high patronage, or great men's support, for success. If we want to do good to souls, we must not look first to the powers of this world. We should begin where the Church of Christ began. We should seek agents filled with the Holy Ghost.

Let us observe, lastly, in these verses, *that one whom our Lord chose to be an apostle, was a false disciple and a traitor.* That man was Judas Iscariot.

We cannot for a moment doubt, that in choosing Judas Iscariot, our Lord Jesus knew well what He was doing. He who could read hearts, certainly saw from the beginning that, notwithstanding his profession of piety, Judas was a graceless man, and would one day betray Him. Why then did He appoint him to be an apostle? The question is one which has perplexed many. Yet it admits of a satisfactory answer. Like everything which our Lord did, it was done advisedly, deliberately, and with deep wisdom. It conveyed lessons of high importance to the whole Church of Christ.

The choice of Judas was meant to teach ministers humility. They are not to suppose that ordination necessarily conveys grace, or that once ordained they cannot err. On the contrary, they are to remember, that one ordained by Christ Himself was a wretched hypocrite. Let the minister who thinketh he standeth, take heed lest he fall.

Again, the choice of Judas was meant to teach the lay-members of the Church, not to make idols of ministers. They are to esteem them highly in love for their work's sake, but they are not to bow down to them as infallible, and honour them with an unscriptural honour. They are to remember that ministers may be successors of Judas Iscariot, as well as of Peter and Paul. The name of Judas should be a standing warning to " cease from man." Let no man glory in men. (1 Cor. iii. 21.)

Finally, our Lord's choice of Judas was meant to teach

the whole Church, that it must not expect to see a
perfectly pure communion in the present state of things.
The wheat and the tares,—the good fish and the bad,—
will always be found side by side, till the Lord comes
again. It is vain to look for perfection in visible
churches. We shall never find it. A Judas was found
even among the apostles. Converted and unconverted
people will always be found mixed together in all
congregations.

NOTES. LUKE VI. 12—19.

12.—[*In prayer to God.*] The peculiarity of the Greek words here
has made some think that the meaning should have been rendered, He continued all night " in a house of prayer," a place set
apart for prayer to God. That the Jews had such praying-
houses, is undeniable. But whether such a house is referred to
here, is very doubtful. Out of the thirty seven places in which
the Greek word occurs in the New Testament, there is only one
other where it could be interpreted "a place of prayer," Acts
xvi. 13, and even there it is a disputed point. There seems no
necessity for leaving the sense given by our translators. Barradius remarks, that the expression which we translate, "prayer
to God," is a Hebraism, meaning "most fervent and earnest
prayer," just as " mountains of God," and "cedars of God," in
the Old Testament, mean "lofty" mountains, and "high" cedars.
(Psalm xxxvi. 6 ; lxxx. 10.)

Isidore Clarius, in his orations on St. Luke, published at Venice
in 1565, has some striking remarks on the disgraceful contrast
between the manner in which the apostles were called to their
office after a night spent in prayer, and the manner in which
ecclesiastical offices were filled up in Italy in his own day. He
exposes the system of jobbing, nepotism, corruption, and covetousness, which universally prevailed on such occasions, and
enters a faithful protest against it.

It is singular enough that the tone of Stella, the Spanish commentator on St. Luke, in expounding this passage, is precisely
similar to that of Clarius.

13.—[*Chose twelve...named apostles.*] Corderius gives a curious
passage from Rabanus Maurus on the number twelve, bringing
together the instances of that number being specially chosen in
the Bible. He says, "The number twelve, which consists of
three times four, points out that the apostles would preach the

faith of the Holy Trinity throughout the four quarters of the
world. The number is prefigured in the Old Testament by
many examples,—by the twelve sons of Jacob,—the twelve
princes of the children of Israel,—the twelve fountains in Elim,
—the twelve stones in Aaron's breast-plate,—the twelve loaves
of shew-bread,—the twelve spies sent forth by Moses,—the
twelve stones of which the altar was made,—the twelve stones
taken out of Jordan,—and the twelve oxen which supported the
brazen laver. In the New Testament, the number is shewn in
the twelve stars on the crown of the woman in Revelation,—and
the twelve foundations, and twelve gates of the heavenly
Jerusalem, seen by John."

It is interesting to remark, that out of the twelve apostles, we
have no less than three pairs of brothers, Peter and Andrew,
James and John, and Jude and James the son of Alphæus.

14.—[*Bartholomew.*] It is thought by many that Bartholomew is
Nathanael, whom we read of in the first chapter of John.
Jansenius, Montanus, and Ferus maintain this. But there
seems no warrant for the conjecture, except it be the fact that
we find Bartholomew always mentioned in close connection with
Philip, who called Nathanael to Christ.

15.—[*James the son of Alphæus.*] This appears to be that James
whom St. Paul calls the "Lord's brother." (Gal. i. 19.) The
fact that he is here called the "son of Alphæus," goes far to
prove that the word "brother" in the New Testament must not
be taken too literally, and admits of being understood as
"cousin." The Alphæus here mentioned must either be a
different person from the father of Matthew, or else Matthew
must have been brother of James and Jude. St. Mark says,
that Matthew or Levi was the son of Alphæus.

It was this James who took the lead in the council, (Acts xv.
19.) and seems to have been regarded as the moderator or chief
of the apostles in Jerusalem. He was also the writer of the
Epistle which bears his name. It is remarkable that like
Matthew and Simon the Canaanite, we never read of his
saying anything, or coming forward in any way, while our
Lord lived. Yet, after our Lord's ascension, none seems to
have had so prominent a position in the Church.

16.—[*Judas the brother of James.*] This apostle is remarkable for
having had three names, Jude, Lebbæus, and Thaddæus. He
it was who wrote the epistle which bears his name.

[*Iscariot.*] Many conjectures have been made as to the
meaning of this name. None of them are satisfactory. Some
think that it means that he was a man of the tribe of Issachar,
—some that he was a man of Kirioth, a small town in Judah,
or Carioth, a town of Ephraim. Nothing certain is known about
the subject.

Let it be noted, among other reasons for our Lord's choice of a traitor to be an apostle, that the choice finally supplied a powerful indirect evidence of the purity, blamelessness, and faultlessness of our Lord's conduct and ministry. When our Lord was accused before the High Priest and Pontius Pilate, if anything could have been proved against Him, the traitor Judas Iscariot was exactly the witness who would have proved it. The mere fact that Judas never came forward to give evidence against our Lord, is a convincing evidence that nothing could be proved against Him. No man is so well qualified to expose another's faults and inconsistencies, if they really exist, as one who has been on intimate terms with him. Judas never appeared against our Lord, because he could not allege anything to his disadvantage. Ford quotes a passage from Anselm, on this point: "Judas is chosen that the Lord might have an enemy among his domestic attendants, for that man is perfect, who has no cause to shrink from the observation of a wicked man, conversant with all his ways."

17.—[*Stood in the plain.*] This expression should be noted. It shows that the discourse which follows is different from that called "the sermon on the mount."

19.—[*Virtue.*] The word so translated is generally rendered "power," or "strength," and must not be taken as a moral quality here.

LUKE VI. 20—26.

20 And he lifted up his eyes on his disciples, and said, Blessed *be ye* poor: for yours is the kingdom of God.

21 Blessed *are ye* that hunger now: for ye shall be filled. Blessed *are ye* that weep now: for ye shall laugh.

22 Blessed are ye when men shall hate you, and when they shall separate you *from their company*, and shall reproach *you*, and cast out your name as evil, for the Son of man's sake.

23 Rejoice ye in that day, and leap for joy: for, behold, your reward *is* great in heaven: for in the like manner did their fathers unto the prophets.

24 But woe unto you that are rich! for ye have received your consolation.

25 Woe unto you that are full! for ye shall hunger. Woe unto you that laugh now! for ye shall mourn and weep.

26 Woe unto you, when all men shall speak well of you! for so did their fathers to the false prophets.

THE discourse of our Lord, which we have now begun, resembles, in many respects, His well-known Sermon on the Mount. The resemblance, in fact, is so striking, that many have concluded that St. Luke and St. Matthew are reporting one and the same discourse, and that St. Luke is giving us, in an abridged form, what St. Matthew reports at length.   There seems no sufficient ground for this conclusion.   The occasions on which the two discourses were delivered, were entirely different.   Our Lord's repetition of the same great lesson, in almost the same words, on two different occasions, is nothing extraordinary.   It is unreasonable to suppose that none of His mighty teachings were ever delivered more than once.   In the present case, the repetition is very significant.   It shows us the great and deep importance of the lessons which the two discourses contain.

Let us first notice in these verses, *who are those whom the Lord Jesus pronounces blessed.*   The list is a remarkable and startling one.   It singles out those who are "poor," and those who "hunger,"—those who "weep," and those who are "hated" by man.   These are the persons to whom the great Head of the Church says, " Blessed are ye ! "

We must take good heed that we do not misunderstand our Lord's meaning, when we read these expressions.   We must not for a moment suppose that the mere fact of being poor, and hungry, and sorrowful, and hated by man, will entitle any one to lay claim to an interest in Christ's blessing.   The poverty here spoken of, is a poverty accompanied by grace.   The want is a want entailed by faithful adherence to Jesus.   The afflictions are the afflictions of the Gospel.   The persecution is persecution for the Son of Man's sake.   Such want, and poverty, and affliction, and persecution, were the inevitable consequences of faith in Christ, at the beginning of Christianity.   Thousands had to give up everything in

this world, because of their religion. It was their case
which Jesus had specially in view in this passage. He
desired to supply them, and all who suffer like them for
the Gospel's sake, with special comfort and consolation.

Let us notice, secondly, in these verses, *who are those to
whom our Lord addresses the solemn words, " Woe unto
you."*   Once more we read expressions which at first
sight seem most extraordinary.   " Woe unto you that
are rich !—Woe unto you that are full !—Woe unto you
that laugh !—Woe unto you when all men shall speak
well of you ! "—Stronger and more cutting sayings than
these can not be found in the New Testament.

Here, however, no less than in the preceding verses,
we must take care that we do not misapprehend our
Lord's meaning.   We are not to suppose that the
possession of riches, and a rejoicing spirit, and the good
word of man, are necessarily proofs that people are not
Christ's disciples. Abraham and Job were rich. David
and St. Paul had their seasons of rejoicing. Timothy
was one who "had a good report from those that were
without." All these, we know, were true servants of God.
All these were blessed in this life, and shall receive the
blessing of the Lord in the day of His appearing.

Who are the persons to whom our Lord says, " Woe
unto you ? "   They are the men who refuse to seek
treasure in heaven, because they love the good things
of this world better, and will not give up their money,
if need requires, for Christ's sake.—They are the men
who prefer the joys and so-called happiness of this world,
to joy and peace in believing, and will not risk the loss
of the one in order to gain the other.—They are those

who love the praise of man more than the praise of God,
and will turn their backs on Christ, rather than not keep
in with the world.—These are the kind of men whom
our Lord had in view when He pronounced the solemn
words, "Woe, woe unto you." He knew well that there
were thousands of such persons among the Jews,—
thousands who, notwithstanding His miracles and sermons, would love the world better than Him. He knew
well that there would always be thousands of such in
His professing Church,—thousands who, though convinced of the truth of the Gospel, would never give up
anything for its sake.—To all such He delivers an awful
warning.—"Woe, woe unto you!"

One mighty lesson stands out plainly on the face of
these verses. May we all lay it to heart, and learn
wisdom! That lesson is the utter contrariety between
the mind of Christ, and the common opinions of mankind,—the entire variance between the thoughts of
Jesus, and the prevailing thoughts of the world. The
conditions of life which the world reckons desirable, are
the very conditions upon which the Lord pronounces
"woes." Poverty, and hunger, and sorrow, and persecution, are the very things which man labours to avoid.
Riches, and fulness, and merriment, and popularity, are
precisely the things which men are always struggling to
attain. When we have said all, in the way of qualifying,
explaining, and limiting our Lord's words, there still
remain two sweeping assertions, which flatly contradict the
current doctrine of mankind. The state of life which
our Lord blesses, the world cordially dislikes. The
people to whom our Lord says, "woe unto you," are the

very people whom the world admires, praises, and imitates. This is an awful fact. It ought to raise within us great searchings of heart.

Let us leave the whole passage with honest self-inquiry and self-examination. Let us ask ourselves what we think of the wonderful declarations that it contains. Can we subscribe to what our Lord says? Are we of one mind with Him? Do we really believe that poverty and persecution, endured for Christ's sake, are positive blessings? Do we really believe that riches and worldly enjoyments, and popularity among men, when sought for more than salvation, or preferred in the least to the praise of God, are a positive curse? Do we really think that the favour of Christ, with trouble and the world's ill word, is better worth having than money, and merriment, and a good name among men, without Christ?—These are most serious questions, and deserve a most serious answer. The passage before us is eminently one which tests the reality of our Christianity. The truths it contains, are truths which no unconverted man can love and receive. Happy are those who have found them truths by experience, and can say "amen" to all our Lord's declarations. Whatever men may please to think, those whom Jesus blesses are blessed, and those whom Jesus does not bless will be cast out for evermore.

NOTES. LUKE VI. 20—26.

20.—[*And he lifted up his eyes.*] It is a disputed point, whether the discourse which begins with this verse, is the same as that recorded in St. Matthew, (chapters v. vi. vii.) and commonly called the Sermon on the mount. The majority of commentators unquestionably regard the two discourses as the same. To this opinion, after much consideration, I feel unable to subscribe.

I regard the two discourses as distinct and different, and consider them as delivered at different times.

For one thing, the occasion of the discourse recorded by St. Luke, is not the same as the occasion of that recorded by St. Matthew. The discourse reported by St. Matthew, was one delivered on " a mountain," and previous to the appointment of the twelve apostles. The discourse reported by St. Luke, was delivered " in the plain," and after the twelve apostles had been ordained. To me it seems impossible to get over this discrepancy.

For another thing, there is a wide difference between the persons called " blessed " in the discourse in St. Matthew, and the persons called " blessed " in the discourse in St. Luke. In St. Matthew the point brought forward in each case is the spiritual character of the person, in St. Luke his temporal circumstances and condition. There is a wide difference, for instance, between " Blessed are the poor *in spirit*," and " Blessed be ye poor."

For another thing, the variance between the two discourses in length is very notable. St. Luke's report can in no sense be called an abridgment of St. Matthew. Many things that St. Matthew reports, he omits altogether. Some things that he inserts, on the other hand, are not to be found in St. Matthew at all.

In the last place, it seems unreasonable to suppose that our Lord never repeated the same lessons on different occasions. All public teachers find it necessary to do so. We cannot doubt that He did also. In the present instance He repeats to a different audience some of the truths which He had before preached at greater length in the Sermon on the Mount. And the repetition was meant to show their importance.

For the above reasons, I believe that St. Luke and St. Matthew are recording two different discourses. In saying this, I consider it only fair to myself to remark that the view I maintain is held by Pool, Cartwright, Doddridge, Whitby, Scott, and Watson.

[*Blessed be ye poor.*] The poverty spoken of here, as well as the hunger, weeping, and being hated, of the rest of the passage, must be taken in a literal sense, remembering only that it is poverty and sorrow for the Gospel's sake to which our Lord refers. The expressions, " rich," and " full," and " laugh," in the latter part of the passage, must evidently be taken in a literal sense. It seems unreasonable to interpret the one set of words spiritually and the other literally.

The promises, of course, in one case, as well as the threatenings in the other, admit of a much wider interpretation. " Ye shall be filled," and " ye shall laugh," are promises which to many of God's saints are never fulfilled in this world. In like manner, "ye shall hunger," and "ye shall mourn and weep," are words of which the wicked, in many cases, will not know the full bitterness till hereafter.

22.—[*Separate you from their company.*] The Greek word so rendered, according to Suicer, is specially applied to ecclesiastical excommunication.

24.—[*Ye have received.*] The Greek word so rendered should rather have a present sense, "ye are receiving or having your consolation."

26.—[*Woe unto you...all...speak well of you.*] Let that expression be carefully noted. Few of our Lord's sayings are more flatly contradictory to the common opinion both of the Church and the world, than this. What is more common in the world than the love of every one's praise? What more frequent in the Church than to hear it said in commendation of a minister, that "every body likes him!" It seems entirely forgotten, that to be liked and approved by every body, is to be of the number of those to whom Jesus says, "Woe unto you." To be universally popular is a most unsatisfactory symptom, and one of which a minister of Christ should always be afraid. It may well make him doubt whether he is faithfully doing his duty, and honestly declaring all the counsel of God.

<hr>

LUKE VI. 27—38.

27 But I say unto you which hear, Love your enemies, do good to them which hate you,

28 Bless them that curse you, and pray for them which despitefully use you.

29 And unto him that smiteth thee on the *one* cheek offer also the other; and him that taketh away thy cloke forbid not *to take thy* coat also.

30 Give to every man that asketh of thee; and of him that taketh away thy goods ask *them* not again.

31 And as ye would that men should do to you, do ye also to them likewise.

32 For if ye love them which love you, what thank have ye? for sinners also love those that love them.

33 And if ye do good to them which do good to you, what thank have ye? for sinners also do even the same.

34 And if ye lend *to them* of whom ye hope to receive, what thank have ye? for sinners also lend to sinners, to receive as much again.

35 But love ye your enemies, and do good, and lend, hoping for nothing again; and your reward shall be great, and ye shall be the children of the Highest: for he is kind unto the unthankful and *to* the evil.

36 Be ye therefore merciful, as your Father also is merciful.

37 Judge not, and ye shall not be judged: condemn not, and ye shall not be condemned: forgive, and ye shall be forgiven:

38 Give, and it shall be given unto you: good measure, pressed down, and shaken together, and running over, shall men give into your bosom. For with the same measure that ye mete withal it shall be measured to you again.

THE teaching of our Lord Jesus Christ, in these verses,

is confined to one great subject. That subject is Christian love and charity. Charity, which is the grand characteristic of the Gospel,—charity, which is the bond of perfectness,—charity, without which a man is nothing in God's sight,—charity is here fully expounded and strongly enforced. Well would it have been for the Church of Christ, if its Master's precepts in this passage had been more carefully studied and more diligently observed !

In the first place our Lord explains *the nature and extent of Christian charity*. The disciples might ask, Whom are we to love ? He bids them "love their enemies, do good to them that hate them, bless them that curse them, and pray for them that despitefully use them." Their love was to be like His own towards sinners—unselfish, disinterested, and uninfluenced by any hope of return.—What was to be the manner of this love ? the disciples might ask. It was to be self-sacrificing and self-denying. "Unto him that smiteth thee on the one cheek offer also the other."—"Him that taketh away thy cloak forbid not to take thy coat also." They were to give up much, and endure much, for the sake of showing kindness and avoiding strife. They were to forego even their rights, and submit to wrong, rather than awaken angry passions and create quarrels. In this they were to be like their Master, long-suffering, meek, and lowly of heart.

In the second place, our Lord lays down *a golden principle for the settlement of doubtful cases*. He knew well that there will always be occasions when the line of duty towards our neighbour is not clearly defined. He knew how much self-interest and private feelings will sometimes dim our perceptions of right and wrong. He supplies us with a precept for our guidance in all such cases, of infinite wisdom; a precept which even infidels have been compelled to admire.—"As ye would that men should do to you, do ye also to them likewise." To do to others as they do to us, and return evil for evil, is the standard of the heathen. To behave to others as we should like others to behave to us, whatever their actual behaviour may be,—this should be the mark at which the Christian should aim. This is to walk in the steps of our blessed Saviour. If He had dealt with the world as the world dealt with Him, we should all have been ruined for ever in hell.

In the third place, our Lord points out to His disciples *the necessity of their having a higher standard of duty to their neighbour than the children of this world*. He reminds them that to love those who love them, and do good to those who do good to them, and lend to those of whom they hope to receive, is to act no better than "the sinner" who knows nothing of the Gospel. The Christian must be altogether another style of man. His feelings of love, and his deeds of kindness, must be like his Master's,—free and gratuitous. He must let men see that he loves others from higher principles than the ungodly do, and that his charity is not confined to those from whom he hopes to get something in return. Anybody can shew kindness and charity, when he hopes to gain something by it. But such charity should never content a Christian. The man who is content with it, ought to remember that his practice does not rise an inch above the level of an old Roman or Greek idolater.

In the fourth place, our Lord shows His disciples *that in discharging their duty to their neighbours, they should look to the example of God.* If they called themselves "children of the Highest," they should consider that their Father is "kind to the unthankful and the evil," and they should learn from Him to be merciful, even as He is merciful. The extent of God's unacknowledged mercies to man can never be reckoned up. Every year he pours benefits on millions who do not honour the hand from which they come, or thank the Giver of them. Yet every year these benefits are continued. "Seed time and harvest, summer and winter, never cease." His mercy endureth for ever. His loving-kindness is unwearied. His compassions fail not. So ought it to be with all who profess themselves to be His children. Thanklessness and ingratitude should not make them slack their hands from works of love and mercy. Like their Father in heaven, they should never be tired of doing good.

In the last place, our Lord assures His disciples that *the practice of the high standard of charity He recommends shall bring its own reward.* "Judge not," He says, "and ye shall not be judged: condemn not, and ye shall not be condemned: forgive, and ye shall be forgiven: give, and it shall be given unto you." And He concludes with the broad assertion, "With the same measure that ye mete withal, shall it be measured to you again." The general meaning of these words appears to be, that no man shall ever be a loser, in the long run, by deeds of self-denying charity, and patient long-suffering love. At times he may seem to get nothing by his conduct. He may appear to reap nothing but ridicule, contempt, and

injury. His kindness may sometimes tempt men to impose
on him. His patience and forbearance may be abused.
But at the last he will always be found a gainer,—often,
very often, a gainer in this life : certainly, most certainly,
a gainer in the life to come.

Such is the teaching of our Lord Jesus Christ about
charity. Few of His sayings are so deeply heart-searching as those we have now been considering. Few passages
in the Bible are so truly humbling as these eleven verses.

How little of the style of charity which our Lord
recommends is to be seen, either in the world or in the
Church! How common is an angry, passionate spirit, a
morbid sensitiveness about what is called *honour*, and a
readiness to quarrel on the least occasion! How
seldom we see men and women who love their enemies,
and do good hoping for nothing again, and bless those
that curse them, and are kind to the unthankful and evil!
Truly we are reminded here of our Lord's words, " Narrow is the way which leadeth unto life, and few there be
that find it." (Matt. vii. 13.)

How happy the world would be, if Christ's precepts
were strictly obeyed! The chief causes of half the sorrows of mankind are selfishness, strife, unkindness, and
want of charity. Never was there a greater mistake than
to suppose that vital Christianity interferes with human
happiness. It is not having too much religion, but too
little, that makes people gloomy, wretched, and miserable.
Wherever Christ is best known and obeyed, there will
always be found most real joy and peace.

Would we know anything by experience of this blessed
grace of charity? Then let us seek to be joined to

Christ by faith, and to be taught and sanctified by His Spirit. We do not gather grapes of thorns, or figs of thistles. We cannot have flowers without roots, or fruit without trees. We cannot have the fruit of the Spirit without vital union with Christ, and a new creation within. Such as are not· born again can never really love in the manner that Christ enjoins.

NOTES. LUKE VI. 27—38.

28.—[*Despitefully use you.*] The word so translated is only found in two other places in the New Testament. In one (Matt. v. 44), it is rendered as it is here. In the other (1 Peter iii. 16), it is "falsely accuse."

The conduct here recommended is beautifully exemplified in the case of our Lord praying for those that crucified Him, and Stephen praying for those who stoned him. Luke xxiii. 34; Acts vii. 60.

29, 30—[*Unto him that smiteth thee, &c.*] The precepts of these two verses must necessarily be interpreted with Scriptural qualification. We must not so expound them as to contradict other passages of God's word. They are strong proverbial forms of expressing a great principle. If we were to press an extreme literal interpretation of them, we should give encouragement to theft, burglary, violence, and murder. The earth would be given into the hands of the wicked.

On the one hand, our Lord did not mean to forbid the repression of crime, or to declare the office of the magistrate and policeman unlawful. Nor yet did He mean to pronounce all war unlawful, or to prohibit the punishment of evil-doers, and disturbers of the peace and order of society. We find Him saying in one place, "He that hath no sword, let him sell his garment and buy one." Luke xxii. 36. We find St. Paul saying of the magistrate, that "he beareth not the sword in vain," that "he is the minister of God, a revenger to execute wrath upon him that doeth evil." Rom. xiii. 4. We find several centurions mentioned in the Gospels and Acts. But we never find their occupation, as soldiers, condemned as unlawful.

On the other hand, it is evident that our Lord condemns every thing like a revengeful, pugnacious, litigious, or quarrelsome spirit. He forbids everything like duelling, or fighting, between individuals, for the settlement of private wrongs. He enjoins forbearance, patience, and long-suffering under injuries and insults. He would have us concede much, submit to much, and put up with much, rather than cause strife. He would have us endure much inconvenience and loss, and even sacrifice some of our just rights, rather than have any contention. It is the same lesson that St. Paul enforces in other words : " If it be possible, as much as lieth in you, live peaceably with all men."—"Avenge not yourselves, but rather give place unto wrath : for it is written, Vengeance is mine; I will repay, saith the Lord."—" Be not overcome of evil, but overcome evil with good." Rom. xii. 18—21.

Few things bring out more painfully the little hold that Christianity has on professing Christians, than the utter neglect of our Lord's injunctions in these verses, which everywhere prevails. Anything more contrary to the mind of Christ than the duelling, and hand to hand conflicts, of which we hear so often in some countries and some ranks of society, it is impossible to conceive. To give blow for blow, and violence for violence, anger for anger, and abuse for abuse, is the conduct of a dog or a heathen, but not of a Christian.

32.—[*Sinners also.*] A. Clarke remarks on the word "sinners," used here and in the two following verses: " I believe this word is used by St. Luke in the same sense in which " publican, or tax-gatherer," is used by St. Matthew. It signifies " heathen," —not only men who have no religion, but who acknowledge none."

33.—[*Do even the same.*] Quesnel remarks on this verse : "A man ought to tremble with fear, if beside the external part of his religion, he finds nothing in his life but what may be found in a Turk or a heathen."

35.—[*Hoping for nothing again.*] The word so translated is not used in any other place in the New Testament. Bishop Pearce would translate "nothing" "no man," and thinks that the meaning is " not cutting off the hope of any man by denying him those things which he requests to preserve him from perishing." De Dieu takes much the same view, "not causing him to despair."

37, 38.—[*Judge not, and ye shall not be judged, &c.*] It is a disputed point whether the promises in these two verses are to be taken in a temporal or spiritual sense. The word " men," in the 38th verse is not in the original, so that no argument can be founded on it. But taking into consideration the whole connection in which the two verses stand, it seems most probable to me that the rewards promised by our Lord are primarily and principally rewards to be received in this world.

I cannot close the notes on this passage, without entering my protest against the rapidly increasing opinion, that we may have the fruits of the Spirit without the doctrine of the Spirit. Nothing is more common now than to find charity, kindness, self-sacrifice, and attention to others, praised and commended by popular writers, who make no secret of their contempt for all the leading doctrines of the Gospel. Once for all, let us understand, that real, genuine, self-denying love, will never grow from any roots but faith in Christ's atonement, and a heart renewed by the Holy Ghost. We shall never make men love one another, unless we teach as St. Paul taught, "Walk in love, as Christ hath loved us." Teaching love on any other principle is, as a general rule, labour in vain.

LUKE VI. 39—45.

39 And he spake a parable unto them, Can the blind lead the blind? shall they not both fall into the ditch?

40 The disciple is not above his master: but every one that is perfect shall be as his master.

41 And why beholdest thou the mote that is in thy brother's eye, but perceivest not the beam that is in thine own eye?

42 Either how canst thou say to thy brother, Brother, let me pull out the mote that is in thine eye, when thou beholdest not the beam that is in thine own eye? Thou hypocrite, cast out first the beam out of thine own eye, and then shalt thou see clearly to pull out the mote that is in thy brother's eye.

43 For a good tree bringeth not forth corrupt fruit; neither doth a corrupt tree bring forth good fruit.

44 For every tree is known by his own fruit. For of thorns men do not gather figs, nor of a bramble bush gather they grapes.

45 A good man out of the good treasure of his heart bringeth forth that which is good; and an evil man out of the evil treasure of his heart bringeth forth that which is evil: for of the abundance of the heart his mouth speaketh.

WE learn, in the first place, from these verses, *the great danger of listening to false teachers in religion.* Our Lord compares such teachers and their hearers to the blind leading the blind, and asks the reasonable question, "Shall they not both fall into the ditch?" He goes on to confirm the importance of His warning by declaring, that "the disciple is not above his master," and the scholar cannot be expected to know more than his teacher. If a man will hear unsound instruction, we cannot expect him to become otherwise than unsound in the faith himself.

The subject which our Lord brings before us here deserves far more attention than it generally receives. The amount of evil which unsound religious teaching has brought on the Church in every age is incalculable. The loss of souls which it has occasioned is fearful to contemplate. A teacher who does not know the way to heaven himself, is not likely to lead his hearers to heaven. The man who hears such a teacher runs a fearful risk himself of being lost eternally. "If the blind lead the blind both must fall into the ditch."

If we would escape the danger against which our Lord warns us, we must not neglect to prove the teaching that we hear by the holy Scriptures. We must not believe things merely because ministers say them. We must not suppose, as a matter of course, that ministers can make no mistakes. We must call to mind our Lord's words on another occasion, "Beware of false prophets." (Matt. vii. 15.) We must remember the advice of St. Paul and St. John: "Prove all things." "Try the spirits whether they are of God." (1 Thess. v. 21 ; 1 John iv. 1.) With the Bible in our hands, and the promise of guidance from the Holy Ghost to all who seek it, we shall be without excuse if our souls are led astray. The blindness of ministers is no excuse for the darkness of the people. The man who from indolence, or superstition, or affected humility, refuses to distrust the teaching of the minister whom he finds set over him, however unsound it may be, will at length share his minister's portion. If people will trust blind guides, they must not be surprised if they are led to the pit.

We learn, secondly, from these verses, that *those who reprove the sins of others should strive to be of blameless life.* Our Lord teaches us this lesson by a practical saying. He shews the unreasonableness of a man finding fault with "a mote," or trifling thing in a brother's eye, while he himself has "a beam," or some large and formidable object sticking in his own eye.

The lesson must doubtless be received with suitable and Scriptural qualifications. If no man is to teach or preach to others, until he himself is faultless, there could be no teaching or preaching in the world. The erring would never be corrected, and the wicked would never be reproved. To put such a sense as this on our Lord's words, brings them into collision with other plain passages of Scripture.

The main object of our Lord Jesus appears to be to impress on ministers and teachers the importance of consistency of life. The passage is a solemn warning not to contradict by our lives what we have said with our lips. The office of the preacher will never command attention, unless he practises what he preaches. Episcopal ordination, university degrees, high-sounding titles, a loud profession of doctrinal purity, will never procure respect for a minister's sermon, if his congregation sees him cleaving to ungodly habits.

But there is much here which we shall all do well to remember. The lesson is one which many besides ministers should seriously consider. All heads of families and masters of households, all parents, all teachers of schools, all tutors, all managers of young people,— should often think of the "mote" and the "beam." All such should see in our Lord's words the mighty lesson, that nothing influences others so much as consistency. Let the lesson be treasured up and not forgotten.

We learn, lastly, from these verses, that *there is only*

*one satisfactory test of a man's religious character. That test
is his conduct and conversation.*

The words of our Lord on this subject are clear and
unmistakeable. He draws an illustration from a tree,
and lays down the broad principle, " every tree is known
by his own fruit." But our Lord does not stop here.
He proceeds further to show that a man's conversation is
one indication of his state of heart. " Of the abundance
of the heart his mouth speaketh." Both these sayings
are deeply important. Both should be stored up among
the leading maxims of our practical Christianity.

Let it be a settled principle in our religion that when
a man brings forth no fruits of the Spirit, he has not the
Holy Ghost within him. Let us resist as a deadly error
the common idea, that all baptized people are born again,
and that all members of the Church, as a matter of
course, have the Holy Ghost. One simple question must
be our rule. What fruit does a man bring forth? Does
he repent? Does he believe with the heart on Jesus?
Does he live a holy life? Does he overcome the world?
Habits like these are what Scripture calls "fruit."
When these "fruits" are wanting, it is profane to talk of a
man having the Spirit of God within him.

Let it be a settled principle again in our religion, that
when a man's general conversation is ungodly, his heart
is graceless and unconverted. Let us not give way to
the vulgar notion, that no one can know anything of the
state of another's heart, and that although men are
living wickedly, they have got *good hearts* at the bottom.
Such notions are flatly contradictory to our Lord's teaching. Is the general tone of a man's communication

carnal, worldly, irreligious, godless, or profane? Then let us understand that this is the state of his heart. When a man's tongue is generally wrong, it is absurd, no less than unscriptural, to say that his heart is right.

Let us close this passage with solemn self-inquiry, and use it for the trial of our own state before God. What fruits are we bringing forth in our lives? Are they, or are they not, fruits of the Spirit?—What kind of evidence do our words supply as to the state of our hearts? Do we talk like men whose hearts are "right in the sight of God?"—There is no evading the doctrine laid down by our Lord in this passage. Conduct is the grand test of character. Words are one great symptom of the condition of the heart.

NOTES. LUKE VI. 39—45..

39.—[*Can the blind lead the blind?*] Let it be noted that this is the second occasion on which our Lord uses this saying. Both here, and in the other place where it is used (Matt. xv. 44), the application is manifest. It is a warning against following unsound religious teachers.

40.—[*The disciple is not above his master, &c.*] It is common to regard this verse as descriptive of the portion of all believers in this world, and as parallel with such sayings as these, "If they have persecuted me they will also persecute you." "If they have kept my saying they will also keep yours." The perfection is looked upon as the being made "perfect through sufferings."

But I feel unable to interpret the verse in this sense. It is good divinity, but not the sense of this passage. The true meaning, I believe, must be sought in connection with the verse which immediately precedes it. In that verse our Lord, under a parable, had been delivering a warning against false teachers. He had been comparing them to blind guides, and showing that if the blind lead the blind, "both must fall into the ditch." He then seems to foresee the common objection that it does not follow because our teachers go astray that we shall go astray also. "Beware of that delusion," He seems to say. "Disciples must not be expected to see more clearly than their teachers. The scholar will become as perfect as his master, but not more so. He will certainly copy his errors, and reproduce his faults. If you choose to follow blind guides, do not wonder if you never get beyond them, and if you share in their final ruin." The marginal reading in the English version appears to bring out this sense more clearly than the text: "Every one shall be per-fected as his master."

How strikingly true this saying of our Lord is, has been painfully proved in England during the last thirty years. All who know anything of our religious history during that period, must have observed, that the leaders of the various new heresies by which we have been plagued, have generally had many ardent followers. These followers have seldom got beyond their masters, and have seldom been able to copy their good points without their bad ones. On the contrary, they have often slavishly reproduced the worst errors of their teachers, and that in a far worse form, and have not imitated their good points at all. They have thus strictly verified our Lord's words, "The disciple is not above his master."

I may remark that the view I have maintained of this text is held by Brentius, Bullinger, Gualter, Stella, and Quesnel.

41.—[*The mote.*] The word so translated is only used here and in the kindred passage in St. Matthew. It means a small bit of straw, or grass, or dry wood.

[*The beam.*] This word means a large piece of timber such as is used for the rafter of a roof. The whole expression is evidently a proverb intended to bring into strong contrast by a figure, little faults and great ones.

43—[*A good tree bringeth not forth.*] Perhaps the sense of the Greek words here would be rendered more literally, if thus paraphrased, "There is no such thing as a good tree bringing forth bad fruit."

44.—[*Men...gather figs.*] Here, as well as in the verse previously noticed (38,) the word "men" is not in the Greek. It is a form of expression equivalent to saying, "figs are not gathered of thorns." It is one that ought to be carefully noted, as it throws light on a difficult passage in another part of St. Luke's Gospel. (Luke xvi. 9.)

LUKE VI. 46—49.

46 And why call ye me, Lord, Lord, and do not the things which I say?

47 Whosoever cometh to me, and heareth my sayings, and doeth them, I will shew you to whom he is like:

48 He is like a man which built an house, and digged deep, and laid the foundation on a rock: and when the flood arose, the stream beat vehement-ly upon that house, and could not shake it: for it was founded upon a rock.

49 But he that heareth, and doeth not, is like a man that without a foundation built an house upon the earth; against which the stream did beat vehemently, and immediately it fell; and the ruin of that house was great.

It has been said, with much truth, that no sermon should conclude without some personal application to the consciences of those who hear it. The passage before us is an example of this rule, and a confirmation of its correctness. It is a solemn and heart-searching conclusion of a most solemn discourse.

Let us mark, in these verses, *what an old and common sin is profession without practice.* It is written, that our Lord said, "Why call ye me Lord, Lord, and do not the things which I say?" The Son of God Himself had many followers, who pretended to honour Him by calling Him Lord, but yielded no obedience to His commandments.

The evil which our Lord exposes here, has always existed in the Church of God. It was found six hundred years before our Lord's time, in the days of Ezekiel: "They come unto thee," we read, "as the people cometh, and they sit before thee as my people, and they hear thy words, but they will not do them, for with their mouth they show much love, but their heart goeth after their covetousness." (Ezek. xxxiii. 31.) It was found in the primitive Church of Christ, in the days of St. James: "Be ye doers of the word," he says, "and not hearers only, deceiving your own selves." (James i. 22.) It is a disease which has never ceased to prevail all over Christendom. It is a soul-ruining plague, which is continually sweeping away crowds of Gospel-hearers down the broad way to destruction. Open sin, and avowed unbelief, no doubt slay their thousands. But profession without practice slays its tens of thousands.

Let us settle it in our minds, that no sin is so foolish and unreasonable as the sin which Jesus here denounces.

Common sense alone might tell us, that the name and form of Christianity can profit us nothing, so long as we cleave to sin in our hearts, and live unchristian lives. Let it be a fixed principle in our religion, that obedience is the only sound evidence of saving faith, and that the talk of the lips is worse than useless, if it is not accompanied by sanctification of the life. The man in whose heart the Holy Ghost really dwells, will never be content to sit still, and do nothing to show his love to Christ.

Let us mark, secondly, in these verses, *what a striking picture our Lord draws of the religion of the man who not only hears Christ's sayings, but does Christ's will.* He compares him to one who "built a house, and digged deep, and laid the foundation on a rock."

Such a man's religion may cost him much. Like the house built on a rock, it may entail on him pains, labour, and self-denial. To lay aside pride and self-righteousness, to crucify the rebellious flesh, to put on the mind of Christ, to take up the cross daily, to count all things but loss for Christ's sake,—all this may be hard work. But, like the house built on the rock, such religion will stand. The streams of affliction may beat violently upon it, and the floods of persecution dash fiercely against it, but it will not give way. The Christianity which combines good profession and good practice, is a building that will not fall.

Let us mark, lastly, in these verses, *what a mournful picture our Lord draws of the religion of the man who hears Christ's sayings, but does not obey them.* He compares him to one who, "without a foundation, built an house upon the earth."

Such a man's religion may look well for a season. An

ignorant eye may detect no difference between the possessor of such a religion, and a true Christian. Both may worship in the same Church. Both may use the same ordinances. Both may profess the same faith. The outward appearance of the house built on the rock, and the house without any solid foundation, may be much the same. But the day of trial and affliction is the test which the religion of the mere outward professor cannot stand. When storm and tempest beat on the house which has no foundation, the walls which looked well in sunshine and fair weather, are sure to come to the ground. The Christianity which consists of merely hearing religion taught, without doing anything, is a building which must finally fall. Great indeed will be the ruin! There is no loss like the loss of a soul!

This passage of Scripture is one which ought to call up in our minds peculiarly solemn feelings. The pictures it presents, are pictures of things which are daily going on around us. On every side we shall see thousands building for eternity, on a mere outward profession of Christianity,—striving to shelter their souls under false refuges,—contenting themselves with a name to live, while they are dead, and with a form of godliness without the power. Few indeed are the builders upon rocks, and great is the ridicule and persecution which they have to endure! Many are the builders upon sand, and mighty are the disappointments and failures which are the only result of their work! Surely if ever there was a proof that man is fallen and blind in spiritual things, it may be seen in the fact that the majority of every generation of baptized people, persist in building on sand.

What is the foundation on which we ourselves are building? This, after all, is the question that concerns our souls.—Are we upon the rock, or are we upon the sand?—We love perhaps to hear the Gospel. We approve of all its leading doctrines. We assent to all its statements of truth about Christ and the Holy Ghost, about justification and sanctification, about repentance and faith, about conversion and holiness, about the Bible and prayer. But what are we *doing?* What is the daily practical history of our lives, in public and in private, in the family and in the world? Can it be said of us, that we not only hear Christ's sayings, but that we also do them?

The hour cometh, and will soon be here, when questions like these must be asked and answered, whether we like them or not. The day of sorrow and bereavement, of sickness and death, will make it plain whether we are on the rock, or on the sand. Let us remember this betimes, and not trifle with our souls. Let us strive so to believe and so to live, so to hear Christ's voice and so to follow Him, that when the flood arises, and the streams beat over us, our house may stand and not fall.

NOTES. LUKE VI. 46—49.

48.—[*He is like a man, &c.*] We must be careful in interpreting and explaining this parable, that we do not lose sight of its proper scope and intention. It is surely not handling Scripture honestly to tell people that the "rock" here is Christ, and the man who builds on it the true believer,—the foundation of earth, false grounds of confidence for justification, and the man who builds on it the deluded Christian who trusts in them. All this may be excellent divinity. But that is not the point in question. The point is, Does the passage teach this lesson? I answer unhesitatingly that it does not.

The object of the parable is not to teach the doctrine of justification, but the folly of Christian profession unaccompanied by

Christian practice, and the certain ruin to which such profession must lead if persisted in. That Christ is the true rock on which we must build our hopes, and that there is no other rock on which we can stand, is abundantly taught elsewhere. But it is not the lesson of the passage before us. The passage is a warning against Antinomianism. Let not that be forgotten.

The habit of accommodating Scripture, and using it in a sense which it was not originally intended to bear, is a dangerous practice. It has indirectly a mischievous effect on our own minds, and is most confusing to the poor and unlearned. When a poor man hears a sense put on texts which does not appear on the face of them, and in reality can only be drawn from them by accommodation, it makes him think that the Bible is a book which none but learned people can understand.

[*Digged deep.*] The English language fails here to give the full force of the Greek words. They would be translated more literally, " digged and deepened."

[*The flood arose, the stream beat.*] To understand this, we must remember that the climate in hot countries is very different from our own. When rains fall in hot countries they often fall very violently, and cause the rivers and streams to swell into a flood very rapidly. Under such circumstances the events described by our Lord might easily take place, and had doubtless often been seen by many of His hearers.

49.—[*He that heareth and doeth not.*] The plain words of John Bunyan, when he describes Talkative in Pilgrim's Progress, are an admirable commentary on this verse. "The soul of religion is the practical part. ' Pure religion and undefiled before God and the Father, is this, to visit the fatherless and widows in their affliction, and to keep himself unspotted from the world.' (James i. 27.) This Talkative is not aware of. He thinks that hearing and saying will make a good Christian, and thus he deceiveth his own soul. Hearing is but the sowing of the seed. Talking is not sufficient to prove that fruit is indeed in the heart and life. Let us assure ourselves, that at the day of doom men shall be judged according to their fruits. It will not then be said, Did you believe? but, Were you a doer, or talker only? And accordingly they shall be judged. The end of the world is compared to our harvest; and you know men at harvest regard nothing but fruit."

LUKE VII. 1—10.

1 Now when he had ended all his sayings in the audience of the people, he entered into Capernaum.

2 And a certain centurion's servant, who was dear unto him, was sick, and ready to die.

3 And when he heard of Jesus, he sent unto him the elders of the Jews, beseeching him that he would come and heal his servant.

4 And when they came to Jesus, they besought him instantly, saying, That he was worthy for whom he should do this:

5 For he loveth our nation, and he hath built us a synagogue.

6 Then Jesus went with them. And when he was now not far from the house, the centurion sent friends to him, saying unto him, Lord, trouble not thyself: for I am not worthy that thou shouldest enter under my roof:

7 Wherefore neither thought I myself worthy to come unto thee: but say in a word, and my servant shall be healed.

8 For I also am a man set under authority, having under me soldiers, and I say unto one, Go, and he goeth; and to another, Come, and he cometh; and to my servant, Do this, and he doeth it.

9 When Jesus heard these things, he marvelled at him, and turned him about, and said unto the people that followed him, I say unto you, I have not found so great faith, no, not in Israel.

10 And they that were sent, returning to the house, found the servant whole that had been sick.

THESE verses describe the miraculous cure of a sick man. A centurion, or officer in the Roman army, applies to our Lord on behalf of his servant, and obtains what he requests. A greater miracle of healing than this, is nowhere recorded in the Gospels. Without even seeing the sufferer, without touch of hand or look of eye, our Lord restores health to a dying man by a single word. He speaks, and the sick man is cured. He commands, and the disease departs. We read of no prophet or apostle, who wrought miracles in this manner. We see here the finger of God.

We should notice in these verses *the kindness of the centurion.* It is a part of his character which appears in three ways. We see it in his treatment of his servant. He cares for him tenderly when sick, and takes pains to have him restored to health.—We see it again in his feeling towards the Jewish people. He did not despise them as other Gentiles commonly did. The elders of the Jews bear this strong testimony, "He loveth our nation."—We see it lastly in his liberal support of the Jewish place of worship at Capernaum. He did not love Israel "in word and tongue only, but in deed." The messengers he sent to our Lord supported their petition by saying, " He hath built us a synagogue."

Now where did the centurion learn this kindness? How can we account for one who was a heathen by birth, and a soldier by profession, showing such a spirit as this? Habits of mind like these were not likely to be gathered from heathen teaching, or promoted by the society of a Roman camp. Greek and Latin philosophy would not recommend them. Tribunes, consuls, prefects and emperors would not encourage them.—There is but one account of the matter. The centurion was what he was "by the grace of God." The Spirit had opened the eyes of his understanding, and put a new heart within him. His knowledge of divine things no doubt was very dim. His religious views were probably built on a very imperfect acquaintance with the Old Testament Scriptures. But whatever light from above he had, it influenced his life, and one result of it was the kindness which is recorded in this passage.

Let us learn a lesson from the centurion's example. Let us, like him, show kindness to every one with whom we have to do. Let us strive to have an eye ready to see, and a hand ready to help, and a heart ready to feel, and a will ready to do good to all. Let us be ready to weep with them that weep, and rejoice with them that rejoice. This is one way to recommend our religion, and make it beautiful before men. Kindness is a grace that all can understand.—This is one way to be like our blessed Saviour. If there is one feature in His character more notable than another, it is His unwearied kindness and love.—This is one way to be happy in the world, and see good days. Kindness always brings its own reward. The kind person will seldom be without friends.

We should notice, secondly, in this passage, *the humility of the centurion.* It appears in his remarkable message to our Lord when He was not far from his house: " I am not worthy that thou shouldest enter under my roof:— neither thought I myself worthy to come unto thee."— Such expressions are a striking contrast to the language used by the elders of the Jews. " He is worthy," said they, " for whom thou shouldest do this."—" I am not worthy," says the good centurion, " that thou shouldest enter under my roof."

Humility like this is one of the strongest evidences of the indwelling of the Spirit of God. We know nothing of it by nature, for we are all born proud. To convince us of sin, to shew us our own vileness and corruption, to put us in our right place, to make us lowly and self-abased, —these are among the principal works which the Holy Ghost works in the soul of man. Few of our Lord's sayings are so often repeated as the one which closes the parable of the Pharisee and Publican : " Every one that exalteth himself shall be abased, and he that humbleth himself shall be exalted." (Luke xviii. 14.) To have great gifts, and do great works for God, is not given to all believers. But all believers ought to strive to be clothed with humility.

We should notice, thirdly, in this passage, *the centurion's faith.* We have a beautiful example of it in the request that he made to our Lord : " Say in a word, and my ser- vant shall be healed." He thinks it needless for our Lord to come to the place where his servant lay dying. He regards our Lord as one possessing authority over diseases, as complete as his own authority over his soldiers, or a Roman Emperor's authority over himself. He believes that a word of command from Jesus is sufficient to send sickness away. He asks to see no sign or wonder. He declares his confidence that Jesus is an almighty Master and King, and that diseases, like obedient servants, will at once depart at His orders.

Faith like this was indeed rare when the Lord Jesus was upon earth. "Show us a sign from heaven," was the demand of the sneering Pharisees. To see something wonderful was the great desire of the multitudes who crowded after our Lord. No wonder that we read the remarkable words, "Jesus marvelled at him," and said unto the people, "I have not found so great faith, no, not in Israel." None ought to have been so believing as the children of those who were led through the wilderness, and brought into the promised land. But the last was first and the first last. The faith of a Roman soldier proved stronger than that of the Jews.

Let us not forget to walk in the steps of this blessed spirit of faith which the centurion here exhibited. Our eyes do not yet behold the book of life. We see not our Saviour pleading for us at God's right hand. But have we the word of Christ's promises? Then let us rest on it and fear nothing. Let us not doubt that every word that Christ has spoken shall be made good. The word of Christ is a sure foundation. He that leans upon it shall never be confounded. Believers shall all be found pardoned, justified, and glorified at the last day. "Jesus says so," and therefore it shall be done.

We should notice, finally, in these verses, *the advantage of being connected with godly families.* We need no clearer proof of this than the case of the centurion's servant. We see him cared for in sickness. We see him restored to health through his master's intercession. We see him brought under Christ's notice through his master's faith. Who can tell but the issue of the whole history, was the conversion and salvation of the man's soul? It was a happy day for that servant, when he first took service in such a household!

Well would it be for the Church, if the benefits of connection with "the household of faith," were more frequently remembered by professing Christians. Often, far too often, a Christian parent will hastily place his son in a position where his soul can get no good, for the sake of mere worldly advantage. Often, far too often, a Christian servant will seek a new place, where religion is not valued, for the sake of a little more wages. These things ought not so to be. In all our moves, our first thought should be the interest of our souls. In all our settlements, our chief desire should be to be connected with godly people. In all our scheming and planning, for ourselves or our children, one question should ever be uppermost in our minds: "What shall it profit to gain the whole world, and lose our own souls?" Good situations, as they are called, are often godless situations, and ruin to all eternity those who take them.

NOTES. LUKE VII. 1—10.

1.—[*Into Capernaum.*] Let it be remembered that a remarkable miracle of healing had already been worked at Capernaum in the cure of the ruler's son, described at the end of the fourth

chapter of St. John. This cure was distinct from that described
here. The Centurion had in all probability heard of it. Few
places, let it be noted, witnessed more of our Lord's miracles
than Capernaum. This circumstance probably throws light on
our Lord's expression, "Capernaum, which art exalted unto
heaven." (Matt. xi. 23.)

2.—[*A certain Centurion's servant.*] Some things in the history
of this miracle call for remarks, which, for convenience sake, may
be made here.

The Centurion here spoken of, was evidently a Gentile by
birth. This is manifest from our Lord's expression, "I have
not found so great faith, no, not in Israel."

In a Roman soldier such faith and love as we see here described, were very extraordinary. "A Roman soldier," says Bunyan,
"was the first fruit of the Gentile world."—"Even the bloody
trade of war," says Bishop Hall, "yielded worthy clients to
Christ. This Roman captain had learned to believe in that
Jesus, whom many Jews despised. No nation, no trade, can
shut out a good heart from God. If he was a foreigner in birth,
yet he was a domestic in heart." It is worthy of remark, that
neither here, nor in the case of soldiers who came to John the
Baptist, nor in the case of Cornelius in the Acts, do we find the
slightest hint that the profession of a soldier is unlawful in the
sight of God. On the contrary, both here and in the history of
such men as Colonel Gardiner and General Havelock, we see proof
that God can give much grace to soldiers, and put much honour
on them.

The Centurion's conduct towards his servant, is very note-
worthy. When we remember the position of servants in Gentile
households, his care and kindness towards this servant are a
strong evidence of the grace which he possessed.

3.—[*He sent unto him the elders.*] Bishop Hall observes here:
"Great variety of visitors resorted to Christ. One comes to Him
for a son, another for a daughter; a third for himself. I see none
come to Him for his servant but this one Centurion. Neither
was he a better man than a master. His servant is sick: he
doth not drive him out of doors, but lays him at home; neither
doth he stand gazing by his bedside, but seeks forth; he
seeks forth not to physicians, but to Christ.—Had the master
been sick the faithfullest servant could have done no more. He
is unworthy to be well served that will not sometimes wait upon
his followers."

5.—[*He hath built us a synagogue.*] The English version here can
hardly be said to give the full sense of the Greek. The meaning
is, "He hath himself built us a synagogue;" that is, at his own
expense and charges.

6—[*Sent friends to him.*] In the parallel passage in St. Matthew, both here and in the beginning of the narrative, the centurion is represented as coming to our Lord in person, and not by the intervention of messengers or friends. This variation in the two accounts has induced some to think that St. Matthew and St. Luke are describing two different miracles. This view is ingeniously defended by Flacius Illyricus. But there seems no sufficient ground for it.—Matthew's account of the miracle is evidently shorter, and more abridged than that of Luke, and he may perhaps speak of the Centurion as doing some things himself, which a more full and complete narrative shows that he did by others. "This," says Trench, "is an exchange of persons, of which all historical narrations, and all the language of common life, is full."—It is highly probable however that the narratives of both the Gospels are literally accurate, and do not require the explanation just given. In all probability the Centurion first sent messengers to our Lord, and afterwards went to speak to Him in person. St. Matthew relates the personal interview, and St. Luke the message. On this view both accounts are true, and do not clash with one another.

Apparent discrepancies between the Gospel narratives, be it noted, are often explainable in this way. Common fairness should make us remember that two men in daily life may describe the same event, and both speak the truth, and yet their accounts may not be precisely the same. And the reason of it is simply this. One man dwells on one circumstance of the story and the other on another. Each brings out his own point more fully than the other. Yet each speaks truth.

The slightly varying accounts which two faithful historians give of the same public events, and the slightly varying evidence which two honest witnesses will often give in a court of justice about the same facts, are striking illustrations of what I mean. In short an entire sameness in the stories told by two separate witnesses is sometimes in itself suspicious, because it looks like concert, collusion, and an attempt to deceive.

[*Trouble not thyself.*] The Greek word so translated is only used three times in the New Testament : here, and at Mark v. 35, and Luke viii. 49 ; and each time in the same sense, as descriptive of persons giving unnecessary trouble and fatigue to our Lord.

7.—[*Say in a word.*] The Portuguese Commentator, Barradius, has some striking remarks on this expression of the Centurion's. He says, " This is a peculiar attribute of God's, to be able to do all things by a word and a command. 'He spake and they were made :' 'He commanded and they were created.' (Psalm cxlviii. 5.) Read the book of Genesis. You will see the world created by the word of God : ' God said, Let there be light, and there was light.' ' God said, Let there be a firmament,' and a firmament was

made," &c. He then shows by a quotation from Augustine,
how all the created beings in existence, whether kings, or angels,
or seraphims, cannot create so much as an ant. But when God
says, " Let the world be made," at once it is made by a word.
And he concludes, " Well therefore does the Centurion say, ' say
in a word only, and my servant shall be healed.'"

9.—[*He marvelled at him.*] There are two occasions where it is
recorded that our Lord Jesus Christ " marvelled," once in this
history, and once in Mark vi. 6. It is remarkable that in one
case He is described as marvelling at "faith," and in the other as
marvelling at "unbelief." Bishop Hall, and Burkitt after him,
both observe, " What can be more wonderful than to see Christ
wonder ? "

The expression is one of those which show the reality of our
Lord's human nature. He was made like unto us in all things,
sin only excepted. As man He grew in wisdom and stature.
As man He hungered, thirsted, was weary, ate, drank, slept,
wept, sorrowed, rejoiced, groaned, agonized, bled, suffered and
died. And so also as man He wondered. Yet all this time
He was very and eternal God, one with the Father, and the
Saviour of the world. This is a great mystery, and one which
we cannot fathom. The union of two natures in one Person,
is a thing passing our weak comprehension. We must believe
and admire, without attempting to define or explain.

In the case in Mark the marvelling is evidently a marvelling
of sorrow. In the case before us it is a marvelling of admiration. Burkitt remarks, " Let it teach us to place our admiration
where Christ placed His. Let us be more affected with the
least measure of grace in a good man, than with all the gaieties
and glories of a great man." Our Lord be it remembered,
did not marvel at the gorgeous and beautiful buildings of the
Jewish temple. But he did marvel at faith.

LUKE VII. 11—17.

11 And it came to pass the day after, that he went into a city called
Nain ; and many of his disciples went
with him, and much people.

12 Now when he came nigh to the
gate of the city, behold there was a
dead man carried out, the only son of
his mother, and she was a widow :
and much people of the city was with
her.

13 And when the Lord saw her, he
had compassion on her, and said unto
her, Weep not.

14 And he came and touched the

bier : and they that bare *him* stood
still. And he said, Young man, I say
unto thee, Arise.

15 And he that was dead sat up,
and began to speak. And he delivered
him to his mother.

16 And there came a fear on all :
and they glorified God, saying, That
a great prophet is risen up among us ;
and, That God hath visited his people.

17 And this rumour of him went
forth throughout all Judæa, and
throughout all the region round
about.

THE wondrous event described in these verses, is only recorded in St. Luke's Gospel. It is one of the three great instances of our Lord restoring a dead person to life, and, like the raising of Lazarus and the ruler's daughter, is rightly regarded as one of the greatest miracles which He wrought on earth. In all three cases, we see an exercise of divine power. In each we see a comfortable proof that the Prince of Peace is stronger than the king of terrors, and that though death, the last enemy, is mighty, he is not so mighty as the sinner's Friend.

We learn from these verses, *what sorrow sin has brought into the world.* We are told of a funeral at Nain. All funerals are mournful things, but it is difficult to imagine a funeral more mournful than the one here described. It was the funeral of a young man, and that young man the only son of his mother, and that mother a widow. There is not an item in the whole story, which is not full of misery. And all this misery, be it remembered, was brought into the world by sin. God did not create it at the beginning, when He made all things "very good." Sin is the cause of it all. "Sin entered into the world" when Adam fell, "and death by sin." (Rom. v. 12.)

Let us never forget this great truth. The world around us is full of sorrow. Sickness, and pain, and infirmity, and poverty, and labour, and trouble, abound on every side. From one end of the world to the other, the history of families is full of lamentation, and weeping, and mourning, and woe. And whence does it all come? Sin is the fountain and root to which all must be traced. There would neither have been tears, nor cares, nor illness, nor deaths, nor funerals in the earth, if there had been no sin. We must bear this state of things patiently. We cannot alter it. We may thank God that there is a remedy in the Gospel, and that this life is not all. But in the mean time, let us lay the blame at the right door. Let us lay the blame on sin.

How much we ought to hate sin! Instead of loving it, cleaving to it, dallying with it, excusing it, playing with it, we ought to hate it with a deadly hatred. Sin is the great murderer, and thief, and pestilence, and nuisance of this world. Let us make no peace with it. Let us wage a ceaseless warfare against it. It is "the abominable thing which God hateth." Happy is he who is of one mind with God, and can say, I "abhor that which is evil." (Rom. xii. 9.)

We learn, secondly, from these verses, *how deep is the compassion of our Lord Jesus Christ's heart.* We see this beautifully brought out in His behaviour at this funeral in Nain. He meets the mournful procession, accompanying the young man to his grave, and is moved with compassion at the sight. He waits not to be applied to for help. His help appears to have been neither asked for nor expected. He saw the weeping mother, and knew well what her feelings must have been, for He had been born of a woman Himself. At once He addressed her with words alike startling and touching :—He "said unto her, Weep not."—A few more seconds, and the meaning of His words became plain. The widow's son was restored to her alive. Her darkness was turned into light, and her sorrow into joy.

Our Lord Jesus Christ never changes. He is the same

yesterday, to-day, and for ever. His heart is still as
compassionate as when He was upon earth. His sympathy with sufferers is still as strong. Let us bear this
in mind, and take comfort in it. There is no friend or
comforter who can be compared to Christ. In all our
days of darkness, which must needs be many, let us first
turn for consolation to Jesus the Son of God. He will
never fail us, never disappoint us, never refuse to take
interest in our sorrows. He lives, who made the widow's
heart sing for joy in the gate of Nain. He lives, to
receive all labouring and heavy-laden ones, if they will
only come to Him by faith. He lives, to heal the brokenhearted, and be a Friend that sticketh closer than a
brother. And He lives to do greater things than these
one day. He lives to come again to His people, that
they may weep no more at all, and that all tears may be
wiped from their eyes.

We learn, lastly, from these verses, *the almighty power
of our Lord Jesus Christ.* We can ask no proof of this
more striking than the miracle which we are now considering. He gives back life to a dead man with a
few words. He speaks to a cold corpse, and at once it
becomes a living person. In a moment, in the twinkling
of an eye, the heart, the lungs, the brain, the senses,
again resume their work and discharge their duty.
"Young man," He cried, "I say unto thee arise."
That voice was a voice mighty in operation. At once
" he that was dead sat up and began to speak."

Let us see in this mighty miracle a pledge of that
solemn event, the general resurrection. That same Jesus
who here raised one dead person, shall raise all mankind

at the last day. "The hour cometh in the which all that
are in the grave shall hear His voice, and shall come forth;
they that have done good unto the resurrection of life, and
they that have done evil unto the resurrection of damnation." (John v. 28, 29.) When the trumpet sounds and
Christ commands, there can be no refusal or escape. All
must appear before His bar in their bodies. And all
shall be judged according to their works.

Let us see, furthermore, in this mighty miracle, a
lively emblem of Christ's power to quicken the dead in
sins. In Him is life. He quickeneth whom He will.
(John v. 21.) He can raise to a new life souls that now
seem dead in worldliness and sin. He can say to hearts that
now appear corrupt and lifeless, "Arise to repentance, and
live to the service of God." Let us never despair of any
soul. Let us pray for our children, and faint not. Our
young men and our young women may long seem travelling on the way to ruin. But let us pray on. Who can
tell but He that met the funeral in the gates of Nain
may yet meet our unconverted children, and say with
almighty power, "Young man, arise." With Christ
nothing is impossible.

Let us leave the passage with a solemn recollection of
those things which are yet to happen at the last day.
We read that "there came a fear on all," at Nain, when
the young man was raised. What then shall be the
feelings of mankind when all the dead are raised at
once? The unconverted man may well fear that day.
He is not prepared to meet God.—But the true Christian
has nothing to fear. He may lay him down and sleep
peacefully in his grave. In Christ He is complete and

safe, and when he rises again he shall see God's face in peace.

11.—[*The day after.*] It would appear from this expression, that the miracle recorded in these verses, was the first instance of our Lord raising a dead person to life. The daughter of Jairus was the second instance, and Lazarus the third. This order of the three miracles is disputed by some. But the internal evidence in favour of it, seems too strong to be put aside. Remembering this, we may understand the sensation that the miracle would create among all Jews who heard of it. No person had been raised from the dead, since the days of Elisha, a period of nine hundred years.

[*A city called Nain.*] This place is nowhere else mentioned in the Bible. It is a small town on the northern slope of the lesser Mount Hermon, of which the ruins and the name remain to the present day. Mr. Burgon says, that an ancient burying place is even now distinguishable at the lower part of the hill, not far from the ruins.

12.—[*A dead man carried out.*] Let us note that the place of burial was outside the city. It is curious to observe how strongly almost all commentators dwell on this point, and urge the impropriety of the practice of burying the dead in church yards, and among the living.

[*Much people...was with her.*] This expression should not be overlooked. It shows the publicity of the great miracle here recorded. It was wrought before many witnesses.

13.—[*When the Lord saw her He had compassion.*] Poole's remarks on this expression are worth reading: "None moved our Lord on behalf of the widow, neither do we read that she herself spake to Him. But our Saviour's bowels were moved at the sight of her sorrows, and consideration of her loss. It is observable that our Saviour wrought His healing miracles, 1, sometimes at the motion and desire of the parties to be healed; 2, sometimes at the desire of others on their behalf; 3, sometimes of His own free motion, neither themselves nor others soliciting Him for any such mercies toward them."—The leper was healed (Luke v. 12,) in reply to his own personal application;—the centurion's servant, (Luke vii. 1,) in reply to the prayer of his master,—and the widow's son was raised without any one interceding on his behalf.

14.—[*The bier.*] The Greek word so translated, is only found here in the New Testament. It would not have been correct to translate it "coffin." The practice of burying in coffins was apparently unknown among the Jews. In the case before us, the young man's body probably laid on a sort of couch. In Bonar's travels in Palestine, he describes a funeral which he saw, and says that the bier was like "a large cradle."

[*I say unto thee arise.*] We should carefully note the wide difference between our Lord's manner of working miracles, and the manner in which they were worked by His prophets and apostles. There is an authority and divine power about the miracles recorded in the Gospels, which we do not see in the history of the other miracles in the Bible. Euthymius remarks, "Of old time indeed the prophet Elijah raised again the son of the widow of Sarepta, but by humbling himself before God, and supplication to Him. (1 Kings xvii. 20, 21.) So also the prophet Elisha raised the son of the Shunammite woman, but only after having stretched himself out upon his body. (2 Kings iv. 34, 35.) But Jesus only touching and commanding, at once raised the dead person."

Burkitt remarks, "The Socinians here own that Christ raised this young man by a divine power, which God had communicated to Him, yet deny Him at the same time to be essentially God. But let them prove, if they can, that a divine power which is proper to God alone, ever was, or ever can, be communicated to a creature, without the communication of the divine nature. True, we find Peter commanding Tabitha to arise. (Acts ix. 40,) but we find all he did was by faith in Christ, and by prayer unto Christ. But Christ here raised the widow's son without prayer, purely by His own power; which undeniably proves Him to be God."

15.—[*Began to speak.*] This fact is mentioned, in order to place it beyond doubt, that the young man was really restored to life. Where there is speech, there must be life.

Let it be observed, that we have no record given to us of anything that was ever said or thought by those who were miraculously raised from the dead. Their experience and knowledge are wisely withheld from us.

16.—[*There came a fear.*] This expression, and the rest of the verse, as well as the verse following, appear to furnish strong proof that this was the first instance of a dead person being restored to life by our Lord, during His ministry on earth.

[*God hath visited His people.*] This expression should be compared with Luke i. 68, and Luke i. 78, and with many places in the Old Testament—such as Ruth i. 6, 1 Sam. ii. 21, Job xxxv. 15, Jerem. vi. 6. It appears to signify any remarkable divine interposition, either in the way of mercy or of judgment, and does not necessarily signify, in this place, a personal visitation. That "God was manifest in the flesh," when Christ became man for us, is an undeniable truth of Scripture. But it cannot be proved that it is taught in this text.

17.—[*This rumour of Him went forth, &c.*] Poole remarks, "The people here saw His divine power manifestly exerted; for the keys of the clouds, the womb, and the grave, are those keys which their teachers had taught them were kept in God's hand alone."

LUKE VII. 18—23.

18 And the disciples of John shewed him of all these things.

19 And John calling *unto him* two of his disciples sent *them* to Jesus, saying, Art thou he that should come? or look we for another?

20 When the men were come unto him, they said, John Baptist hath sent us unto thee, saying, Art thou he that should come? or look we for another?

21 And in the same hour he cured many of *their* infirmities and plagues and of evil spirits; and unto many *that were* blind he gave sight.

22 Then Jesus answering said unto them, Go your way, and tell John what things ye have seen and heard; how that the blind see, the lame walk, the lepers are cleansed, the deaf hear, the dead are raised, to the poor the Gospel is preached.

23 And blessed is *he*, whosoever shall not be offended in me.

THE message which John the Baptist sent to our Lord, in these verses, is peculiarly instructing, when we consider the circumstances under which it was sent. John the Baptist was now a prisoner in the hands of Herod. "He heard in the prison the works of Christ." (Matt. xi. 2.) His life was drawing to a close. His opportunities of active usefulness were ended. A long imprisonment, or a violent death, were the only prospects before him. Yet even in these dark days, we see this holy man maintaining his old ground, as a witness to Christ. He is the same man that he was when he cried, "Behold the Lamb of God." To testify of Christ, was his continual work as a preacher at liberty. To send men to Christ, was one of his last works as a prisoner in chains.

We should mark, in these verses, *the wise fore-thought which John exhibited about his disciples, before he left the world.* He sent some of them to Jesus, with a message of inquiry,—"Art thou he that should come, or do we look for another?" He doubtless calculated that they would receive such an answer as would make an indelible impression on their minds. And he was right. They got an answer in deeds, as well as words,—an answer which probably produced a deeper effect than any arguments which they could have heard from their master's lips.

We can easily imagine that John the Baptist must have felt much anxiety about the future course of his disciples. He knew their ignorance and weakness in the faith. He knew how natural it was for them to regard the disciples of Jesus with feelings of jealousy and envy. He knew how likely it was that petty party-spirit would creep in among them, and make them keep aloof from Christ when their own master was dead and gone. Against this unhappy state of things he makes provision, as far as possible, while he is yet alive. He sends some of them to Jesus, that they may see for themselves what kind of teacher He is, and not reject Him unseen and unheard. He takes care to supply them with the strongest evidence that our Lord was indeed the Messiah. Like his divine Master, having loved his disciples, he loved them to the end. And now, perceiving that he must soon leave them, he strives to leave them in the best of hands. He does his best to make them acquainted with Christ.

What an instructive lesson we have here for ministers, and parents, and heads of families,—for all, in short, who have anything to do with the souls of others! We should endeavour, like John the Baptist, to provide for the future spiritual welfare of those we leave behind, when we die. We should often remind them, that we cannot always be with them. We should often urge them to beware of the broad way, when we are taken from them, and they are left alone in the world. We should spare no pains to make all, who in any way look up to us, acquainted with Christ. Happy are those ministers and parents, whose consciences can testify on their death-beds, that they have told their hearers and children to go to Jesus, and follow Him !

We should mark, secondly in these verses, *the peculiar answer which the disciples of John received from our Lord.* We are told that "in the same hour He cured many of their infirmities and plagues." And then, "He said unto them, Go your way, and tell John what things ye have seen and heard." He makes no formal declaration that He is the Messiah that was to come. He simply supplies the messengers with facts to repeat to their master, and sends them away. He knew well how John the Baptist would employ these facts. He would say to his disciples, "Behold in Him who worked these miracles, the prophet greater than Moses.—This is He whom you must hear and follow, when I am dead.—This is indeed the Christ."

Our Lord's reply to John's disciples, contains a great practical lesson, which we shall do well to remember. It teaches us that the right way to test the value of Churches and ministers, is to examine the works they do for God, and the fruits they bring forth. Would we know whether a Church is true and trust-worthy ?— Would we know whether a minister is really called of God, and sound in the faith ?—We must apply the old rule of Scripture, "Ye shall know them by their fruits." As Christ would be known by His works and doctrine, so must true Churches of Christ, and true ministers of Christ. When the dead in sin are not quickened, and the blind are not restored to sight, and the poor have no glad tidings proclaimed to them, we may generally suspect that Christ's presence is wanting. Where He is, He will be seen and heard. Where He is, there will not only be profession, forms, ceremonies, and a show of religion. There will be actual, visible work in hearts and lives.

We should mark, lastly, in these verses, *the solemn warning which our Lord gave to John's disciples.* He knew the danger in which they were. He knew that they were disposed to question His claim to be the Messiah, because of His lowly appearance. They saw no signs of a king about Him, no riches, no royal apparel, no guards, no courtiers, and no crown. They only saw a man, to all appearance poor as any one of themselves, attended by a few fishermen and publicans. Their pride rebelled at the idea of such an one as this being the Christ! It seemed incredible! There must be some mistake! Such thoughts as these, in all probability, passed through their minds. Our Lord read their hearts, and dismissed them with a searching caution. "Blessed," He said, "is he that is not offended in me."

The warning is one that is just as needful now as it was when it was delivered. So long as the world stands, Christ and His Gospel will be a stumbling block to many. To hear that we are all lost and guilty sinners, and cannot save ourselves,—to hear that we must give up our own righteousness, and trust in One who was crucified between two thieves,—to hear that we must be content to enter heaven side by side with publicans and harlots, and to owe all our salvation to free grace,—this is always offensive to the natural man. Our proud hearts do not like it. We are offended.

Let the caution of these verses sink down deeply into our memories. Let us take heed that we are not offended. Let us beware of being stumbled, either by the humbling doctrines of the Gospel, or the holy practice which it enjoins on those who receive it. Secret pride is one of the worst enemies of man. It will prove at last to have been the ruin of thousands of souls. Thousands will be found to have had the offer of salvation, but to have rejected it. They did not like the terms. They would not stoop to "enter in at the strait gate." They would not humbly come as sinners to the throne of grace. In a word, they were offended. And then will appear the deep meaning of our Lord's words, "Blessed is he who shall not be offended in me."

NOTES. LUKE VII. 18—23.

19.—[*John calling unto him...disciples sent them to Jesus.*] The reason why John the Baptist sent this message to our Lord, is explained by different commentators in widely different ways. Those who wish to see the subject fully discussed should read what Chemnitius and Barradius say about it.

Some think that John sent this message at a time when his faith was failing. They think that like many other saints in the Bible, he had his moments of weakness, and that his imprisonment, together with the fact that our Lord did nothing to deliver him, had made him begin to doubt whether Jesus was the Messiah. This explanation was maintained by Tertullian, but it is not satisfactory.

Some think that John sent his message not from unbelief, but from a desire to obtain information. He regarded himself as delivered to death, and on the brink of the grave. He desired to know whether he was to announce in the world beyond the grave that the Messiah was coming after him. This explanation seems so absurd that it needs no refutation, and were it not that it is maintained (according to Barradius,) by Jerome, Gregory the Great, and Beda, it would not be worth mentioning.

The most probable explanation is that which I have set forth in the exposition of the passage. John's message was not sent on his account, but on account of his disciples. It was not sent because his own faith was failing, but because he wished those he was about to leave behind him to believe in Jesus as the Messiah.—One argument in favour of this view is the great improbability that one so eminently taught of God as John was, and so singularly clear in his past testimony, would forget his first faith and doubt whether Jesus was the Christ.—Another, and far more powerful argument, is the strong language of commendation which our Lord uses about John the Baptist as soon as his messengers had left Him. His expressions are so peculiarly strong, that we might suppose they were specially intended to prevent any slur being thrown on John's character on account of his message. They look as if our Lord would have all men know that John's own faith never failed, and that he was the same man at the end of his course that he was at the beginning.

The view now set forth is maintained by Hilary, Augustine, Chrysostom, Theophylact, and the great majority of the best commentators.

[*He that should come.*] This expression might be rendered more literally, "the coming One." It seems to have been an expression specially applied to the Messiah. John iv. 25. and xi. 27. Chemnitius says, that the word in Hebrew signifies not merely one who comes to a place, but one who comes to enter upon an office, and occupy a position.

20.—[*John Baptist hath sent us.*] It is very difficult to see why our English translators in this place have used the expression "John Baptist," and not "John the Baptist," as at verses 28 and 33. I can detect nothing in the Greek version, to warrant the omission of the word "the."

21.—[*Infirmities...plagues...evil spirits.*] Let it be noted that evil spirits are here mentioned as an affliction distinct from any bodily ailments. Bishop Pearce remarks, "We may conclude that evil spirits are reckoned by St. Luke, (who speaks of distempers with more accuracy than the other evangelists,) as things different from any disorders of the body included in the two former words."

[*He gave sight.*] There is something very peculiar in the Greek words so translated, which our version can hardly convey. It might be rendered, "he made a present of seeing."

22.—[*The dead are raised.*] The question has often been asked, To whom does our Lord refer, in saying this? We only know of one dead person restored to life by Christ up to the present time. That person was the widow's son at Nain.

The answer is simply this. It is mere assumption to say that no dead person was raised to life beside those whose cases are described, during the period of our Lord's earthly ministry. It is unreasonable to suppose that all our Lord's miracles are recorded in the Gospels. He doubtless did many mighty works, beside those which are there described. See John xxi. 25. Augustine in his sermon on this miracle, says: "Who knows how many dead the Lord raised visibly? For all the things that He did are not written. John tells us this. So then there were without doubt many others raised."

[*To the poor the Gospel is preached.*] That this was a sign of Messiah's times appears plain from the words of Isaiah: "In that day the poor among men shall rejoice in the holy one of Israel." (Isa. xxix. 19.) Contempt for the poor, as ignorant and despicable, appears to have been very common in the times of the Gospel. (John vii. 49. ix. 34. and James ii. 24.) Concern and tender interest about the souls of the poor, as souls which would live as long as the souls of rich men, was a distinguishing feature of our Lord's ministry, and of that of His apostles. It is always an evil sign of the state of a Church when the spiritual wants of the lower orders are neglected, and the rich man's way to heaven is made smoother than the way of the poor.

LUKE VII. 24—30.

24 And when the messengers of John were departed, he began to speak unto the people concerning John, What went ye out into the wilderness for to see? A reed shaken with the wind?

25 But what went ye out for to see? A man clothed in soft raiment? Behold, they which are gorgeously apparelled, and live delicately, are in kings' courts.

26 But what went ye out for to see? A prophet? Yea, I say unto you, and much more than a prophet.

27 This is *he*, of whom it is written, Behold, I send my messenger before thy face, which shall prepare thy way before thee.

28 For I say unto you, Among those that are born of woman there is not a greater prophet than John the Baptist: but he that is least in the kingdom of God is greater than he.

29 And all the people that heard *him*, and the Publicans, justified God, being baptized with the baptism of John.

30 But the Pharisees and Lawyers rejected the counsel of God against themselves, being not baptized of him.

THE first point that demands our notice in this passage, is *the tender care which Jesus takes of the characters of His faithful servants.* He defends the reputation of John the

Baptist, as soon as his messengers were departed. He saw that the people around him were apt to think lightly of John, partly because he was in prison, partly because of the inquiry which his disciples had just brought. He pleads the cause of His absent friend in warm and strong language. He bids His hearers dismiss from their minds their unworthy doubts and suspicions about this holy man. He tells them that John was no wavering and unstable character, a mere reed shaken by the wind. He tells them that John was no mere courtier and hanger on about king's palaces, though circumstances at the end of his ministry had brought him into connection with king Herod. He declares to them that John was "much more than a prophet," for he was a prophet who had been the subject of prophecy himself. And he winds up his testimony by the remarkable saying, that "among those that are born of woman there is not a greater prophet than John the Baptist."

There is something deeply touching in these sayings of our Lord on behalf of his absent servant. The position which John now occupied as Herod's prisoner was widely different from that which he occupied at the beginning of his ministry. At one time he was the best-known and most popular preacher of his day. There was a time when "there went out to him Jerusalem and all Judæa,—and were baptized in Jordan." (Matt. iii. 5.) Now he was a solitary prisoner in Herod's hands, deserted, friendless, and with nothing before him but death. But the want of man's favour is no proof that God is displeased. John the Baptist had one Friend who never failed him and never forsook him,—a Friend whose kindness did not ebb and

flow like John's popularity, but was always the same.
That Friend was our Lord Jesus Christ.

There is comfort here for all believers who are sus-
pected, slandered, and falsely accused. Few are the
children of God who do not suffer in this way, at some
time or other. The accuser of the brethren knows well
that character is one of the points in which he can most
easily wound a Christian. He knows well that slanders
are easily called into existence, greedily received and
propagated, and seldom entirely silenced. Lies and
false reports are the chosen weapons by which he labours to injure the Christian's usefulness, and destroy
his peace. But let all who are assaulted in their characters rest in the thought that they have an Advocate in
heaven who knows their sorrows. That same Jesus who
maintained the character of His imprisoned servant before
a Jewish crowd, will never desert any of His people.
The world may frown on them. Their names may be cast
out as evil by man. But Jesus never changes, and will
one day plead their cause before the whole world.

The second point which demands our attention in these
verses is, *the vast superiority of the privileges enjoyed by
believers under the New Testament, compared to those of
believers under the Old.* This is a lesson which appears to
be taught by one expression used by our Lord respecting
John the Baptist. After commending his graces and gifts,
He adds these remarkable words, " He that is least in the
kingdom of God is greater than he."

Our Lord's meaning in using this expression appears to
be simply this. He declares that the religious light of
the least disciple who lived after His crucifixion and re-

surrection, would be far greater than that of John Baptist, who died before those mighty events took place. The weakest believing hearer of St. Paul would understand things, by the light of Christ's death on the cross, which John the Baptist could never have explained. Great as that holy man was in faith and courage, the humblest Christian would, in one sense, be greater than he. Greater in grace and works he certainly could not be. But beyond doubt he would be greater in privileges and knowledge.

Such an expression as this ought to teach all Christians to be deeply thankful for Christianity. We have probably very little idea of the wide difference between the religious knowledge of the best-instructed Old Testament believer and the knowledge of one familiar with the New Testament. We little know how many blessed truths of the Gospel were at one time seen through a glass darkly, which now appear to us plain as noon-day. Our very familiarity with the Gospel makes us blind to the extent of our privileges. We can hardly realize at this time how many glorious verities of our faith were brought out in their full proportions by Christ's death on the cross, and were never unveiled and understood till His blood was shed. The hopes of John the Baptist and St. Paul were undoubtedly one and the same. Both were led by one Spirit. Both knew their sinfulness. Both trusted in the Lamb of God. But we cannot suppose that John could have given as full an account of the way of salvation as St. Paul. Both looked at the same object of faith. But one saw it afar off, and could only describe it generally. The other saw it close at hand, and could describe the reason of his hope particularly. Let us learn to be more thankful. The child who knows the story of the cross, possesses a key to religious knowledge which patriarchs and prophets never enjoyed.

The last point which demands our attention in these verses is, *the solemn declaration which it makes about man's power to injure his own soul.* We read that "The Pharisees and Scribes rejected the counsel of God against themselves." The meaning of these words appears to be simply this, that they rejected God's offer of salvation. They refused to avail themselves of the door of repentance which was offered to them by John the Baptist's preaching. In short they fulfilled to the very letter the words of Solomon: "Ye have set at nought all my counsel and would none of my reproof." (Prov. i. 25.)

That every man possesses a power to ruin himself for ever in hell is a great foundation truth of Scripture, and a truth which ought to be continually before our minds. Impotent and weak as we all are for everything which is good, we are all naturally potent for that which is evil. By continued impenitence and unbelief, by persevering in the love and practice of sin, by pride, self-will, laziness, and determined love of the world, we may bring upon ourselves everlasting destruction. And if this takes place, we shall find that we have no one to blame but ourselves. God has "no pleasure in the death of him that dieth." (Ezek. xviii. 32.) Christ is "willing to gather" men to His bosom, if they will only be gathered. (Matt. xxii. 37.) The fault will lie at man's own door. They that are lost will find that they have "lost their own souls." (Mark viii. 36.)

What are we doing ourselves? This is the chief question that the passage should suggest to our minds. Are we likely to be lost or saved? Are we in the way towards heaven or hell? Have we received into our hearts that Gospel which we hear? Do we really live by that Bible which we profess to believe?—Or are we daily travelling towards the pit, and ruining our own souls? It is a painful thought that the Pharisees are not the only persons who "reject the counsel of God." There are thousands of persons called Christians who are continually doing the very same thing.

Notes. Luke VII. 24—30.

24.—[*What went ye out to see?...a reed, &c.*] Let it be noted that both here and in the two following verses the question is equivalent to a strong and positive affirmation. It is as if our Lord had said, "John the Baptist was not a reed shaken by the wind," —"was not a man clothed in soft raiment,"—"was not merely a prophet."—Such a form of expression is not uncommon in the Bible. A striking example is to be seen in the famous question, "what shall it profit a man to gain the whole world and lose his own soul?" It is equivalent to saying "It shall profit him nothing at all."

[*A reed shaken by the wind.*] Chemnitius observes that this is the very same expression which is used by the heathen satirist, Lucian, in describing the unsettled opinion of the philosophical sects.

25.—[*They which are gorgeously apparelled ... delicately.*] The literal translation of the Greek words here would be, "they that are in gorgeous apparel, and delicate living."

The words translated "delicate living," is only used in one other place in the New Testament, and there rendered, "riot." (2 Peter ii. 13.)

28.—[*Among those...born of women.*] Chrysostom thinks, that by this expression our Lord "tacitly excepted himself. For though He too was born of a woman, yet not as John, for He was not a mere man, neither was He born in like manner as man, but by a strange and wondrous kind of birth." This is not a satisfactory interpretation, and seems to involve dangerous consequences.

[*He that is least...greater than he.*] There are many diverse and strange opinions among the commentators about the meaning of these words. Those who wish to examine them, will find a full account of them in Chemnitius and Barradius.

Some think, that the "least in the kingdom of God," means the least of those who receive Christian baptism, and that John the Baptist never having been baptized, was never regenerated by the Holy Spirit, and therefore was inferior to the humblest person baptized by the Apostles. This is the opinion of Cyril. It is too absurd to require refutation. To say of John who was "filled with the Holy Ghost from his mother's womb," that he was not born again of the Spirit, is preposterous, and revolting to common sense.

Some think, that the "least in the kingdom of God," means the least saint in heaven. This is the opinion of Jerome and Beda.

Some think, that the "least in the kingdom," means the least angel. This is the opinion of Ambrose, Bonaventura, and Thomas Aquinas.

Some think, that the "least in the kingdom," means our Lord Jesus Christ Himself, who humbled Himself and said, "I am a worm and no man." (Psalm xxii. 7.) This is the opinion of Augustine and Chrysostom, and has been maintained by many in every age. But it seems a strained and forced sense to place upon the words.

I believe the true interpretation to be the one I have maintained in the exposition. I believe the "least in the kingdom of God," to mean the least believer who lived after the crucifixion and resurrection of Christ. I believe the weakest member of the Churches planted by St. Paul, had a clearer knowledge of the exact manner in which God would justify the ungodly than John the Baptist, or any one who lived before the crucifixion ever could have. The contrast our Lord is drawing, is between the privileges of those who lived to see the great fountain of sin opened by His blood-shedding, and those who died before that blood was shed. We do not realize the enormous difference in the position of these two classes of persons. We do not sufficiently remember how very dimly and indistinctly many great saving truths must needs have been apprehended, before Christ died and the veil was rent in twain. The "way into the holiest was not made manifest," while John the Baptist lived, and for that reason Jesus says that the least member of the Gospel Church was "greater than he." His grace and gifts were not greater, but His knowledge and privileges decidedly were.

29.—[*And all the people that heard, &c.*] It is a disputed point whether this verse and the following one contain the words of

Christ or of St. Luke, whether they are a continuation of our
Lord's speech or a remark of the Evangelist's. The question
is discussed at length by Maldonatus.

The ancient commentators, including Ambrose, Beda, Euthymius, and, according to Thomas Aquinas, Chrysostom also,
regard the two verses as the words of our Lord. Chemnitius
supports this opinion.

Lyranus and the modern commentators regard the two verses
as the inspired comment of the Evangelist on what our Lord
had just been saying.

The question, perhaps, is not one of much importance. To
me the two verses appear to read awkwardly and unnaturally,
if taken as the words of the Lord. I should never have thought
of regarding them as anything but the words of St. Luke, if the
idea had not been suggested to me by others.

[*Justified God...being baptized.*] The meaning of this expression
appears to be, that "they declared their belief that John was a prophet sent from God, by submitting to his baptism." Burkitt says,
" Those who believe the message that God sendeth, and obey it,
justify God. They that do not believe and obey, accuse and
condemn God." Burgon says, "They acknowledged God's justice, mercy, truth, and goodness."

Let it be noted, that here as elsewhere in the New Testament,
it is impossible to interpret the word "justify" in the sense of
"*to make* just." Man cannot make God just. (see Ps. li. 4.)
The word means always, "To declare, count, or reckon just."
"Justified" persons are not persons who are *made* righteous,
but persons who are *reckoned* and counted righteous.

30.—[*Rejected the counsel of God against themselves.*] The meaning of this expression appears to be, that they despised, and
frustrated, and made of no avail the gracious offer of repentance
and salvation, which God sent to them by John the Baptist.

The Greek word translated "rejected" is more frequently
translated "despised." It is also rendered by the words to
"disannul," to "cast off," to "frustrate," and to "bring to
nothing." Luke x. 16; Gal. iii. 15; 1 Tim. v. 12; Gal. ii. 21;
1 Cor. i. 19.

The "counsel" spoken of here can in no wise be interpreted
as the everlasting counsel of God, whereby He has decreed to
save His own elect by Christ. This counsel shall stand. It is
not in the power of man to disannul or frustrate it. It probably
means here God's gracious purpose in sending John to preach
repentance, and that will of benevolence which God declares
Himself to have towards all mankind, and reveals in the Gospel.

The words "against themselves" might equally well have been

translated, "towards themselves." The marginal reading is "within" themselves, which seems less probable than either of of the other two senses. The general meaning of the whole sentence, which ever sense of the three we take, remains unaltered.

LUKE VII. 31—35.

31 And the Lord said, Whereunto then shall I liken the men of this generation? and to what are they like? 32 They are like unto children sitting in the marketplace, and calling one to another, and saying, We have piped unto you, and ye have not danced ; we have mourned to you, and ye have not wept.

33 For John the Baptist came neither eating bread nor drinking wine; and ye say, He hath a devil. 34 The Son of man is come eating and drinking; and ye say, Behold a gluttonous man, and a winebibber, a friend of Publicans and sinners! 35 But wisdom is justified of all her children.

WE learn in the first place, from these verses, that *the hearts of unconverted men are often desperately perverse as well as wicked.*

Our Lord brings out this lesson in a remarkable comparison, describing the generation of men among whom He lived while He was on earth. He compares them to children. He says, that children at play were not more wayward, perverse, and hard to please, than the Jews of His day. Nothing would satisfy them. They were always finding fault. Whatever ministry God employed among them, they took exception to it. Whatever messenger God sent among them, they were not pleased. First came John the Baptist, living a retired, ascetic, self-denying life. At once the Jews said, "he hath a devil."—After him the Son of Man came, eating and drinking, and adopting habits of social life like the ordinary run of men. At once the Jews accused Him of being "a gluttonous man, and a winebibber."—In short, it became evident that the Jews were determined to receive no message from God at all. Their pretended objections were only a cloak to cover over their hatred of God's truth. What they really disliked was, not so much God's ministers, as God Himself.

Perhaps we read this account with wonder and surprise. We think that never were men so wickedly unreasonable as these Jews were. But are we sure that their conduct is not continually repeated among Christians? Do we know that the same thing is continually going on around us at the present day? Strange as it may seem at first sight, the generation which will neither "dance" when their companions "pipe," nor "lament" when they "mourn," is only too numerous in the Church of Christ.

Is it not a fact that many who strive to serve Christ faithfully, and walk closely with God, find their neighbours and relations always dissatisfied with their conduct? No matter how holy and consistent their lives may be, they are always thought wrong! If they withdraw entirely from the world, and live, like John the Baptist, a retired and ascetic life, the cry is raised that they are exclusive, narrow-minded, sour-spirited, and righteous overmuch. If, on the other hand, they go much into society, and endeavour as far they can to take interest in their neighbour's pursuits, the remark is soon made that they are no better than other people, and have no more real religion than those who make no profession at all. Treatment like this is only too common. Few are the decided Christians who do not know it by bitter experience. The servants of God in every age, whatever they do, are blamed.

The plain truth is, that the natural heart of man hates

God. The carnal mind is enmity against God. It dislikes His law, His Gospel, and His people. It will always find some excuse for not believing and obeying. The doctrine of repentance is too strict for it! The doctrine of faith and grace is too easy for it! John the Baptist goes too much out of the world! Jesus Christ goes too much into the world! And so the heart of man excuses itself for sitting still in its sins.—All this must not surprise us. We must make up our minds to find unconverted people as perverse, unreasonable, and hard to please as the Jews of our Lord's time. We must give up the vain idea of trying to please everybody. The thing is impossible, and the attempt is mere waste of time. We must be content to walk in Christ's steps, and let the world say what it likes. Do what we will we shall never satisfy it, or silence its ill-natured remarks. It first found fault with John the Baptist, and then with his blessed Master. And it will go on cavilling and finding fault with that Master's disciples, so long as one of them is left upon earth.

We learn, secondly, from these verses, that *the wisdom of God's ways is always recognized and acknowledged by those who are wise-hearted.*

This is a lesson which is taught in a sentence of somewhat obscure character : "Wisdom is justified of all her children." But it seems difficult to extract any other meaning from the words, by fair and consistent interpretation. The idea which our Lord desires to impress upon us appears to be, that though the vast majority of the Jews were hardened and unreasonable, there were some who were not,—and that though multitudes saw no wisdom in the ministry of John the Baptist and Himself, there were a chosen few who did. Those few were the "children of wisdom." Those few, by their lives and obedience, declared their full conviction that God's ways of dealing with the Jews were wise and right, and that John the Baptist and the Lord Jesus were both worthy of all honour. In short, they "justified" God's wisdom, and so proved themselves truly wise.

This saying of our Lord about the generation among whom He lived, describes a state of things which will always be found in the Church of Christ. In spite of the cavils, sneers, objections, and unkind remarks with which the Gospel is received by the majority of mankind, there will always be some in every country who will assent to it, and obey it with delight. There will never be wanting a "little flock" which hears the voice of the Shepherd gladly, and counts all His ways right. The children of this world may mock at the Gospel, and pour contempt on the lives of believers. They may count their practice madness, and see no wisdom or beauty in their ways. But God will take care that He has a people in every age. There will be always some who will assert the perfect excellence of the doctrines and requirements of the Gospel, and will "justify the wisdom" of Him who sent it. And these, however much the world may despise them, are they whom Jesus calls wise. They are "wise unto salvation, through faith which is in Christ Jesus." (2 Tim. iii. 15.)

Let us ask ourselves, as we leave this passage, whether we deserve to be called children of wisdom? Have we been taught by the Spirit to know the Lord Jesus Christ?

Have the eyes of our understanding been opened? Have we the wisdom that cometh from above?—If we are truly wise, let us not be ashamed to confess our Master before men. Let us declare boldly that we approve the whole of His Gospel, all its doctrines and all its requirements. We may find few with us and many against us. The world may laugh at us, and count our wisdom no better than folly. But such laughter is but for a moment. The hour cometh when the few who have confessed Christ, and justified His ways before men, shall be confessed and "justified" by Him before His Father and the angels.

NOTES. LUKE VII. 31—35.

32.—[*They are like unto children.*] Let it be noted that the one point to be kept in mind, in the comparison of the generation among whom our Lord lived, to children, is the waywardness and determination not to be pleased, which is often observable in some children. In this respect they were exact types of the Jews when John Baptist and our Lord successively preached to them. Their two ministries were peculiarly unlike one another. But neither pleased the Jews.

To attach deep spiritual meanings to the "market-place," the "piping," "dancing," "mourning," and "weeping," of the similitude, is, to say the least, unprofitable.

[*Ye have not danced.*] The dancing here mentioned must not be tortured into an excuse for modern dancing-parties and balls. The dancing spoken of in Scripture had no resemblance to the dancing of modern times.

34.—[*Eating and drinking.*] The utmost that can be made of this expression amounts to this, that our Lord's habits in the matter of eating and drinking were different from those of John the Baptist, that He was less ascetic, and more like other men.

Comparing this verse with the preceding one, and remembering, also, our Lord's miracle at the marriage in Cana, and the Institution of the Lord's Supper, I certainly think there is a strong probability that our Lord did not altogether abstain from the use of wine. I say this with the utmost respect for the friends of temperance. But 1 do not like to see a good cause injured by its advocates taking up untenable ground.

35.—[*But wisdom is justified of all her children.*] There is some obscurity about these words. At any rate, there is much diversity in the interpretations which commentators put upon them.

Some take the expression "children of wisdom" in a bad sense, and consider the meaning to be, "those who ought to have been, or were reckoned children of wisdom, having rejected wisdom's offers, wisdom is now acquitted and free from all blame at their hands. Divine wisdom tried all things needful for their conversion and salvation, and they would have none of her counsel. She is, therefore, justified, absolved and excused from all blame, if they are lost." This is Chrysostom's view.

Some take the word "justified" in the strange sense of "condemned," and make out the meaning to be as follows. "Those who professed themselves to be children of wisdom have actually condemned wisdom, by refusing her counsels." This, according to Paræus and Chemnitius, is the view maintained by Luther.

I believe the right interpretation is to regard the "children of wisdom" as the truly wise, the elect, the believers, the people who are really taught of God. By them "the wisdom of God's ways is always justified, whatever others may please to think of it. They assent to them, approve of them, and regard them as being entirely right." This sense will be found ably defended in the commentary of Paræus on St. Matthew,—and well and briefly stated by Euthymius.

The "children of wisdom" is a Hebraism for "those who are wise." Thus, the "children of rebellion" means the rebellious, Num. xvii. 10., the "children of wickedness" the wicked, 2 Sam. vii. 10., the "children of pride" the proud, Job xli. 34., the "children of transgression" transgressors, Isai. lvii. 4. The "children of this world," and "children of light," Luke xvi. 8., are similar expressions.

It seems unnecessary to take "wisdom," at the beginning of the verse, in the sense of the Personal Wisdom, Christ Himself. It is more likely a general expression for the "wisdom of God's ways."

The word "but," at the beginning of the verse is more commonly translated "and." Beza and others however show that it should be taken here in the sense of "and yet," or "but," as we have rendered it in our version. Alford points out that "and," should be so rendered in Matt. x. 29. It should be "and yet one," &c.

LUKE VII. 36—50.

36 And one of the Pharisees desired him that he would eat with him. And he went into the Pharisee's house, and sat down to meat.

37 And, behold, a woman in the city, which was a sinner, when she knew that *Jesus* sat at meat in the Pharisee's house, brought an alabaster box of ointment,

38 And stood at his feet behind *him* weeping, and began to wash his feet with tears, and did wipe *them* with the hairs of her head, and kissed his feet, and anointed *them* with the ointment.

39 Now when the Pharisee which had bidden him saw *it*, he spake within himself, saying, This man, if he were a prophet, would have known who and what manner of woman *this is* that toucheth him : for she is a sinner.

40 And Jesus answering said unto him, Simon, I have somewhat to say unto thee. And he saith, Master, say on.

41 There was a certain creditor which had two debtors : the one owed five hundred pence, and the other fifty.

42 And when they had nothing to pay, he frankly forgave them both.

Tell me therefore, which of them will love him most ?

43 Simon answered and said, I suppose that *he*, to whom he forgave most. And he said unto him, Thou hast rightly judged.

44 And he turned to the woman, and said unto Simon, Seest thou this woman ? I entered into thine house, thou gavest me no water for my feet : but she hath washed my feet with tears, and wiped *them* with the hairs of her head.

45 Thou gavest me no kiss : but this woman since the time I came in hath not ceased to kiss my feet.

46 My head with oil thou didst not anoint : but this woman hath anointed my feet with ointment.

47 Wherefore I say unto thee, Her sins, which are many, are forgiven ; for she loved much : but to whom little is forgiven, *the same* loveth little.

48 And he said unto her, Thy sins are forgiven.

49 And they that sat at meat with him began to say within themselves, Who is this that forgiveth sins also ?

50 And he said to the woman, Thy faith hath saved thee ; go in peace.

THE deeply interesting narrative contained in these verses, is only found in the Gospel of St. Luke. In order to see the full beauty of the story, we should read, in connection with it, the eleventh chapter of St. Matthew. We shall then discover the striking fact, that the woman whose conduct is here recorded, most likely owed her conversion to the well-known words, " Come unto me all ye that labour and are heavy-laden, and I will give you rest." That wondrous invitation, in all human probability, was the saving of her soul, and gave her that sense of peace for which we see her so grateful. —A full offer of free pardon is generally God's chosen instrument for bringing the chief of sinners to repentance.

We see in this passage that *men may show some outward respect to Christ, and yet remain unconverted.* The Pharisee before us is a case in point. He showed our Lord Jesus Christ more respect than many did. He even "desired Him that He would eat with him." Yet all this time he was profoundly ignorant of the nature of Christ's Gospel. His proud heart secretly revolted at the sight of a poor contrite sinner being allowed to wash our Lord's feet. And even the hospitality he showed appears to have been cold and niggardly. Our Lord Himself says, "Thou gavest me no water for my feet :— thou gavest me no kiss :—my head with oil thou didst not anoint." In short, in all that the Pharisee did, there was one great defect. There was outward civility, but there was no heart-love.

We shall do well to remember the case of this Pharisee. It is quite possible to have a decent form of religion, and yet to know nothing of the Gospel of Christ,—to treat Christianity with respect, and yet to be utterly blind about its cardinal doctrines,—to behave with great correctness and propriety at Church, and yet to hate justification by faith, and salvation by grace, with a deadly hatred. Do we really feel affection toward the Lord Jesus? Can we say, "Lord, thou knowest all things, thou knowest that I love thee?" Have we cordially embraced His whole Gospel? Are we willing to enter heaven side by side with the chief of sinners, and to owe all our hopes to free grace?—These are questions which we ought to consider. If we cannot answer them satisfactorily, we are in no respect better than Simon the Pharisee; and our Lord might say to us, "I have somewhat to say unto thee."

We see, in the next place, in this passage, *that grateful love is the secret of doing much for Christ.* The penitent woman, in the story before us, showed far more honour to our Lord than the Pharisee had done. She "stood at His feet behind Him weeping." She "washed His feet with tears." She "wiped them with the hairs of her head." She "kissed His feet, and anointed them with costly ointment."—No stronger proofs of reverence and respect could she have given, and the secret of her giving such proofs, was love. She loved our Lord, and she thought nothing too much to do for Him. She felt deeply grateful to our Lord, and she thought no mark of gratitude too costly to bestow on Him.

More "doing" for Christ is the universal demand of all the Churches. It is the one point on which all are agreed. All desire to see among Christians, more good works, more self-denial, more practical obedience to Christ's commands. But what will produce these things? Nothing, nothing but love. There never will be more done for Christ till there is more hearty love to Christ Himself. The fear of punishment, the desire of reward, the sense of duty, are all useful arguments, in their way, to persuade men to holiness. But they are all weak and powerless, until a man loves Christ. Once let that mighty principle get hold of a man, and you will see his whole life changed.

Let us never forget this. However much the world may sneer at "feelings" in religion, and however false or unhealthy religious feelings may sometimes be, the great truth still remains behind, that *feeling* is the secret of doing. The heart must be engaged for Christ, or the hands will soon hang down. The affections must be enlisted into His service, or our obedience will soon stand still. It will always be the loving workman who will do most in the Lord's vineyard.

We see lastly, in this passage, that a *sense of having our sins forgiven is the mainspring and life-blood of love to Christ.* This, beyond doubt, was the lesson which our Lord wished Simon the Pharisee to learn, when He told him the story of the two debtors. "One owed his creditor five hundred pence, and the other fifty." Both had "nothing to pay," and both were forgiven freely. And then came the searching question : "Which of them will love him most?" Here was the true explanation, our Lord told Simon, of the deep love which the penitent woman before Him had displayed. Her many tears, her deep affection, her public reverence, her action in anointing His feet, were all traceable to one cause. She had been much forgiven, and so she loved much.—Her love was the effect of her forgiveness, not the cause,—the consequence of her forgiveness, not the condition,—the result of her forgiveness, not the reason,—the fruit of her forgiveness, not the root. Would the Pharisee know why this woman showed so much love? It was because she felt much forgiven.—Would he know why he himself had shown his guest so little love? It was because he felt under no obligation,—had no consciousness of having obtained forgiveness,—had no sense of debt to Christ.

For ever let the mighty principle laid down by our Lord in this passage, abide in our memories, and sink down into our hearts. It is one of the great corner-stones of the whole Gospel. It is one of the master-keys to unlock the secrets of the kingdom of God. The only way to make men holy, is to teach and preach free and full forgiveness through Jesus Christ. The secret of being holy ourselves, is to know and feel that Christ has pardoned our sins. Peace with God is the only root that will bear the fruit of holiness. Forgiveness must go before sanctification. We shall do nothing till we are reconciled to God.—This is the first step in religion. We must work from life, and not for life. Our best works before we are justified are little better than splendid sins. We must live by faith in the Son of God, and then, and not till then, we shall walk in His ways. The heart which has experienced the pardoning love of Christ, is the heart which loves Christ, and strives to glorify Him.

Let us leave the passage with a deep sense of our Lord Jesus Christ's amazing mercy and compassion to the chief of sinners. Let us see in His kindness to the woman, of whom we have been reading, an encouragement to any one, however bad he may be, to come to Him for pardon and forgiveness. That word of His shall never be broken, "Him that cometh unto me I will in no wise cast out." Never, never need any one despair of salvation, if he will only come to Christ.

Let us ask ourselves, in conclusion, What we are doing for Christ's glory? What kind of lives are we living? What proof are we making of our love to Him who loved us, and died for our sins? These are serious questions. If we cannot answer them satisfactorily, we may well doubt whether we are forgiven. The hope of forgiveness which is not accompanied by love in the life is no hope at all. The man whose sins are really cleansed away will always show by his ways that he loves the Saviour who cleansed them.

NOTES. LUKE VII. 36—50.

36.—[*And one of the Pharisees desired him.*] We know nothing of this Pharisee, except his name, Simon. There is no proof that he was the same as "Simon the leper," mentioned in Mark xiv. 3. He certainly was not Simon Peter, or Simon Zelotes.

We are not told the place at which the circumstances here recorded took place. It is highly probable that it was Nain, where the widow's son was raised.

Our Lord had just been saying, that He was called "the friend of publicans and sinners." St. Luke proceeds at once to show, that He was so indeed, and was not ashamed of the name.

[*He went into the Pharisee's house.*] Our Lord's conduct in eating at the Pharisee's table, is quoted by some Christians in defence of the practice of keeping up intimacy with unconverted people, and going to dinner parties and entertainments at their houses.

Those who use such an argument would do well to remember our Lord's behaviour on this occasion. He carried his "Father's business" with Him to the Pharisee's table. He testified against the Pharisee's besetting sin. He explained to the Pharisee the nature of free forgiveness of sins, and the secret of true love to Himself. He declared the saving nature of faith. If Christians who argue in favour of intimacy with unconverted people, will visit their houses in the spirit of our Lord, and speak and behave as He did, let them by all means continue the practice. But do they speak and behave at the tables of their unconverted acquaintances, as Jesus did at Simon's table? This is a question they would do well to answer.

Bucer's note on this point is worth reading.

[*Sat down to meat.*] The Greek word so translated, means literally "reclined," according to the custom of the country. It is important to note this, in order to understand the remaining part of the passage.

37.—[*And behold a woman in the city.*] The questions, who this

woman was, and at what time in our Lord's ministry the
transactions here described took place, have occasioned much
discussion, and called forth much variety of opinion among
commentators. On one point only almost all are agreed : She
had been a notorious sinner against the seventh commandment.

The Romish writers, Maldonatus and Cornelius á Lapide
maintain strongly that this woman was Mary Magdalene, and
that the anointing here recorded is the same as that which took
place at Bethany, and is described by Matthew, Mark, and John.
Both these opinions seem untenable.

There is not the slightest evidence in Scripture that the
"woman who was a sinner" was Mary Magdalene. Chemnitius
says there is no authority for the opinion but tradition, and
that this tradition began with Gregory the First, and was un-
supported by the earlier fathers, Chrysostom, Origen, Ambrose,
and Jerome.—There is no evidence that Mary Magdalene was
the sister of Martha and Lazarus, and lived at Bethany.—
Above all, there is not the least proof in Scripture that Mary
Magdalene had ever been "a woman that was a sinner"
against the seventh commandment.

On the other hand, there is strong internal evidence that the
event here recorded by St. Luke, took place at an entirely
different time and place from that recorded by Matthew, Mark,
and John. Granting that St. Luke does not always relate events
in regular chronological order, it seems asking too much to suppose that an event which all the other evangelists agree in
placing at the end of our Lord's life on earth, should be so
entirely dragged out of its place by St. Luke as to be brought in
at this early period of His ministry.—Moreover, the expressions
which St. Luke reports in this passage, appear very unlikely to
have been used at the end of our Lord's ministry, and at the
house of friends in Bethany. The question, "who is this that forgiveth sins also?" sounds like a question that would be asked at
a comparatively early period of his ministry, and not like one
that men would ask at the end of three years, and just before
His death.

The true account I believe to be, that the events here recorded
by St. Luke are entirely distinct from those recorded by Matthew,
Mark, and John, and that the woman here mentioned is one
whose name is, for wise and kind reasons, withheld from the
Church. This is the view maintained by the great majority of
all Protestant commentators.

It is a curious fact, that John Bunyan, in his famous sermon
called "The Jerusalem sinner saved," maintains the strange view
that the woman here described by St. Luke was Mary the sister
of Martha, though he confeses that he got the picturesque story
he founds on it, from a book which he saw twenty-four years
before. For once the good man seems to have made a mistake.

[*Which was a sinner.*] It is a common remark, that the Greek words so translated, mean "which used to be, in time past, a sinner." I confess it appears to me doubtful, whether the Greek word for "was," will bear so strong a meaning. How lately this woman had been living in sin, we do not know, but it is highly probable, almost up to the very day when the events here related took place. In short, she "was" even then, by common report, a sinner. But it is evident that she had already repented of her sin, and was already ashamed of it, and this in consequence of our Lord Jesus Christ's teaching and preaching.—If this was not so there would be no meaning in the fact that "when she knew that Jesus sat at meat in the Pharisee's house," she brought her box of ointment, and anointed Him. In short, however recent her conversion, she came to the Pharisee's house a penitent and a believer.

[*Sat at meat.*] The Greek word here, differs from the one in the preceding verse. It means literally, "is lying down at meat."

38.—[*Stood at his feet behind him.*] To understand this we must remember that in the country where our Lord Jesus ministered, people did not sit down at meals, as we do in modern times, but reclined, or lay at full length on couches, with their feet stretched out behind them. It would thus be easy for this woman to do what she did to our Lord's feet.

In addition to this, we must remember that houses in the hot climate, where our Lord was, were very different from houses among ourselves. It was common to have large openings down to the floor, and almost to live, as it were, under a veranda, for the sake of coolness. This necessarily entailed great publicity in the entertainment given, and accounts for the ease with which this woman seems to have found her way into the place where our Lord was.

[*Anointed them.*] Ointments and oils were used in eastern countries, to an extent we can hardly understand. The excessive heat of the climate made it almost necessary, to preserve the skin from cracking. See Psalm civ. 15.

39.—[*This man.*] There is probably something contemptuous and scornful in this expression. It is much the same as " this fellow," like Acts xviii. 13.

[*Would have known.*] Burgon remarks, "The discernment of spirits was accounted the mark of a true prophet; and such knowledge was recognized as the very note of Messiah, as the confession of Nathanael, and the woman of Samaria show." Messiah was to be " of quick understanding." See Isai. xi. 3, 4. John i. 49, and iv. 29.

40.—[*Jesus answering said.*] This expression shows the divine

knowledge of hearts and thoughts which our Lord possessed. He
taught Simon that He not only knew who the woman behind
Him was, but that He also knew what was going on in Simon's
mind. He was " a prophet," and in the highest sense.

42.—[*He frankly forgave them both.*] Let us observe that the debt
was not forgiven because the debtors loved their creditor, but out
of free grace, mercy and compassion. And the love of the debtors
was the consequence of their debts being forgiven. A right understanding of this, is the clue to the whole passage.

47.—[*Her sins,...are forgiven ; for she loved much.*] To explain
these words as meaning that the woman's sins were forgiven,
because she loved much, is to contradict flatly the whole lesson of
the six preceding verses. " For" must be taken as "wherefore,"
and, according to Pearce and Hammond, may fairly be so taken.
Our Lord's meaning must manifestly be : " Her love is a proof of
her forgiveness. She is a person whose many sins are forgiven.

The proof of it is, that she shows much love, and the lesson
of my parable, according to thine own confession, is this, that
much forgiveness produces much love."—Even Stella, the Spanish
Commentator, Roman Catholic as he is, allows that this is the
true sense of the passage.

Lightfoot remarks, that our Lord does not say, " She hath
washed my feet and anointed them, and therefore her sins are
forgiven," but, " therefore *I say* unto thee," or " for this cause *I
declare* unto thee that her sins are forgiven." Her sins were
forgiven before, but now, after this love that she has shown, I
publicly declare unto thee her forgiveness.

48.—[*Thy sins are forgiven.*] We are not, of course, to suppose
that these words mean that the woman's sins were now forgiven
for the first time. Such an interpretation would overthrow again
all the doctrine of the story of the two debtors. The woman
was really forgiven *before* she came to Christ. But she now
received a public and authoritative declaration of it before many
witnesses, as a reward for her open expression of love and gratitude. Before, she had hope through grace. Now, she received
the assurance of hope.

49.—[*Who is this that forgiveth sins ?*] Let it be noted once more,
that this expression is the language that would naturally be used
by persons who were strangers to our Lord, and heard and saw
Him for the first time. It is exceedingly unlikely that such an
expression would have been used at Bethany, a few days before
His crucifixion, in the company of Mary, and Martha, and
Lazarus.

50.—[*Thy faith hath saved thee.*] Let it be observed, that it is not
said, "thy love hath saved thee." Here, as in every other part
of the New Testament, faith is put forward as the key to salva-

tion. By faith, the woman received our Lord's invitation, "come unto me and I will give you rest." By faith, she embraced that invitation, and embracing it, cast off the sins under which she had been so long labouring and heavy-laden. By faith, she boldly came to the Pharisee's house, and confessed by her conduct that she had found rest in Christ. Her faith worked by love, and bore precious fruit. But it was not love but *faith* that saved her soul.

[*Go in peace.*] This was a phrase which was a common valediction among the Jews, like our "goodbye" or "God be with you." Pool thinks that our Lord specially referred to that "peace" which is the fruit of faith, described in Rom. v. 1. He paraphrases the expression thus: "Go thy way, a blessed and happy woman, and in the view and sense of thine own blessedness, be not troubled at the censures and reflections of supercilious persons, who may despise and overlook thee because thou hast been a great sinner"

LUKE VIII. 1—3.

1 And it came to pass afterward, that he went throughout every city and village, preaching and shewing the glad tidings of the kingdom of God: and the twelve *were* with him,

2 And certain women, which had been healed of evil spirits and infirmities, Mary called Magdalene, out of whom went seven devils,

3 And Joanna the wife of Chuza, Herod's steward, and Susanna, and many others, which ministered unto him of their substance.

LET us mark, in these verses, *our Lord Jesus Christ's unwearied diligence in doing good.* We read that "He went throughout every city and village, preaching and showing the glad tidings of the kingdom of God." We know the reception that He met with in many places. We know that while some believed, many believed not. But man's unbelief did not move our Lord, or hinder His working. He was always "about His Father's business." Short as His earthly ministry was in point of duration, it was long when we consider the work that it comprised.

Let the diligence of Christ be an example to all Christians. Let us follow in His steps, however far we may come short of His perfection. Like Him, let us labour to do good in our day and generation, and to leave the world a better world than we found it. It is not for nothing that the Scripture says expressly: "He that abideth in him ought himself also so to walk even as he walked." (1 John ii. 6.)

Time is undoubtedly short. But much is to be done with time, if it is well economised and properly arranged. Few have an idea how much can be done in twelve hours, if men will stick to their business and avoid idleness and frivolity. Then let us, like our Lord, be diligent, and "redeem the time."

Time is undoubtedly short. But it is the only season in which Christians can do any active work of mercy. In the world to come there will be no ignorant to instruct, no mourners to comfort, no spiritual darkness to enlighten, no distress to relieve, no sorrow to make less. Whatever work we do of this kind must be done on this side of the grave. Let us awake to a sense of our individual responsibility. Souls are perishing, and time is flying. Let us resolve, by God's grace, to do something for God's glory before we die. Once more let us remember our Lord's example, and, like Him, be diligent, and "redeem the time."

Let us mark, secondly, in these verses, *the power of the grace of God, and the constraining influence of the love of Christ*. We read that among those who followed our Lord in His journeyings, were "certain women which had been healed of evil spirits and infirmities."

We can well imagine that the difficulties these holy women had to face in becoming Christ's disciples were

neither few nor small.   They had their full share of
the contempt and scorn which was poured on all followers of Jesus by the Scribes and Pharisees.   They
had, besides, many a trial from the hard speeches
and hard usage which any Jewish woman who thought
for herself about religion would probably have to under-
go.   But none of these things moved them.   Grateful
for mercies received at our Lord's hands, they were willing to endure much for His sake. Strengthened inwardly
by the renewing power of the Holy Ghost, they were
enabled to cleave to Jesus and not give way.—And nobly
they did cleave to Him to the very end!   It was *not* a
woman who sold the Lord for thirty pieces of silver.
They were *not* women who forsook the Lord in the garden
and fled.   It was *not* a woman who denied Him three
times in the high priest's house.—But they *were* women
who wailed and lamented when Jesus was led forth to be
crucified.   They *were* women who stood to the last by
the cross.   And they *were* women who were first to visit
the grave "where the Lord lay."   Great indeed is the
power of the grace of God!

Let the recollection of these women encourage all the
daughters of Adam who read of them, to take up the
cross and to follow Christ.   Let no sense of weakness, or
fear of falling away, keep them back from a decided
profession of religion.   The mother of a large family,
with limited means, may tell us that she has no time for
religion.—The wife of an ungodly husband may tell us
that she dares not take up religion.—The young daughter
of worldly parents may tell us that it is impossible for
her to have any religion.—The maid-servant in the midst

of unconverted companions, may tell us that in her place a person cannot follow religion.—But they are all wrong, quite wrong. With Christ nothing is impossible. Let them think again, and change their minds. Let them begin boldly in the strength of Christ, and trust Him for the consequences. The Lord Jesus never changes. He who enabled "many women" to serve Him faithfully while He was on earth, can enable women to serve Him, glorify Him, and be His disciples at the present day.

Let us mark lastly, in these verses, the *peculiar privilege which our Lord grants to His faithful followers*. We read that those who accompanied Him in His journeyings, "ministered to him of their substance." Of course He needed not their help. "All the beasts of the forest were his, and the cattle upon a thousand hills." (Psalm l. 10.) That mighty Saviour who could multiply a few loaves and fishes into food for thousands, could have called forth food from the earth for His own sustenance, if he had thought fit. But He did not do so, for two reasons.—One reason was, that He would show us that He was man like ourselves in all things, sin only excepted, and that He lived the life of faith in His Father's providence.—The other reason was, that by allowing His followers to minister to Him, He might prove their love, and test their regard for Himself. True love will count it a pleasure to give anything to the object loved. False love will often talk and profess much, but do and give nothing at all.

This matter of "ministering to Christ" opens up a most important train of thought, and one which we shall do well to consider. The Lord Jesus Christ is continually proving His Church at the present day. No doubt it would be easy for Him to convert the Chinese or Hindoos in a moment, and to call grace into being with a word, as He created light on the first day of this world's existence.—But He does not do so. He is pleased to work by means. He condescends to use the agency of missionaries, and the foolishness of man's preaching, in order to spread His Gospel. And by so doing, He is continually proving the faith and zeal of the churches. He lets Christians be fellow workers with Him, that He may prove who has a will to "minister" and who has none. He lets the spread of the Gospel be carried on by subscriptions, contributions, and religious Societies, that He may prove who are the covetous and unbelieving, and who are the truly "rich towards God." In short, the visible Church of Christ may be divided into two great parties, those who "minister" to Christ, and those who do not.

May we all remember this great truth and prove our own selves! While we live we are all upon our trial. Our lives are continually showing whose we are and whom we serve, whether we love Christ or whether we love the world. Happy are they who know something of "ministering to Christ of their substance!" It is a thing which can still be done, though we do not see Him with our eyes. Those words which describe the proceedings of the judgment day are very solemn, "I was an hungered and ye gave me no meat, I was thirsty and ye gave me no drink." (Matt. xxv. 42.)

NOTES. LUKE VIII. 1—3.

[1.—*He went throughout.*] The word so translated is only used in one other place in the New Testament: Acts xvii. 1. It is there rendered " passed through." The full idea is that of one going on a journey through a place or country.

2.—[*Mary called Magdalene.*] The origin of this name is differently explained by commentators. Some think that she was so called from a Hebrew word signifying " a plaiter of hair." Some think that she was so called from the town of " Magdala," in Galilee. Talmudic authority favours the first explanation, but the second seems more probable. The question will be found fully discussed in Lightfoot's Horæ Hebraicæ on St. Matthew xxvii., 50.

There is no Scriptural authority for the common opinion that Mary Magdalene was ever a notorious sinner against the seventh commandment. That she had been a sufferer from an extraordinary possession of the devil is plain, from this verse, and Mark xvi. 9., the number " seven devils " being specified in each place with peculiar emphasis. But there is not a whit of satisfactory evidence that she was ever a harlot. Chemnitius considers Gregory the Great to have been the author of the common opinion about Mary Magdalene.

3.—[*Joanna, the wife of Chuza, Herod's steward.*] This person is only mentioned here in the New Testament, and we know nothing more of her. Her case reminds us of Obadiah in Ahab's house, and " the saints in Nero's household."—It also teaches us that not all our Lord's followers were poor. Some rich, though not many, were called.—It also throws light on Herod's anxiety to see our Lord, when He was sent to him by Pilate. He had probably heard of Him through his steward's family.—It also suggests the pleasant idea, that John the Baptist's imprisonment by Herod was a cause of conversion to some of Herod's retainers. Who can tell but Joanna first heard of our Lord through John the Baptist?

[*Chuza, Herod's steward.*] The word translated " steward " is only found here and in two other places: Matt. xx. 8. and Gal. iv. 2. In the latter text it is translated " tutors." Whether Chuza was Herod's treasurer or only the head of his household, we cannot certainly pronounce. The word admits of either sense. At any rate he was a person holding a high and responsible office.

[*Susanna.*] This is the only place in which we find this woman mentioned. Of her past or subsequent history we know nothing.

[*Many others.*] Who these were we do not know. The names of most of them probably are in the book of life, and " the day will declare " them.

[*Ministered to him of their substance.*] Maldonatus in commenting on this expression quotes a passage from Jerome, which throws some light on it. He says, " It was a Jewish custom, and from the ancient habit of the nation it was thought a blameless custom, for women to supply to their instructors food and clothing from their substance."

Hammond, in commenting on this place, thinks that Phœbe, mentioned by St. Paul to the Romans, (Rom. xvi. 1.) was a woman who had travelled with the apostles, and ministered to their wants.

LUKE VIII. 4—15.

4 And when much people were gathered together, and were come to him out of every city, he spake by a parable:

5 A sower went out to sow his seed: and as he sowed, some fell by the way side; and it was trodden down, and the fowls of the air devoured it.

6 And some fell upon a rock; and as soon as it was sprung up, it withered away, because it lacked moisture.

7 And some fell among thorns; and the thorns sprang up with it, and choked it.

8 And other fell on good ground, and sprang up, and bare fruit an hundredfold. And when he had said these things, he cried, He that hath ears to hear, let him hear.

9 And his disciples asked him, saying, What might this parable be?

10 And he said, Unto you it is given to know the mysteries of the kingdom of God: but to others in parables; that seeing they might not see, and hearing they might not understand.

11 Now the parable is this: The seed is the word of God.

12 Those by the way side are they that hear; then cometh the devil, and taketh away the word out of their hearts, lest they should believe and be saved.

13 They on the rock *are they*, which, when they hear, receive the word with joy; and these have no root, which for a while believe, and in time of temptation fall away.

14 And that which fell among thorns are they, which, when they have heard, go forth, and are choked with cares and riches and pleasures of *this* life, and bring no fruit to perfection.

15 But that on the good ground are they, which in an honest and good heart, having heard the word, keep *it*, and bring forth fruit with patience.

THE parable of the sower, contained in these verses, is reported more frequently than any parable in the Bible. It is a parable of universal application. The things it relates are continually going on in every congregation to which the Gospel is preached. The four kinds of hearts it describes are to be found in every assembly which hears the word. These circumstances should make us always read the parable with a deep sense of its importance. We should say to ourselves, as we read it: "This concerns me. My heart is to be seen in this parable. I, too, am here."

The passage itself requires little explanation. In fact, the meaning of the whole picture is so fully explained by our Lord Jesus Christ, that no exposition of man can throw much additional light on it. The parable is pre-eminently a parable of caution, and caution about a most important subject,—the way of hearing the word of God. It was meant to be a warning to the apostles, not to expect too much from hearers. It was meant to be a warning to all ministers of the Gospel, not to look for too great results from sermons. It was meant, not least, to be a warning to hearers, to take heed how they hear. Preaching is an ordinance of which the value can never be overrated in the Church of Christ. But it should never be forgotten, that there must not only be good preaching, but good hearing.

The first caution that we learn from the parable of the sower, is *to beware of the devil when we hear the word.* Our Lord tells us that the hearts of some hearers are like "the wayside." The seed of the Gospel is plucked away from them by the devil almost as soon as it is sown. It does not sink down into their consciences. It does not make the least impression on their minds.

The devil, no doubt, is everywhere. That malicious spirit is unwearied in his efforts to do us harm. He is ever watching for our halting, and seeking occasion to destroy our souls. But nowhere perhaps is the devil so active as in a congregation of Gospel-hearers. Nowhere does he labour so hard to stop the progress of that which is good, and to prevent men and women being saved. From him come wandering thoughts and roving imaginations,—listless minds and dull memories,—sleepy eyes

and fidgetty nerves,—weary ears and distracted attention.
In all these things Satan has a great hand.   People
wonder where they come from, and marvel how it is that
they find sermons so dull, and remember them so badly!
They forget the parable of the sower.   They forget the
devil.

Let us take heed that we are not way-side hearers.
Let us beware of the devil.   We shall always find him
at Church.   He never stays away from public ordinances.
Let us remember this, and be upon our guard.   Heat,
and cold, and draughts, and damp, and wet, and rain,
and snow, are often dreaded by Church-goers, and
alleged as reasons for not going to Church.   But there is
one enemy whom they ought to fear more than all these
things together.   That enemy is Satan.

The second caution that we learn from the parable of
the sower, is to *beware of resting on mere temporary impressions when we have heard the word.*   Our Lord tells us
that the hearts of some hearers are like rocky ground,
The seed of the word springs up immediately, as soon as
they hear it, and bears a crop of joyful impressions, and
pleasurable emotions.   But these impressions, unhappily,
are only on the surface.   There is no deep and abiding
work done in their souls.   And hence, so soon as the
scorching heat of temptation or persecution begins to be
felt, the little bit of religion which they seemed to have
attained, withers and vanishes away.

Feelings, no doubt, fill a most important office in our
personal Christianity.   Without them there can be
no saving religion.   Hope, and joy, and peace, and
confidence, and resignation, and love, and fear, are things

which must be felt, if they really exist. But it must never be forgotten that there are religious affections, which are spurious and false, and spring from nothing better than animal excitement. It is quite possible to feel great pleasure, or deep alarm, under the preaching of the Gospel, and yet to be utterly destitute of the grace of God. The tears of some hearers of sermons, and the extravagant delight of others, are no certain marks of conversion. We may be warm admirers of favourite preachers, and yet remain nothing better than stony-ground hearers. Nothing should content us but a deep, humbling, self-mortifying work of the Holy Ghost, and a heart-union with Christ.

The third caution contained in the parable of the sower is *to beware of the cares of this world.* Our Lord tells us that the hearts of many hearers of the word are like thorny ground. The seed of the word, when sown upon them, is choked by the multitude of other things, by which their affections are occupied. They have no objection to the doctrines and requirements of the Gospel. They even wish to believe and obey them. But they allow the things of earth to get such hold upon their minds, that they leave no room for the word of God to do its work. And hence it follows that however many sermons they hear, they seem nothing bettered by them. A weekly process of truth-stifling goes on within. They bring no fruit to perfection.

The things of this life form one of the greatest dangers which beset a Christian's path. The money, the pleasures, the daily business of the world, are so many traps to catch souls. Thousands of things, which in themselves are innocent, become, when followed to excess, little better than soul-poisons, and helps to hell. Open sin is not the only thing that ruins souls. In the midst of our families, and in the pursuit of our lawful callings, we have need to be on our guard. Except we watch and pray, these temporal things may rob us of heaven, and smother every sermon we hear. We may live and die thorny-ground hearers.

The last caution contained in the parable of the sower, is to *beware of being content with any religion which does not bear fruit in our lives*. Our Lord tells us that the hearts of those who hear the word aright, are like good ground. The seed of the Gospel sinks down deeply into their wills, and produces practical results in their faith and practice. They not only hear with pleasure, but act with decision. They repent. They believe. They obey.

For ever let us bear in mind that this is the only religion that saves souls. Outward profession of Christianity, and the formal use of Church ordinances and sacraments, never yet gave man a good hope in life, or peace in death, or rest in the world beyond the grave. There must be fruits of the Spirit in our hearts and lives, or else the Gospel is preached to us in vain. Those only who bear such fruits, shall be found at Christ's right hand in the day of His appearing.

Let us leave the parable with a deep sense of the danger and responsibility of all hearers of the Gospel. There are four ways in which we may hear, and of these four only one is right.—There are three kinds of hearers whose souls are in imminent peril. How many of these three kinds are to be found in every congregation !—

There is only one class of hearers which is right in the sight of God. And what are we? Do we belong to that one?

Finally, let us leave the parable with a solemn recollection of the duty of every faithful preacher to divide his congregation, and give to each class his portion. The clergyman who ascends his pulpit every Sunday, and addresses his congregation as if he thought every one was going to heaven, is surely not doing his duty to God or man. His preaching is flatly contradictory to the parable of the sower.

NOTES. LUKE VIII. 4—15.

4.—*When much people were gathered, &c.*] Let us note, in this expression, a strong indirect evidence of our Lord's faithfulness and honesty as a public teacher. So far was He from flattering men. and speaking smooth things to procure popularity, that He speaks one of the most heart-searching and conscience-pricking of His parables, when the crowd of hearers was greatest.

Faithful ministers should always denounce sin most plainly, when their churches are most full, and their congregations most large. Then is the time to "cry aloud and spare not," and show people their sins. It is a snare to some ministers, to flatter full congregations and scold thin ones. Such dealing is very unlike that of our Lord.

5.—*[A sower went out to sow.]* It is highly probable that in this parable, our Lord describes something which was actually going on within sight. Many of His parables, we must remember, were spoken in the open air, and the images, in many cases, were borrowed from subjects before his eyes. Hence His lessons were seen as well as heard.

6.—*[Upon a rock.]* The rocky soil of many parts of Palestine makes the circumstances here mentioned far more likely than it appears to us, who live in a country like England.

7.—*[Among thorns.]* The precise nature of the plant or weed here called "thorns," we cannot exactly determine. It is the same word that is used in describing the "crown of thorns," plaited by the soldiers in the day of the crucifixion, and put in mockery on our Lord's head. Whether those thorns were the prickly thorns or briars, with which we are all familiar, has been much doubted, and remains an undecided question.

The description of the growth of the "thorns" here mentioned, would rather lead us to suppose that they were some plant or weed which grew up out of the soil together with the seed corn.

8.—[*He that hath ears to hear let him hear.*] Let it be noted, that this expression is specially recorded by all the three evangelists, Matthew, Mark, and Luke, in their report of this parable. It seems to point out the special importance of the parable.

10.—[*Seeing they might not see.*] The expression used in this verse, is evidently quoted from the words in Isaiah vi. 9. It is worthy of observation that hardly any passage in the Old Testament is so frequently quoted in the New Testament as this. It is found six times, Matt. xiii. 14, 15; Mark iv. 2; John xii. 40; Acts xxviii. 26; Rom. xi. 8, and in this place. On each occasion it is applied to the same subject, the hardened and unbelieving state of mind, in which the Jews were.

11 —[*The seed is the word of God.*] Let us observe here, that the word "is" means, "signifies," or "represents," according to the Hebrew manner of speaking. It is important to remember this, because it throws light on the well-known words used by our Lord at the appointment of the Lord's supper, "This *is* my body. This *is* my blood."

12.—[*Then cometh the devil.*] This is one of those expressions which bring out strongly the existence, personality, and agency of the devil. There is an active, living agent, distinct from man, operating powerfully in man's heart, and to man's injury.

13.—[*Fall away.*] The word so translated, is, in the Greek language, the root of our well-known word "apostacy."

14.—[*Go forth.*] The meaning of this expression has been explained in various ways. Some think that it simply means "going away from the hearing of the word."—Others think it means, " as they pass through life,—in their progress through life," and compare it with Luke i. 6., where Zacharias and Elisabeth are said, " to walk in the ordinances of the Lord." The Greek word there is the same that is used here.

[*Bring...fruit to perfection.*] This expression is rendered in the Greek by a single word, which is found nowhere else in the New Testament.

15.—[*Honest and good heart.*] We must carefully remember that this expression does not imply that any one's heart is naturally "good," or ever can become so, without the grace of God. The fairest sense of the words is, " an unprejudiced heart, willing to be taught," such as was peculiarly lacking among the Jews in our Lord's time. The Bereans are an illustration of this expression. Acts xvii. 9.

[*Keep it.*] The word so translated. is not the word sometimes translated " observe." It rather signifies " hold fast," so as not to let go, and is used in this sense in 1 Thess. v. 21, Heb. iii. 6, and x. 23.

[*Patience.*] The word so translated is sometimes used in an active sense, and sometimes in a passive. Here it is probably active, like Rom. ii. 7, and 2 Cor. i. 6.

LUKE VIII. 16—21.

16 No man, when he hath lighted a candle, covereth it with a vessel, or putteth *it* under a bed; but setteth *it* on a candlestick, that they which enter in may see the light.

17 For nothing is secret, that shall not be made manifest; neither *any thing* hid, that shall not be known and come abroad.

18 Take heed therefore how ye hear: for whosoever hath, to him shall be given; and whosoever hath not, from him shall be taken even that which he seemeth to have.

19 Then came to him *his* mother and his brethren, and could not come at him for the press.

20 And it was told him *by certain* which said, Thy mother and thy brethren stand without, desiring to see thee.

21 And he answered and said unto them, My mother and my brethren are these which hear the word of God, and do it.

THESE verses form a practical application of the famous parable of the sower. They are intended to nail and clench in our minds the mighty lesson which that parable contains. They deserve the especial attention of all true-hearted hearers of the Gospel of Christ.

We learn, firstly, from these verses, that *spiritual knowledge ought to be diligently used*. Our Lord tells us that it is like a lighted candle, utterly useless, when covered with a bushel, or put under a bed,—only useful when set upon a candlestick, and placed where it can be made serviceable to the wants of men.

When we hear this lesson, let us first think of *ourselves*. The Gospel which we possess was not given us only to be admired, talked of, and professed,—but to be practised. It was not meant merely to reside in our intellect, and memories, and tongues,—but to be seen in our lives. Christianity is a talent committed to our charge, and one which brings with it great responsibility. We are not in darkness like the heathen. A glorious light is put before us. Let us take heed that we use it. While we have the light let us walk in the light. (John xii. 35.)

But let us not only think of ourselves. Let us also think of *others*. There are millions in the world who have no spiritual light at all. They are without God, without Christ, and without hope. (Ephes. ii. 12.) Can we do nothing for them?—There are thousands around us, in our own land, who are unconverted and dead in sins, seeing nothing and knowing nothing aright? Can we do nothing for them?—These are questions to which every true Christian ought to find an answer. We should strive, in every way, to spread our religion. The highest form of selfishness is that of the man who is content to go to heaven alone. The truest charity is to endeavour to share with others every spark of religious light we possess ourselves, and so to hold our own candle that it may give light to every one around us. Happy is that soul, which, as soon as it receives light from heaven, begins to think of others as well as itself! No candle which God lights was ever meant to burn alone.

We learn, secondly, from these verses, *the great importance of right hearing*. The words of our Lord Jesus Christ ought to impress that lesson deeply on our hearts. He says, "Take heed how ye hear."

The degree of benefit which men receive from all the means of grace depends entirely on the way in which they use them. Private prayer lies at the very foundation of religion; yet the mere formal repetition of a set of words, when "the heart is far away," does good to no man's soul.—Reading the Bible is essential to the attainment of sound Christian knowledge; yet the mere formal reading of so many chapters as a task and duty, without a humble desire to be taught of God, is little better than a waste of time.—Just as it is with praying and Bible reading, so it is with hearing. It is not enough that we go to Church and hear sermons. We may do so for fifty years, and be " nothing bettered, but rather worse." " Take heed," says our Lord, " how ye hear."

Would any one know how to hear aright? Then let him lay to heart three simple rules. For one thing, we must hear with faith, believing implicitly that every word of God is true, and shall stand. The word in old time did not profit the Jews, "not being mixed with faith in them that heard it." (Heb. iv. 2.)—For another thing, we must hear with reverence, remembering constantly that the Bible is the book of God. This was the habit of the Thessalonians. They received Paul's message, "not as the word of men, but the word of God." (1 Thess. ii. 13.)—Above all, we must hear with prayer, praying for God's blessing before the sermon is preached, praying for God's blessing again when the sermon is over. Here lies the grand defect of the hearing of many. They ask no blessing, and so they have none. The sermon passes through their minds like water through a leaky vessel, and leaves nothing behind.

Let us bear these rules in mind every Sunday morning, before we go to hear the Word of God preached. Let us not rush into God's presence careless, reckless, and unprepared, as if it mattered not in what way such work was done. Let us carry with us faith, reverence, and prayer. If these three are our companions, we shall hear with profit, and return with praise.

We learn, finally, from these verses, *the great privileges of those who hear the word of God, and do it.* Our Lord Jesus Christ declares that He regards them as his "mother and his brethren."

The man who hears the word of God, and does it, is the true Christian. He hears the call of God to repent and be converted, and he obeys it. He ceases to do evil, and learns to do well. He puts off the old man, and puts on the new.—He hears the call of God to believe on Jesus Christ for justification, and he obeys it. He forsakes his own righteousness, and confesses his need of a Saviour. He receives Christ crucified as his only hope, and counts all things loss for the knowledge of Him.—He hears the call of God to be holy, and he obeys it. He strives to mortify the deeds of his body, and to walk after the Spirit. He labours to lay aside every weight, and the sin that so easily besets him.—This is true vital Christianity. All men and women who are of this character are true Christians.

Now the troubles of all who "hear the word of God and do it" are neither few nor small. The world, the flesh, and the devil continually vex them. They often groan, being burdened. (2 Cor. v. 4.) They often find the cross heavy, and the way to heaven rough and narrow. They often feel disposed to cry with St. Paul, " O wretched man that I am, who shall deliver me from the body of this death?" (Rom. vii. 24.)

Let all such take comfort in the words of our Lord
Jesus Christ which we are now considering. Let them
remember that the Son of God himself regards them as
his own near relations! Let them not heed the laughter,
and mockery, and persecution of this world. The woman
of whom Christ says, " She is my mother," and the man
of whom Christ says, " He is my brother," have no cause
to be ashamed.

NOTES. LUKE VIII. 16—21.

16.—[*Under a bed.*] The word rendered "bed," signifies "a couch,"
such as was found in all sitting-rooms in eastern houses, and
under which it is probable many things were put away, when
not wanted.

17.—[*For nothing is secret, &c.*] The application of these words
and their connection with the context are not quite clear. Their
primary sense appears to be that the disciples must not suppose
that our Lord's instructions were intended to be kept secret, and
reserved from the world. They were not to be confined to a few
favoured hearers, like the lessons of the heathen philosophers,
but to be published, proclaimed, and made known to all mankind. In this way the light given to the apostles would be
"placed on a candlestick," and not covered and hidden.

    Some think that the words point to the day of judgment,
and the account which will then be taken of the use which all
who have seen the light of the Gospel, have made of it.

18.—[*Take heed how ye hear.*] Let it be remembered, in reading
such sayings as these, that the bulk of mankind in all ages are
peculiarly dependent on oral teaching. The number of those
who have time and abilities for reading and private study will
always be small. In the days when printing was not invented,
and the writings of men were few, the lesson must have been
specially important. But it will never lose its importance as
long as the world endures.

    [*Whosoever hath.*] This expression evidently means, "who-
soever hath and makes a good use of what he hath." The other
expression in the verse "whosoever hath not," in like manner
means, "whosoever has made no use of what he has received."

19.—[*His mother and his brethren.*] From this expression, many
have concluded that Joseph, the husband of Mary, was now
dead. Whether this was the case we do not know. He
certainly seems to have been dead at the time of the crucifixion,

from the fact of our Lord commending His mother to the care of John. (John xix. 27.)

Who are meant by our Lord's "brethren," cannot now be determined. It is certain that the word so translated, does not necessarily mean the sons of our Lord's mother. It is clear, from many passages in the Bible, that the word " brethren" has frequently a wide signification, and may mean either cousins, or mere distant relations. (Compare Gen. xxxi. 46; Matt. xiii. 55; xxvii. 56; Mark iii. 18; Gal. i. 19.) Some think that these "brethren," were sons of Joseph by a former marriage, before he was Mary's husband. Some think that they were the sons of one of Mary's sisters. Nothing certain is known on the subject.

Whether our Lord's mother clearly saw the nature of His work on earth, at this particular time, may seriously be questioned. There is no reason to suppose that her mind was entirely free from that obscurity under which the holiest and best Jews appear to have been, about the humiliation and sufferings of Messiah.

[*Come at him.*] The word translated "come at," is only found here in the New Testament. According to Parkhurst, it simply means, "to meet with, meet, light upon, or get to." The Syriac version of this place, renders it to "speak with."

LUKE VIII. 22—25.

22 Now it came to pass on a certain day, that he went into a ship with his disciples: and he said unto them, Let us go over unto the other side of the lake. And they launched forth.

23 But as they sailed he fell asleep: and there came down a storm of wind on the lake; and they were filled *with water*, and were in jeopardy.

24 And they came to him, and awoke him, saying, Master, master, we perish. Then he arose, and rebuked the wind and the raging of the water: and they ceased, and there was a calm.

25 And he said unto them, Where is your faith? And they being afraid wondered, saying one to another, What manner of man is this! for he commandeth even the winds and water, and they obey him.

THE event in our Lord's life described in these verses is related three times in the Gospels. Matthew, Mark, and Luke were all inspired to record it. This circumstance should teach us the importance of the event, and should make us "give the more heed" to the lessons it contains.

We see, firstly, in these verses, that *our Lord Jesus Christ was really man as well as God*. We read that as he sailed over the Lake of Gennesaret in a ship with his disciples, " he fell asleep." Sleep, we must be all aware, is one of the conditions of our natural constitution as human beings. Angels and spirits require neither food nor refreshment. But flesh and blood, to keep up a healthy existence, must eat, and drink, and sleep. If the Lord Jesus could be weary, and need rest, He must have had two natures in one person—a human nature as well as a divine.

The truth now before us is full of deep consolation and encouragement for all true Christians. The one Mediator, in whom we are bid to trust, has been Himself "partaker of flesh and blood." The mighty High Priest, who is living for us at God's right hand, has had personal experience of all the sinless infirmities of the body. He has himself hungered, and thirsted, and suffered pain. He has himself endured weariness, and sought rest in sleep.—Let us pour out our hearts before him with freedom, and tell him our least troubles without reserve. He who made atonement for us on the cross is one who " can be touched with the feeling of our infirmities." (Heb. iv. 15.) To be weary of working for God is sinful, but to be wearied and worn in doing God's work is no sin at all. Jesus Himself was weary, and Jesus slept.

We see, secondly, in these verses, *what fears and anxieties may assault the hearts of true disciples of Christ.* We read that " when a storm of wind came down on the lake," and the boat in which our Lord was sailing was filled with water, and in jeopardy, His companions were greatly alarmed. "They came to Him and awoke Him, saying, Master, Master, we perish." They forgot, for a moment, their Master's never-failing care for them in time past. They forgot that with Him they must be safe, whatever happened. They forgot everything but the sight and sense of present danger, and, under the impression of it, could not even wait till Christ awoke. It is only too true that sight, and sense, and feeling, make men very poor theologians.

Facts like these are sadly humbling to the pride of human nature. It ought to lower our self-conceit and high thoughts to see what a poor creature is man, even at his best estate.—But facts like these are deeply instructive. They teach us what to watch and pray against in our own hearts. They teach us what we must make up our minds to find in other Christians. We must be moderate in our expectations. We must not suppose that men cannot be believers if they sometimes exhibit great weakness, or that men have no grace because they are sometimes overwhelmed with fears. Even Peter, James, and John, could cry, "Master, Master, we perish."

We see, thirdly, in these verses, *how great is the power of our Lord Jesus Christ.* We read that when His disciples awoke Him in the storm, "He arose, and rebuked the wind, and the raging of the waters, and they ceased, and there was a calm." This was, no doubt, a mighty miracle. It needed the power of Him who brought the flood on the earth in the days of Noah, and in due season took it away,—who divided the Red Sea and the river Jordan into two parts, and made a path for His people through the waters,—who brought the locusts on Egypt by an east wind, and by a west wind swept them away. (Exod. x. 13, 19.) No power short of this could in a moment turn a storm into a calm. "To speak to the winds and waves" is a common proverb for attempting that which is impossible. But here we see Jesus speaking, and at once the winds and waves obey! As man He had slept. As God He stilled the storm.

It is a blessed and comfortable thought, that all this almighty power of our Lord Jesus Christ is engaged on behalf of His believing people. He has undertaken to save every one of them to the uttermost, and He is "mighty to save." The trials of His people are often many and great. The devil never ceases to make war against them. The rulers of this world frequently persecute them. The very heads of the church, who ought to be tender shepherds, are often bitterly opposed to the truth as it is in Jesus. Yet, notwithstanding all this, Christ's people shall never be entirely forsaken. Though sorely harassed, they shall not be destroyed. Though cast down, they shall not be cast away. At the darkest time let true Christians rest in the thought, that "greater is He who is for them than all they that be against them." The winds and waves of political and ecclesiastical trouble may beat fiercely over them, and all hope may seem taken away. But still let them not despair. There is One living for them in heaven who can make these winds and waves to cease in a moment. The true Church, of which Christ is the Head, shall never perish. Its glorious Head is almighty, and lives for evermore, and His believing members shall all live, also, and reach home safe at last. (John xiv. 19.)

We see, lastly, in these verses, *how needful it is for Christians to keep their faith ready for use.* We read that our Lord said to His disciples, when the storm had ceased, and their fears had subsided, "Where is your faith?" Well might He ask that question! Where was the profit of believing, if they could not believe in the time of need? Where was the real value of faith, unless they kept it in active exercise? Where was the benefit of trusting, if they were to trust their Master in sunshine only, but not in storms?

The lesson now before us is one of deep practical importance. To have true saving faith is one thing. To have that faith always ready for use is quite another. Many receive Christ as their Saviour, and deliberately commit their souls to him for time and eternity, who yet often find their faith sadly failing when something unexpected happens, and they are suddenly tried. These things ought not so to be. We ought to pray that we may have a stock of faith ready for use at a moment's notice, and may never be found unprepared. The highest style of Christian is the man who lives like Moses, "seeing Him who is invisible." (Heb. ii. 27.) That man will never be greatly shaken by any storm. He will see Jesus near him in the darkest hour, and blue sky behind the blackest cloud.

NOTES. LUKE VIII. 22—25.

22.—[*He went into a ship, &c.*] The events here recorded took place on the lake of Gennesaret, or sea of Galilee. At the time of our Lord's earthly ministry, the country round this lake was thickly inhabited, and there seem to have been many boats on it. At present, according to the latest travellers, there are very few boats on it, and the population round it is very thin.

23.—[*There came down a storm of wind.*] All travellers agree in saying, that the lake of Gennesaret is very liable to be visited by such storms. It lies very low, and is surrounded, on almost all sides, by high hills. Sudden gusts, or squalls of wind are consequently very common.

24.—[*They ceased, and there was a calm.*] The well-known story of King Canute, in vain attempting to stop the rising tide by his command, will naturally occur to any reader of English history. There is a striking contrast between the utter failure of Canute's attempt and the almighty power of Christ's words here recorded.

25.—[*Where is your faith.*] Leigh remarks that this would be more accurately rendered " Where is that your faith?" That is, Where is that measure, or degree of faith, which you have showed?

LUKE VIII. 26—36.

26 And they arrived at the country of the Gadarenes, which is over against Galilee.

27 And when he went forth to land, there met him out of the city a certain man, which had devils long time, and ware no clothes, neither abode in *any* house, but in the tombs.

28 When he saw Jesus, he cried out, and fell down before him, and with a loud voice said, What have I to do with thee, Jesus, *thou* Son of God most high? I beseech thee, torment me not.

29 (For he had commanded the unclean spirit to come out of the man. For oftentimes it had caught him: and he was kept bound with chains and in fetters; and he brake the bands, and was driven of the devil into the wilderness.)

30 And Jesus asked him, saying, What is thy name? And he said, Legion: because many devils were entered into him.

31 And they besought him that he would not command them to go out into the deep.

32 And there was there an herd of many swine feeding on the mountain: and they besought him that he would suffer them to enter into them. And he suffered them.

33 Then went the devils out of the man, and entered into the swine: and the herd ran violently down a steep place into the lake, and were choked.

34 When they that fed *them* saw what was done, they fled, and went and told *it* in the city and in the country.

35 Then they went out to see what was done; and came to Jesus, and found the man, out of whom the devils were departed, sitting at the feet of Jesus, clothed, and in his right mind: and they were afraid.

36 They also which saw *it* told them by what means he that was possessed of the devils was healed.

THE well-known narrative which we have now read, is carefully recorded by all the three first Gospel-writers. It is a striking instance of our Lord's complete dominion over the prince of this world. We see the great enemy of our souls for once completely vanquished,—the "strong man" foiled by One stronger than he, and the lion spoiled of his prey.

Let us mark, first, in this passage, *the miserable condition of those over whom the devil reigns.* The picture brought before us is a frightful one. We are told that when our Lord arrived in the country of the Gadarenes, there met Him "a certain man which had devils long time, and ware no clothes, neither abode in any house, but in the tombs." We are also told that although he had been "bound with chains and in fetters, he brake the bands, and was driven of the devil into the wilderness." In short, the case seems to have been one of the most aggravated forms of demoniacal possession. The unhappy sufferer was under the complete dominion of Satan, both in body and soul. So long as he continued in this state, he must have been a burden and a trouble to all around him. His mental faculties were under the direction of a "legion" of devils. His bodily strength was only employed for his own injury and shame. A more pitiable state for mortal man to be in, it is difficult to conceive.

Cases of bodily possession by Satan, like this, are, to say the least, very rarely met with in modern times. Yet we must not, on this account, forget that the devil is continually exercising a fearful power over many hearts and souls. He still urges many, in whose hearts he reigns, into self-dishonouring and self-destroying habits of life. He still rules many with a rod of iron,—goads them on from vice to vice, and from profligacy to profligacy,—drives them far from decent society, and the influence of respectable friends,—plunges them into the lowest depths of wickedness,—makes them little better than self-murderers,—and renders them as useless to their families, the Church, and the world, as if they were dead, and not alive. Where is the faithful minister who could not put his finger on many such cases? What truer account can be given of many a young man, and many a young woman, than that they seem possessed of devils? It is vain to shut our eyes to facts. Demoniacal possession of men's bodies may be comparatively rare. But many, unhappily, are the cases in which the devil appears completely to possess men's souls.

These things are fearful to think upon. Fearful is it to see to what a wreck of body and mind Satan often brings young persons! Fearful is it to observe how he often drives them out of the reach of all good influence, and buries them in a wilderness of bad companions and loathsome sins! Fearful, above all, is it to reflect that yet a little while Satan's slaves will be lost for ever, and in hell! There often remains only one thing that can be done for them. They can be named before Christ in prayer. He that came to the country of the Gadarenes, and healed the miserable demoniac there, still lives in heaven, and pities sinners. The worst slave of Satan in England is not beyond a remedy. Jesus may yet take compassion on him, and set him free.

Let us mark, secondly, in these verses, *the absolute power which the Lord Jesus Christ possesses over Satan.* We are told that he " commanded the unclean spirit to come out of the man," whose miserable condition we have just heard described. At once the unhappy

sufferer was healed. The "many devils" by whom he
had been possessed were compelled to leave him. Nor is
this all. Cast forth from their abode in the man's
heart, we see these malignant spirits beseeching our
Lord that he would "not torment" them, or "command
them to go out into the deep," and so confessing His
supremacy over them. Mighty as they were, they plainly
felt themselves in the presence of One mightier than
themselves. Full of malice as they were, they could not
even hurt the "swine" of the Gadarenes until our Lord
granted them permission.

Our Lord Jesus Christ's dominion over the devil should
be a cheering thought to all true Christians. Without
it, indeed, we might well despair of salvation. To feel
that we have ever near us an invisible spiritual enemy,
labouring night and day to compass our destruction,
would be enough to crush out every hope, if we did not
know a Friend and Protector. Blessed be God! The
Gospel reveals such an One. The Lord Jesus is stronger
than that "strong man armed," who is ever warring
against our souls. The Lord Jesus is able to deliver us
from the devil. He proved His power over him frequently
when upon earth. He triumphed over him gloriously on
the cross. He will never let him pluck any of His sheep
out of His hand. He will one day bruise him under our
feet, and bind him in the prison of hell. (Rom. xvi. 20 ;
Rev. xx. 1, 2.) Happy are they who hear Christ's voice
and follow Him ! Satan may vex them, but he cannot
really hurt them ! He may bruise their heel, but he cannot
destroy their souls. They shall be "more than conquerors"
through Him who loved them. (Rom. viii. 37.)

Let us mark, finally, *the wonderful change which Christ can work in Satan's slaves.* We are told that the Gadarenes "found the man out of whom the devil was departed, sitting at the feet of Jesus, clothed, and in his right mind." That sight must indeed have been strange and astonishing! The man's past history and condition, no doubt, were well known. He had probably been a nuisance and a terror to all the neighbourhood. Yet here, in one moment, a complete change had come over him. Old things had passed away, and all things had become new. The power by which such a cure was wrought must indeed have been almighty. When Christ is the physician nothing is impossible.

One thing, however, must never be forgotten. Striking and miraculous as this cure was, it is not really more wonderful than every case of decided conversion to God. Marvellous as the change was which appeared in this demoniac's condition when healed, it is not one whit more marvellous than the change which passes over every one who is born again, and turned from the power of Satan to God. Never is a man in his right mind till he is converted, or in his right place till he sits by faith at the feet of Jesus, or rightly clothed till he has put on the Lord Jesus Christ.—Have we ever considered what real conversion to God is? It is nothing else but the miraculous release of a captive, the miraculous restoration of a man to his right mind, the miraculous deliverance of a soul from the devil.

What are we ourselves? This, after all, is the grand question which concerns us. Are we bondsmen of Satan or servants of God? Has Christ made us free, or does

the devil yet reign in our hearts ? Do we sit at the feet
of Jesus daily ? Are we in our right minds ? May the
Lord help us to answer these questions aright !

<hr/>

NOTES. LUKE VIII. 26—36.

27.—[*A certain man, which had devils long time.*] There is much
in this case, like all the cases of demoniacal possession in Scripture, which is deeply mysterious. It must needs be so from the
fact that such possession appears to have been far more common, and much more distinctly marked in its symptoms, when
our Lord was upon earth, than it ever has been since.

Let it suffice us to believe implicitly, that diabolical possession of the entire man, both body, mind, and soul. was an undeniable fact during the time of our Lord's earthly ministry,
and that all attempts to explain away the cases described in the
Gospels, by calling them epilepsy, lunacy, and the like, are
utterly unsatisfactory. For the rest, what we cannot thoroughly
understand, we must be content to believe.

That there is such a thing as Satanic possession now, though
comparatively a rare thing, is an opinion held by many able
physicians, who have given special attention to this subject.
Disease of the mind, or madness, is at all times a deeply mysterious subject. It is highly probable that Satan has far more to
do with it than we think.

[*In the tombs.*] Trench quotes a remarkable circumstance,
mentioned by the traveller Warburton, in "The Crescent
and the Cross," which throws some light on this expression. " On descending from the height of Lebanon, I found
myself in a cemetery, where sculptured turbans showed us, that
the neighbouring village was Moslem. The silence of the night
was now broken by fierce yells and howlings, which I discovered
proceeded from a naked maniac, who was fighting with some wild
dogs for a bone. The moment he perceived us, he left his canine
companions, and bounding along with rapid strides, seized my
horse's bridle and almost forced him backwards over the cliff."

The determined propensity to wear no clothes and go naked,
which is a striking symptom of some kinds of mania, is another
curious illustration of the case described in this verse.

28.—[*What have I to do with thee.*] The Greek expression so
rendered, let it be noted, is the same which our Lord uses when
He addresses His mother at the marriage of Cana in Galilee.
(John ii. 4.)

The words here used are the words of the devil by whom the
man was possessed, rather than the man himself. This fact

shows us how entirely all the faculties and powers of the unhappy demoniac were occupied and employed by the evil spirit which possessed him.

[*Jesus, thou Son of God, torment me not.*] These words are a striking incidental proof that there will be a judgment, and a hell. The devils believe this, if men do not.

29.—[*Brake the bands.*] Prodigious muscular strength has often been remarked as accompanying some cases of mania.

30.—[*Legion.*] This is a well-known name by which a division of the Roman army was designated. A Roman Legion is supposed to have contained 5 or 6000 men. The word here is evidently used indefinitely to express a great number.

31.—[*Into the deep.*] The "deep" here means the abyss or pit of hell. It is the same Greek word which is five times translated "bottomless pit," in the book of Revelation. For instance, Rev. xx. 1, 3.

32.—[*An herd of many swine feeding.*] Let it be noted that to keep swine was a breach of the Mosaic law, swine being unclean animals. (Lev. ii. 7.) If therefore the Gadarenes were Jews, and there seems strong reason for supposing they were, they were committing an habitual sin.

[*He suffered them.*] It has often been asked, why our Lord suffered the devils to go into the swine, and permitted the consequent destruction of animal life which ensued. It might suffice to say in reply to this question, that Scripture shows us that animal life was continually taken away by God's own command, when some great spiritual truth was to be taught to man, as in the case of the sacrifices of the law. But in addition to this, it is fair to suppose that our Lord permitted the destruction of the swine, as a mark of God's displeasure against the Gadarenes for keeping them.

After all, the question is ultimately bound up with the deepest of all things:—viz. the origin and permission of evil in creation. To explain this is impossible. Enough for us to see that it exists, and to use the great remedy which God has provided against it.—So doing "what we know not now, we shall know hereafter."

33.—[*The herd ran violently down, &c.*] The extraordinary malice, hatred of God's creation, and love of mischief, which are attributes of Satan, appear strikingly in this fact. Satan must be doing harm. If he cannot harm man, he will harm swine. Well would it be for the world, if Christians were as unwearied and zealous in doing good, as devils are in doing evil.

34.—[*In the country.*] This expression would be rendered more literally "in the fields."

Before leaving this miracle it may be well to say something about the apparent discrepancy between the account given of it by St. Matthew, and those given by St. Mark and St. Luke. St. Matthew speaks of two demoniacs. St. Mark and St. Luke speak of only one.

The explanations of the discrepancy are various. According to Augustine, Theophylact, and Grotius, the one mentioned by Mark and Luke was a more illustrious and well known person than the other. According to Chrysostom, Euthymius, and Maldonatus, he was the fiercest of the two. According to Lightfoot, one of the demoniacs was a Jew and the other a heathen, and the healing of the heathen one is the case which Mark and Luke dwell on.

I venture to suggest that the reason why Mark and Luke only mention one, is the fact that only one of the two asked to be allowed to remain with our Lord, after he was healed, and only one ultimately became a witness to the Lord in the country of the Gadarenes. The case of the other man presented no peculiar circumstances of interest, and therefore Mark and Luke pass it over.

It is hardly necessary to remark that there is no contradiction between the two accounts. Though Mark and Luke only describe the cure of one demoniac, it would be absurd to say that they denied that two were cured. They only describe the case which was most remarkable.

LUKE VIII. 37—40.

37 Then the whole multitude of the country of the Gadarenes round about besought him to depart from them; for they were taken with great fear: and he went up into the ship, and returned back again.

38 Now the man out of whom the devils were departed besought him that he might be with him: but Jesus sent him away, saying,

39 Return to thine own house, and shew how great things God hath done unto thee. And he went his way, and published throughout the whole city how great things Jesus had done unto him.

40 And it came to pass, that, when Jesus was returned, the people *gladly* received him: for they were all waiting for him.

WE see in this passage two requests made to our Lord Jesus Christ. They were widely different one from the other, and were preferred by persons of widely different character. We see, moreover, how these requests were received by our Lord Jesus Christ. In either case the request received a most remarkable answer. The whole passage is singularly instructive.

Let us observe, in the first place, that *the Gadarenes besought our Lord to depart from them, and their request was granted.* We read these painfully solemn words— "He went up into the ship, and returned back again."

Now why did these unhappy men desire the Son of God to leave them? Why, after the amazing miracle of mercy which had just been wrought among them, did they feel no wish to know more of Him who wrought it? Why, in a word, did they become their own enemies, forsake their own mercies, and shut the door against the Gospel?—There is but one answer to these questions. The Gadarenes loved the world, and the things of the world, and were determined not to give them up. They felt convinced, in their own consciences, that they could not receive Christ among them and keep their sins, and their sins they were resolved to keep. They saw, at a glance, that there was something about Jesus with which their habits of life would never agree, and having to choose between the new ways and their own old ones, they refused the new and chose the old.

And why did our Lord Jesus Christ grant the request of the Gadarenes, and leave them? He did it in judgment, to testify His sense of the greatness of their sin. He did it in mercy to His Church in every age, to show how great is the wickedness of those who wilfully reject the truth. It seems an eternal law of His government, that those who obstinately refuse to walk in the light shall have the light taken from them. Great is Christ's patience and longsuffering! His mercy endureth for ever. His offers and invitations are wide, and broad, and sweeping, and universal. He gives every church its day of grace and time of visitation. (Luke xix. 44.) But if men persist in refusing His counsel, He has nowhere promised to persist in forcing it upon them. People who have the Gospel, and yet refuse to obey it, must not be surprised if the Gospel is removed from them. Hundreds of churches, and parishes, and families, are at this moment in the state of the Gadarenes. They said to Christ, " Depart from us," and he has taken them at their word. They were joined to idols, and are now " let alone." (Job xxi. 14; Hosea iv. 17.)

Let us take heed that we do not sin the sin of the Gadarenes. Let us beware lest by coldness, and inattention, and worldliness, we drive Jesus from our doors, and compel Him to forsake us entirely. Of all sins which we can sin, this is the most sinful. Of all states of soul into which we can fall, none is so fearful as to be "let alone."—Let it rather be our daily prayer that Christ may never leave us to ourselves. The old wreck, high and dry on the sand-bank, is not a more wretched sight, than the man whose heart Christ has visited with mercies and judgments, but has at last ceased to visit, because He was not received. The barred door is a door at which Jesus will not always knock. The Gadarene mind must not be surprised to see Christ leaving it and going away.

Let us observe, in the second place, that *the man out of whom the devils were departed, besought our Lord that he might be with Him;—but his request was not granted.* We read that Jesus sent him away, saying, " Return to thine own house, and show how great things God hath done unto thee."

We can easily understand the request that this man made. He felt deeply grateful for the amazing mercy which he had just received in being cured. He felt full of love and warm affection toward Him, who had so wonderfully and graciously cured him. He felt that he could not see too much of Him, be too much in His company, cleave to Him too closely. He forgot everything else under the influence of these feelings. Family, relations, friends, home, house, country, all seemed as nothing in his eyes. He felt that he cared for nothing but to be with Christ.—And we cannot blame him for his feelings. They may have been tinged with something of enthusiasm and inconsideration. There may have been about them a zeal not according to knowledge. In the first excitement of a newly felt cure, he may not have been fit to judge what his future line of life should be. But excited feelings in religion are far better than no feelings at all. In the petition he made, there was far more to praise than to blame.

But why did our Lord Jesus Christ refuse to grant this man's request? Why, at a time when he had few disciples did he send this man away? Why, instead of allowing him to take place with Peter and James and John, did he bid him return to his own house?—Our Lord did what He did in infinite wisdom. He did it for the benefit of the man's own soul. He saw it was more for his good to be a witness for the Gospel at home than a disciple abroad.—He did it in mercy to the Gadarenes. He left among them one standing testimony of the truth of His own divine mission.—He did it, above all, for the perpetual instruction of His whole church. He would have us know that there are various ways of glorifying Him, that He may be honoured in private life as well as in the apostolic office, and that the first place in which we should witness for Christ is our own house.

There is a lesson of deep experimental wisdom in this little incident, which all true Christians would do well to lay to heart. That lesson is our own utter ignorance of what position is good for us in this world, and the necessity of submitting our own wills to the will of Christ. The place that we wish to fill is not always the place that is best for us. The line of life that we want to take up, is not always that which Christ sees to be most for the benefit of our souls. The place that we are obliged to fill is sometimes very distasteful, and yet it may be needful to our sanctification. The position we are compelled to occupy may be very disagreeable to flesh and blood, and yet it may be the very one that is necessary to keep us in our right mind. It is better to be sent away from Christ's bodily presence, by Christ Himself, than to remain in Christ's bodily presence without His consent.

Let us pray for the spirit of "contentment with such things as we have." Let us be fearful of choosing for ourselves in this life without Christ's consent, or moving in this world, when the pillar of cloud and fire is not moving before us. Let us ask the Lord to choose everything for us. Let our daily prayer be, "Give me what Thou wilt. Place me where Thou wilt. Only let me be Thy disciple, and abide in Thee."

37.—[*Besought him to depart.*] It has been remarked by many commentators, that these Gadarenes are an exact type of the men of this world. They saw the miraculous deliverance of a fellow creature from Satan's power, and took no interest in it. But they saw the loss of their swine with deep concern. In a word, they cared more for the loss of swine, than the saving of a soul. There are thousands like them. Tell them of the success of missionaries, and the conversion of souls at home or abroad, they hear it with indifference, if not with a sneer. But if you tell them of the loss of property, or a change in the value of money, they are all anxiety and excitement. Truly the generation of the Gadarenes is not yet extinct!

38.—[*Jesus sent him away.*] Let us note here, that a literal following of Christ, and literal forsaking of relations, friends, and homes, are evidently not essential to salvation. It may be necessary for some persons, and at some times, and under some circumstances. But it is plain from the case before us, that it is not necessary for all. Gualter has some useful remarks on this subject, in his Homily on this passage.

39.—[*Return to thine own house and show, &c.*] It is interesting and instructive to remark how differently our Lord addressed different people, and how different are the commands we find Him laying upon them according to their characters. The young ruler, in Mark x. 21, was commanded to "take up his cross and follow" Christ.—The leper, mentioned in St. Mark i. 43, was strictly charged to "say nothing to any man."—The man, who was called in Luke ix. 19, was not allowed even to go home and bury his father.—The man before us, on the contrary, was commanded to return home, and show every one what Christ had done for him!

Now how shall we account for this strange diversity? There is one simple answer. Our Lord dealt with every case according to what He saw it needed. He knew what was in every man's heart. He prescribed to every man, like a wise physician, the very course of conduct which his state of soul required.

We should surely learn, from our Lord's conduct, not to treat all cases of persons needing spiritual advice, in precisely the same way. All, of course, need the same great doctrines, repentance towards God, faith towards our Lord Jesus Christ, and thorough holiness to be pressed upon them. But all ought not to have one precise rule laid down for their particular course of action, and their particular line of duty. We must consider peculiarities of circumstances, characters, and cases, and advise accordingly. Counsel which may be very good for one man, may not be good for another. A parent's path of duty is one thing, and a child's is another. A master's position is one, and

a servant's another. These things are not sufficiently considered. The wise variety of our Lord's counsels, is a subject
which deserves close study.

LUKE VIII. 41—48.

41 And, behold, there came a man named Jairus, and he was a ruler of the synagogue : and he fell down at Jesus' feet, and besought him that he would come into his house :

42 For he had one only daughter, about twelve years of age, and she lay a dying. But as he went the people thronged him.

43 And a woman having an issue of blood twelve years, which had spent all her living upon physicians, neither could be healed of any,

44 Came behind *him*, and touched the border of his garment : and immediately her issue of blood stanched.

45 And Jesus said, Who touched me ? When all denied, Peter and they that were with him said, Master, the multitude throng thee and press *thee*, and sayest thou, Who touched me ?

46 And Jesus said, Somebody hath touched me : for I perceive that virtue is gone out of me.

47 And when the woman saw that she was not hid, she came trembling, and falling down before him, she declared unto him before all the people for what cause she had touched him, and how she was healed immediately.

48 And he said unto her, Daughter, be of good comfort : thy faith hath made thee whole ; go in peace.

How much misery and trouble sin has brought into the world! The passage we have just read affords a melancholy proof of this. First we see a distressed father in bitter anxiety about a dying daughter. Then we see a suffering woman, who has been afflicted twelve years with an incurable disease. And these are things which sin has sown broad-cast over the whole earth! These are but patterns of what is going on continually on every side. These are evils which God did not create at the beginning, but man has brought upon himself by the fall. There would have been no sorrow and no sickness among Adam's children, if there had been no sin.

Let us see in the case of the woman here described, *a striking picture of the condition of many souls.* We are told that she had been afflicted with a wearing disease for "twelve years," and that she "had spent all her living upon physicians," and that she could not be "healed of any." The state of many a sinner's heart is placed before us in this description as in a glass. Perhaps it describes ourselves.

There are men and women in most congregations who have felt their sins deeply, and been sore afflicted by the thought that they are not forgiven and not fit to die. They have desired relief and peace of conscience, but have not known where to find them. They have tried many false remedies, and found themselves " nothing bettered, but rather worse." They have gone the round of all the forms of religion, and wearied themselves with every imaginable man-made device for obtaining spiritual health. But all has been in vain. Peace of conscience seems as far off as ever. The wound within appears a fretting, intractable sore, which nothing can heal. They are still wretched, still unhappy, still thoroughly discontented with their own state. In short, like the woman of whom we read to day, they are ready to say, "There is no hope for me. I shall never be saved."

Let all such take comfort in the miracle which we are now considering. Let them know that "there is balm in Gilead," which can cure them, if they will only seek it. There is one door at which they have never knocked, in all their efforts to obtain relief. There is one Physician to whom they have not applied, who never fails to heal. Let them consider the conduct of the woman before us in her necessity. When all other means had failed, she went to Jesus for help. Let them go and do likewise.

Let us see, secondly, in the conduct of the woman before us, a *striking picture of the first beginnings of saving faith and its effect.* We are told that she "came behind" our Lord, and "touched the border of His garment, and immediately her issue of blood stanched." The act appeared a most simple one, and utterly inadequate to produce any great result. But the effect of that act was most marvellous! In an instant the poor sufferer was healed. The relief that many physicians had failed to give in "twelve years," was obtained in one moment. It was but one touch, and she was well!

It is hard to conceive a more lively image of the experience of many souls than the history of this woman's cure. Hundreds could testify that, like her, they long sought spiritual help from physicians of no value, and wearied their souls by using remedies which brought no cure. At last, like her, they heard of One who healed labouring consciences, and forgave sinners, " without money and without price," if men would only come to Him by faith.—The terms seemed too easy to be credible. The tidings sounded too good to be true.—But, like the woman before us, they resolved to try. They came to Christ by faith, with all their sins, and to their amazement at once found relief. And now they feel more comfort and hope than they ever felt before. The burden seems rolled off their backs. The weight seems taken off their minds. Light seems breaking in on their hearts. They begin to " rejoice in hope of the glory of God." (Rom. v. 2.) And all, they would tell us, is owing to one simple thing. They came to Jesus just as they were. They touched Him by faith, and were healed.

For ever let it be graven on our hearts that faith in

Christ is the grand secret of peace with God. Without it we shall never find inward rest, whatever we may do in religion. Without it we may go to services daily and receive the Lord's Supper every week,—we may give our goods to the poor, and our bodies to be burned,—we may fast and wear sackcloth, and live the lives of hermits,— all this we may do, and be miserable after all. One true believing touch of Christ is worth all these things put together. The pride of human nature may not like it. But it is true! Thousands will rise up at the last day and testify that they never felt comfort of soul till they came to Christ by faith, and were content to cease from their own works, and be saved wholly and entirely by His grace.

Let us see lastly, in this passage, *how much our Lord desires that those who have received benefit from Him should confess Him before men.* We are told that He did not allow this woman, whose case we have been reading, to retire from the crowd unheeded. He enquired, " who had touched Him." He enquired again, until the woman came forward and "declared" her case before all the people. And then came the gracious words, " Daughter, be of good comfort. Thy faith hath made thee whole."

Confession of Christ is a matter of great importance. Let this never be forgotten by true Christians. The work that we can do for our blessed Master is little and poor. Our best endeavours to glorify Him are weak and full of imperfections. Our prayers and praises are sadly defective. Our knowledge and love are miserably small. But do we feel within that Christ has healed our souls? Then can we not confess Christ before men? Can we not plainly tell others that Christ has done everything for us,—that we were dying of a deadly disease, and were cured,—that we were lost, and are now found,—that we were blind, and now see?—Let us do this boldly, and not be afraid. Let us not be ashamed to let all men know what Jesus has done for our souls. Our Master loves to see us doing so. He likes His people not to be ashamed of His name. It is a solemn saying of St. Paul, "If thou shalt confess with thy mouth the Lord Jesus, and believe in thy heart that God hath raised him from the dead, thou shalt be saved." (Rom. x. 9.)—It is a still more solemn saying of Christ Himself, "Whosoever shall be ashamed of me and my words, of him shall the Son of man be ashamed." (Luke ix. 26.)

NOTES. LUKE VIII. 41—48.

41.—[*And behold.*] Chemnitius remarks, that all the three Gospel writers who record the miracle of the raising of Jairus' daughter begin their account with this expression " behold !" It seems intended to call our attention partly to the greatness of the miracle, and partly to the singular goodness of God in raising up friends to the Gospel even in the synagogues.

Let it be noted that Jairus lived at Capernaum, and that the Gospels mention no less than three persons of rank and influence in Capernaum, for whom our Lord wrought special miracles. One is the nobleman whose son was healed. (John iv. 46.) Another is the centurion whose servant was healed. (John vii. 2.) The third is Jairus, the ruler of the synagogue.

42.—[*She lay a dying.*] The Greek word so translated would be rendered more literally, " she was dying—at the point of death."

[*The people thronged him.*] Let us mark the pious observation of Quesnel on this circumstance :—"Abundance of Christians, as it were, press upon Christ, in hearing His word, receiving the sacraments, and performing the outward part of religion ; but few touch Him by a lively faith, a true Christian life, the prayer of charity, and the meditation, love, and imitation of his mysteries. The numerous assemblies and multitudes of people who fill the churches, and make the crowd at sermons, and yet cease not to go on in their usual course, in following the world and their own passions, throng and press Christ, but do not touch Him."

43.—[*A woman having an issue of blood.*] In order to realize this woman's case, and the greatness of the miracle here recorded, we should read Leviticus xv. 19. We shall then see that her disease rendered her ceremonially unclean. Bearing this in mind, we shall understand her desire to avoid publicity and observation. At the same time, let us not fail to note the high position which our Lord occupies in working this cure. He works it as our great High Priest. He bestows health and ceremonial cleanness, and yet in doing so contracts no uncleanness himself.

44.—[*Border of His garment.*] Parkhurst, in his lexicon, says, that this was " a tassel, or tuft of the garment, which the Jews in general, and our blessed Lord in particular, wore in obedience to the Mosaic law (Numb. xxii. 12), and which the Scribes and Pharisees affected to wear remarkably large, as badges of extraordinary piety, and of uncommon obedience to the divine commandment."

45.—[*Who touched me!*] This expression would be translated more literally, " who is the person that touched me."

[*Master.*] Let it be noted that the word so translated is only used by St. Luke in the New Testament, and is only applied to Christ. It signifies literally, " one who is set over anything to take care of it." It is a title of respect, and an acknowledgment of authority.

46.—[*Virtue.*] The word so translated is more frequently rendered " power," "might," or " strength." The whole expression of the verse is a very peculiar one.

48.—[*Hath made whole.*] The word so rendered might have been equally well translated " hath saved." There is, probably, an intentional use of a word of deep double meaning.

LUKE VIII. 49—56.

49 While he yet spake, there cometh one from the ruler of the synagogue's *house,* saying to him, Thy daughter is dead ; trouble not the Master.

50 But when Jesus heard *it,* he answered him, saying, Fear not : believe only, and she shall be made whole.

51 And when he came into the house, he suffered no man to go in, save Peter, and James, and John, and the father and the mother of the maiden.

52 And all wept, and bewailed her : but he said, Weep not ; she is not dead, but sleepeth.

53 And they laughed him to scorn, knowing that she was dead.

54 And he put them all out, and took her by the hand, and called,

saying, Maid, arise.

55 And her spirit came again, and she arose straightway : and he commanded to give her meat.

56 And her parents were astonished : but he charged them that they should tell no man what was done.

THE verses we have now read, contain one of the three great instances which the Holy Ghost has thought fit to record of our Lord restoring a dead person to life. The other two instances are those of Lazarus and the widow's son at Nain. There seems no reason to doubt that our Lord raised others beside these three. But these three cases are specially described as patterns of His almighty power. One was a young girl, who had just breathed her last. One was a young man, who was being carried to his burial. One was a man, who had already lain four days in the grave. In all three cases alike we see life at once restored at Christ's command.

Let us notice, in the verses before us, *how universal is the dominion which death holds over the sons of men.* We see him coming to a rich man's house, and tearing from him the desire of his eyes with a stroke. "There cometh one from the ruler of the synagogue's house, saying to him, thy daughter is dead." Such tidings as these are the bitterest cups which we have to drink in this world. Nothing cuts so deeply into man's heart as to part with beloved ones, and lay them in the grave. Few griefs are so crushing and heavy as the grief of a parent over an only child.

Death is indeed a cruel enemy ! He makes no distinction in his attacks. He comes to the rich man's hall, as well as to the poor man's cottage. He does not spare the young, the strong, and the beautiful, any more than the old, the infirm, and the grey-haired. Not all the gold of Australia, nor all the skill of doctors, can keep the hand of death from our bodies, in the day of his power. When the appointed hour comes, and God permits him to smite, our worldly schemes must be broken off, and our darlings must be taken away and buried out of our sight.

These thoughts are melancholy, and few like to hear of them. The subject of death is one that men blink, and refuse to look at. "All men think all men mortal but themselves." But why should we treat this great reality in this way? Why should we not rather look the subject of death in the face, in order that when our turn comes we may be prepared to die? Death will come to our houses, whether we like it or not. Death will take each of us away, despite our dislike to hearing about it. Surely it is the part of a wise man to get ready for this great change. Why should we not be ready? There is One who can deliver us from the fear of death. (Heb. ii. 15.) Christ has overcome death, and "brought life and immortality to light through the Gospel." (2 Tim. i. 10.) He that believeth on Him hath everlasting life, and though he were dead yet shall he live. (John vi. 47 ; xi. 25.) Let us believe in the Lord Jesus, and then death will lose his sting. We shall then be able to say with Paul, "To me to die is gain." (Phil. i. 21.)

Let us notice, secondly, in the verses before us, *that faith in Christ's love and power is the best remedy in time of trouble.* We are told that when Jesus heard the tidings, that the ruler's daughter was dead, He said to him, "Fear not, believe only, and she shall be made whole."—These words, no doubt, were spoken with

immediate reference to the miracle our Lord was going
to perform.   But we need not doubt that they were also
meant for the perpetual benefit of the Church of Christ.
They were meant to reveal to us the grand secret of
comfort in the hour of need.   That secret is to exercise
faith, to fall back on the thought of Christ's loving heart
and mighty hand,—in one word, to believe.

Let a petition for more faith form a part of all our
daily prayers.   As ever we would have peace, and calm-
ness, and quietness of spirit, let us often say, "Lord
increase our faith."   A hundred painful things may
happen to us every week in this evil world, of which
our poor weak minds cannot see the reason.   Without
faith we shall be constantly disquieted and cast down.
Nothing will make us cheerful and tranquil but an abiding
sense of Christ's love, Christ's wisdom, Christ's care over
us, and Christ's providential management of all our
affairs.   Faith will not sink under the weight of evil tidings.
(Psa. cxii. 7.)   Faith can sit still and wait for better times.
Faith can see light even in the darkest hour, and a
needs-be for the heaviest trial.   Faith can find room
to build Ebenezers under any circumstances, and can
sing songs in the night in any condition.   "He that
believeth shall not make haste."   "Thou wilt keep
him in perfect peace whose mind is staid on thee."   (Isa.
xxviii. 16 ; xvi. 3.)   Once more let the lesson be graven
on our minds.   If we would travel comfortably through
this world, we must "believe."

Let us notice, finally, in these verses, *the almighty
power which our Lord Jesus Christ possesses even over
death*.   We are told that He came to the house of Jairus

and turned the mourning into joy. He took by the hand the breathless body of the ruler's daughter, "and called saying, damsel arise." At once by that all-powerful voice life was restored. "Her spirit came again, and she arose straightway."

Let us take comfort in the thought that there is a limit to death's power. The king of terrors is very strong. How many generations he has mowed down and swept into the dust! How many of the wise, and strong, and fair, he has swallowed down and snatched away in their prime! How many victories he has won, and how often he has written, "vanity of vanities," on the pride of man! Patriarchs, and kings, and prophets, and apostles, have all in turn been obliged to yield to him. They have all died. But thanks be unto God, there is One stronger than death. There is One who has said, "O death I will be thy plagues : O grave I will be thy destruction ! " (Hosea xiii. 14.) That One is the Friend of sinners, Christ Jesus the Lord. He proved His power frequently, when He came to earth the first time, in the house of Jairus, by the tomb of Bethany, in the gate of Nain. He will prove it to all the world when He comes again. "The last enemy that shall be destroyed is death." (1 Cor. xv. 26.) "The earth shall cast out the dead." (Isa. xxvi. 19.)

Let us leave the passage with the consoling thought, that the things which happened in Jairus' house are a type of good things to come. The hour cometh and will soon be here, when the voice of Christ shall call all His people from their graves, and gather them together to part no more. Believing husbands shall once more see

believing wives.   Believing parents shall once more see
believing children.   Christ shall unite the whole family
in the great home in heaven, and all tears shall be wiped
from all eyes.

NOTES. LUKE VIII. 49—56.

49 .—[*Thy daughter is dead.*]   Chemnitius remarks, that, with one
exception (Mark i. 30), we never read in the Gospels of children
coming to Christ on behalf of their parents, though we frequently
read of parents applying on behalf of their children.   He makes
the deep observation, that "love is more prone to descend than
to ascend."

[*The Master.*]   Let it be noted that the Greek word so translated is not the same as that used in the 45th verse.   It here
signifies " the Teacher."

51.—*Peter, and James, and John.*]   These three apostles, it should
be remembered, were three times singled out from the rest
of the twelve, and allowed to be our Lord's companions on
special occasions.   They were with him on the Mount of Transfiguration, and in the Garden of Gethsemane, and on the occasion of this miracle.   None of the apostles had such a clear
revelation of our Lord's divinity, our Lord's humanity, and our
Lord's power and compassion towards the sorrowful and sinful.

52.—[*She is not dead, but sleepeth.*]   Much has been said about the
difficulty of this expression, but without any just cause.   The
strength of it has led some to assert, that the daughter of Jairus
was not really and literally dead, but only in a trance.   Such
an assertion contradicts the context, while there is really no
difficulty in the expression, that does not admit of explanation.

Burkitt says, that our Lord's meaning was this :—" She is
dead to you, but asleep to me ; not so dead as to be beyond my
power to raise her to life."

Alford says—" The words are most probably used with reference to the speedy awakening which was to follow."

Jones, of Nayland, says—" As we have but imperfect notions
of the relation and difference between life and death, our
Saviour, when he was about to raise a maid to life, said to those
who were present, ' the damsel is not dead, but sleepeth.'   He
did not say, She is dead, and I will raise her to life ; but, she is
asleep, whence it was to be inferred that she would awake.
They who were not skilled in the language of signs and figures
laughed him to scorn, as if he had spoken in ignorance what
was expressed with consummate truth and wisdom.   The
substitution of sleep for death has the force and value of a whole
sermon in a single word."

54.—[*He put them all out.*] When we read this expression, we
should remember the words in the preceding verse, "They laughed Him to scorn." It seems a rule in Christ's dealings with men
not to force evidence upon them, but rather to withhold from
scorners and scoffers those proofs of His own mission which He
affords to others. And as it was when He was upon earth, so it
is now. The scoffing spirit is the spirit which is often left to
itself.

55.—[*Her spirit came again.*] This is one of those texts which
show plainly the separate existence of spirits, and their indepen-
dence of the body. Matthew Henry remarks—"This proves
that our souls exist and act in a state of separation from the
body, and therefore are immortal, that death does not extinguish
the candle of the Lord, but takes it out of a dark lantern. It is
not, as Grotius observes, the temperament of the body, or anything that dies with it; but something that subsists by itself,
which, after death, is somewhere else than where the body is.
Where the soul of the child was in the interval we are not told.
It was in the hand of the Father of spirits, to whom all souls at
death return."

[*To give her meat.*] This would be proof positive that her
body was really alive again, and that her parents saw no vision,
but real material flesh and blood. It is the same evidence of
resurrection which our Lord gave His disciples after His own
rising from the dead: "Have ye here any meat? And he did eat
before them." (Luke xxiv. 41—43.)

56.—[*Tell no man.*] Let us note here, as in many places, how little
our Lord desired publicity. To do great works, and say nothing
about them—to work powerfully, and yet noiselessly and
quietly, is to walk in Christ's steps. The shallowest streams
and emptiest vessels make most noise.

LUKE IX. 1—6.

1 Then he called his twelve disciples together, and gave them power
and authority over all devils, and to
cure diseases.

2 And he sent them to preach the
kingdom of God, and to heal the sick.

3 And he said unto them, Take
nothing for *your* journey, neither
staves, nor scrip, neither bread, neither money; neither have two coats
apiece.

4 And whatsoever house ye enter
into, there abide, and thence depart.

5 And whosoever will not receive
you, when ye go out of that city, shake
off the very dust from your feet for a
testimony against them.

6 And they departed, and went
through the towns, preaching the
Gospel, and healing every where.

THESE verses contain our Lord's instructions to His

twelve apostles, when He sent them forth the first time
to preach the Gospel. The passage is one which throws
much light on the work of Christian ministers in every
age. No doubt the miraculous powers which the apostles
possessed, made their position very unlike that of any
other body of men in the Church. No doubt, in many
respects, they stood alone, and had no successors. Yet
the words of our Lord in this place must not be confined
entirely to the apostles. They contain deep wisdom for
Christian teachers and preachers, for all time.

Let us observe, that *the commission to the apostles contained special reference to the devil and bodily sickness.* We
read that Jesus gave them "authority over all devils,
and to cure diseases."

We see here, as in a glass, two of the principal parts
of the Christian minister's business. We must not expect him to cast out evil spirits, but we may fairly
expect him to "resist the devil and all his works," and to
keep up a constant warfare against the prince of this
world.—We must not expect him to work miraculous
cures, but we may expect him to take a special interest
in all sick people, to visit them, sympathize with them,
and help them, if needful, as far as he can.—The
minister who neglects the sick members of his flock is no
true pastor. He must not be surprised if people say that
he cares for the fleece of his sheep more than for their
health. The minister who allows drunkenness, blasphemy, uncleanness, fighting, revelling, and the like, to
go on among his congregation unreproved, is omitting a
plain duty of his office. He is not warring against the
devil. He is no true successor of the apostles.

Let us observe, secondly, that *one of the principal works which the apostles were commissioned to take up was preaching.* We read that our Lord " sent them to preach the kingdom of God," and that " they went through the towns preaching the Gospel."

The importance of preaching, as a means of grace, might easily be gathered from this passage, even if it stood alone. But it is but one instance, among many, of the high value which the Bible everywhere sets upon preaching. It is, in fact, God's chosen instrument for doing good to souls. By it sinners are converted, inquirers led on, and saints built up. A preaching ministry is absolutely essential to the health and prosperity of a visible church. The pulpit is the place where the chief victories of the Gospel have always been won, and no Church has ever done much for the advancement of true religion in which the pulpit has been neglected. Would we know whether a minister is a truly apostolical man ? If he is, he will give the best of his attention to his sermons. He will labour and pray to make his preaching effective, and he will tell his congregation that he looks to preaching for the chief results on souls. The minister who exalts the sacraments, or forms of the Church, above preaching, may be a zealous, earnest, conscientious, and respectable minister ; but his zeal is not according to knowledge. He is not a follower of the apostles.

Let us observe, thirdly, that our Lord charges His apostles, when He sends them forth, *to study simplicity of habits, and contentment with such things as they have.* He bids them " take nothing for their journey, neither staves, nor scrip, neither bread nor money; neither have two coats a piece. And whatsoever house ye enter into there abide, and thence depart." In part, these instructions apply only to a peculiar period. There came a day when our Lord Himself bade every one who had "no sword, to sell his garment and buy one." (Luke xxii. 36.) But, in part, these instructions contain a lesson for all time. The spirit of these verses is meant to be remembered by all ministers of the Gospel.

The leading idea which the words convey is, a warning against worldliness and luxurious habits. Well would it be for the world and the Church if the warning had been more carefully heeded! From no quarter has Christianity received such damage as it has from the hands of its own teachers. On no point have its teachers erred so much, and so often, as in the matter of personal worldliness and luxury of life. They have often destroyed, by their daily lives, the whole work of their lips. They have given occasion to the enemies of religion to say, that they love ease, and money, and good things, far more than souls. From such ministers may we pray daily that the Church may be delivered! They are a living stumbling-block in the way to heaven. They are helpers to the cause of the devil, and not of God. The preacher whose affections are set on money, and dress, and feasting, and pleasure-seeking, has clearly mistaken his vocation. He has forgotten his Master's instructions. He is not an apostolic man.

Let us observe, lastly, that *our Lord prepares His disciples to meet with unbelief and impenitence in those to whom they preached.* He speaks of those "who will not receive them" as a class which they must expect to see. He tells them how to behave, when not received, as if it was a state of things to which they must make up their mind.

All ministers of the Gospel would do well to read carefully this portion of our Lord's instructions. All missionaries, and district visitors, and Sunday-school teachers, would do well to lay it to heart. Let them not be cast down if their work seems in vain, and their labour without profit. Let them remember that the very first preachers and teachers whom Jesus employed were sent forth with a distinct warning, that not all would believe. Let them work on patiently, and sow the good seed without fainting. Duties are theirs. Events are God's. Apostles may plant and water. The Holy Ghost alone can give spiritual life. The Lord Jesus knows what is in the heart of man. He does not despise his labourers because little of the seed they sow bears fruit. The harvest may be small. But every labourer shall be rewarded according to his work.

Notes. Luke IX. 1—6.

1.—[*His twelve disciples.*] Let it be noted, that Judas Iscariot, the false apostle and traitor, was one of those twelve whom our Lord sent forth to preach and heal the sick. It must not surprise us, if we see unconverted men preachers and ministers of the Gospel. Our Lord permitted one to be in the number of His apostles, in order to show that we must expect to see the evil mingled with the good in this world. The highest ecclesiastical office and dignity afford no proof that a man has the grace of God.

[*Gave them power.*] Theophylact remarks, what an evidence we have here of our Lord's divine power. He could not only work miracles Himself, but could give power to others to work them.

2.—[*He sent them to preach.*] Let it be carefully noted, that, speaking literally and accurately, there is no such thing as apostolical succession. The office of the apostles was isolated, peculiar, and distinct, and ceased with themselves. Ministers of the churches of Christ are successors of Timothy and Titus, but not of the apostles.

3.—[*Take nothing for your journey, &c.*] The words of Quesnel on this verse are worth reading. "Men will never be able to establish the kingdom of God in the hearts of people, so long as they do not appear fully persuaded themselves of those truths which they preach. And how can they appear so, if they plainly contradict them in their practice and behaviour? In order to persuade others to be unconcerned for superfluities, a man must not himself appear too much concerned, even about necessaries."

[*Scrip.*] The word so translated, means, a little bag to carry provisions in.

4.—[*There abide, and thence depart.*] The object of this injunction is evident. The apostles were to beware of appearing changeable, fickle, luxurious, and hard to please. Like men who regard all the world as an inn, and heaven as their home, they were to be content with any lodging, and any kind of entertainment.

6.—[*Preaching the Gospel.*] It is a very awful thought, that one of those who did this, was Judas Iscariot. There seems no reason to suppose that he preached less faithfully or powerfully than the other apostles. Yet his heart was all the time wrong in the sight of God. It is no proof that a man is a converted man, because he preaches the Gospel! See Philipp. i. 15. A man may preach Christ from false motives.

LUKE IX. 7—11.

7 Now Herod the tetrarch heard of all that was done by him : and he was perplexed, because that it was said of some, that John was risen from the dead ;
8 And of some, that Elias had appeared ; and of others, that one of the old prophets was risen again.
9 And Herod said, John have I beheaded : but who is this of whom I hear such things? And he desired to see him.

10 And the apostles, when they were returned, told him all that they had done. And he took them, and went aside privately into a desert place belonging to the city called Bethsaida.
11 And the people, when they knew *it*, followed him : and he received them, and spake unto them of the kingdom of God, and healed them that had need of healing.

LET us mark, in this passage, *the power of a bad conscience.* We are told, that when "Herod the tetrarch heard of all

that was done by our Lord, he was perplexed." He
said, "John have I beheaded, but who is this?" Great
and powerful as he was, the tidings of our Lord's ministry called his sins to remembrance, and disturbed him
even in his royal palace.   Surrounded as he was by everything which is considered to make life enjoyable, the report
of another preacher of righteousness filled him with alarm.
The recollection of his own wickedness in killing John the
Baptist flashed on his mind.   He knew he had done wrong.
He felt guilty, self-condemned, and self-dissatisfied.   Faithful and true is that saying of Solomon's, "The way of
transgressors is hard." (Prov. xiii. 15.)   Herod's sin had
found him out.   The prison and the sword had silenced
John the Baptist's tongue, but they could not silence
the voice of Herod's inward man.   God's truth can
neither be silenced, nor bound, nor killed.

Conscience is a most powerful part of our natural
constitution.   It cannot save our souls.   It never leads
a man to Christ.   It is often blind, and ignorant, and
misdirected.   Yet conscience often raises a mighty testimony against sin in the sinner's heart, and makes him feel
that "it is an evil and a bitter thing" to depart from God.
Young persons ought especially to remember this, and,
remembering it, to take heed to their ways.   Let them
not flatter themselves that all is right, when their sins
are past, and done, and forgotten by the world.   Let
them know that conscience can bring up each sin before
the eyes of their minds, and make it bite like a serpent.
Millions will testify at the last day that Herod's experience was their own.   Conscience called old sins from
their graves, and made them walk up and down in their

hearts. In the midst of seeming happiness and prosperity they were inwardly miserable and distressed. Happy are they who have found the only cure for a bad conscience! Nothing will ever heal it but the blood of Christ.

Let us mark, secondly, *the importance to Christians of occasional privacy and retirement.* We are told, that when the apostles returned from their first ministerial work, our Lord "took them and went aside privately into a desert place." We cannot doubt that this was done with a deep meaning. It was meant to teach the great lesson that those who do public work for the souls of others, must be careful to make time for being alone with God.

The lesson is one which many Christians would do well to remember. Occasional retirement, self-inquiry, meditation, and secret communion with God, are absolutely essential to spiritual health. The man who neglects them is in great danger of a fall. To be *always* preaching, teaching, speaking, writing, and working public works, is, unquestionably, a sign of zeal. But it is not always a sign of zeal according to knowledge. It often leads to untoward consequences. We *must* make time occasionally for sitting down and calmly looking within, and examining how matters stand between our own selves and Christ. The omission of the practice is the true account of many a backsliding which shocks the Church, and gives occasion to the world to blaspheme. Many could say with sorrow, in the words of Canticles, "They made me keeper of the vineyards, but my own vineyard have I not kept." (Cant. i. 6.)

Let us mark, lastly, in this passage, *our Lord Jesus*

Christ's readiness to receive all who came to Him. We are told, that when the multitude followed Him into the desert, whither He had retired, "he received them, and spake unto them of the kingdom of God, and healed them that had need of healing." Unmannerly and uninvited as this intrusion on His privacy seems to have been, it met with no rebuff from our Lord. He was always more ready to give instruction than people were to ask it, and more willing to teach than people were to be taught.

But the incident, trifling as it may seem, exactly tallies with all that we read in the Gospels of the gentleness and condescension of Christ. We never see Him dealing with people according to their deserts. We never find Him scrutinizing the motives of His hearers, or refusing to allow them to learn of Him, because their hearts were not right in the sight of God. His ear was always ready to hear, and His hand to work, and His tongue to preach. None that came to Him were ever cast out. Whatever they might think of His doctrine, they could never say that Jesus of Nazareth was "an austere man."

Let us remember this in all our dealings with Christ about our own souls. We may draw near to Him with boldness, and open our hearts to Him with confidence. He is a Saviour of infinite compassion and lovingkindness. He will not break the bruised reed, nor quench the smoking flax. The secrets of our spiritual life may be such as we would not have our dearest friends know. The wounds of our consciences may be deep and sore, and require most delicate handling. But we need not fear anything, if we commit all to Jesus, the Son of God.

We shall find that His kindness is unbounded. His own words shall be found abundantly true : "I am meek and lowly of heart, and ye shall find rest to your souls." (Matt. ii. 29.)

Let us remember this, finally, in our dealing with other people, if we are called upon to give them help about their souls. Let us strive to walk in the steps of Christ's example, and, like Him, to be kind, and patient, and always willing to aid. The ignorance of young beginners in religion is sometimes very provoking. We are apt to be wearied of their instability, and fickleness, and halting between two opinions. But let us remember Jesus, and not be weary. He "received all," spake to all, and did good to all. Let us go and do likewise. As Christ deals with us, so let us deal one with another.

Notes. Luke IX. 7—11.

7.—[*He was perplexed.*] The Greek word so translated, is rendered, in Luke xxiv. 4., "much perplexed." In the only three other places where it is used in the New Testament, it is translated, "doubted," or, "was in doubt." (Acts ii. 12 ; v. 24 ; x. 17.)

[*Risen from the dead.*] Let it be noted, that a resurrection from the dead is spoken of here, and in the following verses, as a thing which was commonly believed and acknowledged as true among the Jews. The notion, that the Jews, before Christ, knew nothing of a resurrection or another life, is utterly untenable.

9.—[*I beheaded...I hear.*] Let it be noted, that the Greek word for " I," is twice repeated in this verse. Alford thinks that the repetition "implies personal concern and alarm at the growing fame of Jesus."

10.—[*He took them and went aside privately.*] Let the words of Cecil, on this subject, be carefully weighed. "If a man would seriously set himself to work, he must retire from the crowd. He must not live in a bustle. If he is always driving through the business of the day, he will be so in harness, as not to observe the road he is going."

Again, he says; " I know not how it is that some Christians

can make so little of recollection and retirement. I find the spirit of the world a strong assimilating principle. I find it hurrying away minds in its wake, and sinking men among the dregs and filth of a carnal nature. Even my ministerial employment would degenerate into a mere following of my trade, and crying of my wares. I am obliged to withdraw myself regularly, and say to my heart, 'What are you doing? Where are you?'"

LUKE IX. 12—17.

12 And when the day began to wear away, then came the twelve, and said unto him, Send the multitude away, that they may go into the towns and country round about, and lodge, and get victuals: for we are here in a desert place.

13 But he said unto them, Give ye them to eat. And they said, We have no more but five loaves and two fishes; except we should go and buy meat for all this people.

14 For they were about five thousand men. And he said to his disciples,

Make them sit down by fifties in a company.

15 And they did so, and made them all sit down.

16 Then he took the five loaves and the two fishes, and looking up to heaven, he blessed them, and brake, and gave to the disciples to set before the multitude.

17 And they did eat, and were all filled: and there was taken up of fragments that remained to them twelve baskets.

THE miracle described in these verses is more frequently related in the Gospels than any that our Lord wrought. There is no doubt a meaning in this repetition. It is intended to draw our special attention to the things which it contains.

We see, for one thing, in these verses, *a striking example of our Lord Jesus Christ's divine power.* He feeds an assembly of five thousand men with five loaves and two fishes. He makes a scanty supply of victuals, which was barely sufficient for the daily wants of Himself and His disciples, satisfy the hunger of a company as large as a Roman legion. There could be no mistake about the reality and greatness of this miracle. It was done publicly, and before many witnesses. The same power which at the beginning made the world out of nothing, caused food to exist, which before had not existed. The circumstances of the whole event made deception impossible. Five thousand hungry men would not have agreed that they were "all filled," if they had not received real food. "Twelve baskets full of fragments" would never have been taken up, if real material loaves and fishes had not been miraculously multiplied. Nothing, in short, can explain the whole transaction, but the finger of God. The same hand which sent manna from heaven in the wilderness to feed Israel, was the hand which made five loaves and two fishes supply the wants of five thousand men.

The miracle before us is one among many proofs that with Christ nothing is impossible. The Saviour of sinners is Almighty. He "calleth those things which be not as though they were." (Rom. iv. 17.) When He wills a thing, it shall be done. When He commands a thing, it shall come to pass. He can create light out of darkness, order out of disorder, strength out of weakness, joy out of sorrow, and food out of nothing at all. For ever let us bless God that it is so! We might well despair, when we see the corruption of human nature, and the desperate hardness and unbelief of man's heart, if we did not know the power of Christ.—" Can these dry bones live? Can any man or woman be saved? Can any child, or friend of ours, ever become a true Christian? Can we ourselves ever win our way through to heaven?"—Questions like these could never be answered, if Jesus was not Almighty. But thanks be to God, Jesus has all power in heaven and earth. He lives in heaven for us, able to save to the uttermost, and therefore we may hope.

We see, for another thing, in these verses, a *striking emblem of Christ's ability to supply the spiritual wants of mankind*. The whole miracle is a picture. We see in it, as in a glass, some of the most important truths of Christianity. It is, in fact, a great acted parable of the glorious Gospel.

What is that multitude which surrounded our Lord in the wilderness, poor and helpless, and destitute of food? It is a figure of mankind. We are a company of poor sinners, in the midst of a wicked world, without strength, or power to save ourselves, and sorely in danger of perishing from spiritual famine.

Who is that gracious Teacher who had compassion on this starving multitude in the wilderness, and said to His disciples, "Give ye them to eat?" It is Jesus Himself, ever pitiful, ever kind, ever ready to shew mercy, even to the unthankful and the evil. And He is not altered. He is just the same to day as He was eighteen hundred years ago. High in heaven at the right hand of God, He looks down on the vast multitude of starving sinners, who cover the face of the earth. He still pities them, still cares for them, still feels for their helplessness and need. And He still says to His believing followers, "Behold this multitude, give ye them to eat."

What is that wonderful provision which Christ miraculously made for the famishing multitude before Him? It is a figure of the Gospel. Weak and contemptible as that Gospel appears to many, it contains "enough and to spare" for the souls of all mankind. Poor and despicable as the story of a crucified Saviour seems to the wise and prudent, it is the power of God unto salvation to every one that believeth. (Rom. i. 16.)

What are those disciples who received the loaves and
fishes from Christ's hand, and carried them to the multitude, till all were filled? They are a figure of all
faithful preachers and teachers of the Gospel. Their
work is simple, and yet deeply important. They are
appointed to set before men the provision that Christ has
made for their souls. Of their own invention they are
not commissioned to give anything. All that they convey
to men, must be from Christ's hands. So long as they
faithfully discharge this office, they may confidently
expect their Master's blessing. Many, no doubt, will
always refuse to eat of the food that Christ has provided.
But if ministers offer the bread of life to men faithfully,
the blood of those who are lost will not be required at
their hands.

What are we doing ourselves? Have we discovered
that this world is a wilderness, and that our souls must
be fed with bread from heaven, or die eternally?
Happy are they who have learned this lesson, and
have tasted by experience, that Christ crucified is the
true bread of life! The heart of man can never be
satisfied with the things of this world. It is always
empty, and hungry, and thirsty, and dissatisfied, till it
comes to Christ. It is only they who hear Christ's voice,
and follow Him, and feed on Him by faith, who are "filled."

NOTES. LUKE. IX. 12—17.

14.—[*By fifties in a company.*] The word translated "company,"
is only used in this place in the New Testament. It signifies
"a company of people reclining at meat."

Our Lord's love of order and dislike to confusion, appear
strongly in the description here given about the disposition of
the multitude, before He fed them. He teaches us the importance of doing everything in an orderly methodical way.

17.—[*Of fragments...twelve baskets.*] Let our Lord's disapproba-
tion of waste be noted. If "the great Housekeeper of the world,"
Burkitt says, "is so particular about saving fragments, what
account will they give in the day of judgment, who think
nothing of wasting time, money, health, and strength, in the
service of sin and the world?"

The remark of Brentius on this miracle is worth notice. He
says, "the whole sixth chapter of St. John is the true explanation
of the use of this miracle. Christ is the bread of life, and he
who eats of Him shall live for ever."

[*Baskets.*] The Greek word so translated is only used in the New
Testament, in the account given by Matthew, Mark, Luke, and
John, of this miracle. It means a wicker basket such as the
Jews were remarkable for carrying with them, as remarked even
by the Roman poet, Juvenal. It is worthy of notice, that in the
second miracle of feeding the multitude, recorded by Matthew
and Mark only, where *seven baskets* of fragments were taken
up, the word translated "basket," is entirely different from that
used here. It signifies, in that miracle, a large wicker basket,
and is said by Hesychius to be a vessel for corn. At any rate, it
means a very large basket, for it is the same word used where it
is said that St. Paul was "let down in a basket from the wall."
(Acts ix. 25.)

LUKE IX. 18—22.

18 And it came to pass, as he was alone praying, his disciples were with him : and he asked them, saying, Whom say the people that I am?

19 They answering said, John the Baptist ; but some *say,* Elias ; and others *say,* that one of the old prophets is risen again.

20 He said unto them, But whom say ye that I am? Peter answering said, The Christ of God.

21 And he straitly charged them, and commanded *them* to tell no man that thing ;

22 Saying, The Son of man must suffer many things, and be rejected of the elders and Chief Priests and Scribes, and be slain, and be raised the third day.

LET us notice in this passage, *the variety of opinions
about our Lord Jesus Christ, which prevailed during His
earthly ministry.* We are told that some said that He
was John the Baptist ;—some that He was Elias ;—and
some that one of the old prophets was risen again. One
common remark applies to all these opinions. All were
agreed that our Lord's doctrine was not like that of the

Scribes and Pharisees.   All saw in Him a bold witness
against the evil that was in the world.

Let it never surprise us, to find the same variety
of opinions about Christ and His Gospel in our own
times.   God's truth disturbs the spiritual laziness of men.
It obliges them to think.   It makes them begin to talk,
and reason, and speculate, and invent theories to account
for its spread in some quarters, and its rejection in others.
Thousands in every age of the Church spend their lives
in this way, and never come to the point of drawing
near to God.   They satisfy themselves with a miserable
round of gossip about this preacher's sermons, or that
writer's opinions.   They think "this man goes too far," and
"that man does not go far enough."   Some doctrines they
approve, and others they disapprove.   Some teachers they
call "sound," and others they call "unsound."   They cannot
quite make up their own minds what is true, or what is
right.   Year rolls on after year, and finds them in the same
state,—talking, criticising, fault-finding, speculating, but
never getting any further,—hovering like the moth round
religion, but never settling down like the bee, to feed on
its treasures.   They never boldly lay hold of Christ.
They never set themselves heartily to the great business
of serving God.   They never take up the cross, and
become thorough Christians.   And at last, after all their
talking, they die in their sins, unprepared to meet God.

Let us not be content with a religion of this kind.
It will not save us to talk and speculate, and bandy
opinions about the Gospel.   The Christianity that saves,
is a thing personally grasped, personally experienced,
personally felt, and personally possessed.   There is not

the slightest excuse for stopping short in talk, opinion, and speculation. The Jews of our Lord's time might have found out, if they had been honest inquirers, that Jesus of Nazareth was neither John the Baptist, nor Elias, nor an old prophet, but the Christ of God. The speculative Christian of our own day, might easily satisfy himself on every point which is needful to salvation, if he would really, candidly, and humbly seek the teaching of the Spirit. The words of our Lord are weighty and solemn, "If any man will do God's will, he shall know of the doctrine whether it be of God." (John vii. 17.) Honest, practical obedience, is one of the keys of the gate of knowledge.

Let us notice, secondly, in this passage, *the singular knowledge and faith displayed by the Apostle Peter.* We read, that when our Lord said to His disciples, "Whom say ye that I am? Peter answering, said, the Christ of God."

This was a noble confession, and one of which, in these days, we can hardly realize the full value. To estimate it aright we should place ourselves in the position of our Lord's disciples. We should call to mind that the great, and wise, and learned of their own nation, saw no beauty in their Master, and would not receive Him as the Messiah. We should recollect that they saw no royal dignity about our Lord,—no crown,—no army,—no earthly dominion. They saw nothing but a poor man, who often had no place in which to lay his head. And yet it was at this time, and under these circumstances, that Peter boldly declares his belief that Jesus is the Christ of God. Truly, this was a great faith! It was mingled, no doubt,

with much of ignorance and imperfection. But such as
it was, it was a faith that stood alone. He that had it
was a remarkable man, and far in advance of the age in
which he lived.

We should pray frequently that God would raise up
more Christians of the stamp of the apostle Peter.
Erring, and unstable, and ignorant of his own heart as
he sometimes proved, that blessed apostle was in some
respects one in ten thousand. He had faith, and zeal,
and love to Christ's cause, when almost all Israel was
unbelieving and cold. We want more men of this sort. We
want men who are not afraid to stand alone, and to cleave
to Christ when the many are against Him. Such men, like
Peter, may err sadly at times, but in the long run of life
will do more good than any. Knowledge, no doubt, is
an excellent thing; but knowledge without zeal and
warmth will never do much for the world.

Let us notice, thirdly, in this passage, *our Lord's prediction of His own coming death.* We read that He said,
"The Son of Man must suffer many things, and be
rejected of the elders, and chief priests, and scribes, and
be slain, and be raised the third day." These words, as
we read them now, sound simple and plain; but there
lie beneath the surface of them two truths which ought
to be carefully remembered.

For one thing our Lord's prediction shows us, that His
death upon the cross was the voluntary act of His own
free will. He was not delivered up to Pilate and crucified because He could not help it, and had no power to
crush His enemies. His death was the result of the
eternal counsels of the blessed Trinity. He had under-

taken to suffer for man's sin, the just for the unjust, that He might bring us to God. He had engaged to bear our sins, as our Substitute and Surety, and He bore them willingly in His own person on the tree. He saw Calvary and the cross before Him all the days of His ministry. He went up to them willingly, knowingly, and with full consent, that He might pay our debts in His own blood. His death was not the death of a mere weak son of man, who could not escape ; but the death of One who was very God of very God, and had undertaken to be punished in our stead.

For another thing, our Lord's prediction shows us the blinding effect of prejudice on men's minds. Clear and plain as His words now seem to us, His disciples did not understand them. They heard as though they heard not. They could not understand that Messiah was to be "cut off." They could not receive the doctrine that their own Master must needs die. And hence, when His death really took place, they were amazed and confounded. Often as He had told them of it, they had never realized it as a fact.

Let us watch and pray against prejudice. Many a zealous man has been grievously misled by it, and has pierced himself through with many sorrows. Let us beware of allowing traditions, old preconceived notions, unsound interpretations, baseless theories in religion, to find root in our hearts. There is but one test of truth— "What saith the Scripture?" Before this let every prejudice go down.

NOTES. LUKE IX. 18—22.

18.—[*He was alone praying.*] Let us not forget to notice how frequently our Lord's habit of private prayer is mentioned in the Gospels. He sets an example to all who work for God. Much private prayer is one secret of success.

19.—[*John the Baptist...Elias...one of the old prophets.*] Let it be remembered, that talk and speculation about Christ and His Gospel, are one of Satan's great traps for ruining souls. Many a man cloaks his indolence and laziness about religion, under a pretence of the variety of opinions, and the difficulty of knowing who is right.

20.—[*The Christ of God.*] This expression, it should be noted, is tantamount to saying the Messiah of God, the predicted Saviour of whom Daniel spoke. (Dan. ix. 21.)

21.—[*Tell no man.*] There is a time to be silent as well as to speak. Our Lord knew that the public proclamation of His being Messiah, would cause Him to be cut off before His time.

22.—[*Must suffer.*] The Greek word translated "must" in this place, does not quite bear the sense of force and necessity, which our English word "must" conveys. It rather means, "it is becoming, it is suitable, it is necessary for certain great ends and purposes." In Luke xxiv. 26., the same expression is rendered, "*ought* not Christ to have suffered."

LUKE IX. 23—27.

23 And he said to *them* all, If any *man* will come after me, let him deny himself, and take up his cross daily, and follow me.

24 For whosoever will save his life shall lose it: but whosoever will lose his life for my sake, the same shall save it.

25 For what is a man advantaged, if he gain the whole world, and lose himself, or be cast away?

26 For whosoever shall be ashamed of me and of my words, of him shall the Son of man be ashamed, when he shall come in his own glory, and in *his* Father's, and of the holy angels.

27 But I tell you of a truth, there be some standing here, which shall not taste of death, till they see the kingdom of God.

THESE words of our Lord Jesus Christ contain three great lessons for all Christians. They apply to all ranks and classes without exception. They are intended for every age and time, and for every branch of the visible church.

We learn, for one thing, *the absolute necessity of daily self-denial.* We ought every day to crucify the flesh, to overcome the world, and to resist the devil. We ought to keep under our bodies, and bring them into subjection. We ought to be on our guard, like soldiers in an enemy's country. We ought to fight a daily battle, and war a daily warfare. The command of our Master is clear and plain: "If any man will come after Me, let him deny himself, and take up his cross daily, and follow Me."

Now what do we know of all this? Surely this is a question which ought to be asked. A little formal church-going, and a decent attendance at a place of worship, can never be the Christianity of which Christ speaks in this place.—Where is our self-denial? Where is our daily carrying of the cross? Where is our following of Christ?—Without a religion of this kind we shall never be saved. A crucified Saviour will never be content to have a self-pleasing, self-indulging, worldly-minded people. No self-denial—no real grace! No cross —no crown! "They that are Christ's," says St. Paul, "have crucified the flesh with its affections and lusts." (Gal. v. 24.) "Whosoever will save his life," says the Lord Jesus, "shall lose it; but whosoever will lose his life for My sake shall save it."

We learn, for another thing, from our Lord's words in this passage, *the unspeakable value of the soul*. A question is asked, which admits of only one answer—"What is a man advantaged if he gain the whole world and lose himself, or be cast away."

The possession of the whole world, and all that it contains, would never make a man happy. Its pleasures are false and deceptive. Its riches, rank, and honours, have no power to satisfy the heart. So long as we have not got them they glitter, and sparkle, and seem desir-

able.   The moment we have them we find that they are
empty bubbles, and cannot make us feel content.   And,
worst of all, when we possess this world's good things, to
the utmost bound of our desire, we cannot keep them.
Death comes in and separates us from all our property for
ever.   Naked we came upon earth, and naked we go forth,
and of all our possessions we can carry nothing with us.
Such is the world, which occupies the whole attention of
thousands !   Such is the world, for the sake of which
millions are every year destroying their souls !

The loss of the soul is the heaviest loss that can befal
a man.   The worst and most painful of diseases—the
most distressing bankruptcy of fortune—the most dis-
astrous shipwrecks—are a mere scratch of a pin compared
to the loss of a soul.   All other losses are bearable, or
but for a short time, but the loss of the soul is for evermore.   It is to lose God, and Christ, and heaven, and
glory, and happiness, to all eternity.   It is to be cast
away for ever, helpless and hopeless in hell !

What are we doing ourselves ?   Are we losing our
souls ?   Are we, by wilful neglect or by open sin—by
sheer carelessness and idleness, or deliberate breach of
God's law—compassing our own destruction ?   These
questions demand an answer.   The plain account of
many professing Christians is this, that they are daily
sinning against the sixth commandment.   They are
murdering their own souls !

We learn, in the last place, from our Lord's words,
*the guilt and danger of being ashamed of Christ and His
words.*   We read that He says—" Whosoever shall be
ashamed of Me and of My words, of Him shall the Son

of Man be ashamed when He shall come in His own glory, and in His Father's, and of the holy angels."

There are many ways of being ashamed of Christ. We are guilty of it whenever we are afraid of letting men know that we love His doctrines, His precepts, His people, and His ordinances. We are guilty of it whenever we allow the fear of man to prevail over us, and to keep us back from letting others see that we are decided Christians. Whenever we act in this way, we are denying our Master, and committing a great sin.

The wickedness of being ashamed of Christ is very great. It is a proof of unbelief. It shows that we care more for the praise of man whom we can see, than that of God whom we cannot see.—It is a proof of ingratitude. It shows that we fear confessing Him before man who was not ashamed to die for us upon the cross. Wretched indeed are they who give way to this sin. Here, in this world, they are always miserable. A bad conscience robs them of peace. In the world to come they can look for no comfort. In the day of judgment they must expect to be disowned by Christ to all eternity, if they will not confess Christ for a few years upon earth.

Let us resolve never to be ashamed of Christ. Of sin and worldliness we may well be ashamed. Of Christ and His cause we have no right to be ashamed at all. Boldness in Christ's service always brings its own reward. The boldest Christian is always the happiest man.

NOTES. LUKE IX. 23—27.

23.—[*Will come.*] The word "will" here, and in the expression in the following verse, "*will* save," must be interpreted as, "wills to," or, "is willing to." It is not a future tense, but the same Greek word that is used in John v. 40. ; "Ye will not come unto me that ye might have life;" which means, "ye have no will, or wish to come."

[*Take up his cross.*] Campbell remarks on this expression, "Every one condemned by the Romans to crucifixion, was compelled to carry the cross on which he was to be suspended to the place of execution. In this manner our Lord was treated."

"As this was not a Jewish but a Roman punishment, the mention of it on this occasion may justly be looked on as the first hint given by Jesus, of the death He was to suffer. If it had been usual in the country to execute criminals in this manner, the expression might have been thought proverbial for preparing for the worst."

Quesnel remarks on the whole verse. "Take particular notice of the three words, "to them all," and "daily." No person is excused, and no day is excepted. Of what therefore, do those think, and to what do they aspire, who make every day a day of pleasure, luxury, and diversion? Who has a right to shake off the yoke of the cross, but only he who designs to have a right to nothing but hell?"

24.—[*Will save his life shall lose it.*] There is here, as it were, a play upon words. He that is determined to save his life,—in the sense of keeping it and all that is good in this world connected with life,—shall lose it, shall lose that which is after all the great object of our existence, his immortal soul. It is the same use of words in two different senses that we have in the expression, "let the dead bury the dead," which means, "let those who are spiritually dead, attend to such matters as the burial of the naturally dead."

25.—[*Lose himself.*] Let it be noted, that our Lord speaks of this as a perfectly possible event. A man may lose or destroy himself.

26.—[*When he shall come, &c.*] This means our Lord's second coming to judge the world. Let it be noted, that there are three kinds of glory mentioned here, as accompanying the second advent of Christ, His own, the Father's, and the glory of the angels.

27.—[*Not taste of death till they see.*] These words are interpreted two ways. Some think that they mean "They shall not die till they see the Church of Christ established and settled on earth." This is a very unsatisfactory explanation. The right view appears to be that which connects the verse with the transfiguration, and regards the glorious vision of the kingdom, which the transfiguration supplied, as the fulfilment of the promise of the verse. This is the view of Jerome, Hilary, Chrysostom, Theophylact, and many more.

To apply the expression, as some do, to people "not dying until they are converted," is a very unjustifiable accommodation of the words, and a most improper use of Scripture.

LUKE IX. 28—36.

28 And it came to pass about an eight days after these sayings, he took Peter and John and James, and went up into a mountain to pray.

29 And as he prayed, the fashion of his countenance was altered, and his raiment *was* white *and* glistering.

30 And, behold, there talked with him two men, which were Moses and Elias:

31 Who appeared in glory, and spake of his decease which he should accomplish at Jerusalem.

32 But Peter and they that were with him were heavy with sleep: and when they were awake, they saw his glory, and the two men that stood with him.

33 And it came to pass, as they departed from him, Peter said unto Jesus, Master, it is good for us to be here: and let us make three tabernacles; one for thee, and one for Moses, and one for Elias: not knowing what he said.

34 While he thus spake, there came a cloud, and overshadowed them: and they feared as they entered into the cloud.

35 And there came a voice out of the cloud, saying, This is my beloved Son: hear him.

36 And when the voice was past, Jesus was found alone. And they kept *it* close, and told no man in those days any of those things which they had seen.

THE event described in these verses, commonly called "the transfiguration," is one of the most remarkable in the history of our Lord's earthly ministry. It is one of those passages which we should always read with peculiar thankfulness. It lifts a corner of the veil which hangs over the world to come, and throws light on some of the deepest truths of our religion.

In the first place, this passage shows us *something of the glory which Christ will have at His second coming.* We read that "the fashion of His countenance was altered, and His raiment was white and glistering," and that the disciples who were with Him "saw His glory."

We need not doubt that this marvellous vision was meant to encourage and strengthen our Lord's disciples. They had just been hearing of the cross and passion, and the self-denial and sufferings to which they must submit themselves, if they would be saved. They were now cheered by a glimpse of the " glory that should follow," and the reward which all faithful servants of their Master would one day receive. They had seen their Master's day of weakness. They now saw, for a few minutes, a pattern and specimen of His future power.

Let us take comfort in the thought, that there are good things laid up in store for all true Christians, which shall make ample amends for the afflictions of this present time. Now is the season for carrying the cross, and sharing in our Saviour's humiliation. The crown, the kingdom, the glory, are all yet to come. Christ and His people are now, like David in the cave of Adullam, despised, and lightly esteemed by the world. There seems no form nor comeliness in Him, or in His service. But the hour cometh, and will soon be here, when Christ shall take to Himself His great power and reign, and put down every enemy under His feet. And then the glory which was first seen for a few minutes, by three witnesses on the Mount of Transfiguration, shall be seen by all the world, and never hidden to all eternity.

In the second place, this passage shows us *the safety of all true believers who have been removed from this world.* We are told that when our Lord appeared in glory, Moses and Elijah were seen with Him, standing and speaking with Him. Moses had been dead nearly fifteen hundred years. Elijah had been taken up by a whirlwind from the earth more than nine hundred years before this time. Yet here these holy men were seen once more alive, and not only alive, but in glory !

Let us take comfort in the blessed thought that there is a resurrection and a life to come. All is not over, when the last breath is drawn. There is another world beyond the grave. But, above all, let us take comfort in the thought, that until the day dawns, and the resurrection begins, the people of God are safe with Christ. There is much about their present condition, no doubt, which is deeply mysterious.—Where is their local habitation?—What knowledge have they of things on earth? These are questions we cannot answer. But let it suffice us to know that Jesus is taking care of them, and will bring them with Him at the last day. He showed Moses and Elijah to His disciples on the Mount of Transfiguration, and He will show us all who have fallen asleep in Him, at His second advent. Our brethren and sisters in Christ are in good keeping. They are not lost, but gone before.

In the third place, this passage shows us that *the Old Testament saints in glory take a deep interest in Christ's atoning death.* We are told that when Moses and Elijah appeared in glory with our Lord on the Mount of Transfiguration, they "talked with Him." And what was the subject of their conversation? We are not obliged to make conjectures and guesses about this. St. Luke tells us, "they spake of His decease, which He should accomplish at Jerusalem." They knew the meaning of that death. They knew how much depended on it. Therefore they "talked" about it.

It is a grave mistake to suppose that holy men and women under the Old Testament knew nothing about the sacrifice which Christ was to offer up for the sin of the world. Their light, no doubt, was far less clear than ours. They saw things afar off and indistinctly, which we see, as it were, close at hand. But there is not the slightest proof that any Old Testament saint ever looked to any other satisfaction for sin, but that which God promised to make by sending Messiah. From Abel downwards the whole company of old believers appear to have been ever resting on a promised sacrifice, and a blood of almighty efficacy yet to be revealed. From the beginning of the world there has never been but one foundation of hope and peace for sinners—the death of an Almighty Mediator between God and man. That foundation is the centre truth of all revealed religion. It was the subject of which Moses and Elijah were seen speaking when they appeared in glory.—They spoke of the atoning death of Christ.

Let us take heed that this death of Christ is the ground of all our confidence. Nothing else will give us comfort in the hour of death and the day of judgment. Our own works are all defective and imperfect. Our sins are more in number than the hairs of our heads. (Psalm xl. 12.) Christ dying for our sins, and rising again for our justification, must be our only plea, if we wish to be saved. Happy is that man who has learned to cease from his own works, and to glory in nothing but the cross of Christ! If saints in glory see in Christ's death so much beauty, that they must needs talk of it, how much more ought sinners on earth!

In the last place, the passage shows us *the immense distance between Christ and all other teachers whom God has given to man.* We are told that when Peter, " not knowing what he said," proposed to make three tabernacles on the mount, one for Jesus, one for Moses, and one for Elias, as if all three deserved equal honour, this proposal was at once rebuked in a remarkable way : " There came a voice out of the cloud, saying, This is my beloved Son, hear Him." That voice was the voice of God the Father, conveying both reproof and instruction. That voice proclaimed to Peter's ear that however great Moses and Elijah might be, there stood One before him far greater than they. They were but servants ; He was the King's Son. They were but stars ; He was the Sun. They were but witnesses ; He was the Truth.

For ever let that solemn word of the Father ring in our ears, and give the key note to our religion. Let us honour ministers for their Master's sake. Let us follow them so long as they follow Christ. But let it be our principal aim to hear Christ's voice, and follow Him whithersoever He goeth. Let some talk, if they will, of the voice of the Church. Let others be content to say, " I hear this preacher, or that clergyman." Let us never be satisfied unless the Spirit witnesseth within us that we hear Christ Himself, and are His disciples.

NOTES. LUKE IX. 28—36.

28.—[*After these sayings.*] This expression seems to make it plain that the words, " seeing the kingdom of God," in the preceding verse, were spoken with special reference to the vision of the transfiguration.

[*Peter, and James, and John.*] Let it be noted that these three disciples were chosen to be witnesses on three special occasions, the raising of Jairus' daughter, the agony in the garden, and the transfiguration.

[*A mountain.*] It is a common tradition that this mountain

was Tabor. But the opinion of well informed modern travellers is unfavourable to the tradition.

29.—[*As he prayed.*] Let it be noted, that we are specially told that it was when our Lord was "praying" at His baptism the Holy Ghost descended and the Father's voice was heard. So also prayer ushers in the great vision of glory in this place.

Bishop Hall remarks, " Behold how Christ entered upon all His great works, with prayers in His mouth. When He was to enter into that great work of His humiliation in His passion, He went into the garden to pray. When He is to enter into this great work of His exaltation in His transfiguring, He went up into the mountain to pray. He was taken up from His knees to both. O noble example of piety and devotion to us!"

[*The fashion.*] This expression is only used six times in the New Testament, and in other places is translated "shape." " sight," or " appearance." (John v. 37. 2 Cor. v. 7. 1 Thess. v. 22.)

[*Was altered.*] This is a peculiar expression. It would be more literally rendered, "other," that is, " other than it generally appeared." (See Mark xvi. 12.)

[*Glistering.*] This word is only used once in the New Testament. Parkhurst explains it as meaning, "to emit flashes of light, to shine or glister as lightning." See Nahum iii. 3.

30.—[*Moses and Elias.*] It is a true and common remark that Moses in this vision represented the law, and Elijah the prophets. Both agreed in acknowledging and recognizing Christ, as Him of whom the law and the prophets testified.

It is also highly probable that they were meant to be types and emblems of the saints who will appear with Christ in glory at His second advent. Moses is the type of those who are found dead, and will be raised at the Lord's coming. Elijah is the type of those who are found alive, and " caught up to meet the Lord in the air." 1 Thess. iv. 17.

31.—[*His decease.*] This expression is remarkable. It means literally, his " Exodus," or departure. It is used for " death" by St. Peter, speaking of his own death. (2 Pet. i. 15.) It is also remarkable that in Acts xiii. 24, we have a Greek word used for our Lord's " coming " to take the office of a Saviour, which might be translated literally His " entrance." Both expressions are singularly applicable to Him who came into the world and was made flesh, and after doing the work He came to do, left the world and went to the Father. The beginning of His ministry was an " Eisodus," or entrance; His death, an " Exodus," or departure.

[*He should accomplish.*] This expression would be more literally rendered, " He should fulfil." It is a very peculiar form of speech, and singularly applicable to Christ. Watson remarks,

" to depart from life is the common lot : but to *fulfil* his decease or departure from the world, was peculiar to Christ, because His death was the grand subject of prophecy, and the event upon which the salvation of the world was suspended."

32.—[*Were heavy with sleep.*] Let it be noted, that the very same disciples who here slept during a vision of glory, were also found sleeping during the agony in the garden of Gethsemane. Flesh and blood does indeed need to be changed before it can enter heaven ! Our poor, weak bodies can neither watch with Christ in His time of trial, nor keep awake with Him in His glorification. Our physical constitution must be greatly altered before we could enjoy heaven.

[*When they were awake, they saw.*] It is evident that they awoke before the vision was over, and saw and heard much of what happened.

33.—[*It is good for us to be here.*] There is doubtless much to be blamed in this expression of Peter's ;—partly because he placed Moses and Elijah on a level with his divine Master, and partly because he would fain have tarried in the mount, and kept his Master there when there was work to be done in the world. The comment of St. Luke, " not knowing what he said," is a gentle hint that his wish was not commendable, but blameworthy. Nevertheless we cannot but admire the outburst of Peter's delight when he saw his Master surrounded with such glory, and with such glorified companions. It was the outburst of a truly burning heart. Archbishop Usher remarks, " When Peter saw Moses and Elias with Christ in His transfiguration, though he had but a glimpse of glory, yet he says, ' It is good for us to be here.' But Oh ! how infinitely good will it be to be in heaven. How shall we then be rapt up with glory, when we shall be for ever with the Lord ! "

35.—[*Hear him.*] There can be no doubt that this expression was meant to point to the prophecy of Moses in Deuteronomy, where Moses says of the prophet like unto himself, " Unto him shall ye hearken," (Deut. xviii. 15.) and that under so great a penalty that all who refused should be " destroyed from among the people."

Calvin remarks, " We are placed under His tuition alone, and commanded from Him alone to seek the doctrine of salvation, to depend upon and listen to One—to adhere to One—in a word, as the terms import, to hearken to One only."

36.—[*Jesus was found alone.*] The disappearance of Moses and Elias, together with the words, " Hear him," were doubtless meant to teach that the law of ceremonies was about to pass away, and that the true Lamb of God and true prophet was come.

LUKE IX. 37—45.

37 And it came to pass, that on the next day, when they were come down from the hill, much people met him.

38 And, behold, a man of the company cried out, saying, Master, I beseech thee, look upon my son: for he is mine only child.

39 And, lo, a spirit taketh him, and he suddenly crieth out; and it teareth him that he foameth again, and bruising him hardly departeth from him.

40 And I besought thy disciples to cast him out; and they could not.

41 And Jesus answering said, O faithless and perverse generation, how long shall I be with you, and suffer you? Bring thy son hither.

42 And as he was yet a coming, the devil threw him down, and tare *him*. And Jesus rebuked the unclean spirit, and healed the child, and delivered him again to his father.

43 And they were all amazed at the mighty power of God. But while they wondered every one at all things which Jesus did, he said unto his disciples,

44 Let these sayings sink down into your ears: for the Son of man shall be delivered into the hands of men.

45 But they understood not this saying, and it was hid from them, that they perceived it not: and they feared to ask him of that saying.

THE event described in these verses took place immediately after the transfiguration. The Lord Jesus, we should remark, did not tarry long on the Mount of Olives. His communion with Moses and Elias was very short. He soon returned to His accustomed work of doing good to a sin-stricken world. In His life on earth, to receive honour and have visions of glory was the exception. To minister to others, to heal all who were oppressed by the devil, to do acts of mercy to sinners, was the rule. Happy are those Christians who have learned of Jesus to live for others more than for themselves, and who understand that it is "more blessed to give than to receive." (Acts xx. 35.)

We have, first, in these verses, *an example of what a parent should do when he is troubled about his children.* We are told of a man in sore distress about his only son. This son was possessed by an evil spirit, and grievously tormented by him, both in body and soul. In his distress the father makes application to our Lord Jesus Christ for relief. "Master," he says, "I beseech Thee look upon my son: for he is mine only child."

There are many Christian fathers and mothers at this day who are just as miserable about their children as the man of whom we are reading. The son who was once the "desire of their eyes," and in whom their lives were bound up, turns out a spendthrift, a profligate, and a companion of sinners. The daughter who was once the flower of the family, and of whom they said, "this same shall be the comfort of our old age," becomes self-willed, worldly-minded, and a lover of pleasure more than a lover of God. Their hearts are well nigh broken. The iron seems to enter into their souls. The devil appears to triumph over them, and rob them of their choicest jewels. They are ready to cry, "I shall go to the grave sorrowing. What good shall my life do to me?"

Now what should a father or mother do in a case like this? They should do as the man before us did. They should go to Jesus in prayer, and cry to Him about their child. They should spread before that merciful Saviour the tale of their sorrows, and entreat Him to help them. Great is the power of prayer and intercession! The child of many prayers shall seldom be cast away. God's time of conversion may not be ours. He may think fit to prove our faith by keeping us long waiting. But so long as a child lives, and a parent prays, we have no right to despair about that child's soul.

We have, secondly, in these verses, *an example of Christ's readiness to show mercy to young persons.* We are told in the case before us, that the prayer of the afflicted parent was graciously granted. He said to him, "Bring thy son hither." And then "He rebuked the unclean spirit, and healed the child, and delivered him again to his father." We have many similar cases in the Gospels. The daughter of Jairus, the nobleman's son at Capernaum, the daughter of the Canaanitish woman, the widow's son at Nain, are all instances of our Lord's interest in those who are young. The young are exactly those whom the devil labours to lead captive and make His own. The young seem to have been exactly the persons whom our Lord took a special delight in helping. Three He plucked out of the very jaws of death. Two, as in the case before us, He rescued from the complete dominion of the devil.

There is a meaning in facts like these. They are not recorded without a special purpose. They are meant to encourage all who try to do good to the souls of the young. They are meant to remind us that young men and young women are special objects of interest to Christ. They supply us with an antidote to the common idea that it is useless to press religion on the attention of young people. Such an idea, let us remember, comes from the devil and not from Christ. He who cast out the evil spirit from the child before us, still lives, and is still mighty to save. Let us then work on, and try to do good to the young. Whatever the world may think, Jesus is well pleased.

We have, lastly, in these verses, an example of *the spiritual ignorance which may be found even in the hearts of good men*. We are told that our Lord said to His disciples, "The son of man shall be delivered into the hands of men." They had heard the same thing from His lips little more than a week before. But now, as then, the words seemed lost upon them. They heard as though they heard not. They could not realize the fact that their Master was to die. They could not realize the great truth that Christ was to be "cut off" before He was to reign, and that this cutting off was a literal death upon the cross. It is written, "They understood not this saying,"—"it was hid from them,"—"they perceived it not."

Such slowness of understanding may surprise us much at this period of the world. We are apt to forget the power of early habits of thought, and national prejudices, in the midst of which the disciples had been trained. "The throne of David," says a great divine, "did so fill their eyes that they could not see the cross." Above all, we forget the enormous difference between the position we occupy who know the history of the crucifixion and the Scriptures which it fulfilled, and the position of a believing Jew who lived before Christ died and the vail was rent in twain. Whatever we may think of it, the ignorance of the disciples should teach us two useful lessons, which we shall all do well to learn.

For one thing, let us learn that men may understand spiritual things very feebly, and yet be true children of God. The head may be very dull, when the heart is right. Grace is far better than gifts, and faith than knowledge. If a man has faith and grace enough to give up all for Christ's sake, and to take up the cross and follow Him, he shall be saved in spite of much ignorance. Christ shall own him at the last day.

Finally, let us learn to bear with ignorance in others, and to deal patiently with beginners in religion. Let us not make men offenders for a word. Let us not set our brother down as having no grace, because he does not exhibit clear knowledge. Has he faith in Christ? Does he love Christ? These are the principal things. If Jesus could endure so much weakness in His disciples, we may surely do likewise.

NOTES. LUKE IX. 37—45.

38.—[*Cried out.*] The Greek word so translated implies a crying out with a very loud voice. It is the same word that is used of our Lord's "crying with a loud voice" on the cross; (Matt. xxvii. 46.) and "the multitude crying out to Pilate to do as he had ever done to them." (Mark xv. 8.)

[*Mine only child.*] Let us remember that the daughter of Jarius, whom our Saviour raised from the dead, was an *only* daughter, and the widow's son at Nain an *only* son. These things are worth notice. St. Luke is the only Gospel writer who specially mentions them.

39.—[*Hardly.*] Let it be noted that this word must be taken with "departed." It means "scarcely," or "with difficulty."

40.—[*They could not.*] The reality of Satanic possession is shown by this fact. We read of no *disease* which the disciples could not cure. But here we are told of a demoniac whose case baffled them. There was a degree of Satanic possession, with which their weak faith was unable to grapple. It was evidently something quite distinct from any merely bodily ailment.

41.—[*O faithless and perverse generation.*] The question has been often raised, "To whom were these words addressed? and with what purpose were they spoken?" Were they meant to apply to the disciples only, and to be a rebuke to their unbelief? This is the opinion of Origen.—Were they, on the other hand, addressed to the whole multitude of the Jews, as well as to the disciples? This is the opinion of Hilary, Chrysostom, and Jerome.—Did our Lord refer to the contrast between the vision of glory he had just left in the Mount of Transfiguration, in the company of Moses and Elias, and the unbelief and wickedness of the generation among whom He was sojourning? This is the opinion of Burgon.

It may however be doubted whether these words could fairly

326   EXPOSITORY THOUGHTS.

be applied to the man whose son was afflicted. He did what he could. He brought his son to the disciples. If the cure was not wrought, the fault was surely their's more than his. In fact, when the disciples, as recorded by St. Matthew, xvii. 20, asked our Lord why they could not cast out this devil, He answered them at once, "Because of your unbelief." The father, on the contrary, when our Lord said to him, "If thou canst believe all things are possible," cried out, "Lord I believe."

The words of our Lord would therefore appear to be directed partly to His own disciples, and partly to the whole generation of the Jews among whom He lived.

44.—[*Let these sayings sink down into your ears.*] The literal translation of these words would be, "Put these sayings into your ears."

LUKE IX. 46—50.

46 Then there arose a reasoning among them, which of them should be greatest.

47 And Jesus, perceiving the thought of their heart, took a child, and set him by him,

48 And said unto them, Whosoever shall receive this child in my name receiveth me : and whosoever shall receive me receiveth him that sent me : for he that is least among you all, the same shall be great.

49 And John answered and said, Master, we saw one casting out devils in thy name ; and we forbade him, because he followeth not with us.

50 And Jesus said unto him, Forbid *him* not : for he that is not against us is for us.

THE verses we have now read contain two most important warnings. They are directed against two of the commonest evils which are to be found in the Church of Christ. He who gave them knew well what was in the heart of man. Well would it have been for the Church of Christ, if His words in this passage had received more attention !

In the first place, the Lord Jesus gives us *a warning against pride and self-conceit.* We are told that "there arose a reasoning among the disciples which of them should be the greatest." Wonderful as it may seem, this little company of fishermen and publicans was not beyond the plague of a self-seeking and ambitious spirit. Filled with the vain notion that our Lord's kingdom was to appear immediately, they were ready to wrangle about their place and precedency in it. Each thought his own claim the strongest. Each thought his own deserts and right to honour most unquestionable. Each thought that, whatever place was assigned to his brethren, a principal place ought to be assigned to himself. And all this happened in the company of Christ Himself, and under the noon-tide blaze of His teaching. Such is the heart of man!

There is something very instructive in this fact. It ought to sink down deeply into the heart of every Christian reader. Of all sins there is none against which we have such need to watch and pray, as pride. It is a pestilence that walketh in darkness, and a sickness that destroyeth at noon day.—No sin is so deeply rooted in our nature. It cleaves to us like our skin. Its roots never entirely die. They are ready, at any moment, to spring up, and exhibit a most pernicious vitality.—No sin is so specious and deceitful. It can wear the garb of humility itself. It can lurk in the hearts of the ignorant, the ungifted, and the poor, as well as in the minds of the great, the learned, and the rich. It is a quaint and homely saying, but only too true, that no pope has ever received such honour as pope "self."

Let a prayer for humility, and the spirit of a little child, form part of our daily supplications. Of all creatures none has so little right to be proud as man, and of all men none ought to be so humble as the Christian. Is it really true that we confess ourselves to be "miserable

sinners," and daily debtors to mercy and grace? Are we
the followers of Jesus, who was "meek and lowly of heart,"
and "made Himself of no reputation" for our sakes?
Then let that same mind be in us which was in Christ
Jesus. Let us lay aside all high thoughts and self-
conceit. In lowliness of mind, let us esteem others
better than ourselves. Let us be ready, on all occasions,
to take the lowest place. And let the words of our
Saviour ring in our ears continually, "He that is least
among you all, the same shall be great."

In the second place, our Lord Jesus Christ gives us *a
warning against a bigotted and illiberal spirit.* As in the
preceding verses, so here, the occasion of the warning is
supplied by the conduct of His own disciples. We read
that John said to Him, "Master, we saw one casting
out devils in thy name : and we forbade him, because
he followeth not with us." Who this man was, and
why he did not consort with the disciples, we do not
know. But we do know that he was doing a good work
in casting out devils, and that he was doing what he
did in the name of Christ. And yet John says,
"we forbade him."—Very striking is the reply which the
Lord at once gave him : "Forbid him not : for he that
is not against us is for us."

The conduct of John and the disciples on this occasion
is a curious illustration of the oneness of human nature,
in every age. Thousands, in every period of Church
history, have spent their lives in copying John's mistake.
They have laboured to stop every man who will not work
for Christ in their way, from working for Christ at all.
They have imagined, in their petty self-conceit, that no

man can be a soldier of Christ, unless he wears their uniform, and fights in their regiment. They have been ready to say of every Christian who does not see everything with their eyes, "Forbid him! Forbid him! for he followeth not with us."

The solemn remark of our Lord Jesus Christ, on this occasion, demands our special notice. He pronounces no opinion upon the conduct of the man of whom John speaks. He neither praises nor blames him for following an independent course, and not working with His disciciples. He simply declares that he must not be forbidden, and that those who work the same kind of work that we do, should be regarded not as enemies, but allies. "He that is not against us is for us."

The principle laid down in this passage is of great importance. A right understanding of it will prove most useful to us in these latter days. The divisions and varieties of opinion which exist among Christians are undeniably very great. The schisms and separations which are continually arising about Church-government, and modes of worship, are very perplexing to tender consciences.—Shall we approve those divisions? We cannot do so. Union is strength. The disunion of Christians is one cause of the slow progress of vital Christianity.—Shall we denounce, and hold up to public reprobation, all who will not agree to work with us, and to oppose Satan in our way? It is useless to do so. Hard words never yet made men of one mind. Unity was never yet brought about by force.— What then ought we to do? We must leave alone those who do not agree with us, and wait quietly till God shall

think fit to bring us together. Whatever we may think
of our divisions, the words of our Lord must never be
forgotten : "Forbid them not."

The plain truth is, that we are all too ready to say, " We
are the men, and wisdom shall die with us." (Job xii. 2.)
We forget that no Church on earth has an absolute
monopoly of all wisdom, and that people may be right in
the main, without agreeing with us. We must learn
to be thankful if sin is opposed, and the Gospel
preached, and the devil's kingdom pulled down, though
the work may not be done exactly in the way we like.
We must try to believe that men may be true-hearted
followers of Jesus Christ, and yet for some wise reason
may be kept back from seeing all things in religion just
as we do. Above all, we must praise God if souls are
converted, and Christ is magnified,—no matter who the
preacher may be, and to what Church he may belong.
Happy are those who can say with Paul, "If Christ be
preached, I rejoice, yea and will rejoice," (Phil. i. 18.)
and with Moses, "Enviest thou for my sake ? Would
God that all the Lord's people were prophets, and that
all did prophecy." (Num. xi. 29.)

NOTES. LUKE IX. 46—50.

46.—[*A reasoning.*] The word so translated is the same that is
rendered "thought" in the following verse.

[*Which of them should be the greatest.*] The expectation of
a temporal kingdom about to be set up by the Messiah, must
have been the foundation of this desire of pre-eminence.

48.—[*This child.*] We must beware that we do not wrest our
Lord's language about children here and elsewhere, into the
false notion that children are naturally innocent, and without
sin. The simplicity, unworldliness, and dependent spirit of a
little child, arising from its sense of weakness, and feebleness,

and ignorance of the world's standard of good, are the real points in which the child is to be the Christian's pattern.

50.—[*Forbid him not.*] It is curious to observe the various practical applications of the great principle contained in this passage, which men have made at various periods of the Church's history.

Bucer directs the passage against the Anabaptists and fanatics of his own time in Germany. He argues that it justifies Christians making use of the support and countenance of kings, princes, and other great persons in the world, if they are disposed to help the Gospel, even though they are not converted to God themselves.

Scott applies the passage to religious revivals, and argues that it should teach us neither lightly to condemn nor lightly to approve them.

Our own times appear to point out plainly that we should apply the passage to the subject of our relations with other religious denominations. In the face of such a Scripture as this, Churchmen should beware how they condemn and reprobate Dissenters, and Dissenters should beware how they denounce and revile Churchmen. Both parties would do well to leave off contention, and to learn to rejoice in any good that is doing in the world, by whatsoever means it may be done. If devils are cast out, we ought to be glad, though those who cast them out follow not with us.

One qualification only should always accompany our use of this passage of Scripture. We must not allow it to make us indifferent to sound doctrine. We must not think and talk as if it mattered nothing whether men are Jews, Socinians, Papists, or Protestants, so long as they seem earnest-minded men. The persons to whom the passage specially applies, are persons who do apostolic work in the name of Jesus,—who labour to pull down the kingdom of Satan by the use of Gospel weapons. Let us beware how we ever forbid such persons, or hinder them in their work.

LUKE XIX. 51—56.

51 And it came to pass, when the time was come that he should be received up, he stedfastly set his face to go to Jerusalem.

52 And sent messengers before his face: and they went, and entered into a village of the Samaritans, to make ready for him.

53 And they did not receive him, because his face was as though he would go to Jerusalem.

54 And when his disciples James and John saw *this*, they said, Lord, wilt thou that we command fire to come down from heaven, and consume them, even as Elias did?

55 But he turned, and rebuked them, and said, Ye know not what manner of spirit ye are of.

56 For the Son of man is not come to destroy men's lives, but to save *them*. And they went to another village.

LET us notice in these verses, *the steady determination with which our Lord Jesus Christ regarded His own crucifixion and death.* We read that "when the time was come that He should be received up, He steadfastly set His face to go to Jerusalem." He knew full well what was before Him. The betrayal, the unjust trial, the mockery, the scourging, the crown of thorns, the spitting, the nails, the spear, the agony on the cross,— all, all were doubtless spread before His mind's eye, like a picture. But He never flinched for a moment from the work that He had undertaken. His heart was set on paying the price of our redemption, and going even to the prison of the grave, as our surety. He was full of tender love towards sinners. It was the desire of His whole soul to procure for them salvation. And so, "for the joy set before Him, He endured the cross, despising the shame." (Heb. xii. 2.)

For ever let us bless God that we have such a ready and willing Saviour. For ever let us remember that as He was ready to suffer, so He is always ready to save. The man that comes to Christ by faith should never doubt Christ's willingness to receive Him. The mere fact that the Son of God willingly came into the world to die, and willingly suffered, should silence such doubts entirely. All the unwillingness is on the part of man, not of Christ. It consists in the ignorance, and pride, and unbelief, and half-heartedness of the sinner himself. But there is nothing wanting in Christ.

Let us strive and pray that the same mind may be in us which was in our blessed Master. Like Him, let us be willing to go anywhere, do anything, suffer anything, when the path of duty is clear, and the voice of God calls. Let us set our faces steadfastly to our work, when our work is plainly marked out, and drink our bitter cups patiently, when they come from a Father's hand.

Let us notice, secondly, in these verses, *the extraordinary conduct of two of the apostles, James and John.* We are told that a certain Samaritan village refused to show hospitality to our Lord. "They did not receive him, because his face was as though he would go to Jerusalem." And then we read of a strange proposal which James and John made. "They said, Lord, wilt thou that we command fire to come down from heaven and consume them, even as Elias did?"

Here was zeal indeed, and zeal of a most plausible kind,—zeal for the honour of Christ! Here was zeal, justified and supported by a Scriptural example, and that the example of no less a prophet than Elijah! But it was not a zeal according to knowledge. The two disciples, in their heat, forgot that circumstances alter cases, and that the same action which may be right and justifiable at one time, may be wrong and unjustifiable at another. They forgot that punishments should always be proportioned to offences, and that to destroy a whole village of ignorant people for a single act of discourtesy, would have been both unjust and cruel. In short, the proposal of James and John was a wrong and inconsiderate one. They meant well, but they greatly erred.

Facts like this in the Gospels are carefully recorded for our learning. Let us see to it that we mark them well, and treasure them up in our minds. It is possible to have much zeal for Christ, and yet to exhibit it in most unholy and unchristian ways. It is possible to mean well and have good intentions, and yet to make most grievous mistakes in our actions. It is possible to fancy that we have Scripture on our side, and to support our conduct by Scriptural quotations, and yet to commit serious errors. It is clear as daylight, from this and other cases related in the Bible, that it is not enough to be zealous and *well-meaning*. Very grave faults are frequently committed with good intentions. From no quarter perhaps has the Church received so much injury as from ignorant but well-meaning men.

We must seek to have knowledge as well as zeal. Zeal without knowledge is an army without a general, and a ship without a rudder. We must pray that we may understand how to make a right application of Scripture. The word is no doubt "a light to our feet, and a lantern to our path." But it must be the word rightly handled, and properly applied.

Let us notice, lastly, in these verses, *what a solemn rebuke our Lord gives to persecution carried on under colour of religion.* We are told that when James and John made the strange proposal on which we have just been dwelling, "he turned and rebuked them, and said, Ye know not what manner of spirit ye are of. For the Son of man is not come to destroy men's lives, but to save them." Uncourteous as the Samaritan villagers had been, their conduct was not to be resented by violence. The mission of the Son of man was to do good, when men would receive Him, but never to do harm. His kingdom was to be extended by patient continuance in well doing, and by meekness and gentleness in suffering, but never by violence and severity.

No saying of our Lord's, perhaps, has been so totally overlooked by the Church of Christ as that which is now before us. Nothing can be imagined more contrary to the will of Christ than the religious wars and persecutions which disgrace the annals of Church history. Thousands and tens of thousands have been put to death for their religion's sake all over the world. Thousands have been burned, or shot, or hanged, or drowned, or beheaded, in the name of the Gospel, and those who have slain them have actually believed that they were doing God service! Unhappily, they have only shown their own ignorance of the spirit of the Gospel, and the mind of Christ.

Let it be a settled principle in our minds, that whatever men's errors may be in religion, we must never persecute them. Let us, if needful, argue with them, reason with them, and try to show them a more excellent way. But let us never take up the "carnal" weapon to promote the spread of truth. Let us never be tempted, directly or indirectly, to persecute any man, under pretence of the glory of Christ and the good of the Church. Let us rather remember, that the religion which men profess from fear of death, or dread of penalties, is worth nothing at all, and that if we swell our ranks by fear and threatening, in reality we gain no strength. "The weapons of our warfare," says St. Paul, "are not carnal." (2 Cor. x. 4.) The appeals that we make must be to men's consciences and wills. The arguments that we use must not be sword, or fire, or prison, but doctrines, and precepts, and texts. It is a quaint and homely saying, but as true in the Church as it is in the army, that "one volunteer is worth ten pressed men."

NOTES. LUKE IX. 51—56.

51.—[*The time that he should be received up.*] The Greek word so translated is peculiar, and is only found here in the New Testament. It would be rendered more literally, "the days of his reception up." About the meaning of the expression there is a curious difference of opinion.

Some think, with Heinsius and Hammond, that the meaning is, "the time of his death and being lifted up upon the cross."

Others think, with Suicer and Bengel, that the meaning is, "the time of his ascension, or being taken up to heaven."

This latter sense seems far the more probable of the two, and is confirmed by the fact that the Syriac and Arabic versions both render the word, "his ascension." Besides this, the Greek verb which is several times used to describe the ascension, is the very verb from which the word before us is derived. See Mark xvi. 19. Acts i. 2. xi. 22.

53.—[*They did not receive him.*] The wretched state of feeling between the Samaritans and the Jews is painfully illustrated by the circumstance here mentioned. Charity was indeed well-nigh extinct, where such a state of things existed. Those who wish to see the origin of the estrangement between the Jews and Samaritans, should read 2 Kings xvii; and Ezra iv.

54.—[*His disciples, James and John, &c.*] There is something very remarkable in the spirit exhibited by these two disciples on this occasion. It shows us that it was not without good reason that our Lord called them Boanerges, or sons of thunder, when He first ordained them to be apostles. Mark iii. 17. It shows us also the gradually transforming power of the grace of God in John's character. Three times we have sins against charity recorded in the Gospels as committed by John. Once we find him and his brother asking to sit at Christ's right and left hand in His kingdom, and to be preferred before all the other apostles.—Once we find him forbidding a man to cast out devils, because he did not follow the apostles.—Here again we find him showing a fierce and cruel spirit against the Samaritan villagers for not receiving our Lord. Yet this was the apostle who proved at last most remarkable for preaching love and charity. No change is too great for the Lord to work.

[*Even as Elias did.*] Appeals to the Old Testament, like this, have often been made by fanatical men in order to justify violent actions. The case of Oliver Cromwell and many of his followers will naturally occur to some readers.

The examples of men who were raised up to do special works in the times of the Old Testament must not be followed in all things. The man who presumes to imitate Joshua and Elijah in all their dealings with the enemies of God, must furnish proof of his call and commission to walk in their steps.

55.—[*He turned and rebuked them, &c.*] Our Lord's entire disapproval of all persecution for religion's sake is very plainly taught in this passage. Whatever we may think of men's doctrines or practices, we are not to persecute them.

Poole says, "Christ did not approve of the Samaritan worship, yet he did not think that the way to change their minds was to call for fire from heaven against them. It is not the will of God that we should approve of any corrupt worship, and join with those who use it. But neither is it his will that we should by fire and sword go about to suppress it, and bring men off from it."

Quesnel remarks, "It often happens that the ministers of the Church, under pretence of zeal for her interests, offend against Christian meekness. The Church knows no such thing as revenge, and her ministers ought not to know it either. Their wrath should be incensed against sin, not against the sinner. The fire of heaven is one day to come down to purify the world by destruction. At present it comes down only to sanctify it by edification."

[*What manner of spirit ye are of.*] The disciples were forgetting the nature of that Spirit by whom they professed, as Christ's disciples, to be guided. They were forgetting that He was a Spirit of love and meekness and gentleness, and that all acts of a revengeful and violent character were grievous to Him. "The fruit of the Spirit is love, joy, peace, longsuffering, gentleness." (Gal. v. 22.) Their own Master had taught them that if any man smote them on one cheek they were to turn to him the other also. (Matt. v. 39.) But all this for the time was forgotten. A fierce temper and a sense of injured dignity make men bad reasoners, and drive good instruction out of their memories.

Bengel remarks, that we should compare with the conduct of these two disciples "the fact that when Jesus prayed on the cross, employing the very words of the twenty-second and thirty-first Psalms, he did not pray against his enemies, but for them."

It is an interesting fact, that the apostle John, at a later period in his life, came down to Samaria in a very different spirit. He came with Peter on a special mission from Jerusalem, to confer spiritual blessings on Samaritan believers. And we are told that he "preached the Gospel in many villages of the Samaritans." (Acts viii. 25.)

LUKE IX. 57—62.

57 And it came to pass, that, as they went in the way, a certain *man* said unto him, Lord, I will follow thee whithersoever thou goest.

58 And Jesus said unto him, Foxes have holes, and birds of the air *have* nests; but the Son of man hath not where to lay *his* head.

59 And he said unto another, Follow me. But he said, Lord, suffer me first to go and bury my father.

60 Jesus said unto him, Let the dead bury their dead: but go thou and preach the kingdom of God.

61 And another also said, Lord, I will follow thee; but let me first go bid them farewell, which are at home at my house.

62 And Jesus said unto him, No man, having put his hand to the plough, and looking back, is fit for the kingdom of God.

THE passage of Scripture we have just read is a very remarkable one. It contains three short sayings of peculiar solemnity, addressed by our Lord Jesus Christ to three different persons. We know nothing of the names of those persons. We know nothing of the effect which our Lord's words produced upon them. But we need not doubt that each was addressed in the way which his character required, and we may be sure that the passage is specially intended to promote self inquiry.

The first of these sayings was addressed to *one who offered to be a disciple unconditionally, and of his own accord.* "Lord," said this man, "I will follow thee whithersoever thou goest."—That offer sounded well. It was a step in advance of many. Thousands of people heard our Lord's sermons who never thought of saying what this man said. Yet he who made this offer was evidently speaking without thought. He had never considered what belonged to discipleship. He had never counted the cost. And hence he needed the grave reply which his offer called forth:—"Foxes have holes, and birds of the air have nests, but the Son of Man hath not where to lay his head."—He must weigh well what he was taking in hand. He must not suppose that Christ's service was all pleasure and smooth sailing. Was he prepared for this? Was he ready to "endure hardness?" (2 Tim. ii. 3.) If not, he had better withdraw his application to be a disciple.

Let us learn, from our Lord's words on this occasion, that He would have all who profess and call themselves Christians reminded that they must carry the cross. They must lay their account to be despised, and afflicted, and tried, like their Master. He would have no man enlisted on false pretences. He would have it distinctly understood that there is a battle to be fought, and a race to be run,—a work to be done, and many hard things to be endured,—if we propose to follow Him. Salvation He is ready to bestow, without money and without price. Grace by the way, and glory in the end, shall be given to every sinner who comes to Him. But He would not have us ignorant that we shall have deadly enemies,—the world, the flesh, and the devil, and that many will hate us, slander us, and persecute us, if we become His disciples. He does not wish to discourage us, but He does wish us to know the truth.

Well would it have been for the church if our Lord's warning had been more frequently pondered! Many a man begins a religious life full of warmth and zeal, and by and bye loses all his first love, and turns back again to the world. He liked the new uniform, and the bounty money, and the name of a Christian soldier.—He never considered the watching, and warring, and wounds, and conflicts, which Christian soldiers must endure. Let us never forget this lesson. It need not make us afraid to begin serving Christ, but it ought to make us begin carefully, humbly, and with much prayer for grace. If we are not ready to take part in the afflictions of Christ, we must never expect to share His glory.

The second of our Lord's sayings is addressed to *one whom He invited to follow Him.* The answer He received was a very remarkable one. " Lord," said the man, " suffer me first to go and bury my father."—The thing he requested was in itself harmless. But the time at which the request was made was unseasonable. Affairs of far greater importance than even a father's funeral demanded the man's immediate attention. There would always be plenty of people ready and fit to take charge of a funeral. But there was at that moment a pressing want of labourers to do Christ's work in the world. And hence the man's request drew from our Lord the solemn reply,— " Let the dead bury their dead, but go thou and preach the kingdom of God."

Let us learn, from this saying, to beware of allowing family and social duties to interfere with our duty to Christ. Funerals, and marriages, and visits of courtesy, and the like, unquestionably are not in themselves sinful. But when they are allowed to absorb a believer's time, and keep him back from any plain religious duty, they become a snare to his soul. That the children of the world, and the unconverted, should allow them to occupy all their time and thoughts is not wonderful. They know nothing higher, and better, and more important. " Let the dead bury their dead."—But the heirs of glory, and children of the King of kings, should be men of a different stamp. They should declare plainly, by their con-duct, that the world to come is the great reality which fills their thoughts. They should not be ashamed to let men see that they have no time either to rejoice or to sorrow like others who have no hope. (1 Thess. iv. 13.) Their Master's work waits for them, and their Master's work must have the chief place in their hearts. They are God's priests in the world, and, like the priests of old, their mourning must be kept carefully within bounds. (Lev. xxi. 1.) "Weeping," says an old divine, "must not hinder working," and mourning must not be allowed to run into excess.

The third of our Lord's sayings in this passage was addressed to *one who volunteered to follow Him, but marred the grace of his offer by interposing a request.* "Lord," he said, "I will follow thee; but let me first go bid them farewell which are at home at my house."—The answer he received shows plainly that the man's heart was not yet thoroughly engaged in Christ's service, and that he was therefore unfit to be a disciple. "Jesus said unto him, No man having put his hand to the plough, and looking back, is fit for the kingdom of God."

We learn from this saying that it is impossible to serve Christ with a divided heart. If we are looking back to any thing in this world we are not fit to be disciples. Those who look back, like Lot's wife, want to go back. Jesus will not share His throne with any one,—no, not with our dearest relatives. He must have all our heart, or none. No doubt we are to honour father and mother, and love all around us. But when love to Christ and love to relatives come in collision, Christ must have the preference. We must be ready, like Abraham, if needs be, to come out from kindred and father's house for Christ's sake. We must be prepared in case of necessity, like Moses, to turn our backs even on those who have brought us up, if God calls us, and the path is plain. Such decided conduct may entail sore trials on our affections. It may wring our hearts to go contrary to the opinions of those we love.—But such conduct may sometimes be positively necessary to our salvation, and without it, when it becomes necessary, we are unfit for the kingdom of God. The good soldier will not allow his heart to be entangled too much with his home. If he daily gives way to unmanly repinings about those he has left behind him, he will never be fit for a campaign. His present duties —the watching, the marching, the fighting,—must have the principal place in his thoughts. So must it be with all who would serve Christ. They must beware of soft- ness spoiling their characters as Christians. They must endure hardness, as good soldiers of Jesus Christ. (2 Tim. ii. 3.)

Let us leave the whole passage with many searchings of heart. The times are undoubtedly much changed since our Lord spoke these words. Not many are called to make such real sacrifices for Christ's sake as when Christ was upon earth. But the heart of man never changes. The difficulties of salvation are still very great. The atmosphere of the world is still very unfavourable to spiritual religion. There is still need for thorough, un- flinching, whole-hearted decision, if we would reach heaven. Let us aim at nothing less than this decision. Let us be willing to do anything, and suffer anything, and give up everything for Christ's sake. It may cost us something for a few years, but great will be the reward in eternity.

57.—[*A certain man said.*] St. Matthew tells us that this man was a scribe. This offer appears to have been made at an early period of our Lord's earthly ministry. (Matt. viii. 19.) St. Luke mentions it in this place, because it is his habit to relate events in groups, and not in strict chronological order. See Luke i. 3, and the note thereon.

58.—[*Foxes have holes, &c.*] This expression throws strong light on the poverty and lowliness in which our Lord was pleased to pass the time of His ministry.

Let our Lord's reply to this man's offer be carefully noted. Both here and elsewhere we find Him putting forward prominently the cross which must be borne, if the man becomes a Christian. The conduct of those ministers and Christians who keep back the trials of Christianity from inquirers, and suppress the cross in order to swell the ranks of their own sect, or party, or congregation, is very unlike the conduct of Christ. To obtain adherents to our ranks by incorrect and partial statements, is a procedure to which no Christian should ever condescend. Better a small congregation honestly obtained, than a large one gathered by false representations.

59.—[*First to go and bury my father.*] There is probably more implied in this expression than at first sight appears. It means something more than merely attending the funeral of a deceased parent.

Theophylact and Pellican think that it means, "to take care of a father until he is dead," and that it implies a wish to attend upon an aged father during all the infirmities of his latter days, until he was released by death.

Heinsius thinks that there is a reference to the many tedious and superstitious practices of the Jews in connexion with deaths and funerals, such as a seven days' lamentation before the burial of a father, and a year's special mourning after his funeral.

There is some probability in both these opinions.

60.—[*Let the dead bury their dead.*] The first word, "dead," in this expression, means the "spiritually dead," the second the "naturally dead." The meaning evidently is, that funerals may be safely left to those who, being without spiritual life themselves, attach importance to all ceremonies and customs belonging to this life, and are sure to attend to them.

[*Go thou and preach.*] It is not unlikely that this command to go and preach was delivered just before our Lord selected the seventy preachers mentioned in the next chapter. If this man had been ready he might have been one of the seventy.

61.—[*Bid...farewell.*] The Greek word so translated is peculiar. In Mark vi. 40, it is rendered "sent away;" in Luke xiv. 33, it is "forsaketh;" but in Acts xviii. 18, 21, and 2 Cor. ii. 13, it is "taking leave," and "bidding farewell."

Heinsius thinks that it should be translated, "suffer me first to go and give my commands" to them at home, as if the man was about to die, or take a long journey.

It is probable, that, like the expression, "bury my father," more is implied than appears. Had the desire to bid farewell been like the simple wish of Elisha, "to kiss his father and mother," when Elijah called him, our Lord would hardly have said what He did. (1 Kings xix. 20.) It is evident at any rate that our Lord saw the man's heart was more at his home than at his work.

62.—[*Fit for the kingdom.*] In this proverb the Greek word rendered, "fit," is remarkable, and only used here and Luke xiv. 35, and Heb. vi. 7. It means literally, "well-placed," or "well-disposed."—It implies that a man wanting to go home to take leave of his friends is not rightly disposed for Gospel work, any more than a man looking behind him is rightly placed for ploughing.

Let it be noted in the whole passage, that both in the second and third cases the grand fault manifestly was the desire to do something "first," (59, 61 verses) before doing Christ's work.

LUKE X. 1—7.

1 After these things the Lord appointed other seventy also, and sent them two and two before his face into every city and place, whither he himself would come.

2 Therefore said he unto them, The harvest truly *is* great, but the labourers *are* few: pray ye therefore the Lord of the harvest, that he would send forth labourers into his harvest.

3 Go your ways: behold, I send you forth as lambs among wolves.

4 Carry neither purse, nor scrip, nor shoes: and salute no man by the way.

5 And into whatsoever house ye enter, first say, Peace *be* to this house.

6 And if the Son of peace be there, your peace shall rest upon it: if not, it shall turn to you again.

7 And in the same house remain, eating and drinking such things as they give: for the labourer is worthy of his hire. Go not from house to house.

THE verses before us relate a circumstance which is not recorded by any Gospel writer except St. Luke. That circumstance is our Lord's appointment of seventy disciples to go before His face, in addition to the twelve

apostles. We do not know the names of any of these
disciples. Their subsequent history has not been revealed
to us. But the instructions with which they are sent
forth are deeply interesting, and deserve the close attention of all ministers and teachers of the Gospel.

The first point in our Lord's charge to the seventy
disciples is *the importance of prayer and intercession.*
This is the leading thought with which our Lord
opens His address. Before He tells His ambassadors
what to do, He first bids them to pray. "Pray ye the
Lord of the harvest that he would send forth labourers
into his harvest."

Prayer is one of the best and most powerful means of
helping forward the cause of Christ in the world. It is
a means within the reach of all who have the Spirit of
adoption. Not all believers have money to give to mis-
sions. Very few have great intellectual gifts, or exten-
sive influence among men. But all believers can pray for
the success of the Gospel,—and they ought to pray for it
daily. Many and marvellous are the answers to prayer
which are recorded for our learning in the Bible. "The
effectual fervent prayer of a righteous man availeth
much." (James v. 16.)

Prayer is one of the principal weapons which the
minister of the Gospel ought to use. To be a true
successor of the apostles, he must give himself to prayer as
well as to the ministry of the word. (Acts vi. 4.) He must
not only use the sword of the Spirit, but pray always, with
all prayer and supplication. (Eph. vi. 17, 18.) This is the
way to win a blessing on his own ministry. This, above all,
is the way to procure helpers to carry on Christ's work. Col-

leges may educate men. Bishops may ordain them. Patrons may give them livings. But God alone can raise up and send forth "labourers" who will do work among souls. For a constant supply of such labourers let us daily pray.

The second point in our Lord's charge to the seventy disciples, is *the perilous nature of the work in which they were about to be engaged.* He does not keep back from them the dangers and trials which are before them. He does not enlist them under false pretences, or prophecy smooth things, or promise them unvarying success. He tells them plainly what they must expect. "Behold," He says, "I send you forth as lambs amongst wolves."

These words, no doubt, had a special reference to the life-time of those to whom they were spoken. We see their fulfilment in the many persecutions described in the Acts of the Apostles. But we must not conceal from ourselves that the words describe a state of things which may be seen at this very day. So long as the church stands believers must expect to be like "lambs among wolves." They must make up their minds to be hated, and persecuted, and ill treated, by those who have no real religion. They must look for no favour from unconverted people, for they will find none. It was a strong but a true saying of Martin Luther, that "Cain will murder Abel, if he can, to the very end of the world." "Marvel not," says St. John, "if the world hate you." "All that will live godly in Jesus Christ," says St. Paul, "shall suffer persecution." (1 John iii. 13; 1 Pet. iii. 8.)

The third point in our Lord's charge to the seventy disciples is, *the thorough devotion to their work which He enjoins upon them.* They were to abstain even from the appearance of covetousness, or love of money, or luxury : " Carry neither purse, nor scrip, nor shoes."—They were to behave like men who had no time to waste on the empty compliments and conventional courtesies of the world : " Salute no man by the way."

These remarkable words must doubtless be interpreted with some qualification. The time came when our Lord Himself, at the end of His ministry, said to the disciples, " He that hath a purse let him take it, and likewise his scrip." (Luke xxii. 36.) The apostle Paul was not ashamed to use salutations. The apostle Peter expressly commands us to "be courteous." (1 Pet. iii. 8.) But still, after every deduction and qualification, there remains a deep lesson beneath these words of our Lord, which ought not to be overlooked. They teach us that ministers and teachers of the Gospel should beware of allowing the world to eat up their time and thoughts, and to hinder them in their spiritual work. They teach us that care about money, and excessive attention to what are called " the courtesies of life," are mighty snares in the way of Christ's labourers, and snares into which they must take heed lest they fall.

Let us consider these things. They concern ministers especially, but they concern all Christians more or less. Let us strive to show the men of the world that we have no time for their mode of living. Let us show them that we find life too precious to be spent in perpetual feasting, and visiting, and calling, and the like, as if there were no death, or judgment, or life to come.—By all means let us be courteous. But let us not make the courtesies of life an idol, before which everything else must bow down. Let us declare plainly that we seek a country beyond the grave, and that we have no time for that incessant round of eating, and drinking, and dressing, and civility, and exchange of compliments, in which so many try to find their happiness, but evidently try in vain. Let our principle be that of Nehemiah, " I am doing a great work, so that I cannot come down." (Neh. vi. 3.)

The fourth point in our Lord's charge to the seventy disciples is *the simple-minded and contented spirit which He bade them to exhibit.* Wherever they tarried, in travelling about upon their Master's business, they were to avoid the appearance of being fickle, changeable, delicate livers, or hard to please about food and lodging. They were to "eat and drink such things" as were given them. They were not to "go from house to house."

Instructions like these no doubt have a primary and special reference to the ministers of the Gospel. They are the men above all who, in their style of living, ought to be careful to avoid the spirit of the world. Simplicity in food and household arrangements, and readiness to put up with any accommodation, so long as health can be preserved uninjured, should always be the mark of the " man of God." Once let a preacher get the reputation of being fond of eating and drinking and worldly comforts, and his ministerial usefulness is at an end. The sermon about " things unseen " will produce little effect when the life preaches the importance of the " things that are seen."

But we ought not to confine our Lord's instructions to ministers alone. They ought to speak loudly to the

consciences of all believers, of all who are called by the
Holy Ghost and made priests to God. They ought to remind us of the necessity of simplicity and unworldliness in
our daily life. We must beware of thinking too much about
our meals, and our furniture, and our houses, and all those
many things which concern the life of the body. We
must strive to live like men whose first thoughts are
about the immortal soul. We must endeavour to pass
through the world like men who are not yet at home,
and are not overmuch troubled about the fare they meet
with on the road and at the inn. Blessed are they who
feel like pilgrims and strangers in this life, and whose best
things are all to come !

NOTES. LUKE X. 1—7.

1.—[*Appointed*.] The Greek word so translated is only found in
one other place in the New Testament, Acts i. 24., where it is
rendered "shew." According to Parkhurst, it signifies " to mark
out, or, appoint to an office by some outward sign, and is often
used in this sense by profane writers and in the apocryphal
books." John the Baptist's "shewing" to Israel, Luke i. 80, is
a substantive derived from this word.

[*Other seventy*.] We know nothing of the names, or subsequent
history of these seventy disciples. They are nowhere else mentioned in the New Testament. Most commentators remark on
the selection of the number seventy, and assign reasons for it.
Grotius says, that they were chosen according to the number of
the Jewish Sanhedrim, and so were seventy-two, six being
chosen out of every tribe of Israel. Wordsworth remarks, that
" the number seventy was that of the heads of the families of Israel
(Gen. xlvi. 27.,) and of the elders constituted by Moses. (Numb.
xi. 16. 25) and of the palm trees at Elim. (Exod. xv. 27.) And
the Jews supposed that the languages of the world were seventy."

[*Sent them two and two*.] The mission of the disciples in
pairs deserves remark, and ought to be remembered in modern
missionary work. " Two are better than one." (Eccles. iv. 9.)
Cornelius à Lapide has a long and interesting note, to show
the wisdom of the arrangement.

[*He would come*.] The Greek expression would be more
literally rendered, " was about to come."

2.—[*Send forth.*] The Greek word so rendered is peculiar. It signifies literally " to cast forth," or, " send forth with a degree of force." It implies that nothing but God's powerful and con-straining call will ever move men to become ministers and labourers in the Gospel harvest.

3.—[*Go your ways.*] The Greek here is simply one word, " go away,—depart."

[*I send you forth.*] The Greek for " I " is here emphatically inserted, as if to show the dignity of the disciple's office.

4.—[*Nor shoes.*] We find in St. Mark vi. 9., that when the apostles went forth, our Lord commanded them to be " shod with sandals." It should be remembered therefore, that the sandal and the shoes among the Jews, essentially differed. The sandal only covered the sole of the foot and was fastened about the foot and ancle with straps. The shoe, on the contrary, was a more luxurious thing, and covered the whole foot. In the passage before us the prohibition is only against shoes and not against sandals. This is Major's explanation, and seems the most probable one. Shoes were not so suitable as sandals to men whose only business was to preach the kingdom of God.

[*Salute no man by the way.*] This expression has given rise to many explanatory remarks. One thing is perfectly clear. Our Lord did not intend His disciples to neglect common courtesy. The very next verse enjoins the use of a courteous salutation on visiting a house.

Schoettgen thinks that our Lord refers to a custom among the Jews, according to which people journeying, or praying, and meditating, were exempted from giving or returning salutations.

Others think that our Lord refers to the long and ceremonious salutations which prevail in Eastern countries, and desired His disciples not to waste time in conforming to them. Barnes says, " If two Arabs of equal rank meet each other, they extend to each other the right hand, and having clasped hands, they elevate them, as if to kiss them. Each one then draws back his hand, and kisses it instead of his friend's, and then places it upon his forehead. The parties then continue the salutation by kissing each other's beards. They give thanks to God that they are once more permitted to see their friend,—they pray to the Almighty in his behalf. Sometimes they repeat not less than ten times this ceremony of grasping hands and kissing."

The explanation of Euthymius seems most natural. He thinks our Lord meant that His disciples should devote them-selves entirely to the work they were engaged in, and not waste precious opportunities of preaching, on things which were not of paramount necessity. He also very properly refers us to the case of Elisha and Gehazi : "He said to Gehazi, gird up thy

loins, and take thy staff in thine hand, and go thy way . if
thou meet any man, salute him not, and if any man salute thee
answer him not again." (2 Kings iv. 29.)

The plain practical lesson to ministers ought never to be forgotten. They should be careful not to waste their time in
leaving cards, and paying unmeaning morning calls, as others
do who have nothing better to do with their time. The man of
God ought to have no leisure for any work but that of his
Master. The man of the world who expects clergymen to be as
ready as other people to leave cards, and pay morning calls, and
dine out, only displays his own ignorance of what a Christian
minister ought to be.

5.—[*Peace be to this house.*] It is probable that this was a common Jewish form of salutation. (See 1 Sam. xxv. 6 : Psalm
cxxii. 7, 8.)

6.—[*If the Son of peace be there, &c.*] Bishop Pearce's explanation
of this verse is worth quotation. "In the Jewish style a man
who has any good or bad quality, is called the son of it. So
here the son of peace is mentioned : and in Matt. xi. 19, and
Luke vii. 35, are men called children of wisdom. So likewise
what a man is doomed to, he is called the son of. Wicked men
are children of wrath. (Ephes. ii. 3.) Judas is the son of per-
dition. (John xvii. 12.) So also a man desiring to die is called
a son of death. (2 Sam. xii. 5.)" The expression therefore means,
"If a worthy person, or one deserving your good wishes, be
there, your peace shall rest upon it." The conclusion of the
verse is like the expression in the Psalms, "My prayer returned
into mine own bosom." (Psalm xxxv. 13.)

7.—[*In the same house remain.*] The meaning of this direction is
made clear from the end of the verse, "go not from house to
house." The disciples were to be content with such lodgings as
were provided for them, and not to be hard to please either in
the matter of bed or board.

[*Such things as they give.*] The first expression so translated
would be rendered more literally, "The things from them."
Major thinks it means, "That which belongs to them, and such
things as they themselves eat."

[*The labourer is worthy of his hire.*] This expression is a
proverbial one. It is remarkable as being the only expression
in the Gospels, which is quoted in the Epistles. St. Paul uses
it in writing to Timothy, in connection with the expression "the
Scripture saith." (1 Tim. v. 18.) This has led many to conclude
with much probability that St. Luke's Gospel was finished, and
regarded as part of Holy Scripture, at the time when St. Paul
wrote to Timothy.

Mr Ford quotes some admirable remarks from Cecil and

Scougal on the duties of ministers, which throw some light on the general lessons of the whole verse. Cecil says, "It is one thing to be humble and condescending: it is another to make yourself common, cheap, and contemptible. The men of the world know when a minister is out of his place."

Scougal says, "Another occasion of contempt is too much frequenting the company of laity, and a vain and trifling conversation among them. The saying of Jerome to Nepotian, is very observable, 'A clergyman soon becomes contemptible if, when often invited to dinner, he generally accepts the invitation.'"

LUKE X. 8—16.

8 And into whatsoever city ye enter, and they receive you, eat such things as are set before you:

9 And heal the sick that are therein, and say unto them, The kingdom of God is come nigh unto you.

10 But into whatsoever city ye enter, and they receive you not, go your ways out into the streets of the same, and say,

11 Even the very dust of your city, which cleaveth on us, we do wipe off against you: notwithstanding, be ye sure of this, that the kingdom of God is come nigh unto you.

12 But I say unto you, that it shall be more tolerable in that day for Sodom, than for that city.

13 Woe unto thee, Chorazin! woe unto thee, Bethsaida! for if the mighty works had been done in Tyre and Sidon, which have been done in you, they had a great while ago repented, sitting in sackcloth and ashes.

14 But it shall be more tolerable for Tyre and Sidon at the judgment, than for you.

15 And thou, Capernaum, which art exalted to heaven, shalt be thrust down to hell.

16 He that heareth you heareth me; and he that despiseth you despiseth me, and he that despiseth me despiseth him that sent me.

THESE verses comprise the second part of our Lord Jesus Christ's charge to the seventy disciples. Its lessons, like those of the first part, have a special reference to ministers and teachers of the Gospel. But they contain truths which deserve the serious attention of all members of the Church of Christ.

The first point we should notice in these verses is *the simplicity of the tidings which our Lord commanded some of His first messengers to proclaim.* We read that they were commissioned to say, "The kingdom of God is come nigh unto you."

These words we should probably regard as the key-note to all that the seventy disciples said. We can hardly suppose that they said nothing else but this single sentence. The words no doubt implied far more to a Jewish hearer at the time when they were spoken, than they convey to our minds at the present day. To a well-instructed Israelite, they would sound like an announcement that the times of Messiah had come,—that the long promised Saviour was about to be revealed,—that the "desire of all nations" was about to appear. (Hag. ii. 7.) All this is unquestionably true. Such an announcement suddenly made by seventy men, evidently convinced of the truth of what they said, travelling over a thickly peopled country, could hardly fail to draw attention and excite inquiry. But still the message is peculiarly and strikingly simple.

It may be doubted whether the modern way of teaching Christianity, as a general rule, is sufficiently simple. It is a certain fact that deep reasoning and elaborate arguments are not the weapons by which God is generally pleased to convert souls. Simple plain statements, boldly and solemnly made, and made in such a manner that they are evidently felt and believed by him who makes them, seem to have the most effect on hearts and consciences. Parents and teachers of the young, ministers and missionaries, Scripture-readers and district visitors, would all do well to remember this. We need not be so anxious as we often are about fencing, and proving, and demonstrating, and reasoning, out the doctrines of the Gospel. Not one soul in a hundred was ever brought to Christ in this fashion. We want more simple, plain, solemn, earnest, affectionate statements of simple Gospel truths. We may safely leave such statements to work and take care of themselves. They are arrows from God's own quiver, and will often pierce hearts which have not been touched by the most eloquent sermon.

The second point we should notice in these verses is *the great sinfulness of those who reject the offer of Christ's Gospel.* Our Lord declares that it shall be "more tolerable at the last day for Sodom," than for those who receive not the message of His disciples. And He proceeds to say that the guilt of Chorazin and Bethsaida, cities in Galilee, where He had often preached and worked miracles, but where the people had nevertheless not repented, was greater than the guilt of Tyre and Sidon.

Declarations like these are peculiarly awful. They throw light on some truths which men are very apt to forget. They teach us that all will be judged according to their spiritual light, and that from those who have enjoyed most religious privileges, most will be required. —They teach us the exceeding hardness and unbelief of the human heart. It was possible to hear Christ preach, and to see Christ's miracles, and yet to remain unconverted.—They teach us, not least, that man is responsible for the state of his own soul. Those who reject the Gospel, and remain impenitent and unbelieving, are not merely objects of pity and compassion, but deeply guilty and blameworthy in God's sight. God called, but they refused. God spoke to them, but they would not regard. The condemnation of the unbelieving will be strictly just. Their blood will be upon their own heads. The Judge of all the earth will do right.

Let us lay these things to heart, and beware of unbelief.   It is not open sin and flagrant profligacy alone
which ruin souls.   We have only to sit still and do
nothing, when the Gospel is pressed on our acceptance,
and we shall find ourselves one day in the pit.   We
need not run into any excess of riot.   We need not
openly oppose true religion.   We have only to remain
cold, careless, indifferent, unmoved, and unaffected, and
our end will be in hell.   This was the ruin of Chorazin
and Bethsaida.   And this, it may be feared, will be the
ruin of thousands, as long as the world stands.   No sin
makes less noise, but none so surely damns the soul, as
unbelief.

The last point that we should notice in these verses is
*the honour which the Lord Jesus is pleased to put upon
His faithful ministers.*   We see this brought out in the
words with which He concludes His charge to the seventy
disciples.   He says to them, "He that heareth you heareth
me, and he that despiseth you despiseth me, and he that
despiseth me despiseth him that sent me."

The language here used by our Lord is very remarkable, and the more so when we remember that it was
addressed to the seventy disciples, and not to the twelve
apostles.   The lesson it is intended to convey is clear and
unmistakeable.   It teaches us that ministers are to be
regarded as Christ's messengers and ambassadors to a
sinful world.   So long as they do their work faithfully,
they are worthy of honour and respect for their Master's
sake.   Those who despise them, are not despising them
so much as their Master.   Those who reject the terms of
salvation which they are commissioned to proclaim, are

doing an injury not so much to them as to their King.
When Hanun, king of Ammon, ill-used the ambassadors
of David, the insult was resented as if it had been done
to David himself. (2 Sam. x. 1—19.)

Let us remember these things, in order that we may form
a right estimate of the position of a minister of the Gospel. The subject is one on which error abounds. On the
one side the minister's office is regarded with idolatrous
and superstitious reverence. On the other side it is often
regarded with ignorant contempt. Both extremes are
wrong. Both errors arise from forgetfulness of the plain
teaching of Scripture. The minister who does not do
Christ's work faithfully, or deliver Christ's message correctly, has no right to look for the respect of the people.
—But the minister who declares all the counsel of God,
and keeps back nothing that is profitable, is one whose
words cannot be disregarded without great sin. He is on
the King's business. He is a herald. He is an ambassador. He is the bearer of a flag of truce. He brings
the glad tidings of terms of peace. To such a man the
words of our Lord will prove strictly applicable. The rich
may trample on him. The wicked may hate him.
The pleasure-lover may be annoyed at him. The covetous may be vexed by him. But he may take comfort
daily in his Master's words, "He that despiseth you
despiseth me." The last day will prove that these words
were not spoken in vain.

NOTES. LUKE X. 8—16.

8.—[*Eat such things as are set before you.*] Quesnel remarks on
this verse, "An evangelical labourer, to satisfy the necessities of
life, may make use of all such things as are set before him, and
are not forbidden, provided it be done without eagerness or

affectation. If a missionary, a pastor, or a preacher do not show a great indifferency towards everything which relates to bodily wants, he will never be able much to advance the work of God."

11.—[*Be ye sure of this.*] The literal translation of the Greek expression used here, would be, "Know this."

12.—[*It shall be more tolerable, &c.*] Let it be noted here that there are degrees of guilt and punishment in hell, even as there are degrees of grace and glory in heaven.

Let it also be noted, that our Lord speaks of Sodom as a real city which once existed; and of the story of the guilt of its inhabitants, as a real and true story. There is no foundation here for the theory that the historical parts of the Old Testament are only mythical inventions, intended to point a moral, or convey a spiritual lesson.

Let it also be noted, that both in the present and the three following verses, the grand truth is manifestly implied that man is accountable for his belief, and that not believing the Gospel is a sin which leads to hell as really as not keeping the ten commandments. It is doubtless true that no man can come to Christ except the Father draws him. But it is also no less true that God regards man as a responsible being, and that his not coming to Christ will be part of his guilt, and add to his condemnation at the last day.

13.—[*Chorazin,—Bethsaida.*] Let it be noted that these places were in the district where all our Lord's chiefest miracles were wrought; and where at least five of the apostles are supposed to have lived, Peter, Andrew, Philip, James, and John. It is not the seeing miracles alone that is necessary to convert souls.

[*Tyre and Sidon.*] These two cities were great commercial ports, famous for their riches, luxury, and idolatry. Ezekiel prophecies against them. (Ezek. xxxviii.) They are now little better than ruins.

15.—[*Thrust down to hell.*] It is worthy of remark, that Capernaum, of which this strong expression is spoken, has so completely passed away, that not even its ruins remain, and the place where it stood is matter of dispute.

It should be noted that "heaven" and "hell" are probably used here as allegorical expressions, signifying the highest exaltation and the lowest degradation. (See Isa. xiv. 13.)

16.—[*He that heareth you heareth me.*] There is probably no stronger language than this in the New Testament about the dignity of a faithful minister's office, and the guilt incurred by those who refuse to hear his message. It is language, we must remember, which is not addressed to the twelve apostles, but to seventy disciples, of whose names and subsequent history we know nothing. Scott remarks, "To reject an ambassador, or to treat him with contempt, is an affront to the prince who commissioned and sent him, and whom he represents. The apostles and seventy disciples were the ambassadors and representatives of Christ; and they who rejected and despised them, in fact rejected and despised Him."

It is one thing to take a Roman Catholic view of the ministry, maintain apostolical succession, and regard ministers as mediators between God and man, by virtue of their office and orders. It is quite another thing to despise their office, and regard their warnings and exhortations as of no importance. Both extremes are grievous errors, and should be carefully avoided.

LUKE X. 17—20.

17 And the seventy returned again with joy, saying, Lord, even the devils are subject unto us through thy name.

18 And he said unto them, I beheld Satan as lightning fall from heaven.

19 Behold, I give unto you power to tread on serpents and scorpions, and over all the power of the enemy : and nothing shall by any means hurt you.

20 Notwithstanding in this rejoice not, that the spirits are subject unto you; but rather rejoice, because your names are written in heaven.

WE learn, from this passage, *how ready Christians are to be puffed up with success.* It is written, that the seventy returned from their first mission with joy, "saying, Lord, even the devils are subject unto us through thy name." There was much false fire in that joy. There was evidently self-satisfaction in that report of achievements. The whole tenor of the passage leads us to this conclusion. The remarkable expression which our Lord uses about Satan's fall from heaven, was most probably meant to be a caution. He read the hearts of the young and inexperienced soldiers before Him. He saw how much they were lifted up by their first victory. He wisely checks them in their undue exultation. He warns them against pride.

The lesson is one which all who work for Christ should mark and remember. Success is what all faithful labourers in the Gospel field desire. The minister at home and the missionary abroad, the district visitor and the city missionary, the tract distributor and the Sunday-school teacher, all alike long for success. All long to see Satan's kingdom pulled down, and souls converted to God. We cannot wonder. The desire is right and good. Let it, however, never be forgotten, that the time of success is a time of danger to the Christian's soul. The very hearts that are depressed when all things seem against them, are often unduly exalted in the day of prosperity. Few men are like Samson, and can kill a lion without telling others of it. (Judges xiv. 6.) No wonder that St. Paul says of a bishop, that he ought not to be "a novice, lest being lifted up with pride, he fall into the condemnation of the devil." (1 Tim. iii. 6.) Most of Christ's labourers probably have as much success as their souls can bear.

Let us pray much for humility, and especially for humility in our days of peace and success. When everything around us seems to prosper, and all our plans work well,—when family trials and sicknesses are kept from us, and the course of our worldly affairs runs smooth,—when our daily crosses are light, and all within and without like a morning without clouds,—then, then is the time when our souls are in danger! Then is the time when we have need to be doubly watchful over our own hearts. Then is the time when seeds of evil are sown within us by the devil, which may one day astound us by their growth and strength. There are few Christians who can carry a full cup with a steady hand. There are few whose souls prosper in their days of uninterrupted success. We are all inclined to sacrifice to our net, and burn incense to our own drag. (Hab. i. 16.) We are ready to think that our own might and our own wisdom have procured us the victory. The caution of the passage before us ought never to be forgotten. In the midst of our triumphs, let us cry earnestly, "Lord, clothe us with humility."

We learn, for another thing, from these verses, that *gifts, and power of working miracles, are very inferior to grace.* It is written that our Lord said to the seventy disciples, "In this rejoice not, that the spirits are subject unto you, but rather rejoice because your names are written in heaven." It was doubtless an honour and a privilege to be allowed to cast out devils. The disciples were right to be thankful. But it was a far higher privilege to be converted and pardoned men, and to have their names written in the register of saved souls.

The distinction here drawn between grace and gifts is one of deep importance, and often and sadly overlooked in the present day. Gifts, such as mental vigour, vast memory, striking eloquence, ability in argument, power in reasoning, are often unduly valued by those who possess them, and unduly admired by those who possess them not. These things ought not so to be. Men forget that gifts without grace save no one's soul, and are the characteristic of Satan himself. Grace, on the contrary, is an everlasting inheritance, and, lowly and despised as its possessor may be, will land him safe in glory. He that has gifts without grace is dead in sins, how-

ever splendid his gifts may be.   But he that has grace
without gifts is alive to God, however unlearned and
ignorant he may appear to man.   And "a living dog is
better than a dead lion." (Eccles. ix. 4.)

Let the religion which we aim to possess be a religion
in which grace is the main thing.   Let it not content us
to be able to speak eloquently, or preach powerfully, or
reason ably, or argue cleverly, or profess loudly, or talk
fluently.   Let it not satisfy us to know the whole system
of Christian doctrines, and to have texts and words at our
command.   These things are all well in their way.   They
are not to be undervalued. They have their use. But these
things are not the grace of God, and they will not deliver
us from hell.   Let us never rest until we have the witness
of the Spirit within us that we are " washed, and sanctified, and justified, in the name of the Lord Jesus and by
the Spirit of God." (1 Cor. vi. 11.)   Let us seek to know
that " our names are written in heaven," and that we are
really one with Christ and Christ in us.   Let us strive
to be "epistles of Christ known and read of all men," and
to show by our meekness, and charity, and faith, and
spiritual-mindedness, that we are the children of God.
This is true religion.   These are the real marks of saving
Christianity.   Without such marks, a man may have
abundance of gifts and turn out nothing better than a follower of Judas Iscariot, the false apostle, and go at last to
hell. With such marks, a man may be like Lazarus, poor
and despised upon earth, and have no gifts at all. But his
name is written in heaven, and Christ shall own him as
one of His people at the last day.

NOTES. LUKE X. 17—20.

17.—[*The seventy returned again.*] How long the mission of the seventy lasted we do not know. It may be safely conjectured that it was of short duration.

18.—[*I beheld Satan as lightning fall, &c.*] There are two meanings assigned by Commentators to these remarkable words.

Some think that our Lord is speaking of the effect produced on Satan's kingdom by the preaching of the seventy disciples:— "I saw in spirit, or with my mind's eye, Satan's power declining, and himself rapidly losing his dominion over men in consequence of your ministry." This is the view held by many modern Commentators, but it does not seem satisfactory. The strong language used by our Lord will hardly admit of being explained and fined down by such an interpretation as this.

Others think that our Lord is speaking of what He had witnessed when Satan and his angels fell from heaven, and were cast down into hell, because they kept not their first estate.—"There was a time when I saw Satan, great and mighty as he was, fall suddenly from his high position, and become a lost spirit." This last interpretation appears to me far the more satisfactory of the two, and is that which is held by Cyprian, Ambrose, Chrysostom, Jerome, Gregory, Bede, Theophylact, Bernard, Erasmus, Pellican, Doddridge, Gill, and Alford.

The application of our Lord's words, assuming that He refers to Satan's original fall, is differently explained.

Theophylact, Heinsius, and Gill, consider that our Lord's meaning was; "Marvel not that the devils are subject unto you, for I beheld their prince fall, and it is no wonder that his servants now fall before you."

Cyprian, Jerome, Gregory, Bede, Erasmus, and Pellican, consider that our Lord's intention was to warn the disciples against vain glory; "Be not puffed up because the devils are subject to you. Remember that Satan fell through pride, as I myself saw."

I believe this last view to be the true one, and I think it is confirmed by St. Paul's warning to Timothy, when he bids him not make a novice a Bishop, lest "being lifted up with pride, he fall into the condemnation of the devil." (1 Tim. iii. 6.)

19.—[*Power to tread on serpents, &c.*] It may be doubted, whether these words are to be interpreted figuratively or literally. In favour of the literal view, may be placed our Lord's promise in Mark xvi. 18, and the fact that St. Paul took up a viper and was unhurt. (Acts xxviii. 5.) In favour of the figurative view, may be placed the fact, that Satan is called the " old serpent," that his agents partake of his nature, and that there is a promise in Genesis iii. 15, that " the seed of the woman shall bruise the serpent's head," in which all Christ's members are interested. (See also Psalm xli. 14.)

[*Scorpion.*] A scorpion is a poisonous insect about four inches long, with a sting in its tail, found in tropical climates. Its sting is very dangerous. When coiled up it has some resemblance to an egg. (See Luke xi. 12.)

[*The Enemy.*] This means Satan, the great enemy of God and man.

20.—[*Your names are written in heaven.*] This means that "you are registered in heaven as citizens of God's kingdom, and persons who are chosen to salvation through Christ, pardoned, accepted, and saved." It is the same as St. Paul's saying "whose names are in the book of life." (Phil. iv. 3.) See also Dan. xii. 1; and Rev. xiii. 8; xx. 12. We find the contrary expression, " written in the earth," in Jerem. xvii. 13.

LUKE X. 21—24.

21 In that hour Jesus rejoiced in spirit and said, I thank thee, O Father, Lord of heaven and earth, that thou hast hid these things from the wise and prudent, and hast revealed them unto babes : even so, Father; for so it seemed good in thy sight.

22 All things are delivered to me of my Father : and no man knoweth who the Son is, but the Father; and who the Father is, but the Son, and he to whom the Son will reveal *him*.

23 And he turned him unto *his* disciples, and said privately, Blessed *are* the eyes which see the things that ye see :

24 For I tell you, that many prophets and kings have desired to see those things which ye see, and have not seen *them*; and to hear those things which ye hear, and have not heard *them*.

THERE are five remarkable points in these verses which deserve the attention of all who wish to be well-instructed Christians. Let us take each of the five in order.

We should observe, in the first place, *the one instance on record of our Lord Jesus Christ rejoicing*. We read, that in that hour " Jesus rejoiced in spirit." Three times we are told in the Gospels that our Lord Jesus Christ wept. Once only we are told that He rejoiced.

And what was the cause of our Lord's joy ? It was the conversion of souls. It was the reception of the

Gospel by the weak and lowly among the Jews, when the "wise and prudent" on every side were rejecting it. Our blessed Lord no doubt saw much in this world to grieve Him. He saw the obstinate blindness and unbelief of the vast majority of those among whom He ministered. But when He saw a few poor men and women receiving the glad tidings of salvation, even His heart was refreshed. He saw it and was glad.

Let all Christians mark our Lord's conduct in this matter, and follow His example. They find little in the world to cheer them. They see around them a vast multitude walking in the broad way that leadeth to destruction, careless, hardened, and unbelieving. They see a few here and there, and only a few, who believe to the saving of their souls. But let this sight make them thankful. Let them bless God that any at all are converted, and that any at all believe. We do not realize the sinfulness of man sufficiently. We do not reflect that the conversion of any soul is a miracle,—a miracle as great as the raising of Lazarus from the dead. Let us learn from our blessed Lord to be more thankful. There is always some blue sky as well as black clouds, if we will only look for it. Though only a few are saved, we should find reason for rejoicing. It is only through free grace and undeserved mercy that any are saved at all.

We should observe, secondly, *the sovereignty of God in saving sinners*. We read that our Lord says to His Father, "Thou hast hid these things from the wise and prudent, and revealed them unto babes." The meaning of these words is clear and plain. There are some from

whom salvation is " hidden." There are others to whom
salvation is " revealed."

The truth here laid down is deep and mysterious.
"It is high as heaven: what can we do? It is deep as
hell: what do we know?" Why some around us are
converted and others remain dead in sins, we cannot
possibly explain. Why England is a Christian country
and China buried in idolatry, is a problem we cannot
solve. We only know that it is so. We can only acknowledge that the words of our Lord Jesus Christ
supply the only answer that mortal man ought to give:
"Even so, Father, for so it seemed good in thy sight."

Let us, however, never forget that God's sovereignty
does not destroy man's responsibility. That same God
who does all things according to the counsel of His own
will, always addresses us as accountable creatures,—as
beings whose blood will be on their own heads if they
are lost. We cannot understand all His dealings. We
see in part and know in part. Let us rest in the conviction that the judgment day will clear up all, and that
the Judge of all will not fail to do right. In the mean
time, let us remember that God's offers of salvation are
free, wide, broad, and unlimited, and that "in our doings
that will of God is to be followed which we have expressly declared unto us in the Word of God." (17th
Article of Church of England.) If truth is hidden from
some and revealed to others, we may be sure that there
is a cause.

We should observe, thirdly, *the character of those from
whom truth is hidden, and of those to whom truth is
revealed.* We read that our Lord says, "Thou hast hid

these things from the wise and prudent and hast revealed them unto babes."

We must not gather from these words a wrong lesson. We must not infer that any persons on earth are naturally more deserving of God's grace and salvation than others. All are alike sinners, and merit nothing but wrath and condemnation. We must simply regard the words as stating a fact. The wisdom of this world often makes people proud, and increases their natural enmity to Christ's Gospel. The man who has no pride of knowledge, or fancied morality, to fall back on, has often fewest difficulties to get over in coming to the knowledge of the truth. The publicans and sinners are often the first to enter the kingdom of God, while the Scribes and Pharisees stand outside.

Let us learn from these words to beware of self-righteousness. Nothing so blinds the eyes of our souls to the beauty of the Gospel as the vain, delusive idea, that we are not so ignorant and wicked as some, and that we have got a character which will bear inspection. Happy is that man who has learned to feel that he is "wretched, and miserable, and poor, and blind, and naked." (Rev. iii. 17.) To see that we are bad, is the first step towards being really good. To feel that we are ignorant is the first beginning of all saving knowledge.

We should observe, in the fourth place, *the majesty and dignity of our Lord Jesus Christ.* We read that He said, "All things are delivered to me of my Father: and no man knoweth who the Son is but the Father; and who the Father is but the Son, and he to whom the Son will reveal him."

These are the words of one who was very God of very
God, and no mere man. We read of no patriarch, or
prophet, or apostle, or saint, of any age, who ever used
words like these. They reveal to our wondering eyes a
little of the mighty mystery of our Lord's nature and
person. They show Him to us, as the Head over all
things, and King of kings: "All things are delivered to
me of my Father."—They show Him as one distinct
from the Father, and yet entirely one with Him, and
knowing Him in an unspeakable manner. "No man
knoweth who the Son is but the Father: and who the
Father is but the Son."—They show Him, not least, as
the Mighty Revealer of the Father to the sons of men,
as the God who pardons iniquity, and loves sinners for His
Son's sake: "No man knoweth who the Father is but
he to whom the Son will reveal him."

Let us repose our souls confidently on our Lord Jesus
Christ. He is one who is "mighty to save." Many and
weighty as our sins are, Christ can bear them all.
Difficult as is the work of our salvation, Christ is able to
accomplish it. If Christ was not God as well as man
we might indeed despair. But with such a Saviour as
this we may begin boldly, and press on hopefully, and
await death and judgment without fear. Our help is
laid on one that is mighty. (Psalm lxxxix. 19.) Christ
over all, God blessed for ever, will not fail any one that
trusts in Him.

Let us observe, finally, *the peculiar privileges of those
who hear the Gospel of Christ.* We read that our Lord
said to His disciples, "Blessed are the eyes which see the
things that ye see. For I tell you that many prophets

and kings have desired to see those things which ye see, and have not seen them, and to hear those things which ye hear, and have not heard them."

The full significance of these words will probably never be understood by Christians until the last day. We have probably a most faint idea of the enormous advantages enjoyed by believers who have lived since Christ came into the world, compared to those of believers who died before Christ was born. The difference between the knowledge of an Old Testament saint and a saint in the apostle's days is far greater than we conceive. It is the difference of twilight and noon day, of winter and summer, of the mind of a child and the mind of a full grown man. No doubt the Old Testament saints looked to a coming Saviour by faith, and believed in a resurrection and a life to come. But the coming and death of Christ unlocked a hundred Scriptures which before were closed, and cleared up scores of doubtful points which before had never been solved. In short, " the way into the holiest was not made manifest, while the first tabernacle was standing." (Heb. ix. 8.) The humblest Christian believer understands things which David and Isaiah could never explain.

Let us leave the passage with a deep sense of our own debt to God and of our great responsibility for the full light of the Gospel. Let us see that we make a good use of our many privileges. Having a full Gospel, let us beware that we do not neglect it. It is a weighty saying, "To whomsoever much is given, of them will much be required." (Luke xii. 48.)

NOTES. LUKE X. 21—24.

21.—[*I thank thee, O Father, &c.*] The meaning of this remarkable expression appears to be, " I thank thee, that, having hid these things from the wise and prudent, thou hast revealed them unto babes."—The same kind of expression is found in Rom. vi. 17. " God be thanked, that ye were the servants of sin, but ye have obeyed from the heart that form of doctrine." The thanks are not given because they were the servants of sin, but because they had obeyed the Gospel. Campbell remarks, that the same kind of expression may be found in Isaiah xii. 1, which literally rendered would be, " Lord, I will praise thee, because thou wast angry with me; thine anger is turned away."

[*Wise and prudent.*] These were the Scribes, and Pharisees, and Priests, and Elders of the Jews, who were "wise in their own eyes, and prudent in their own sight," and refused to receive the Gospel of Christ.

[*Babes.*] These were the fishermen, and publicans, and other poor and unlearned Jews, who became our Lord's disciples, and followed Him, when the majority of the nation would not believe.

Let it be noted, that this remarkable expression, and that in the verse following, appear to have been used by our Lord more than once. The words in Matt. xi. 25 seem to have been spoken on an entirely different occasion.

22.—[*All things are delivered unto me, &c.*] Let the words of Whitby on this verse be noted. "All things, that is all power both in heaven and earth, (Matt. xxviii. 18.) all judgment, (John i. 27.) and power over all flesh to give eternal life. (John xvii. 2.) Now this includes power to raise the dead, and to pass judgment on them according to their works, and secret thoughts, and so a power and wisdom which is plainly divine, and consequently the divine nature from which these attributes are inseparable. This is an argument for the divinity of Christ!"

[*Kings.*] By these "kings" we must suppose such men are meant as David, Solomon, Hezekiah, Jehoshaphat, and Josiah."

LUKE X. 25—28.

25 And, behold, a certain Lawyer stood up, and tempted him, saying, Master, what shall I do to inherit eternal life?

26 He said unto him, What is written in the law? how readest thou?

27 And he answering said, Thou shalt love the Lord thy God with all thy heart, and with all thy soul, and with all thy strength, and with all thy mind; and thy neighbour as thyself.

28 And he said unto him, Thou hast answered right: this do, and thou shalt live.

WE should notice in this passage, *the solemn question which was addressed to our Lord Jesus Christ.* We are told that a certain lawyer asked Him, " What shall I do to inherit eternal life? " The motive of this man was evidently not right. He only asked this question to " tempt " our Lord, and to provoke Him to say something on which His enemies might lay hold. Yet the question he propounded was undoubtedly one of the deepest importance.

It is a question which deserves the principal attention of every man, woman, and child on earth. We are all sinners—dying sinners, and sinners going to be judged after death. "How shall our sins be pardoned? Wherewith shall we come before God? How shall we escape the damnation of hell? Whither shall we flee from the wrath to come? What must we do to be saved?"—These are inquiries which people of every rank ought to put to themselves, and never to rest till they find an answer.

It is a question which unhappily few care to consider. Thousands are constantly inquiring, " What shall we eat? What shall we drink? Wherewithal shall we be clothed? How can we get money? How can we enjoy ourselves? How can we prosper in the world? " Few, very few, will ever give a moment's thought to the salvation of their souls. They hate the subject. It makes them uncomfortable. They turn from it and put it away. Faithful and true is that saying of our Lord's, " Wide is the gate and broad is the way that leadeth unto destruction, and many there be that go in thereat." (Matt. vii. 13.)

Let us not be ashamed of putting the lawyer's

question to our own souls. Let us rather ponder it, think
about it, and never be content till it fills the first place in
our minds. Let us seek to have the witness of the Spirit
within us, that we repent us truly of sin, that we have
a lively faith in God's mercy through Christ, and that
we are really walking with God. This is the character
of the heirs of eternal life. These are they who shall
one day receive the kingdom prepared for the children of
God.

We should notice, secondly, in this passage, *the high
honour which our Lord Jesus Christ places on the Bible.*
He refers the lawyer at once to the Scriptures, as the
only rule of faith and practice. He does not say in reply
to his question,—"What does the Jewish Church say
about eternal life? What do the Scribes, and Pharisees,
and priests think? What is taught on the subject in
the traditions of the elders?"—He takes a far simpler
and more direct course. He sends his questioner at
once to the writings of the Old Testament:—"What is
written in the law? How readest thou?"

Let the principle contained in these words, be one of
the foundation principles of our Christianity. Let the
Bible, the whole Bible, and nothing but the Bible, be the
rule of our faith and practice. Holding this principle we
travel upon the king's highway. The road may sometimes seem narrow, and our faith may be sorely tried,
but we shall not be allowed greatly to err.—Departing
from this principle we enter on a pathless wilderness.
There is no telling what we may be led to believe or do.
For ever let us bear this in mind. Here let us cast
anchor. Here let us abide. It matters nothing who

says a thing in religion, whether an ancient father, or a modern Bishop, or a learned divine. Is it in the Bible? Can it be proved by the Bible? If not, it is not to be believed.—It matters nothing how beautiful and clever sermons or religious books may appear. Are they in the smallest degree contrary to Scripture? If they are, they are rubbish and poison, and guides of no value.—What saith the Scripture? This is the only rule, and measure, and guage of religious truth. "To the law and to the testimony;" says Isaiah, "if they speak not according to this word, it is because there is no light in them." (Isaiah viii. 20.)

We should notice, lastly, in this passage, *the clear knowledge of duty to God and man, which the Jews in our Lord's time possessed.* We read that the lawyer said, in reply to our Lord's question, "Thou shalt love the Lord thy God with all thy heart, and with all thy soul, and with all thy strength, and with all thy mind ; and thy neighbour as thyself." That was well spoken. A clearer description of daily practical duty, could not be given by the most thoroughly instructed Christian in the present day. Let not this be forgotten.

The words of the lawyer are very instructive in two points of view. They throw a strong light on two subjects, about which many mistakes abound.—For one thing, they show us how great were the privileges of religious knowledge which the Jews enjoyed under the Old Testament, compared to the heathen world. A nation which possessed such principles of duty as those now before us, was immeasurably in advance of Greece and Rome.—For another thing, the lawyer's words show us how much

clear head-knowledge a person may possess, while his
heart is full of wickedness.   Here is a man who talks of
loving God with all his soul, and loving his neighbour as
himself, while he is actually "tempting" Christ, and
trying to do Him harm, and anxious to justify himself
and make himself out a charitable man!   Let us ever
beware of this kind of religion.   Clear knowledge of the
head, when accompanied by determined impenitence of
heart, is a most dangerous state of soul.   "If ye know
these things," says Jesus, "happy are ye if ye do them."
(John xiii. 7.)

Let us not forget, in leaving this passage, to apply the
high standard of duty which it contains, to our own
hearts, and to prove our own selves.   Do we love God with
all our heart, and soul, and strength, and mind?   Do we
love our neighbour as ourselves?   Where is the person
that could say with perfect truth, "I do?"   Where is the
man that ought not to lay his hand on his mouth, when
he hears these questions?   Verily we are all guilty in this
matter!   The best of us, however holy we may be,
come far short of perfection.   Passages like this, should
teach us our need of Christ's blood and righteousness.
To Him we must go, if we would ever stand with boldness
at the bar of God.   From Him we must seek grace, that
the love of God and man may become ruling principles of
our lives.   In Him we must abide, that we may not
forget our principles, and that we may show the world
that by them we desire to live.

NOTES. LUKE X. 25—28.

25.—[*A certain Lawyer stood up.*]   An English reader must remember that the "Lawyers" spoken of in the Gospels were men who devoted themselves to the study of the law of God.

[*What shall I do, &c.*] The literal rendering of the Greek would be, "What having done, shall I inherit eternal life?" Let us note that this kind of question was asked of our Lord three times. Once it was asked by the rich young ruler, whose case is mentioned in all the three first Gospels. Once it was at the end of our Lord's ministry, by one who said, "Which is the great commandment?" The third case is the one before us now, which is related only by St. Luke.

It is probable that questions like these were much discussed and disputed among the Jews.

26.—[*How readest thou?*] Let the following quotation from Quesnel, the Roman Catholic writer, be observed. "Jesus Christ himself refers us to the law of God, though he was truth itself, and could give souls holy instruction. In vain do we seek after other lights and ways besides those which we find there. It is the Spirit of God which dictated the law and made it the rule of our life. It is injurious to him for us either not to study it, or to prefer the thoughts of man before it.—The first question which will be put to a Christian at the tribunal of God will be to this effect. 'What is written in the law? What have you read in the Gospel? What use have you made thereof?' What answer can that person return who has not so much as read it, though he has sufficient ability and opportunity to do it?"

27.—[*Thou shalt love the Lord, &c.*] This seems to have been a formulary or confession of faith with which Jews were well acquainted.

Vitringa observes, "What the lawyer replies, Thou shalt love the Lord, &c., was daily read in their synagogues."

Doddridge says, "This passage of Scripture is still read by the whole assembly of a Jewish synagogue, both in their morning and evening prayers, and is called, from the first word of it, the Shemah. Only it is observable that they leave out the clause, Thou shalt love thy neighbour as thyself."

28.—[*This do, and thou shalt live.*] These words must needs mean that if a man really and truly lived up to the standard described in the formulary quoted by the lawyer, he would be justified by his life. But that no man ever did or could so live, and that consequently all need the righteousness of another, even Christ, is clear from the whole tenor of the Gospel. To this our Lord would gradually lead the lawyer's conscience.

LUKE X. 29—37.

29 But he, willing to justify himself, said unto Jesus, And who is my neighbour?

30 And Jesus answering said, A certain *man* went down from Jerusalem to Jericho, and fell among thieves, which stripped him of his raiment, and wounded *him*, and departed, leaving *him* half dead.

31 And by chance there came down a certain Priest that way: and when he saw him, he passed by on the other side.

32 And likewise a Levite, when he was at the place, came and looked *on him*, and passed by on the other side.

33 But a certain Samaritan, as he journeyed, came where he was: and when he saw him, he had compassion on *him*,

34 And went to *him*, and bound up his wounds, pouring in oil and wine, and set him on his own beast, and brought him to an inn, and took care of him.

35 And on the morrow when he departed, he took out two pence, and gave *them* to the host, and said unto him, Take care of him: and whatsoever thou spendest more, when I come again, I will repay thee.

36 Which now of these three, thinkest thou, was neighbour unto him that fell among the thieves?

37 And he said, He that shewed mercy on him. Then said Jesus unto him, Go, and do thou likewise.

THESE words contain the well-known parable of the good Samaritan. In order to understand the drift of this parable, we must carefully remember the occasion on which it was spoken. It was spoken in reply to the question of a certain lawyer, who asked, "who is my neighbour." Our Lord Jesus Christ answers that question by telling the story we have just read, and winds up the narrative by an appeal to the lawyer's conscience. Let these things not be forgotten. The object of the parable is to show the nature of true charity and brotherly love. To lose sight of this object, and discover deep allegories in the parable, is to trifle with Scripture, and deprive our souls of most valuable lessons.

We are taught, first, in this parable, *how rare and uncommon is true brotherly love*. This is a lesson which stands out prominently on the face of the narrative before our eyes. Our Lord tells us of a traveller who fell among thieves, and was left naked, wounded, and half dead on the road. He then tells us of a priest and a Levite, who, one after the other, came travelling that way, and saw the poor wounded man, but gave him no help. Both were men, who from their office and profession, ought to have been ready and willing to do good to one in distress. But both, in succession, were too selfish, or too unfeeling to offer the slightest assistance. They doubtless reasoned with themselves, that they knew nothing of the wounded traveller,—that he had perhaps got into trouble by his own misconduct,—that they had no time to stop to help him,—and that they had enough to do to mind their own business, without troubling themselves with strangers. And the result was, that one after the other, they both "passed by on the other side."

We have in this striking description, an exact picture of what is continually going on in the world. Selfishness is the leading characteristic of the great majority of mankind. That cheap charity which costs nothing more than a trifling subscription or contribution, is common enough. But that self-sacrificing kindness of heart, which cares not what trouble is entailed, so long as good can be done, is a grace which is rarely met with. There are still thousands in trouble who can find no friend or helper. And there are still hundreds of "priests and Levites" who see them, but "pass by on the other side."

Let us beware of expecting much from the kindness of man. If we do, we shall certainly be disappointed. The longer we live the more clearly we shall see that few people care for others except from interested motives, and that unselfish, disinterested, pure brotherly love, is as scarce as diamonds and rubies. How thankful we ought to be that the Lord Jesus Christ is not like man! His kindness and love are unfailing. He never disappoints any of His friends. Happy are they who have learned to say, "my soul, wait thou only upon God; my expectation is from him." (Psalm lxii. 5.)

We are taught, secondly, in this parable, *who they are to whom we should shew kindness, and whom we are to love as neighbours.* We are told that the only person who helped the wounded traveller, of whom we are reading, was a certain Samaritan. This man was one of a nation who had "no dealings" with the Jews. (John iv. 9.) He might have excused himself by saying that the road from Jerusalem to Jericho was through the Jewish territory, and that cases of distress ought to be cared for by the Jews. But he does nothing of the sort. He sees a man stripped of his raiment, and lying half dead. He asks no questions, but at once has compassion on him. He makes no difficulties, but at once gives aid. And our Lord says to us, "go and do thou likewise."

Now, if these words mean anything, a Christian ought to be ready to show kindness and brotherly love to every one that is in need. Our kindness must not merely extend to our families, and friends, and relations. We must love all men, and be kind to all, whenever occasion requires. We must beware of an excessive strictness in scrutinizing the past lives of those who need our aid. Are they in real trouble? Are they in real distress? Do they really want help? Then, according to the teaching of this parable, we ought to be ready to assist them. We should regard the whole world as our parish, and the whole race of mankind as our neighbours. We should seek to be

the friend of every one who is oppressed, or neglected, or
afflicted, or sick, or in prison, or poor, or an orphan, or
a heathen, or a slave, or an idiot, or starving, or dying.
We should exhibit such world-wide friendship, no doubt,
wisely, discreetly, and with good sense, but of such
friendship we never need be ashamed. The ungodly
may sneer at it as extravagance and fanaticism. But we
need not mind that. To be friendly to all men in this
way, is to show something of the mind that was in
Christ.

We are taught, lastly, in this parable, *after what
manner, and to what extent we are to show kindness and love
to others.* We are told that the Samaritan's compassion
towards the wounded traveller was not confined to feelings.
and passive impressions. He took much trouble to give
him help. He acted as well as felt. He spared no pains
or expense in befriending him. Stranger as the man was,
he went to him, bound up his wounds, set him on his
own beast, brought him to an inn, and took care of him.
Nor was this all. On the morrow he gave the host of
the inn money, saying, " take care of him, and whatsoever
thou spendest more, when I come again I will repay thee."
And our Lord says to each of us, " go and do thou likewise."

The lesson of this part of the parable is plain and
unmistakeable. The kindness of a Christian towards
others should not be in word and in tongue only, but in
deed and in truth. His love should be a practical love,
a love which entails on him self-sacrifice and self-denial,
both in money, and time, and trouble. His charity
should be seen not merely in his talking, but his acting,

—not merely in his profession, but in his practice. He should think it no misspent time to work as hard in doing good to those who need help, as others work in trying to get money. He should not be ashamed to toil as much to make the misery of this world rather smaller, as those toil who hunt or shoot all day long. He should have a ready ear for every tale of sorrow, and a ready hand to help every one in affliction, so long as he has the power. Such brotherly love the world may not understand. The returns of gratitude which such love meets with may be few and small. But to show such brotherly love, is to walk in the steps of Christ, and to reduce to practice the parable of the good Samaritan.

And now let us leave the parable with grave thoughts and deep searchings of heart.—How few Christians seem to remember that such a parable was ever written! What an enormous amount of stinginess, and meanness, and ill-nature, and suspicion there is to be seen in the Church, and that even among people who repeat the creed and go to the Lord's table!—How seldom we see a man who is really kind, and feeling, and generous, and liberal, and good-natured, except to himself and his children! Yet the Lord Jesus Christ spoke the parable of the good Samaritan, and meant it to be remembered.

What are we ourselves? Let us not forget to put that question to our hearts. What are we doing, each in our own station, to prove that this mighty parable is one of the rules of our daily life? What are we doing for the heathen, at home and abroad? What are we doing to help those who are troubled

in mind, body, or estate? There are many such in
this world. There are always some near our own doors.
What are we doing for them? Anything, or nothing at
all? May God help us to answer these questions! The
world would be a happier world if there was more
practical Christianity.

NOTES. LUKE X. 29—37.

29.—[*He willing to justify himself.*] It may be doubted whether
the word translated "willing," would not have been better rendered "desiring." It is so translated in the following passages
in St. Luke, (Luke v. 39. viii. 20: x. 24: xx. 46: xxiii. 8.), as
well as in other places in the New Testament.

The expression makes clear the true character of the lawyer.
He was a self-righteous man, and flattered himself that he could
deserve the eternal life he had inquired about by his own doings.

[*Who is my neighbour?*] The lawyer, no doubt, expected that
our Lord would answer according to the narrow-minded prejudices of the Jewish nation at that time, that Jews alone were his
neighbours. Major quotes two remarkable passages from Tacitus
and Juvenal, proving that even among the heathen Romans the
Jews were notorious for bitterness and ill-feeling towards all who
were not of their own nation.

The feeling of the Jews towards other nations is a remarkable
instance of man's readiness to pervert and misapply God's laws.
The law of Moses about intercourse and intermarriage with
foreigners, was undoubtedly meant for the good of the Jews, to
keep them a separate people among the nations of the earth.
But it was never meant to sanction unkindness and want of
charity.

30.—[*From Jerusalem to Jericho.*] The road between these two
places passed through a wild and rocky country, and was notorious for being infested by robbers. On this account, Jerome
says, it was called "the bloody way." It is a curious fact, that
Dr. Bonar, one of the latest travellers in Palestine, mentions,
that even now it is a dangerous road for people to travel alone,
and that a lady in his company well-nigh "fell among thieves."

31.—[*By chance.*] The Greek word so rendered is only found here
in the New Testament. It means literally, " by coincidence,—
as it happened."

[*A certain Priest.*] There is a propriety in the mention of a
Priest and a Levite on this road. Jericho was a city specially

appointed for the residence of Priests and Levites. No less than 12,000 of them, according to Lightfoot, lived there. At Jerusalem was the temple, which Priests and Levites had to attend in monthly courses. These circumstances make it quite natural for a Priest and a Levite to be on the road.

[*Passed by on the other side.*] Parkhurst suggests that the Priest was afraid of being legally polluted by touching a dead carcase, and thinks that his conduct is an example of hypocritical pretence to excessive ceremonial purity, like that recorded in Matt. xxvii. 6; John xviii. 28.

32.—[*Came and looked on him.*] The conduct of the Levite, be it remarked, was worse than that of the Priest. Both "saw" the wounded man, but the Levite seems to have "come" to him, and then passed by.

33.—[*Came where he was.*] It may be doubted whether the Greek words here would not have been more literally rendered, "came unto him."

34.—[*Pouring in oil.*] A note in Schoettgen throws light on this expression. He says, "Some one might naturally ask whence this traveller got his oil and wine on a journey? It has occured to me that travellers in hot eastern countries made a point of carrying oil with them, that they might anoint and strengthen their limbs wearied with continual heat. We have an example in the case of Jacob, who, even when he slept on the bare ground in Bethel, and journeyed alone with only a staff, nevertheless had oil with him, with which he anointed the stone, and oil which he poured out to the glory of God." (Gen. xxviii. 18.)

35.—[*Two pence.*] Let it be noted, that this sum was in reality much larger than it appears at first sight to an English reader. The value of money was very different then from what it is now. A "penny a day," according to Matthew xx. 2, was a fair day's wages.

36.—[*Thinkest thou, was.*] The Greek here is literally, "seems to thee to have been."

Before leaving this parable, a question of some importance demands consideration:—"Is the parable of the good Samaritan an allegory or not? Is it meant to teach the mercy of our Lord Jesus Christ to man? Was the conduct of the good Samaritan intended to be interpreted by us as a type and figure of our Lord Jesus Christ's great work of redemption?"—Let the question be rightly understood. The question is not whether the passage may be accommodated and fitted by man, so as to illustrate the work of Christ on behalf of sinners. The question is simply this:—"Did our Lord Jesus Christ speak the parable with this double meaning, and intend us to interpret it in this way?"

The question is one which the great majority of Commentators at once answer in the affirmative. According to them, the traveller represents human nature,—the falling among thieves, Adam's fall,—the lying naked, wounded, and half dead, the condition of mankind,—and the failure of the priest and Levite to help, the inability of ceremonies and forms to raise man from his low estate. The good Samaritan is Jesus Christ. The oil and wine are the blood of Christ and the Holy Spirit. The inn is the Church. The host is the ministry. The two pence are the two sacraments. The promised coming again to repay what is spent more, the Lord's second advent.

This, with some minor variations, is the sense which many Commentators, both ancient and modern, extract from the parable. Mr. Alford even speaks of those who cannot receive it, as "the superficial school of critics."—There is no denying the praise of ingenuity to the interpretation. To many it is sure to appear very clever, just because it is not natural. But the serious question remains still to be answered : "Did our Lord Jesus Christ really intend this meaning to be placed upon the parable?"—My own conviction decidedly is, that He did not; and that the allegorical sense which has been placed on the parable, is a gratuitous invention of man.

My reasons for not holding the allegorical interpretation of the parable are three-fold.

1. I see nothing either in the passage, or in the context, to lead me to suppose that our Lord meant to convey more than one plain lesson by it. That lesson is the true nature of love to our neighbours.

2. I see much in the circumstances of the parable itself which appears to me to overthrow entirely the idea that it is an allegory of man's redemption. Without twisting and straining it in the most violent and unwarrantable manner, the parable, upon the allegorical interpretation, involves manifest absurdities.—Grant that the traveller represents human nature. At best, it is an awkward figure. The traveller was an object of pity, and only half dead. Man is more than pitiable : he deserves blame, and is dead in sins. But who then can the priest and Levite be who fail to give aid? They are part of human nature themselves!—Grant, in order to avoid this awkwardness, that the traveller means the Gentile, and the failure of priest and Levite to help him, the weakness of the Mosaic law. Again, the question arises, what are we to make of the inn and the host, if they mean the Church and the ministry? At this rate, the Gentiles are handed over to the care of the Gentiles, since there was no Gentile Church till Christ called and formed it! All this may seem to some minds to admit of explanation. To my own it appears to involve inextricable confusion.

3. My third and last reason is this. I hold it to be a most dangerous mode of interpreting Scripture, to regard everything which its words may be tortured into meaning, as a lawful interpretation of the words. I hold undoubtedly that there is a mighty depth in all Scripture, and that in this respect it stands alone. But I also hold that the words of Scripture were intended to have one definite sense, and that our first object should be to discover that sense, and adhere rigidly to it. I believe that, as a general rule, the words of Scripture are intended to have, like all other language, one plain definite meaning, and that to say that words *do* mean a thing, merely because they *can* be tortured into meaning it, is a most dishonourable and dangerous way of handling Scripture.—If any one wants to see to what absurdities such a mode of interpreting Scripture leads, he has only to read the commentaries of the Fathers. Hardly any, except perhaps Chrysostom, seem satisfactory and sound on this point.

I am quite aware that in holding the views which I have endeavoured to defend, about the parable of the good Samaritan, I hold the views of a small minority of commentators. But that those with whom I agree are not all "superficial," I think the following five names prove,—Gualter, Baxter, Scott, Poole, and Adam Clarke. Even Stella, the Roman Catholic Spanish commentator, denounces the allegorical interpretation, and Maldonatus, is evidently unwilling to endorse it.

The question will probably never be settled as long as the world stands, but I have thought it right to bear my testimony fully and frankly to what I believe to be the truth.

LUKE X. 38—42.

38 Now it came to pass, as they went, that he entered into a certain village : and a certain woman named Martha received him into her house.
39 And she had a sister called Mary, which also sat at Jesus' feet, and heard his word.
40 But Martha was cumbered about much serving, and came to him, and said, Lord, dost thou not care that my sister hath left me to serve alone ? bid her therefore that she help me.
41 And Jesus answered and said unto her, Martha, Martha, thou art careful and troubled about many things :
42 But one thing is needful : and Mary hath chosen that good part, which shall not be taken away from her.

The little history which these verses contain, is only recorded in the Gospel of St. Luke. So long as the world stands, the story of Mary and Martha will furnish the Church with lessons of wisdom which ought never to be forgotten. Taken together with the eleventh chapter of St. John's Gospel, it throws a most instructive light on the inner life of the family which Jesus loved.

Let us observe, for one thing, how *different the characters and temperaments of true Christians may be.* The two sisters of whom we read in this passage were faithful disciples. Both had believed. Both had been converted. Both had honoured Christ when few gave Him honour. Both loved Jesus, and Jesus loved both of them.—Yet they were evidently women of very different turn of mind. Martha was active, stirring, and impulsive, feeling strongly, and speaking out all she felt. Martha was quiet, still, and contemplative, feeling deeply, but saying less than she felt. Martha, when Jesus came to her house, rejoiced to see Him, and busied herself with preparing a suitable entertainment. Mary, also, rejoiced to see Him, but her first thought was to sit at His feet and hear His word. Grace reigned in both hearts, but each showed the effect of grace at different times, and in different ways.

We shall find it very useful to ourselves to remember this lesson. We must not expect all believers in Christ to be exactly like one another. We must not set down others as having no grace, because their experience does not entirely tally with our own. The sheep in the Lord's flock have each their own peculiarities. The trees in the Lord's garden are not all precisely alike. All true servants of God agree in the principal things of religion. All are led by one Spirit. All feel their sins, and all trust in Christ. All repent, all believe, and all are holy. But in minor matters they often differ widely. Let not one despise another on this account. There will be Marthas and there will be Marys in the Church until the Lord comes again.

Let us observe, for another thing, *what a snare to our souls the cares of this world may be, if allowed to take up too much attention.* It is plain from the tone of the passage before us, that Martha allowed her anxiety to provide a suitable entertainment for our Lord, to carry her away. Her excessive zeal for temporal provisions, made her forget, for a time, the things of her soul. "She was cumbered about much serving."—By and bye her conscience pricked her, when she found herself alone serving tables, and saw her sister sitting at Jesus' feet and hearing His word. Under the pressure of a conscience ill at ease, her temper became ruffled, and the old Adam within broke out into open complaint. "Lord," she said, "dost not thou care that my sister hath left me to serve alone? Bid her therefore that she help me." In so saying, this holy woman sadly forgot what she was, and to whom she was speaking. She brought down on herself a solemn rebuke, and had to learn a lesson which probably made a lasting impression. Alas! "how great a matter a little fire kindleth." The beginning of all this was a little over-anxiety about the innocent household affairs of this world!

The fault of Martha should be a perpetual warning to all Christians. If we desire to grow in grace, and to enjoy soul-prosperity, we must beware of the cares of this world. Except we watch and pray, they will insensibly eat up our spirituality, and bring leanness on our souls. It is not open sin, or flagrant breaches of

God's commandments alone, which lead men to eternal
ruin. It is far more frequently an excessive attention to
things in themselves lawful, and the being "cumbered
about much serving." It seems so right to provide for
our own! It seems so proper to attend to the duties
of our station! It is just here that our danger lies.
Our families, our business, our daily callings, our household affairs, our intercourse with society, all, all may
become snares to our hearts, and may draw us away
from God. We may go down to the pit of hell from the
very midst of lawful things.

Let us take heed to ourselves in this matter. Let us
watch our habits of mind jealously, lest we fall into sin
unawares. If we love life, we must hold the things of
this world with a very loose hand, and beware of allowing
anything to have the first place in our hearts, excepting
God. Let us mentally write "poison" on all temporal
good things. Used in moderation they are blessings, for
which we ought to be thankful. Permitted to fill our
minds, and trample upon holy things, they become a
positive curse. Profits and pleasures are dearly purchased,
if in order to obtain them we thrust aside eternity from
our thoughts, abridge our Bible-reading, become careless
hearers of the Gospel, and shorten our prayers. A little
earth upon the fire within us will soon make that fire
burn low.

Let us observe, for another thing, *what a solemn rebuke
our Lord Jesus Christ gave to His servant Martha.* Like
a wise physician He saw the disease which was preying
upon her, and at once applied the remedy. Like a
tender parent, He exposed the fault into which His

erring child had fallen, and did not spare the chastening which was required. "Martha, Martha," He said, "thou art careful and troubled about many things: but one thing is needful." Faithful are the wounds of a friend! That little sentence was a precious balm indeed! It contained a volume of practical divinity in a few words.

"One thing is needful." How true that saying! The longer we live in the world, the more true it will appear. The nearer we come to the grave, the more thoroughly we shall assent to it. Health, and money, and lands, and rank, and honours, and prosperity, are all well in their way. But they cannot be called *needful*. Without them thousands are happy in this world, and reach glory in the world to come. The "many things" which men and women are continually struggling for, are not really necessaries. The grace of God which bringeth salvation is the one thing needful.

Let this little sentence be continually before the eyes of our minds. Let it check us when we are ready to murmur at earthly trials. Let it strengthen us when we are tempted to deny our Master on account of persecution. Let it caution us when we begin to think too much of the things of this world. Let it quicken us when we are disposed to look back, like Lot's wife. In all such seasons, let the words of our Lord ring in our ears like a trumpet, and bring us to a right mind. "One thing is needful." If Christ is ours, we have all and abound.

We should observe, lastly, *what high commendation our Lord Jesus Christ pronounced on Mary's choice*. We read that He said, "Mary hath chosen that good part, which

shall not be taken from her." There was a deep meaning
in these words. They were spoken not for Mary's sake
only, but for the sake of all Christ's believing people in
every part of the world. They were meant to encourage
all true Christians to be single-eyed and whole-hearted,
—to follow the Lord fully, and to walk closely with God,
—to make soul-business immeasurably their first business, and to think comparatively little of the things of
this world.

The true Christian's portion is the grace of God. This
is the "good part" which he has chosen, and it is the only
portion which really deserves the name of "good."
It is the only good thing which is substantial, satisfying,
real, and lasting. It is good in sickness and good in
health,—good in youth and good in age,—good in adver-
sity and good in prosperity,—good in life and good in
death—good in time and good in eternity. No circumstance and no position can be imagined in which it is
not good for a man to have the grace of God.

The true Christian's possession shall never be taken
from him. He alone, of all mankind, shall never be
stripped of his inheritance. Kings must one day leave
their palaces. Rich men must one day leave their money
and lands. They only hold them till they die.—But the
poorest saint on earth has a treasure of which he will
never be deprived. The grace of God, and the favour of
Christ, are riches which no man can take from him.
They will go with him to the grave when he dies. They
will rise with him in the resurrection morning, and be
his to all eternity.

What do we know of this " good part " which Mary

chose? Have we chosen it for ourselves? Can we say with truth that it is ours? Let us never rest till we can. Let us " choose life," while Christ offers it to us without money and without price. Let us seek treasure in heaven, lest we awake to find that we are paupers for evermore.

NOTES. LUKE X. 38—42.

38.—[*As they went.*] It is not quite clear at what period of our Lord's earthly ministry the history here recorded comes in, nor what is the connexion between it and the preceding passage. Stier conjectures that one object is to supply a serviceable caution against the idea that active working charity, like that of the good Samaritan, was the only way to serve Christ, and to show that sitting still and hearing is just as useful in its season as relieving distressed people.—He says, "Is not the inmost fundamental thought of the words directed to busy Martha, a warning against the tendency to an unquiet bustling character? "Do" was the word of the Lord in the parable of the good Samaritan; but now He says, "rest."—"Do not forget the hearing in thy much doing."

In any point of view one thing is certain. The Martha and Mary here spoken of, are the same sisters of whom we read in the eleventh chapter of John.

40.—[*Was cumbered.*] The Greek word so translated, means literally, "was drawn about, distracted."

[*Came to him.*] The word translated "came" implies a sudden coming. See Luke xxi. 34, and xxiv. 4.

41.—[*Troubled.*] The word so rendered is only used here in the New Testament. It means literally "to be in a tumult; to be disturbed."

Our Lord, we must remember, does not mean to say that Martha's occupation was wrong, but that, for the time, Mary's occupation was better than Martha's.

42.—[*One thing is needful.*] Not a few commentators consider this to mean, "one dish of meat is needful," and think that our Lord was only referring to the many dishes which Martha was preparing in order to entertain Him.

I cannot entertain this notion for a moment. There is no proof that Martha was preparing a banquet at all, though she was undoubtedly busy about household affairs. Our Lord's words have a far deeper signification. "Of one thing, even of salvation, there is necessity." That this is His meaning His subsequent words about Mary appear abundantly to prove. If "one thing is needful" means only "one dish," we might just as well say, that the "good part" which Mary chose, was the good portion of the feast which she had selected for herself!

Doddridge remarks, "This is one of the greatest and most important apophthegms that was ever uttered, and one can scarce pardon the frigid impertinence of Theophylact and Basil who explain it as if our Lord had only meant one dish of meat."

The whole verse is a deep elliptical sentence, and can only be rendered by a large paraphrase.

[*That good part.*] This is a general expression, and meant to be interpreted with a reference to the conduct of Mary, at the time when her sister interposed. She was choosing soul-benefit. She was seeking more grace. She was striving after nearer and closer communion with God and His Christ. This was the portion which she preferred to everything else, and to which she was willing for a time to postpone all earthly care. Those who seek such a portion shall never be disappointed. Their treasure shall never be taken from them.

In leaving this passage, we should be careful not to fall into the error of thinking slightly of Martha's grace, or speaking, as some do occasionally, as if the good woman had no grace at all. This is a grave error. In the day of affliction Martha's grace shone clearly and brightly. There is hardly any confession in all the four Gospels, of our Lord's office, which will compare with that which she made in the eleventh chapter of John.

The Roman Catholic writers are fond of quoting the whole passage, in favour of a monastic or conventual life; and insinuate that monks and nuns are like Mary, and people in secular occupations like Martha. Unhappily, their comparison fails completely. If all monks and nuns had been people who "sat at Christ's feet and heard His words," there might have been something in what they say. Unfortunately, convents and monasteries have been proved to be the very last places where successors of Mary are likely to be found. Bucer, in his commentary on the Gospels, dwells ably on this point.

END OF VOL. I.